DIGITAL COMPUTERS'
MEMORY TECHNOLOGY

Digital Computers' Memory Technology

D. Dutta Majumder
J. Das
Indian Statistical Institute
Calcutta

A HALSTED PRESS BOOK

John Wiley & Sons
New York Chichester Brisbane Toronto

Copyright © 1980, WILEY EASTERN LIMITED
New Delhi

Published in the U.S.A., Canada and
Latin America by Halsted Press,
a Division of John Wiley & Sons, Inc., New York

Library of Congress Cataloging in Publication Data

Dutta Majumder, Dwijesh.
  Digital computers' memory technology.

  "A Halsted Press book."
  Includes index.
  1. Computer storage devices. I. Das, J., joint author. II. Title.
TK7895. M4D87   621. 3819'5833   80-18160
ISBN 0-470-26932-4

Printed in India at Rajkamal Electric Press, Delhi.

FOREWORD

Memory technology spans a wide range of cost and performance and has consequently a hierarchal structure. While in terms of speed semiconductor memory is the fastest, followed by disc storage and magnetic tape, in terms of costs the reverse situation obtains. In a technological sense the most rapid evolution has taken place in mainframe memory which has evolved from the early delay line, to the ferrite core and the present semicondutor Random Access Memory which is now beginning to dominate the field. Further improvements are likely in this area using Josephson junctions. Similarly, the disc store is being threatened by developments in magnetic bubble memory and charge couple devices. All these developments in turn have had a significant impact on computers and computing vastly extending its scope of application.

It is interesting to note that most of the new technologies are based on developments in Physics which have occurred over the last 30 years, be it the transistor effect, the 'magnetic bubble' or the Josephson effect. Interestingly enough, all these effects exploit microelectronic technology.

The authors have made a very useful contribution to the literature in the field by reviewing comprehensively the entire field of memory technology to the present day. My association with the Indian Statistical Institute and Professor Dutta Majumder goes back 25 years. This author's own interests extend beyond the area of memory technology and he has also made useful contributions in the field of speech and pattern recognition as also cybernetics. This volume provides an extremely useful reference to both the computer scientist as well as the memory technologist. Teachers and students will immensely benefit by this work as it encompasses the various facets and choices of technology of digital computers' memory.

B. NAG

Chairman
Electronics Commission
Government of India

PREFACE

The important factors in the advancement of computer technology are the memory performance speed, size and cost. Though development in other areas of software and hardware sub-systems contributed immensely, search for a faster and cheaper memory has always been there. It can be remarked that the capabilities of future computer and information processing systems will also be determined principally by developments in memory technology.

In the earlier period of the development of the electronic computers several nonmagnetic material technology were experimented with for suitable devices. Notable among the nonmagnetic storage devices, some of which are still useful, are punched paper tapes, films, and cards, photographic films, acoustic delay lines and electrostatic storage tubes. Storage systems which make use of the properties of permanence inherent in the magnetic materials of different configuration appeared to offer the most likely solution to the problem, and since then immense efforts have been devoted to the development of diverse type of magnetic memory devices with increasingly better performances. The extended ferromagnetic layer surface memories with particulate materials have occupied an important place as auxiliary and peripheral memories in large scale data processing and process-control systems today. Peripheral memories are rapidly becoming as important to a computer system of same characteristics as main memory in terms of cost per bit.

The other group of magnetic devices which made use of the properties of ferrite materials with rectangular hysteresis loop are toroidal cores, and apertured plates and magnetic films. Inspite of all the development efforts in other directions, ferrite core matrix memory systems are playing a crucial role as main memory. Magnetic memories, in spite of so many strong points in their favour have not improved fast enough to provide an alternative to the improved logic and to the ever-expanding needs of memory that evolving data processing systems have been shown to require. To meet this need an amazing array of physical effects and devices have been investigated in the last two decades, and at great expanse. Such a short list would include, superconducting switches (cryotrons), bistable diodes (cryosar, tunnel diode, Ovshinsky diode), photochronics, thin magnetic films (flat and cylindrical), propagating magnetic domains (magnetic bubble memory), magneto-optics, parametrons (phase storage), ferroelectrics, sonic delay lines, thermoplastics, surface change storage and transistor flip-flops (bipolar, MOS).

The development of MOS, bipolar, and other semiconductor memories has attracted the interest of computer engineers in the seventies. With their low power dissipation, the circuits can be densely packed on a chip. They have found their place in main storage and in Read Only Memories (ROM), Programmable ROM (PROM); and in associative memories with bipolars appreciably high speed is achieved. Large-Scale-Integration (LSI) through MOS technology has enhanced the performance and cut the cost of random-access memories. Developments and obsolescenes in semiconductor technology are taking place so quickly that it is very difficult for any author to claim his writings as contemporary state of the art in this sphere.

Two major factors that may be responsible for the impact of semiconductor memory technology on memory/computer industry are: (a) the technology is developing to the point where a degree of standardisation has to be evolved, and (b) some major computer manufacturers have converted to semiconductor main frame memory. Speed increases and power reductions are constantly being made. Recently n-channel MOS (COMS) technologies have come up with exciting possibilities. In packaging techniques, ceramic and plastic Dual in-Line-Packages (DIP) are gaining ground. But in a large semiconductor memory, costs other than those for the memory devices, such as power supplies, printed circuit boards, error correction circuitry (ECC), etc. must also be considered.

To make a comparative statement between the core memory and semiconductor memory, it can be conjectured that just as core technology is well capitalized, so also the semiconductor memory—this being an out growth of overall semiconductor technology with a large production base. So unless some more significant breakthroughs are achieved, core and semiconductor technologies will assume their more natural complementary role with a continuing market for both for some time to come. And in our opinion, regardless of whatever wins the core vs. solid state memory contest, the need for a memory with much better price performance than either will still exist, and furthermore, it may be possible to develop such a memory in the near future.

This book is an attempt to present the advances in computer memory technology or a large part of it in some form of a text and a reference book for the benefit of computer science and electrical engineering students, professional engineers, and researchers. From the experience of the past three decades it can be remarked that better memories are developed as a result of the immense interdisciplinary efforts of system designers, physicists and electrical engineers. This book will be helpful in improving the understanding between the different disciplines. The system designer gets the specifications at the system and subsystem level, the physicist can learn which material properties are most relevant to the proper functioning of the memory device, and the electrical engineer will find a description of the physical principles of the storage elements he is using or proposing to use. The book provides a comprehensive introduction to this interesting field. Those who want to make an in depth study of the subjects are referred to the original literatures as given in the text.

Some of the material presented in the book are based on the result of the research and development work and training activities carried out by the authors (one for about twenty-five years and the other for ten years) on digital computers in general and memory technology in particular. The chapters are arranged in a manner so as to trace the historical growth of the technology except for the cryogenic memory which was developed in the mid-fifties. But in order of sophistication and application potentiality it should be grouped with some of the advanced technologies, and we have presented it in a later chapter.

A brief introduction on the role of memory in computer technology along with their different characteristics are given in Chapter 1. The second chapter covers the memory systems used in first generation computers which are still used as peripheral devices, such as, magnetic drums, disks and tapes using magnetic particulate layer surfaces. Chapter 3 contains an elaborate design study of digital magnetic core memory systems including automatic testing methods of individual cores and planes. Chapter 4 present special ferrite storage devices including NDRO methods. A study on magnetic thin film memory including planar, cylindrical and plated film technology is presented in Chapter 5. An attempt is made to present the growth of the semiconductor memory systems in a nutshell including its advantages and disadvantages in Chapter 6. Chapter 7 contains brief studies on Cryogenic memory, Magnetic Bubble Memory, and Optical memories. A study of Associative Memory and Read Only Memories are presented in Chapter 8. In the end, a chapter has been added on some studies about existing computer memories in relation to biological memories. An attempt has been made to present an up-to-date and representative bibliography for each chapter at the end of the book.

We express our sincere gratitude to the Late Professor P.C. Mahalanobis, Founder-Director of Indian Statistical Institute; Professor C.R. Rao, Former-Director, Indian Statistical Institute and Professor S.K. Mitra, former Head of the Electronic Computer Division of Indian Statistical Institute who were instrumental in starting electronic computer R and D work in our laboratory in the Institute. We also express our thanks to the present Director of the Institute for his help and encouragement in carrying out the research programmes on computers and allied information processing technology.

It is our pleasure to thank all our colleagues in the Electronics and Communication Sciences Laboratory of Indian Statistical Institute, for their help in the writing of this book. We also express our thanks to Mr. S. Biswas and also to Mr. S. Seal and Mr. J. Gupta for typing the manuscript and Mr. S.K. Chakravarti for drawing all the diagrams.

D. Dutta Majumder
J. Das

CONTENTS

1. INTRODUCTION TO DIGITAL COMPUTERS' MEMORY TECHNOLOGY

The modern history of computing dates back to 1944 when the Harvard Mark I Calculator was constructed. Other machines, such as the ENIAC, MANIAC, and ORDVAC, followed in quick succession. These high speed computers of the late forties became the laggards of the early fifties, when computer designers looked for new techniques to improve speed and reliability in the next generation of computing devices. Thus began a cyclic pattern of innovation and obsolescence which has since repeated on the average of every six years. Although the development of a new class of computing machines has been completed which are now being pressed into service, the burden of computing has kept pace with this technological advancement and computer designers are once again looking for new ways to increase computing speeds.

There are three basic approaches to high speed computer research, viz., (a) logical organization, (b) programming organization and (c) hardware innovation, and each of these holds promise in its own right. However, we can hope to make speed improvements of several orders of magnitude only through hardware innovation. Memory performance and cost are the twin keys to computer technology. Although new electronic device processor organizations and software systems have contributed enormous advances in computer technology, they would have been less effective without faster, more reliable, and cheaper memories that were developed with them.

The history of electronic digital computer has been connected with the development of suitable memories. Initially the development of high speed computers was seriously handicapped by lack of a suitable method of storing information. Some of the early computers used cathode-ray tubes for storage—the information being retained by electrostatic charges on the screen—but these devices were somewhat bulky and unreliable. Acoustic delay line and magnetic drums were used quite extensively but these had the drawback that access time was too long for the high speed operation required in fast computers. The development of square loop ferrite materials was undertaken to provide storage devices which would overcome all these disadvantages. The ferrite core made the large scale use of discrete elements for the storage of each binary digit economical and thus made possible random access system in which the access time is independent of the location of the infrmations in the store. Moreover, these storage devices are non-volatile and the reliability of ferrite core stores proved to be much higher than of previous high speed storage mechanisms, which became obsolete and were gradually replaced in all major computer developments.

Subsequently tunnel diode, cryogenic memories have been developed. The problems associated with cryogenic memories are both fundamental and economic. The major technical problem is uniformity. Meanwhile, continued advances in thin films and plated wire have pushed these technologies into contention.

Research and development in the field of storage systems, however, continued on an accelerated pace. As requirements for higher and higher volume of direct access storage increase, it appears that the production of memories from discrete storage elements becomes economically unfeasible. Consequently, new methods of mass and batch fabrication were required to render these systems economically possible. The resulting new devices have been utilized by memory developers to mechanize and to organize memories which offer the system-engineer new levels of performance.

1.1 ORGANIZATION OF DIGITAL COMPUTER IN RELATION TO MEMORY

Regardless of whether a computer is used for scientific work or for processing data, a computing system requires five major elements, as shown in the block diagram of Figure 1.1. These are input, output, storage, arithmetic unit, and control. Computer memory is analogous to work sheet and instruction list of the hand computation; the memory stores the initial data to be operated upon, the intermediate results, the final results, and also the instructions regarding the operation to be performed, the arguments to be operated upon, and the instruction to be chosen next. The actual operations indicated by the instructions are performed in the arithmetic unit. The input and output units can be punched paper-tape or card readers and punchers, or magnetic tape readers and writers, or character reading machines and high speed printers, etc.

From the point of view of economic impact, the history of computers might be said to begin in 1946 when the University of Pennsylavania's 'ENIAC' initiated the era of electronic computers. The significance of this event can be appreciated by comparing electronics with the other technologies with which computer pioneers had experimented.

The development that changed the simple organization of Von Neumann's computer (Figure 1.1) into today's system of processors of a large-scale computing centre occurred in small steps. The first innovation was caused by the great disparity in speed between the memory, control and arithmetic unit, which operate at electronic speeds, and the input-output (I/O) unit, which usually involves moving parts. The solution to this was straightforward, but had far reaching implications. When data have to be taken out, the control transfers this information to a buffer, signals the I/O unit to take care of it, then proceeds with the main calculation. When the work of I/O unit is finished, it interrupts the main processor with a message that it is ready for further work. We thus have two independent machines, the central processing unit (CPU) and the I/O processor.

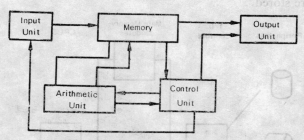

Figure 1.1 Block diagram of an electronic digital computer.

The number of different I/O units, or peripherals, soon mushroomed. To the paper tape reader and punch were added card readers and punches, line printers, magnetic tapes, plotters, visual displays and, for applications such as process control, real time inputs and outputs that interface through analog/digital converters. And, since the main memory is never large enough, backup storage devices, such as drums and disks, were added.

Coordinating the action of some or all of these units became a major task, well worth the services of one or two smaller computers, the satellite processor. Thus a basic disparity in speed of operation and the desire to use a costly computer in the most efficient way led to a system as shown in Figure 1.2.

Figure 1.2 would not be complete without remote consoles. Time sharing, or the use of one computer by many (apparently) simultaneously, arose from a nostalgia for the old days, when it was customary to ponder over a problem at the console and to keep the computer idle during most of this time. The basic idea of time sharing is simple. Time is sliced into short intervals, anywhere from a fraction of a second to minutes, and the slices are given according to some priority scheme in turn to the various users who sit at consoles and request time. An additional advantage is that these consoles, which are at present usually teletypewriter units, can be far from central computer, linked by a telephone line, so that a user has direct access to a large computer from his office or home.

However, the memory, a basic requirement of all data processing systems, is a place for storing a quantity of data and instructions, either temporarily or permanently. It holds all working data and instructions and makes them available to the data processing circuits when needed. Each cell, where a data number is stored in the memory, is identified by a location number called an *address*. It permits the machine instruction to call for the data by asking for the contents of the cell. It also permits the data to be stored at a particular cell, indentified by an individual address. Usually the cells are numbered in sequence. Data and machine instructions, when stored together in the memory, are so coded that the machine recognizes one from the other. They may also be stored separately in the memory, with the computer having a prior knowledge of where the machine instructions and data are stored.

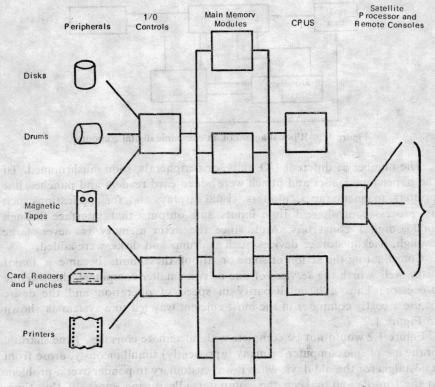

Figure 1.2   A typical computer system configuration.

The storage unit of a general purpose computer, as shown in Figure 1.3, may be classified according to the requirements into different sections, namely, the main store from which all the operations are carried out, the backing store and auxiliary store which supplement the main store. If block transfers can take place automatically between the main and backing stores required, the system can be used as if it is one store, with a capacity equal to the combined capacities of the two levels.

1.1.1   Main Memory

The memory of a large computer is not actually concentrated at one place, but storage devices are distributed throughout the machine. For instance, the storage device of a machine consists of the *operation registes*, which comprise the storage devices used in the arithmetic and control elements of the computer. However, the combination of the two blocks labelled *digital operational storage* and *address register,* may be termed as the main storage unit. During operation a number (usually a part of the word) is entered into the address register. The address register section controls the address selection system of the storage section in such a manner that one particular 'location' or 'address' is selected for the particular number. Then the word is stored in or read out from that particular location according to the operand part of the instruction.

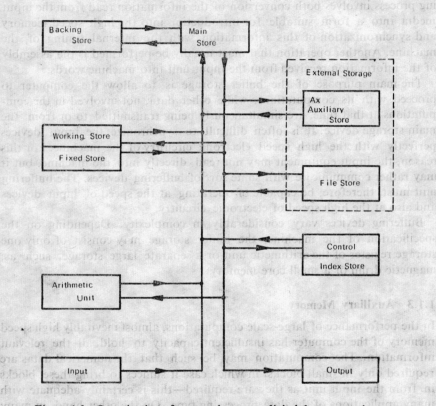

Figure 1.3 Organization of a general purpose digital data processing sytem.

Nowadays, large computing systems use semiconductor, magnetic thin film, magnetic core, tape, disk and drum memories. In these cases, the cores, the films, or semiconductors are used as the high speed, low capacity main memory, backed by a lower speed, higher capacity magnetic tape memory. In such systems, data is first brought into the main memory before it is actually used in computation, as the computation always involves a large number of data transfers between the main memory and the arithmetic unit.

1.1.2   Buffer Memory

In computing systems information is exchanged between input-output unit and internal memory. The input-output device is generally much slower in operation than internal memory or computing circuits. Furthermore, most of the input-output devices involve mechanical motion, and clearly, the effects of inertia and friction must make it difficult to synchronize them with the internal circuitry. This situation is worst in serial synchronous machines and least troublesome in parallel asynchronous machines. In such cases the expressive term *bufferings* has been applied to this transfer process. Buffering process involves both conversion of the information read from the input media into a form suitable for introduction into the high speed memory and synchronization of this information with the internal timing of the machine. Another operation that must usually be performed is the assembly of the information received from the input unit into machine words.

The main purpose of the buffer storage is to allow the computer to proceed with its computations, while other data, not involved in the computations at that time, are simultaneously being transmitted to or from the main storage device. It is often difficult to synchronize the input devices perfectly with the high speed electronic circuitry of the machine. For this reason, the input equipment may not read directly into the machine, but it may rather communicate with some sort of buffering devices. The buffering unit must, therefore, be capable of operating at the speed of input devices and also at the high speed of electronic circuitry.

Buffering devices vary considerably in complexity. Depending on the specification of the machine, the buffer storage may consist of only one storage register of the arithmetic unit or a separate large storage, such as, magnetic drum or a small core memory.

1.1.3   Auxiliary Memory

In the performance of large-scale computations, almost inevitably high speed memory of the computer has insufficient capacity to hold all the relevant information. The computation may be such that the numerical datas are required only in small blocks, in which case it suffices to bring these blocks in from the input unit as they are required—this is certainly adequate with many applications of the data processing type. On the other hand, in many applications a large volume of intermediate results may be generated from time to time which must be used in later stage of the computation. In such applications it is necessary to have an auxiliary memory to which information beyond the capacity of the high speed memory can be transferred and where it can be held until needed.

Auxiliary storage units are generally incorporated such that the size of the main storage unit can be kept within a reasonable limit. This section of the computers' memory is characterized by the low cost per digit stored. Whenever necessary, blocks of data and/or instructions can be transferred from the auxiliary storage unit to the main storage unit and *vice versa*. This section of the memory is sometimes designated as the *back-up-store*, because its function is to handle quantities of data which are excess of the storage capacity of the main memory.

The external or the auxiliary memory is usually a bulk storage medium, capable of holding large amounts of data and, therefore, mainly consists of slow-speed, large-capacity and low-cost units.

1.2 BRIEF HISTORY OF COMPUTERS' MEMORY

Conceptually, any element or phenomenon, that exhibits two or more stable states or a delay property, can be utilized for storage. In general, the design effort devoted to the improvement of random access memory is directed towards either the refinement of existing memory types or the development of basically new types of memories. Many other different techniques for memory devices have been used or proposed. These memory devices are varied in capacity, speed, reliability and cost. They can be classified in a variety of ways—static or dynamic, erasable or nonerasable, volatile or non-volatile, synchronous or asynchronous, serial or parallel, and so on. The most widely used memory devices discussed here are: (i) delay line storage, (ii) electrostatic and ferroelectric storage, (iii) magnetic drums, disks, and tapes, (iv) arrays of magnetic cores, (v) magnetic thin film, and (vi) semiconductor memory devices.

1.2.1 Delay Line Store

Delay lines have been used for digital storage since the early period of digital computers. Although it is one of the oldest forms of memory, it still remains a viable technology in small serial computers and electronic calculators, as well as in communication networks, television and radar systems. There are three basic types of passive delay lines in use today. The oldest, is the solid delay line, a prism of glass material in which signals are internally reflected at several faces while propagating from an input to an output transducer. Next is the wire line, in which a mechanical vibration is induced by a magnetostrictive transducer. The newest form is the surface delay line, in which the signals travel across the surface of the material rather than through its volume. And then there are acoustic delay lines of the semiconductor material. In these devices a sound wave creates electrical effects which in the presence of an electric field, react upon the sound wave to amplify it. These are shown in Figure 1.4.

Attenuation of the input pulses in the storage medium is considerable and as a result, restoring amplifiers are required at the receiving end. In many cases, a carrier frequency is required to transmit data efficiently in the medium. As a consequence, the input amplifier is often a modulator, and the receiving amplifier is a demodulator. All passive delay lines are subject

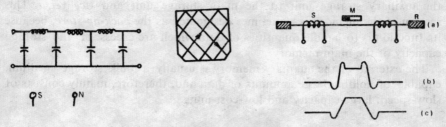

Figure 1.4   Delay line storage.

to certain fundamental limitations. One of these is associated with the way the sound attenuates as it is propagated through a material.

Delay line memory is basically a serial memory. In delay line memory, as the stored information appears at the output, it is immediately reloaded at the input. Thus, it is continuously recirculated with a time address rather than the physical location address. This time address—the moment at which a particular bit appears at the output—is in step with the data. It is available for use only when the data appear at the output of the delay line; and only at that moment can new data be loaded in it.

The use of purely electrical delay lines for storage is not suitable for more than a few bits due to size, cost and bandwidth limitations, whereas ultrasonic delay lines in the form of nickel wire or blocks of glass show significant improvement in cost, size, and weight factor.

Another form of delay lines that were used in some machines are the magnetostrictive delay lines. *Magnetostriction is the property of materials by virtue of which they change their length under the influence of a magnetic field.* Magnetostrictive delay lines consist of a length of magnetostrictive material with a transmitter at one end and a receiver at the other.

Although the variation of delay with temperature can be made negligibly small in magnetostrictive delay lines, the same in mercury delay lines is a significant factor limiting the maximum capacity of the unit. Also, the magnetostrictive delay lines are rugged, cheap and compact. In some applications their delay can be continuously varied simply by changing the position of the receiving transducer. Their chief drawback is their frequency response, which is not as good as that of mercury delay lines.

1.2.2   Electrostatic and Ferroelectric Store

The first available random-access memories made use of electrostatic storage tubes of which several types were developed. In 1949, F.C. Williams and others published a method of using a conventional cathode-ray tube as a memory tube. The electron beam of a cathode-ray tube directed to a definite target, causes the target to change its potential with respect to a common collector plate. The pulse thus stored is withdrawn by redirecting the beam to the targets, which is then permitted to discharge its stored potential to a common plate. This is the underlying principle of electrostatic storage and requires that means must be provided for retaining or regenerating the target potential.

An essential requirement for the operation of all electrostatic storage tubes is that the secondary emission ratio of the storage surface should be greater than unity for certain range of primary electron velocity. In Williams' tube, the charge patterns on small areas of the screen of a cathode-ray tube are used to store binary information. These small areas or spots, each representing one binary digit, are arranged in a two-dimensional array and are selected by means of the normal X and Y deflection plates. To detect the rate of change of charge on the surface during reading, a signal plate is placed close to the screen of cathode-ray tube. When the electron beam impinges on a target spot, the electrons cause a 'hole' to appear on the face of the tube. This produces a charge which can be detected on the collector plate when scanned. If, during writing, the electron beam is deflected slightly, a second 'hole' is produced. When the separation of the spots is less than a certain critical distance, some of the secondary electrons emitted from the second spot are attracted by the positive potential of the first. The potential at the first spot is, therefore, reduced and an overall potential distribution is set up between the two spots. This potential distribution can be used to represent the digit '0' and '1'—the single spot or 'dot' representing '0' and the double spot, which can be drawn out into a 'dash' representing '1'. In this method, the record is lost by leakage unless regenerated periodically.

Improvements in Williams' tube have been made later on. The dot-dash replaces the dot-dot method of recording—a '0' being recorded by focussing the beam on the target, and a '1' being recorded by permitting the beam to move a short distance under control of wide pulse. Other types of electrostatic storage devices, such as, 'barrier grid' storage tube, 'holding gun' tube, the 'selectron', 'diode-capacitor' storage were developed, though none of them have been found suitable for the present day memory system.

Quite recently much interest has been shown in the possible exploitation of the so-called *ferroelectric materials* in the construction of storage devices. Ferroelectric storage utilizes the rectangular hysteresis loop characteristics of some dielectric materials such as Rochelle salt, and barium titanate. The two remanent states of polarization may be taken to represent the digits '0' and '1'. The state of an element can be read by detecting the displacement current which flows when a field is applied. If the element was initially in the '1' state, a large displacement current flows as the polarization is changed. Similarly, a small current flows, for the element storing a '0'. The writing of information in the ferroelectric element is done by the coincidence of two voltage pulses, neither of which is sufficient enough to change the polarization.

Although ferroelectric store has the apparent advantages of simplicity of manufacture and high packing density, it has some practical difficulties. A defect of ferroelectric memory elements in comparison to magnetic elements is the comparatively high dissipation of energy during switching. As a result, to-dates ferroelectric memories have not emerged from the experimental stage.

1.2.3   Magnetic Drum, Disk and Tape Store

The familiar principles of magnetic recording have been applied in computers for the storage of information. The various moving-magnetic mediums used for recording can be conveniently considered in two classes—the noncontact recording systems such as drums and disks, and the incontact recording systems such as tapes and magnetic cards. The noncontact systems involve much higher velocities of the medium and are, therefore, faster systems. At the same time the binary data must be somewhat less densely packed on the surface so that flux variations from bit to bit can be detected across the air gap.

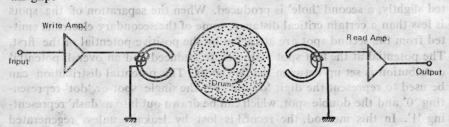

Figure 1.5   Read/write system of a magnetic drum.

The principles of writing and reading are generally the same for all these three moving memory systems, but the packing density and other details may vary widely. The arrangement of magnetic drum store is shown in Figure 1.5 and the modulation techniques for recording information are shown in Figure 1.6. The recording medium is deposited onto a nonmagnetic metal drum or cylinder. The read/write heads are fitted very close to the recording surface. The writing of information into the memory is done by turning on an electromagnet intermittently. The rate at which information can be transferred to or from a magnetic surface depends on the density with which the digits are packed along the surface and the velocity of the surface relative to the heads. Different types of magnetic memory recording have been used, although these can be considered as variations of two distinct families—return to zero (RZ) type, and nonreturn to zero (NRZ) type. The RZ and NRZ methods of recording may be regarded as amplitude modulation methods. Also, it is possible to record information by phase modulation method (PM), with positive rate of change of flux at the strobing instant representing one binary digit, and with negative rate of change of flux representing the other binary digit. So far as speed is concerned, the speed of magnetic drum is limited by the current in the braking coils, and hence the drum rotation is often maintained frequently at a nominal value of 3,600 rpm and sometimes at 6,900 rpm, as on Remington Rand (ERA) 1102, and on the Harvard Mark II, and sometimes at 12,000 rpm as on IBM 650 computer. High speed drum memory in the range of 18,000 rpm to 36,000 rpm has been successfully developed and used.

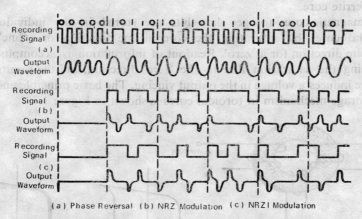

(a) Phase Reversal (b) NRZ Modulation (c) NRZI Modulation

Figure 1.6 Modulation techniques used in drum, disk, tape and film storage system.

Magnetic tapes and cards employ incontact recording. Thus the packing density is typically somewhat greater and the velocity lower than those with disks and drums. However, improvements in noncontact recording have diminished the difference between the two, so that maximum densities of 15,000 bits per inch are now obtainable both with contact and non-contact recordings. Surface speeds for contact recording run as high as 11.5 in/s in one commercial tape system.

The use of magnetic tape involves engineering problems different from those encountered with disks and drums. Tape is not ordinarily continuous and, therefore, cannot be continuously in motion. Quick starting and stopping of the tapes involve some severe mechanical problems. Another serious problem in the use of magnetic tapes is the presence of minor pinholes on the magnetic surface, which can cause "drop-outs" of recorded digits. Moreover, particles of dust on the tape can also cause "drop-outs". For these reasons parity checking is usually done in the tape transfer.

However, magnetic drums can be designed to store a large amount of information. For high speed, medium capacity, scientific computers, the use of a relatively small size core storage backed by a matched magnetic drum storage was the trend even in the second generation computers. For applications where economy is of major importance, magnetic drums and disks are the most prominent type of peripheral memories in use.

1.2.4 Magnetic Core Store

The use of square loop ferrite cores as storage elements was first suggested in 1947 by Forrester and others. The early work of Forrester was based on cores made of several wraps of metal tape. These were, however, not suitable for high-speed, large capacity storage systems. Later on, development of a magnesium-manganese ferrite resulted in the production of a more suitable ferrite core.

In magnetic cores torages data bits are stored in the individual tiny toroidal cores by saturating the core in one direction for a 'one' and in opposite direction for a 'zero'. Readout of information is accomplished by reversing the saturation flux in the 'zero' direction, and the resulting flux change induces a voltage in the output vincing. The basic principle underlying the storage mechanism in toroidal cores is shown in Figure 1.7.

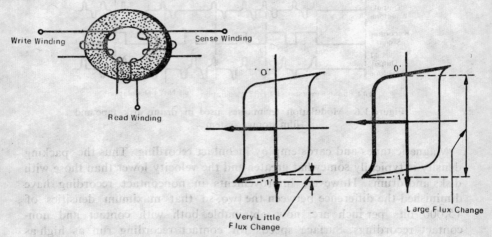

Figure 1.7 Basic switching mechanism of magnetic core.

Three types of core memory organizations are in use currently. These are known as coincident current 3D (bit organized memories), linear select 2D (word organized memories) and $2\frac{1}{2}$D systems. The $2\frac{1}{2}$D system is a three-wire hybrid of 2D and 3D systems and is faster than 3D system, having no inhibit noise on the sense wire. The method of reading from a core in one plane is to use two augmenting coincident current on the selected X and Y coordinates, so that only one core in one plane that receives these two currents will be selected for switching. Though the unselected cores on the selected rows and columns do not switch, they do generate additional noise in the sense wire. This noise problem is rather severe for large capacity core memories. The tiny toroidal cores are also very sensitive to temperature. The various organizations of core memories, the problem of noise, the drive current tolerances and the effect of temperature have been discussed elaborately in a subsequent chapter.

Basically, two techniques, namely, the destructive read-out (DRO) and the non-destructive read-out (NDRO) are employed in designing magnetic core memories. One of the methods requires the application of the reversible flux, as mentioned earlier and the other method utilizes the property of irreversible flux changes. However, various techniques of NDRO operation, using either the conventional cores or the specially designed core structures have been developed and these are briefly discussed in Chapter III.

Special ferrite devices were sometimes used for storing digital data. The ferrite aperture plate, as developed by J.A. Rajchman of RCA Laboratories, provides a complete magnetic memory plane in a single element. It is a small square plate in which holes are drilled in a matrix array. On this plate is etched a winding, linking all cores and this is conveniently used as the sense winding. The X and Y select windings must, therefore, be threaded through the holes. The individual 'core' requires a fairly small (about 330 mA) current to be driven to its saturation, and the switching time is about the same as that for ordinary toroidal cores. This, again forms a matrix that can presumably be produced quite cheaply on a mass scale.

1.2.5 Tunnel Diode Store

Various nonmagnetic memory elements have been developed and these are advantageous in certain applications. The tunnel diode, simply a negative resistance element, has been incorporated in several storage systems. Since the diode is not a hysteric device, like magnetic elements, its memory must have a d.c. holding power. A tunnel diode memory cell usually consists of one or two tunnel diodes and other circuit elements such as resistors, capacitors, rectifying diodes, etc. These additional circuit components are required to provide the proper d.c. holding bias and the means for write-in and read-out.

The current/voltage characteristic of a tunnel diode is shown in Figure 1.8(a) and a simple tunnel diode store for word organized system is shown in Figure 1.8(b). A rectifier diode has been added to increase the discrimination property. To read the information a negative voltage pulse is applied to word line A; this causes the rectifier diode to become forward biased in the elements where the tunnel diode is in the low voltage or 1 state

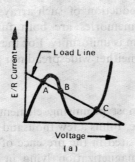
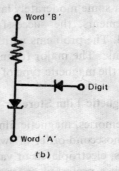

Figure 1.8 (a) Tunnel diode nagative resistance characteristic; and
(b) Tunnel diode storage element per word organized system.

and a current flows in the digit line. The voltage drop across those tunnel diodes in the high voltage state prevents the rectifier diodes from conducting. In the case of a stored 0, when writing, the tunnel diode is returned to its low voltage state by the application of a negative pulse to word line B, while the digit line is driven negative to write 1, or left at its normal potential to write 0.

Tunnel diode memory schemes can be operated in both destructive and nondestructive readout modes. The tunnel diode memory system requires a large number of components and, hence, the cost of the system is comparatively high. Also, due to large number of connections per element, the packing density decreases and the risk of failure increases. In addition to the advantage of high operating speed, the tunnel diode storage system requires only moderate currents and low voltages from the drive circuits as compared to magnetic elements.

1.2.6 Superconductive Store

Another class of random access memories utilizing the superconductive effects, is known as cryogenic memories. Tin and lead are the materials which exhibit superconductivity at low temperature. In continuous sheet memory, a tin film, a lead sense line, and a lead drive strip are fabricated by vacuum deposition techniques on a two inch square substrate. The sense line is beneath the storage plane and is oriented diagonally to and directly under the intersections of the two sets of drive strips which are orthogonal to one another. Coincidence of the X and Y drive currents at an intersection of the drive strips produces a magnetic field strong enough to switch the region of storage plane, beneath the intersection and out of the superconducting state, thus permitting magnetic flux to link through the plane in that region. When the currents are removed, the flux linking the small region of the continuous sheet is trapped, and the persistent currents are established in the storage plane to support this trapped flux. The stored information can proper polarity, and then sensing the voltage, change on the same line.

Although some moderately large memory arrays have been built with cryoelectric elements, the successful mass production of such arrays is yet to be achieved. The problems with cryogenic memories are both fundamental and economic. The major technical problem is uniformity. For these reasons, their use as the magnetic type of memory is neither widespread nor promising.

1.2.7 Magnetic Film Store

For fast memories, magnetic films are the most promising elements because of their nanosecond order of switching time. Films a few thousand angstroms in thickness, electroplated or vacuum deposited in the presence of magnetic field, exhibit a preferred or 'easy' axis of magnetization lying in the plane of the film, and the direction of magnetization along this axis can be reversed in a few nanoseconds. In the conventional planer film memory the word lines run parallel to the easy axis of magnetization, creating a field pattern in the 'hard' direction. The digit and the sense lines run parallel to the hard axis of magnetization, creating a field pattern in the 'easy' direction. A word line rotates all bit positions of a word in the 'hard' direction, but they tend to flip back, when released. A relatively small digit signal pushes them into the 'one' state or back to the 'zero' state, as desired. The flux is only rotated rather than switched.

The most promising type of magnetic film, which has received great attention for presentday computer memories, is known as plated wire. This is fabricated by plating a magnetic film on a wire substrate. The wire substrate then serves as one of the electrical conductors in the system. A closed flux path can be obtained by using the magnetic film surrounding the wire in a small region.

Nowadays plated wire memories operating at 500 nsec cycle times have a diode in series with each word line, permitting a very economical transistor switch matrix to select the word lines. These matrices would be feasible for operating cycle time down to about 200 nsec. Advantages cited for plated wire memories include low cost, high speed, easier fabrication and capability of nondestructive readout operation.

Another form of cylindrical thin film memory, known as 'Magnetic Rods', has been used in many experimental and commercial computers. These films are isotropic and are made of materials having high coercive force. Also, the problems of magnetostriction, skew, and dispersion, which plagued designers of planer thin film memories and the plated wires with circumferential storage states are avoided here. This rod memory element has the advantage of fast switching speed and larger output signals.

1.2.8   Semiconductor Store

The most obvious storage application of integrated circuit techniques is in discrete bit storage and registers, where each bit position of the register is mechanized with a single integrated circuit flip-flop. Prototype memories have been built in which special integrated circuit storage elements are utilized in a matrix configuration. One such element uses a p-n-p and a n-p-n transistor as a latching switch which is simpler than the conventional flip-flop. As integrated circuit technology yields improvement of the fabrication, significantly higher speed, lower cost, and larger capacity, random access memories are possible through the use of planer epitaxial transistor and metal oxide semiconductor (MOS) elements.

The circuits on these chips can be either static or dynamic. Information is stored in MOS memory elements either in the form of conventional cross-coupled pair of d.c. 'nor' gates, or in the form of a charge on a capacitor in a dynamic circuit. The charge is maintained by periodic refreshing. Such dynamic circuits dissipate very little power and can be packed very densely on a small chip. However, large scale integration (LSI) through MOS technology promises to enhance the performance and cut the cost of random access memories. The typical size of this cell, with addressing lines, is about 40 square mils of silicon wafer and it dissipates less than one milliwatt of power.

The factors that limit speed in the simplest MOS designs are the transistor's resistance and capacitance, which form an RC network with an intrinsic time constant.

1.2.9 Optical Store

Optical techniques, though still in an early stage of development, offer a number of advantages in mass storage applications. Optical methods permit information packing densities greater than those possible with magnetic recording, which provides a different approach to problem of power consumption, weight and mechanical complexity. The development of optical memories takes the advantage of all the latest tricks of the trade, such as, holography, high resolution photographic emulsion and photochromism. They use the laser to vaporize material or to heat it above some critical temperature, where it can be affected by external magnetic or electric field.

Magnetic materials when combined with optical systems lead to several novel approaches for reversible storage media. Considerable progress has been made on the problem of developing beam accessed memories using magnetic film as storage medium. Writing is accomplished by heating above the curie point, using either an electron or light beam. In principle, reading can be accomplished by the same beam of electrons or light. Read-out using light is more favourable since the interaction between light and the magnetic materials, called the *magneto-optical effect*, is strong enough to yield excellent signal-to-noise ratio from a single bit even as small as one micron in diameter.

Another approach to optical memories, known as *optoelectronic memories*, is to use some form of light emitting storage elements. Optoelectronic memories contain an array of electrically bistable light emitting elements, any of which can be turned on or off, so binary data can be stored. Much of the interest in optoelectronic stems from its low cost potential, which depends on the fact that (a) individual active and passive circuit elements such as, inductors, capacitors, transistors, etc. are not required, and (b) relatively large and complex arrays may be fabricated using polycrystalline materials and simple manufacturing techniques.

The optoelectronic technique also possesses a number of other significant properties. The availability of visible radiation provides useful nondestructive readout properties in memory function, as well as excellent isolation between control and signal paths in the logic function. In addition, electroluminscent arrays are sources of broad area, diffuse light emission; thus it is possible to form compact groups of individually controllable light emitting areas, which respond very rapidly to direct electrical excitation.

1.2.10 Magnetic Bubble Store

A uniaxial magnetic film with its easy axis normal to the film exhibits serpentine domains in the demagnetizing state. When a stable d.c. bias magnetic field is applied along the easy axis, those serpentine domains with magnetization opposite to the applied field will shrink and become a cylindrical domain which are called magnetic bubbles. Such cylindrical domains or bubbles represent cluster of magnetic spins stable under the combined influences of the applied field, domain wall energy, and the magnetostatic energy.

The magnetic bubble technology has now reached a point where it is destined to play a leading role in the future development of computer hardware. The generation, propagation and sensing of the magnetic bubble domains are different aspects of the same phenomena—the interaction of bubble domains with its magnetic environment. In binary storage applications, individual bubble domains are manipulated in the garnet medium by either current loops or permalloy propagation tracks.

1.3 CHARACTERISTICS AND CLASSIFICATION OF MEMORY SYSTEMS

It can safely be remarked that the development work of high-speed electronic computer has progressed simultaneously with the development of adequate memory systems. Various memory devices discussed so far differ widely in size, speed of operation, cost and complexity. They can be classified in several ways. An incomplete list of classification based on their location, physical characteristics, mode of operation, usage, etc. is discussed below.

(i) *Location*. The memory systems of a large computer are not actually concentrated in one place, but are distributed throughout the machine. Memories may be classified as internal or external to the computer or central processor, depending on their location.

(ii) *Physical type*. Memory design may be of different types of which the more popular types include:

(a) Semiconductor memories (LSI).
(b) Magnetic cores, thin films, cylindrical films.
(c) Magnetic drums, disks and tapes.
(d) Delay lines.
(e) Electrostatic and ferroelectric memories.
(f) Miscellaneous types consisting of cryogenic, aperture plate, tunnel diode, optical memories and magnetic bubble memory.

(iii) *Physical characteristic*. Memories can be classified according to their physical characteristics, such as, erasable or nonerasable; volatile or nonvolatile. In a *volatile* memory, information either decays naturally or is lost when electrical power is switched off, e.g. electrostatic and delay line memories. However, in a *nonvolatile* memory, information once recorded remains without deterioration until deliberately changed. The examples of this class of memory are the different types of magnetic memories. Information stored in dynamic registers, flip-flop registers, core memory, magnetic drum and tape is *erasable*, while information stored in punched cards, paper tapes, and photographic plates is *nonerasable*.

(*iv*) *Mode of transfer*. Serial or parallel word transfer is also an important distinction which serves to classify memories.

(*v*) *Principle of operation*. Storage devices can also be divided according to whether they are static or dynamic. A static storage device is one in which the information does not change position. Flip-flop registers, magnetic core registers, punched cards or tapes are examples of the static storage devices. Dynamic storage devices, on the other hand, are devices in which the information stored is continuously changing position.

(*vi*) *Mode of access*. The procedure for locating information may be divided into two classes—random access and sequential access. A random access storage device is one in which any location in the memory may be selected at random, and access to the information stored is direct. Examples of this type are flip-flop register and magnetic core memory system. A sequential access device is one in which the arrival at the location desired, may be preceded by sequencing through other locations. Magnetic drums, tapes and disks are the examples of sequential access memory.

(*vii*) *Capacity*. Memories can be subject to a less specific or more relative classification according to speed and capacity. The different types are high speed-low capacity, medium speed-medium capacity and low speed-high capacity systems. Usually, large capacity system includes memories with a capacity greater than 10^7 binary digits, medium-capacity is from 10^5 to 10^7 binary digits, and low capacity is below 10^5 binary digits. Similarly, for the speed ranges, low speed includes the access time greater than 1 millisecond, medium speed access times are between 1 millisecond and 10 microseconds, and high speed access times are less than 10 microseconds.

(*viii*) *Usage*. Memories can be classified according to use. For example, in some cases the data will never change; a table of logarithms or trigonometric functions would thus constitute a permanent memory. In other uses, the memory contents are continually changed as the problem solution proceeds to alter the memory.

All these classifications overlap and the characteristic which is most useful to the designer depends a great deal on the application. The magnetic core memories, which are random access, static, erasable storage devices, are used principally in the inner memory because of their high operating speeds and low cost per bit.

References

Anderson, J.R. (1953) : 'Electrical delay lines for digital computer applications', *IRE Trans. on Electronic Computers*, V. EC-2, pp. 5-13, June.

Ayling, J.K. and Moore, R.D. (1971): 'Main monolithic memory', *IEEE. J. Solid State Circuits* V. SC-6, pp. 276-79.

Salvitt, D.A., et. al. (1961): 'Tunnel diode storage using current sensing', *Proc. Western Joint Computer Conf.*, May, pp. 427-42.

Back, R.M. (1960): 'A high speed serial general purpose computer using magnetestrictive delay line storage', *Proc. Eastern Joint Computer Conf.*, December, pp. 283-97.

Bate, G. and Alstad, J.K. (1969): 'A critical review of magnetic recording materials', *Trans. on Magnetics. IEEE* V. MAG-5, pp. 821-39.

Bobeck, A.H. (1967): 'Properties and device applications of magnetic domains in orthoforrites', *Bell. Syst. Tech. J.* V. 46, pp. 1901-925.

Booth, A.D. (1948): 'A magnetic digital storage system', Electronic Engineering, V. 21, no. 257, pp. 234-38.

Bowden, B.V. (1955): 'Faster than thought', Isaac Pitman, London.

Bradley, E.M. (1960): 'A computer storage matrix using ferromagnetic thin films', *J. Brit. IRE.*, V.20, pp. 765-84.

Buck, D.A. (1956): 'The cryctron—a superconductive computer component', *Proc. IRE*, V. 44, pp. 482-493, April.

Conti, C.J. (1969): 'Concepts for buffer storage', *IEEE Comp. Group News*, V.2, No. 8, pp. 9-13.

Dakin, C.J. and Cooke, C.E.G. (1967): 'Circuits for digital equipment', Lonxon Iliffe Books, London.

Eckert, J.P. (1953): 'A survey of digital computer memory systems', *Proc. IRE*, V. 41 no. 10, pp. 1393-1406.

Forrester, J.W. (1951): 'Digital information storage in three dimensions', *J. Appl. Phys.*, V. 22, pp. 44-48.

Gleen, W.E. and Wolf, J.E. (1962): 'Thermoplastic recording', *Intern. Science and Technology*, pp. 28-35.

Gleen, W.E. (1959): 'Thermoplastic recording', *J. Appl. Phys.* V. 30, December.

Hartres, D.R. (1946): 'The ENIAC and electronic computing machine', *Nature*, V. 158, pp. 500.

Holland, J.H. (1960): 'On iterative circuit computers constructed on microelectronic components and system I, *Proc. Western Joint Computer Conf.*

Hoover L.W., Hough, G. and Herrott, D.R. (1959): System design of the flying spot store', *Bell Syst. Tech. J.* V. 38, pp. 363.

Huskey, H.D. and Korn, G.A. (1962): 'Computer handbook', New York, McGraw-Hill.

Kaufman, M.M. (1960): 'Tunnel diode 10 μsec memory', *IRE Intern. Convention Records*, pt. II, pp. 114-23.

Kilburn, W., Toolill, G.C. and Williams, F.C. (1951): 'Universal high speed digital computer', *Proc. IEE*, V. 96, pt. II, pp. 13-28.

Langmuir, D.B. (1937): Theoretical limitations of cathode ray tubes', *Proc. IRE.*, V. 25 pp. 977-91.

Lentx, T. and Miyata, J. (1961): Magneto-optical readout of magnetic recording', *Electronics*, V. 34 pp. 36-9.

Mayer, L. (1958): Magnetic writing with an electron beam', *J. Appl. Phys.*, V. 29 pp. 1454-56.

Miller, J.C. et. al., (1960) : 'The tunnel diode as a storage element', *Inern. Solid State Circuit Conf.*, Digest, pp. 52-3.

Moore School of Engineering (Electrical) (1948): 'The EDVAC, a preliminary report on logic and design', Univ. of Pennsylvania, Philadelphia.

Pasqualini, R. (1967): 'Design consideration for a parallel bit organized MOS memory', *IEEE Trans. on Electronic Computers*, V.EC-16, pp. 551-57.

Petritx, R.L. (1967): 'Current status of large scale integration', Fall, Joint Computer Conf., *AFIPS. Proc.*, V. 31, pp. 551-557.

Pugh, E.W. (1971): 'Storage hierarchies: gaps, cliffs and trends', *IEEE Trans. on Magnetics,*, V. MAG-7, pp. 810-14.

Rajchman, J.A. (1953): 'A Myriabit magnetic core matrix memory', *Proc. IRE*, V. 41, no. 10 pp. 1407-1421.

Richards, R.K. (1957): 'Digital computer components and circuits,' D. Van Nostrand Inc., Princeton, N.J.

Hoagland, A. (1972): 'Mass storage—past, present and future, AFIPS, Proc. Fall Joint Comp. Conf. V. 41, pp. 985-991.

Schmidt, J.D. (1965): 'Integrated MOS transistor random access memory', *Solid State Design*, V. 6, pp. 21-25.

Sinkins, Q.W. (1967): 'Planar magnetic films memories,' *Fall, Joint Computer Conf.*, V. 31, pp. 593-94.

Speliotis, D.E. (1967): 'Magnetic recording materials', *J. Appl. Phys.*, V. 38, pp. 1207-14.

Takahashi, S., Ishii, O. et. al. (1962) : 'A tunnel diode high speed digital memory', *IFIP Congress Proc.*, Munich, September.

Wilkes, M.V. and Renwick, W. (1948) : 'An ultrasonic memory unit for EDSAC', *Electronic Engineering*, V. 20, pp. 208-213, July.

Williams, F.C. and Kilburn, T. (1949): 'A storage system for use with binary digital computers,' *Proc. IEEE*, V. 96, pt. II, pp. 81-100, March.

Williams, F.C. and Kilburn, T. et. al. (1953): 'Recent advances in cathode ray tube storage,' *Proc. IEEE.*, Pt. II, V. 100, pp. 523-539, October.

2. STORAGE SYSTEMS FOR ELECTRONIC COMPUTERS, USING MAGNETIC LAYER SURFACES AND THEIR DESIGN STUDY

The role of storage section in all information processing systems (IPS) has been explained briefly in Chapter 1. In this chapter, studies on the design of magnetic particulate layer medium stores for electronic computers, such as, magnetic drums, disks and tapes, are presented, mostly from system requirement considerations along with the physics of memory devices. The possibilities and limitations of these stores are discussed and to what extent the design can be optimized is indicated.

2.1 PHYSICAL PRINCIPLES INVOLVED IN MAGNETIC PARTICULATE LAYER MEMORY

The basic requirements of a storage device or memory system of any of the IPS are as follows:

(a) Physical stability of the stored data, so that the information can be retained for an extended period, if desired.
(b) Combination of the physical properties of nonvolatility and alterability.
(c) Sufficiently high total capacity to hold binary information.
(d) Small enough access time or maximum waiting time for reading from or writing on to a desired location.

Digital information storage systems employing magnetic surfaces are built to satisfy the above requirements for specific applications. Magnetic drum and disk memory systems use a rotating nonmagnetic metallic drum and disk respectively, with a magnetizable surface coating as its memory organ. Basic requirements in connection with a memory, that is, both its ability to record two states of a binary digit and availability of the stored data for consultation at any time, are satisfied in this type. It is customary to divide the magnetic surface into cells, each having a finite area. Either state of a binary digit is defined by the magnetic configuration of the cell. The state of magnetization of a cell represents a static storage. When the medium is moved relative to a pick-up head in close proximity of the digit cell, it is converted to a dynamic storage. The fluxes associated with a digit cell will take up the minimum reluctance path along the pick-up head, and a voltage will be developed across the windings in the head approximately proportional to the time and space derivative of the stored flux pattern. The nature of the voltage waveform will give a clear indication of the state of magnetization of the medium. For recording the appropriate digit polarity in the specified cell the pulse current is fed into a coil wound on a magnetic core which is almost complete magnetically except for a small air gap in the vicinity of the recording medium which is moved relative to this head.

Since any practical computer store should satisfy the requirements of large storage capacity and easy accessibility to the stored data, the design of memory involves a storage problem as well as a switching problem.

2.2 MAGNETIC DRUM AND DISK STORES IN DIFFERENT ELECTRONIC COMPUTER SYSTEMS

Depending on the class of computer and the type of use, in principle a magnetic drum and disk can conveniently be used either as the main store, buffer store or as the auxiliary store of an automatic digital computing system. It should be remembered that these rotating wheel magnetic memories were used as main store in several first generation digital computers. The first digital computers were built for mathematicians under their guidance. The functional elements, of which memory is the most important single member, took certain sizes and shapes, depending on the fact that for solving mathematical problems digitally, large number of arithmetical operations need to be performed on a comparatively small number of data. Computers belonging to this class are known as scientific and engineering computers. First generation computers such as UNIVAC and IBM 704 and many other smaller machines such as IBM 650, DATATRON, HEC, URAL, etc. were developed primarily as scientific computers. Magnetic drums were used as the main store in these computers, whenever a low speed, cost limited computer was desired to be built, with both drum and disk as the backing up (auxiliary) store whenever required.

2.2.1 Magnetic Drums in Data Processors

In the next stage of development computers were built for proccessing business data. These had to have different interrelations between functional parts, as in a business machine large amount of data is to be processed, the number of arithmetic operations being smaller. First generation data processors that are still in use were essentially scientific computers with special features that made them useful for business and statistical problems which are characterized by large amount of data and frequent input. Manipulating these data requires large storage capacity, frequency sorting and decisions or branch routine operations. Table 2.1 shows the characteristics of large-scale calculators and business data processors in which systems magnetic drums were extensively used as main store, and almost universally used as the auxiliary store. Table 2.2 shows the use of magnetic drums in some large scale calculators and business data processors of the first generation machines.

2.2.2 Magnetic Drums and Disks in Factory Control and Real Time Applications

When the research and development of scientific computers and data processors were aiming at refinements and improvements, a relatively later trend in line of the development has been the use of digital computers for the control of production processes. The parameters involved in a process control or manufacturing control computer are less critical but must be very reliable. A quantitative consideration drawn from a hypothetical example of a computer controlling a factory producing automobiles will be helpful for understanding. Production per hour is, say, 100 automobiles, and there are about 2000 automobiles at various stages of production. If there are 50 decision points in the process, and each car assembly on arriving at a decision point needs an entry into the computer and requires a decision from the computer. If the variables of a car are defined in 200 bits, the total storage requirement will not exceed 500,000 bits. So it would be an extremely wasteful exercise with respect to storage capacity and entry rate capacity to use scientific computer or business machines for factory control processes. Magnetic drums provided a very suitable memory device for application in such computers in the early years of automation.

Digital computers are used as the central component of the large-scale real time systems. In such a system, input data from a large number of independent asynchronous sources are fed automatically into the computer where they are processed under programmed control. A complete compilation of the real time situation is made by the computer and presented to operators. The computer automatically generates control command for the external environment in response to corrections and command information fed into it by the operators. We do not intend to go into the complexities of logical design for real time computers, which must have outstanding features considering its particular real time applications. Greater emphasis is naturally placed on reliability, speed, capacity and flexibility than is usual in scientific or commercial applications.

In a process control system the various independent synchronous or asynchronous sources operate at a much lower speed than that of the computer. It may not be operationally feasible to interrupt the computer operations to accept each piece of data as it arrives. So buffering mechanisms are designed to gather the data at the slow incoming rate and then pass on the large block of the data to the computer at the computers speed. The desirable features for such a system can be characterized as follows:

(a) Input data should be written on the memory as soon as possible after they are received and definitely before another piece of data is received from the same source.

TABLE 2.1

Characteristic of some early first generation computers

Manufacturer	Year	Model	Word length bits	Basic circuits	Clock rate Kc	Type of storage	Typical capacity (word)	Access time μsec	Special features
English Electric	1955	DEUCE	32	Vac. tube	1	Drum	8K	15	Serial binary computer
Ferranti Ltd.	1956	PEGASUS	39	-do-	330	Nic. delay line	—	—	Accumulators
Bull, France	1956	GAMMA 3 ET	12 digit	Vac. tube, diode	280	Delay line drum 4K 100	135 4K	500 10,000	—
Ramington Rand	1957	UNIVAC-II	12 chr.	Vac. tube, transistor	—	Core drum	4K 10K	20	M. Speed Sc. Comp.
Ferranti Ltd.	1957	MERCURY	40	Vacuum tube	1000	Core drum	1K 16K	20 10,000	Division by subroutine only
International Business MAC. Corp.	1957	704	Variable 12 deci. digital and sign	Transistor diode	—	Core	2K/32K	12	High speed general purpose computer
Siemens	1958	SIEMENS 2002		Diode transistor	200	Core drum	100K 1000K	5 10,000	Real time input
Datamatic Corp.	1958	DATAMATIC 1000		Diode transistor	100	Core	2K	10	High speed general purpose computer
Standard Elec.	1959	ER-56	7 deci. digits	Diode transistor	—	Core drum	9K 72K	5 10,000	—
Ferranti Ltd.	1959	SIRIUS	10 deci. digits	Core transistor	500	Nickel delay line	10 K	4,000	—

EMI Electronic	1960	EMIDEC 1100	36	Transistor	100	Core	4K	10	Aut. deci. binary conv.
Olivetti, Italy	1960	ELEA 9003	Variable	Diode transistor	100	Core drum	20K 120K	10 10,000	Three simult. prog. sequences
Philips	1960	PASCAL	42	Vac. tube diode transistor	660	Core drum	2K 16K	3 —	—
Computer Dev. ICT	1961	STEVIN ICT-1301	12 deci.	Diode transistor	1000	Core drum	2K 80K	4 300	Automatic error correction
Leo Comp. Ltd.	1961	LEO-III	42	Diode transistor	—	Core	4K	7	—
Eng. Elec.	1962	KDF-9	48	Core, diode, transistor	2	Core	4K/32K	3	Use of spl. working storage

TABLE 2.2

Use of magnetic drums in some first generation calculators and business data processors

Calculators	IBM-type 701	ERA-1103A	IBM-type 704	ILLIAC	702	IBM-type 702	IBM-type 705	UNIVAC file computer	Underwood Corp ELECOM 125	RCA BIZMAC	Ferrantio- Orion
Magnetic-drum capacity	8,192 or 16,384 words	Integrated drum of 16,384 words	8,192 or 16,384 words	12,800 words	36,848 words	Up to 30 drums or 60,000 characters	Same as 702	10,880 characters	10-100,000 characters	Core+ drum 4096+ 32,736 characters	Core +drum 16,384 (incore) any number of drums each holding 16,384 words
Access time	50 ms	17 ms	12 ms	17 ms	8.3 ms		Variable word length	5 ms	1.7 ms		24 ms
Speed	800 words per second	30,000 words per second (depending on inter-race)	10,000 words per second		25,000 characters per second			Fixed word variable block	0.02 ms (core) 5.2 ms (drum)		
Word size	18 or 36 bits	36 bits	36 bits	40 bits	Variable word length					Variable word block	Can be fitted
Arithmetic number system	Parallel binary	Parallel binary	Parallel binary	Parallel binary	Parallel binary	Characters serially, decimal alphanumeric	Same as 702	Characters serial alphanumeric	Characters serial numeric	Characters Alpha-numeric	Alpha-numeric

(b) The writing of input data on the memory should not interfere with the reading of data by the computer.

(c) The computer should be able to read the data selectively from the memory, that is, to read data from only one source at a time.

(d) The buffering system must be able to combine the data received from many sources. All these requirements can be conveniently incorporated in a magnetic drum and disk storage systems. The dual access system, with one set of heads for the computer side, another set for the outside world, avoids interference and makes the system very reliable.

In most control systems various quantities change relatively little between computing cycles. A special type of digital computer called the digital differential analyzer (DDA) works with incremental changes in quantities other than their absolute values. This family of special purpose computers, started with magnetic drum as its main memory.

2.3 DESIGN PARAMETERS FOR ROTATING MAGNETIC MEMORIES IN COMPUTING SYSTEMS

The computing speed of a machine depends mainly on the action of the high speed parts of the machine. During the system design, either using Von Neumann's elaborate method or some simplified method, an optimum combination for the working speeds of the arithmetical system and the operational information storage is to be calculated, from which the tentative parameters of the storage system are found. The most important technical indices of the storage system of universal automatic digital machines are: *service delay*, i.e., the period from the instant of the generation of the read/write signal and the memory operation complete signal; *capacity*, measured by the general quantity of information stored in the system; *working reliability*; *economy*; *easy* obliteration of stored information; *overall size*, etc.

The service delay determines the computing speed. If the computing system operates at a moderate speed then there is no sense in stepping up the quick action of the storage system excessively. It is also unreasonable to attach a storage system with a large service delay to a high speed computing system. An optimum combination must be found out. Increasing the working speed of these systems often decreases reliability, for complicating the design and forcing circuit conditions.

Let us take the overall duration of the operations as a fully determined value τ_{op} conditioned by the parameters of its circuits, then the dependence of the comuputing speed V_0 on the average service delay τ_0 can be expressed by the following relationship:

$$V = \frac{1}{\tau_{op}[1 + n/\eta]} \tag{1}$$

where $\eta = \tau_{op}/\tau_0$ can be termed as the coefficient of the working efficiency of the storage system. It shows how many times τ_{op} is greater than τ_0. The term n characterizes the number of times reference to the operational storage is essential for executing each operation on the arithmetical system . n depends on machine design. In the simple case, $n = 1$ for a single address machine and goes up to 4 for a 3 or 4 address machine.

If we represent $V \tau_{op} = f(\eta)$ on a graph it can be seen that as η increases in the initial sections of the curve, the computing speed rises considerably (approximately to 0.9-0.8 for $n = 1$-4 in accord for $\eta = 10$-20). After that even a substantial increase in η will no longer result in a rise in computing speed which attains the maximum value $V \tau_{op} = 1$ with $\eta = \infty$, i.e in the case where $\tau_0 = 0$ (in practice such a case never occurs). So the purpose of the designer is not to aim at achieving $\tau_0 = 0$, but to have harmonious combination of the quick action of the various systems of the machine. In this respect values of η between 10 and 20 may, in practice, be considered optimum for $n = 1$-4.

Before we go deep into the subject we shall define the following terms:

D = number of digits/words
W = number of words/track
A = access time in seconds
T = number of tracks
S = scanning rate
d = diameter of the magnetic drum
δ = packing density per linear inch
Δ = packing density per square inch
s = area of the magnetizable material which must be scanned in order to provide the required capacity
P = number of revolutions of the drum per unit time
τ_n = duration of the word code with serial recording along strip (with parallel recording $\tau_n = 0$)
τ_d = delay time in line
f_s = repetition rate of pulses
τ_t = time needed for transforming a discrete address code into electrical control quantities corresponding to the code
τ_{rp} = duration of the process of recording

It has been stressed earlier that accurate knowledge about the limiting values of design parameters is essential to reach a safe design which must be satisfied by an optimum design. In previous section we have made a brief comparative survey of the ultimate performance criteria of some memory systems and also indicated about the optimality criteria. Using those notations we shall study the technical variables involved in the design of a complete magnetic drum store.

Without considering their mutual interrelations, the variables may be listed as: (1) scanning rate; (2) drum and disk size; (3) pulse packing density; (4) access time and service delay; (5) properties of the coating material and coating thickness; (6) record/read head design; (7) aerodynamic effects at high speed; and (8) switching the desired location. So it seems that inspite of the applicability of the general principles of magnetic recording and playback, the variables involved in the process of pulse recording on a rotating magnetic wheel are sufficiently complex to render the process ineffective unless the interrelationship among the large and generally impractical number of parameters is found. Nonlinear characteristics of parameter variations, conflicting requirements of speed, reliability and cost and numerous other factors, often cause the bulk of the design procedure to consist of empirical studies on the work bench. We shall attempt here to insert the desired conditions in a few well-selected formulae to obtain the design as is possible in other branches of technology.

2.3.1 Scanning Rate

By remote implications scanning rate depends on almost all other variables. It may be defined as

$$S = \frac{TWD}{A} \text{ digits/second} \tag{2}$$

It appears from Eq. (2) that scanning rate is to be increased by maximizing the total memory capacity and by minimizing access time without decreasing total memory capacity.

To maximize total memory capacity we have to increase either the digit packing density for a fixed drum diameter or the total number of tracks at a fixed digit packing density (say, maximum reliable packing density) or the drum diameter. The drum diameter, again, affects maximum reliable packing density and also indirectly the access time. So it calls for an optimum drum diameter.

2.3.2 Drum Size

By optimum drum size we shall mean optimum drum diameter and maximum number of tracks. Total number of tracks possible is limited largely by the difficulty of switching the location with very large number of tracks and also to some extent by the mechanical considerations for rotating a long cylinder.

Increasing the diameter of the drum increases the length of the track, but the number of digits which can be stored does not increase in proportion after a certain diameter. This is due to the fact that the packing density depends to an extent on the spacing between the head and the magnetizable surface of the drum and the head dimensions. The minimum permissible spacing is determined by the mechanical tolerance of the drum which has to be relaxed after a certain size. Similarly, making a drum of smaller diameter reduces the information that can be stored in a single track, but again not proportionately, since finer tolerances and smaller heads can up to a point be used. Also, to minimize access time, drum diameter should be kept small, since the maximum speed at which the drum can be rotated without risk of breaking up is proportional to its peripheral speed.

If the drum is to be used as an intermediate store or as an auxiliary store where minimization of access time is not so important, a large amount of design flexibility is permissible. From practical point of view drum diameter should be kept small, and a drum of 5-10 inch diameter with grease packed super-procession ball bearing and integral high frequency motor capable of running up to a speed of 24,000 rpm can be safely used.

2.3.3 Packing Density

The area of the magnetizable material which must be scanned in order to provide the required capacity is given by

$$s = \frac{TWD}{\Delta} \text{ sq. inch} \tag{3}$$

Thus from the dimension of the recorded dipole packing densities are very important parameters which, together with total memory capacity specified, indicate the scale of design of the memory system. The packing density is essentially dependent on the geometry of the head and drum, their relative speed and properties of the coating materials.

In actual calculations we have to consider the safety margins both with respect to length and breadth of an elementary recorded dipole. The points to be considered are: (i) goemetric span between the extremities of the recorded dipole; (ii) rate of decline of the recorded flux at the ends of the dipole; (iii) duration of the recording current pulse during the recording process; (iv) geometry of the head (as there are tapers in the magnetic coupling coefficient at the two sides of the head in front of the drum). Parameter (i) is related to the span of the head, obviously a very small gap is necessary if a high density of recorded information is to be obtained, while (ii) indicates that the nature of the field at some distance is also important. Hence, better 'pulse resolution' is to be achieved by minimizing these 'trailing effects' beyond the 'span' by proper head design and choice of coating material. Parameter (iii) can be minimized to negligible value by reducing the duration of the recording pulse at the limit. An approximate estimate of the dipole span and the flux pattern at the extremities can be made experimentally by using heads of negligible width. Detailed theoretical and experimental study of these points along with study of the potential between the corners of the head and distribution of magnetic field in the ferromagnetic layer of the drum, variation of the field with permeability, airgap, layer thickness, drum eccentricity, etc. will be presented in later section.

The most important engineering parameters involved in the design of a magnetic drum store, as mentioned in this chapter, viz. read/record head design, properties of the coating material and coating thickness, aerodynamic effects at high speed, etc. will be presented along with the description of a magnetic drum storage system designed, developed and constructed by one of the authors, in the next sections.

2.3.4 Memory Cost and Performance

To establish a framework for relating memory performance in terms of capacity, access time, and cost with recording and circuit effects, the following relationship is suggested:

$$C = K \left(\frac{B_c}{A_{av}} \right)^{1/2} \tag{4}$$

where C = cost, K = a constant for a particular technology and cost structure, B_c = bit capacity and A_{av} = average access time.

The storage factors in Eq. (4) above can further be related to the drum recording parameters as follows:

$$C = K \, (2B_f T_N)^{1/2} \tag{5}$$

where B_f = bit frequency, T_N = number of tracks.

Therefore, if we assume a fixed recording frequency and number of tracks, the cost of the memory system will be constant from Eq. (5) and the capacity will be linearly related to the access time from Eq. (4).

Thus, from Eq. (4) $\dfrac{C^2}{K^2} = \dfrac{B_c}{A_{av}}$ $\tag{6}$

and from Eq. (5) $\dfrac{C^2}{K^2} = 2B_f T_N$ $\tag{7}$

Therefore $B_c = 2B_f T_N \times A_{av}$ $\tag{8}$

This approach offers the unique opportunity to weigh the performance factors and estimate their influence upon memory cost. For example, in designing an auxiliary store for a data processing system, we see from these relationships, that a two megabit-3 millisecond system is equivalent technologically and cost-wise to an eight megabit-12 millisecond system employing the same technology. From this relationship it is also possible to weigh the performance of drum memory with that obtained from other devices.

2.4 DESIGN, CONSTRUCTION AND OPERATION OF MAGNETIC DRUM STORE

Most of the classical work on design and development of magnetic drum stores was carried out during the growth of the first generation computers, such as by Bigelow et al. (1948), Booth (1953), Willams et al. (1952), Dutta Majumder (1959, 1961, 1963).

In this section constructional details of magnetic drum memory satisfying data storage requirements of different information processing systems are discussed. A practical magnetic drum store for a parallel or a serial parallel operation providing a reasonable balance between access time, storage capacity, reliability, size and cost is described by Dutta Majumder (1959, 1961) and this is suitable for a low cost system in Indian conditions.

As stated earlier, the data stored on a magnetic drum are usually represented by magnetized spots on an oxide coated surface (or a nickel plated surface), in a temporary or a permanent form, depending on the system requirements. The binary code is used for the representation of digits on a magnetic drum. Each binary digit is represented by a small area or cell on a magnetic track, magnetically conditioned in either the one or the other of the saturation states. These two states are induced by passing the appropriate writing current waveform through the magnetic write-head coil while the drum is rotating. The information thus stored in the cell is recorded or read out by a similar magnetic read head or, if convenient, by the same head.

Successive cells on a magnetic track are packed closely together. The type of magnetic recording is longitudinal, the cells being magnetized along the peripheral length of the track with a minimum depth of magnetization. The magnetization pattern should be such that the area directly under the magnetic pole pieces is saturated.

A number of practical methods of recording are available. In general, each method is named in relation to the fundamental principle underlying the operation, e.g. phase modulation (PM), nonreturn to zero (NRZ), return-to-zero (RZ), nonreturn to zero inverted (NRZI). The form of digital representation as mentioned above is suitable for all these methods, the difference being only in the magnetic configuration of the storage cells.

Application of the ferromagnetic coating on a drum is a delicate job and involves certain technical know-how. The technique described here has been found to result in a coating that is very resistant to abrasion and other mechanical damages. It has the further advantage that, if damages should occur, it could be repaired.

2.4.1 Selection Problem

Computer store presents the problem of selecting automatically that portion of the memory, the content of which is to be read out or on to which information is to be written. Treating the problem in a rather philosophical way, from an ensemble of bits stored somehow in space, any of the bits can be selected in two distinct ways:

(i) To provide read/write station for each of the bits, so that instead of selecting the bits we select the R/W stations.

(ii) To provide a relative movement between R/W station and the stored bits, so that as the bits pass under the R/W heads sequentially, the problem reduces to the determination of time instant exactly when the bits pass under the head.

The above two methods may be termed as space selection (S-selection) and time selection (T-selection) respectively. There are associated problems of logical design in connection with each method. In almost all magnetic drum memory systems both T-selection and S-selection are simultaneously applied. In binary memory it is very convenient as total memory capacity is expressed in powers of two. In the serial drum memory system each of the channels is S-selected along the axis of the drum, and each of the words in each channel along the periphery is T-selected. In the address of a storage location there is a combination of S- and T-addresses.

In the parallel storage as shown in Figure 2.1 system which can be used with either a parallel or a serial parallel logic, total words are arranged sequentially along the circumferences, all the bits of each word being packed along the axis. So each word is T-selected in synchronism with the corres-

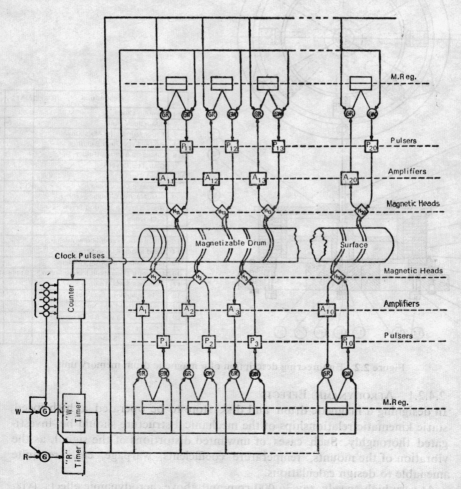

Figure 2.1   The logical block diagram of a magnetic drum memory.

ponding clock pulses emanating from the phonic wheel or synchronization track as it is called.

2.4.2 Mechanical Design of Magnetic Drum

The magnetic drum used in memory system presented was designed constructed, coated, and finished by ourselves in the laboratory as shown in Figure 2.2 in the early sixties.

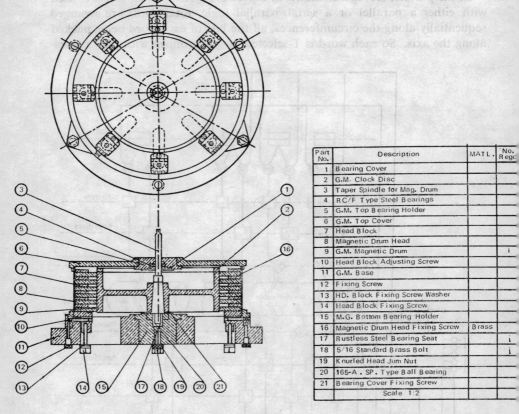

Part No.	Description	MATL.	No. Reqd.
1	Bearing Cover		
2	G.M. Clock Disc		
3	Taper Spindle for Mag. Drum		
4	RC/F Type Steel Bearings		
5	G.M. Top Bearing Holder		
6	G.M. Top Cover		
7	Head Block		
8	Magnetic Drum Head		
9	G.M. Magnetic Drum		i
10	Head Block Adjusting Screw		
11	G.M. Base		
12	Fixing Screw		
13	HD. Block Fixing Screw Washer		
14	Head Block Fixing Screw		
15	M.G. Bottom Bearing Holder		
16	Magnetic Drum Head Fixing Screw	Brass	
17	Rustless Steel Bearing Seat		i
18	5/16 Standard Brass Bolt		i
19	Knurled Head Jum Nut		
20	165-A . SP . Type Ball Bearing		
21	Bearing Cover Fixing Screw		
	Scale 1:2		

Figure 2.2 Engineering description of a magnetic drum memory unit.

2.4.2.1 AERODYNAMIC EFFECTS

In designing a magnetic drum and disk store to be operated at high speed, static kinematic relationships of the mechanical structure should be investigated thoroughly. Such cases of unwanted distortions of the signal, as the vibration of the mounts, temperature coefficients, warpage, etc. are quite amenable to design calculations.

At very high speeds, say 36,000 rpm and above, aerodynamic effects (viz.

drag, losses due to aerodynamic friction and vibration effects due to turbulence) become serious obstacles. It is well known that fluid resistance is proportional to velocity at low speeds and to square of velocity at high speeds. Also that, generally, as Reynold's number exceeds 2000 the fluid flow becomes turbulent. (Reynold's number is defined as the dimensionless ratio

$$R = \frac{\rho VL}{\mu} = \frac{VL}{\nu} \tag{9}$$

where ρ = density, μ = dynamic viscosity, $\nu = \mu/\rho$ = kinematic viscosity, V a typical velocity and L = representative linear dimension.)

Of course, the onset of turbulence can be greatly delayed by using sufficiently smooth boundary walls and rounded entrances up to about $R =$ 75,000. There is an apparent violation of the physical experience, that the symmetric causes produce symmetric effects, it is probably that nearly symmetric causes may produce most unsymmetric effects. However, if the causes that make a symmetric system nearly symmetric at high speed could be minimized, the effects of turbulence may further be minimized.

2.4.2.2 BEARING PROBLEM
About the bearing problem, commercial type bearings in cascade on concentric sleeve so as to subdivide the angular motion, can be used up to 15,000 rpm. But in the vicinity of 36,000 rpm and above, air lubricated journal bearings are necessary. To rotate the drum at such a high speed, the diameter will have to be decreased to, say, 4 inch and the entire assembly enclosed in a partly evacuated housing.

2.4.2.3 ENGINEERING DESCRIPTION OF THE DRUM
Figure 2.2 illustrates completely the construction of the drum assembly. The drum is 7 inch in diameter by $2\frac{1}{2}$ inch in axial length, and is made of cast brass of high machinable quality. It is mounted vertically on a steel tapered spindle with two high precision angular contact bearings and one precision thrust bearing, the latter being fitted at the bottom to bear the vertical load. The bearings were originally lubricated on assembly with grease, but there are arrangements made to lubricate with oil subsequently, mainly because of the drag experienced with grease. It is advisable to use self-contained pressure-feed lubricating systems, with built-in failure alarm, to supply each bearing with a predetermined quantity of oil at regular intervals. Care should be taken in the selection of the circulating oil and materials which come in contact with it, in order to prevent any harmful chemical reaction resulting in deterioration of the lubricating efficiency.

2.4.2.4 SPEED CONTROL AND DRIVE MOTOR
The drum is driven synchronously by a motor, the shaft of which is mounted on a projection of the drum shaft above the top bearing. The rotor

and the drum shafts are coupled by a flexible coupling to minimize transmission of any motor vibrations to the drum. This type of arrangement was adopted in order to allow interchangeability of various types of motors for experimental purposes. For normal usage, the drive motor is an inverted squirrel-cage type with a high inertia to weight ratio. To ensure a long life the stability of the motor is equally important as that of the drum. Speed control of the drum may be achieved by using the eddy current breaking disk, fitted to the rear of the motor shaft. The disk is dynamically balanced independently, thus allowing its removal without destroying the dynamic balance of the drum unit.

On top of the drum is mounted the toothed phonic wheel, as it is called, which provides clock pulse for the drum system. In the final design, synchronization tracks are provided for deriving different timing pulses.

There are eight radial slots cut at the base of the framework, in each of which complete head blocks can be moved forward and backward by means of micrometer arrangement and then can be clamped from the bottom. Individual heads can also be adjusted within certain limits for obtaining uniform response characteristics. The heads can be accurately positioned and fixed to aluminium alloy mountings which have been designed for rigidity in shape and choice of material. The head mountings can be spring loaded as a precautionary measure so that when the clamps in the slots are released, the head/assembly move away from surface. Number of heads to be accommodated in each block depends on head design requirements. Different types of heads were studied with arrangements for holding them. Terminations for connections to heads and leading out cables are incorporated in the mountings.

2.4.2.5 STABILITY OF THE ROTATING DRUM

One of the most important tasks during the engineering fabrication of the device is minimization of eccentricity of the rotating drum. If the center of gravity lies at a distance e inch from the shaft centre, then when the drum of mass m rotates with an angular speed ω, the rotating centrifugal force is $m\omega^2 e$, which will have its horizontal and vertical components, and also have equivalent horizontal and vertical vibratory forces. When the horizontal and vertical vibrations are in resonance with the natural frequency, i.e. when the angular speed ω coincides with the natural frequency of the nonrotating disk, we expect the disk to vibrate violently and also cease to transmit rotating forces to the bearings. The speeds at which such violent vibrations occur are known as *critical speeds* which are calculated from *influence numbers* and is a problem of the subject of strength of materials.

The vibration and the bearing forces are made to disappear by balancing the structure. Its centre of gravity can be made to coincide with the shaft centre by either applying suitable 'correction masses' or by removing certain quantity of materials. This process is known as *static balancing*. But in the case of a rotating drum static balancing alone is not sufficient. However, when in rotation the centrifugal forces on m_1 and m_2 form a moment which causes rotating reactions on the bearings. The drum is said to be statically balanced but dynamically unbalanced, and this type of unbalance can be detected by a dynamic test only. The degree and location of the existing unbalances in a given rotor can be determined by a *dynamic balancing* machine. All unbalances (static, dynamic or combined) of a rigid rotating structure can be corrected by several methods. The rotating drum under discussion was balanced both statically and dynamically by the methods that are described in detail in Denhertog's book, *Mechanical Vibrations*.

Variations due to eccentricity and other factors are much below the limits of unsatisfactory operation. Any further introduction of eccentricity during coating is minimized by dressing the drum surface with a diamond cutter, while the drum is rotated in its own bearings and in its normal running position.

2.5 VARIOUS ASPECTS OF COATING TECHNIQUES

The magnetic properties of the coating depend on the material used. The theoretical investigation undertaken to study the effect of the potential between the corners of the head, distribution of the magnetic field in the ferromagnetic layer of the drum, variation of the field with permeability, airgap, layer thickness, etc. that was necessary to have the required insight into the problem, is presented.

The coating materials and the coating techniques described here have been found to result in a coating that is highly resistant to abrasion and other mechanical damages and are quite satisfactory for this purpose.

2.5.1 Choice of Coating Material

In digital computers, the binary system of notation, where every digit is either '0' or '1' is invariably used. This in magnetic recording data storage means that the magnetic material is saturated in either a positive or a negative sense. In such a method of recording amplitude fidelity is not of much importance and so recording linearity is not required. Maximum pulse amplitude is limited only by the maximum change in magnetization which can be accommodated in the recording medium, that is, the step from minus remanence $(-B_r)$ to plus remanence $(+B_r)$. High frequency response of a medium depends on the ability to maintain st eep magnetization which in turn depends on the ratio of coercive force to remanence (H_c/B_r). This steepness factor, which should be better termed specific magnetic reluctance (SMR) of the medium, is the major deciding factor in the choice of coating material.

Several satisfactory commercial processes for production of magnetic recording media are in force nowadays. Cobalt-nickel alloy or only nickel plated on a nonmagnetic metal base is one solution to the problem. The coercive force and remanence of the plated media are of the order of 200 oersteds and 10,000 gausses respectively; consequently SMR (H_c/B_r) is poor. It has been found that the plated drums give a wideband signal to noise ratio of only 10-20 db. Most of the noise was at low frequency due to uneven stresses in the plated layer.

The commercial magnetic drum manufacturing firms, however, can eliminate these difficulties. The drum recording surface can be copper plated, machined and finally nickel plated to a controlled thickness. Throughout the manufacturing and plating processes, controls are to be applied to ensure maximum adhesion, nonporosity, maximum stability and uniformity of thickness of both the copper and nickel plating. The nickel plating is examined microscopically, and if the surface defects are found to exceed a certain amount (5-10 $\times$ 10^{-7} sq in) the unit is rejected.

Coating material employed is acicular ν-Fe_2O_3 power, where the steepness factor (H_c/B_r) can be artificially increased. The particle length varies from 0.2 to 0.8 micron and length to breadth ratio from 2 : 1 to 6 : 1 reducing the dehydrated α-Fe_2O_3 to Fe_2O_4 and then oxidizing the Fe_2O_4 under carefully controlled conditions to ν-Fe_2O_3. The oxidizing process is carried out slowly in the presence of a limited supply of oxygen and a relatively low temperature; otherwise the oxide will run away to α-Fe_2O_3. There are different types of 'acicular reds and yellows' and in deciding on the preferred type, stability during the process of oxidation and SMR (H_c/B_r) are taken into account. A very important point is that the values of the quantities H_c and B_r are influenced by the thoroughness of the conversion process and manufacturing refinements in dispersion and coating. Another very important factor is the oxide-binder ratio. It generally lies between 60 and 75 per cent. Other things being equal, the sensitivity of the medium does depend on the quantity of magnetic oxide present per unit length.

High coercivity and low permeability in the case of iron oxide powder, with which we are almost exclusively concerned, can be interpreted by domain theory postulated by Weiss. In the case of iron oxide the crystals are cubic in shape and the preferred directions are along the crystal edges. As there are three such axes, and the direction can be either positive or negative along anyone of them, it is clear that there are in all six preferred directions.

The application of a very weak field, corresponding to magnetization from toe to instep, is associated with the change in position of the block walls. This region is reversible. Stronger forces, which raise the magnetization between the instep and the knee, cause changes in orientation of the domains from one preferred direction to another that is nearest to the direction of the magnetizing force. As all the six preferred directions are equally likely, there is no change in induction on removal of the magnetizing force. The change is irreversible and substantial magnetizing force in the reverse direction is required to return the material to original condition. Stronger magnetizing forces take it over the knee to saturation. This region is reversible.

In addition, when powdered in very fine particles, these individually constitute one domain. In that case, there is no possibility of block-wall movement, and it is therefore impossible for magnetization to take place other than through irreversible and reversible changes in the orientation. Moreover, that SMR of the medium is increased in this method is self-explanatory from the figures of sheared hysteresis loop due to the presence of minute particles in the dispersed medium.

The dispersed material behaves like a homogeneous material so long as the particle sizes and their distances are both small in comparison with the lowest wavelength to be recorded. In magnetic iron oxide ν-Fe_2O_3 cubic and spinel crystal structure, coercivity of the order of 250-500 oersteds and remanence of 600-1000 gausses can be achieved which lead to a rather satisfactory SMR.

2.5.2   Coating Thickness

The influence of coating thickness is explained from physical considerations from the analysis of the frequency response curve of a magnetic recording medium (Figure 2.3). The detailed theoretical and experimental studies of these parameters on digital data recording are presented in a next section.

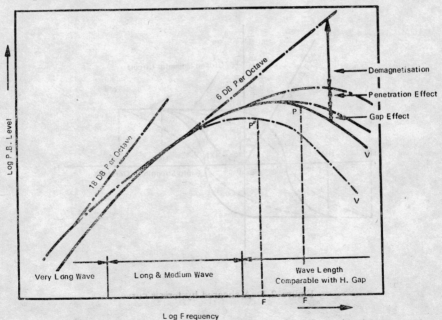

Figure 2.3   Analysis of the response curve of a magnetic recording medium.

Several factors combine to fix up the overall frequency response of a magnetic recording medium. For very long wavelength response rises at 18 db per octave (this range is not important for recording purposes), and then with decreasing wavelength response rises at 6 db per octave. This is due to the fact that the voltage induced in the playback head is proportional to the rate of change of flux. So doubling the frequency would double the rate of change of flux and so increase the output voltage by 6 db. Over a range of about two octaves the response is sensibly level, beyond this the response falls. With further increase in frequency as the wavelength becomes shorter, the slope even reverses the trend.

Most important effects are attributed to self-demagnetization and mutual interaction between the adjacent elementary magnets. The 'demagnetization effect' is purely a function of the geometry of the sample. In the coated surface, the magnetic material employed consists of a large number of small particles, distributed more or less evenly, some particles touching one another, others are isolated by the binder material. The length of the elementary bar magnets or short magnetic dipoles in the case of pulse recording produced during the process of recording depends on peripheral speed and frequency of the signal, other things being equal. In any type of recording, width of the magnets will remain constant. The demagnetization factor, which can be defined as the slope of the shearing line of the sheared hysterisis loop, as shown in Figure 2.4, decreases with increase in the ratio of length to diameter.

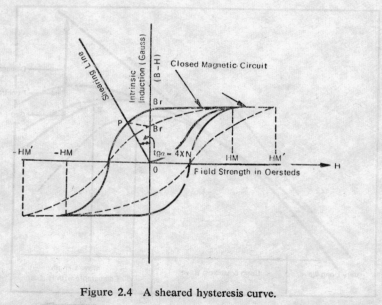

Figure 2.4   A sheared hysteresis curve.

Demagnetization effect is not exactly predictable, as the short magnetic dipoles interact with each other and are themselves shortened by pole-tips across the scanning gap. The situation is much more complicated by the fact that the short magnets are not made up of solid material but of large number of small particles each of which is a magnet in its own right.

In fact, the characteristics of the individual particles, particularly their shape and size, have a very appreciable effect on the degree of demagnetization. Mathematical treatment on the subject including all the factors stated is presented in a next section.

From the above concept of demagnetization effect it may be concluded that the frequency response of a thin medium will be superior to that of thick one. But the experimental observations reveal that other conditions being equal, within the thickness of a few thou, the response does not differ much. Disregarding the absolute value, the position of maximum reproduced level is at a higher frequency with the thinnest medium. The above fact is interpreted by what is known as *penetration effect*. The useful magnetic fluxes associated with longer wavelengths penetrate more than the shorter ones, and this penetration depth is normally less than a thou. So even if the thickness of the medium is more, the whole of the depth is not penetrated by the useful magnetic fluxes; that is why the thickness variation does not affect much the frequency response. If the thickness is reduced to the order of depth of penetration, the high frequency will be favoured. But if the thickness is reduced further, there will not be any selective behaviour, and the frequency response will be controlled by demagnetization effect only.

2.5.3   Primer Technique

Application of ferromagnetic coating on a drum is a piece of highly specializ-ed precision work and involves certain technical know-how which, of course, may vary from worker to worker, and also with coating material. The facts and recommendations made in this section are based on a labo-ratory experience and have been found to be reliable.

The whole technique consists of methods of dilution, primer techniques, and spraying process (or dipping process with which we are not concerned). The importance of preparing the dispersion and methods of dilution has been explained in an earlier section. Coating experiments were carried out with several different coating materials such as red magnetic oxide (111 type) with an intrinsic coercivity of dispersion 260 oersteds and retentivity of coating about 450 gauss, black magnetic oxide (110 type) with intrinsic coercivity of dispersion 310 oersteds and retentivity of coating about 450 gauss, and a ferromagnetic varnish prepared from a powder of ferrocobalt ferrite with intrinsic coercivity of dispersion 300 oersteds and retentivity of coating about 600 gauss.

The surface that is to be coated must first be clear and absolutely free from dirt, grease, dust or other foreign material. If practicable, the surface to be coated should be cleaned with soap and water and then rinsed thoroughly and dried. If water cannot be used, the surface itself should be free from irregularities which would produce variations in coating thickness. However, a mirror smooth surface should be avoided.

The metallic surface should be given a light etch with ordinary phos-phoric acid to produce an evenly roughened precoat which will ensure proper bonding of the primer to a metal. This step is specially important when preparing to coat aluminium or aluminium alloys. The phosphoric acid that is used is common o-phosphoric acid diluted to 6-8 per cent by volume solution with water.

After using the primer solution, gun apparatus must be cleaned thoroughly and immediately in methyl ethyl ketone if congestion of the equipment is to be avoided. For priming brass or bronze, the zinc chromate primers may be used followed by a cure cycle. There are also various vinyl "wash" primers now in the market which do not require curing and which afford excellent adhesion to copper alloys. The finished primed surface should be sanded and polished to ensure a perfectly uniform surface.

2.5.4   Spray-Coating Process

Both from the physical and experimental considerations, the coating thickness should be held to a minimum consistent with head design and signal requirements (optimum coating thickness), to ensure sufficient flexibility. The dispersion as supplied is much too thick to be sprayed directly and must be diluted before use. The following solvent combination is prepared for dilution:

By weight :   25%—Hi-flash coal naptha
25%—toluol
50%—butyl acetate

This solvent combination has been found to be satisfactory, although other combinations can obviously be developed. The amount of diluent to be added depends on the type of gun to be used and the thickness of coat desired. Diluent is best added slowly and the dispersion agitated vigorously. After dilution, the dispersion should be filtered through at least three layers of 125 mesh silk screen having a fineness classification better than 10x. It is then ready for spraying.

The pressure to be used in the spray gun depends on the size of the gun. Approximately 50 pounds of atomizing pressure gives satisfactory result. The technique employed in spraying is of paramount importance. The article to be coated should be mounted and rotated during spraying, the speed of rotation for best results is an individual problem. The gun is adjusted to give a spray cone of average width, very narrow or very wide cones are avoided. The gun should be held away from the object far enough to prevent the air-pressure from rippling the coating but not so far away that the dispersion dries before it reaches the object. The total thickness of coating should be deposited in several passes; each pass should be allowed to set up before the next possible magnetic surface, free from perturbances. Methods used for polishing and finishing surfaces are given below.

2.5.5   Finishing and Polishing of Surfaces

The surface of the magnetic coating obtainable from the ferrocobalt ferrite or the other two types of oxide coatings depends on the method of application and on drying conditions. The air dry surface is adequate even though it may contain small holes or modules of lumped magnetic oxide or dirt. To produce a highly finished surface, each coat should be wet-sanded with wet or dry 400 grit sand paper, taking care that not too much of the coating is removed. This treatment will remove large imperfections and present a planer surface but scratches and minor non-uniformities will still exist. After coating has been rough finished with sand paper, the surface is polished and further cut by any of the cutting compounds sold for the purpose. After all these operations the final polishing is done with a diamond cutter at working speed (6000 rpm) by means of a micrometer cross-feed.

2.6 GAP-EFFECT

With increase in frequency, as the wavelength approaches the dimension of scanning gap, the response falls rapidly and the first zero is reached when the wavelength is equal to the scanning slit.

The gap effect which exists in any method of scanning is discussed in the book of magnetic recording. The db loss in our case can be calculated as:

Let F_0 be the frequency, and λ the slit width.

Then,

$$F_0 = \frac{\text{Velocity of the medium in inches per sec}}{\text{Slit width in inches}} \tag{10}$$

and the loss in db due to the slit loss at any other lower frequency F is given by

$$\text{db loss} = 20 \log_{10} \left\{ \frac{\sin F/F_0}{F/F_0} \right\} \tag{11}$$

The graphs in Figure 2.3 give the general appearance of an observed response together with the contribution of demagnetization, penetration and gap-effect. The method of converting a response curve established at a velocity v of the medium into the curve at any other velocity v' is also shown.

Several studies have been made of the play back (PB) process of magnetic recording. The first contribution was the determination of the approximate flux PB response of a magnetic head in contact with an infinitely thin recorded tape. The approximate flux response was found to be of the form:

$$\frac{\sin 2\pi/\lambda}{2\pi/\lambda} \cos (2\pi/\lambda)\, t$$

where λ is the wavelength of the recorded signal in the units of half gap length. The output voltage of the head is the time derivative of the flux-response, and therefore, the voltage amplitude varies as $\sin (2\pi/\lambda)$. Wallace solved for the effects of finite head to surface separation, and finite thickness of the surface.

The next major step was taken by Westmijze (1953). He showed that the simple sin $2\pi/\lambda$ voltage response is only a rough estimate. The formula predicts a zero output at $\lambda = 2/n$, where n is an integer, and shown on the basis of an exact calculation that these null points are shifted towards longer wavelengths. He also determined the effect of head to surface separation and surface thickness by using a reciprocity theorem. We shall deal with this aspect in a next section in some detail.

We shall discuss three models of magnetic head. In first type, the infinite gap is formed by two parallel planes $x = -l/2$ and $x = +l/2$. It is for this simple model, that the above gap-loss formula of the form

$$\frac{\sin \pi\, l/\lambda}{\pi\, l/\lambda} \tag{12}$$

holds. The corresponding flux equation is

$$\phi = \phi' G\left(\frac{\pi l}{\lambda}\right) \tag{13}$$

where

$$G(x) = \frac{\sin x}{x} \tag{14}$$

The second type is formed by two thin sheets, extending in the plane $Y = 0$, one from $x = -\infty$ to $x = -l/2$ and $x = l/2$ to $x = +\infty$. The corresponding flux equation is

$$\phi = \phi' \left(\frac{1-\exp\,(-2\pi a/\lambda)}{2\pi d/\lambda}\right) \exp\,(-2\pi a/\lambda)\, J_0\left(\frac{\pi\, l}{\lambda}\right)\cos \omega t \tag{15}$$

The three factors describing the influence of surface thickness d, space between head and tape a and the gap length l are occurring separately. The gap-loss is given by the Bessel function $J_0\,(\pi l/\lambda)$ which is independent of d and a. The first terms of the asymptotic expansion of the Bessel functions is

$$J_0\left(\frac{\pi\, l}{\lambda}\right) \simeq \frac{\sin\left(\dfrac{\pi l}{\lambda}+\dfrac{\pi}{4}\right)}{\pi\,\sqrt{l/2\lambda}} \tag{16}$$

which show that the decrease of amplitude of the maximum and minima is slower than in the first case.

In the third type, that is, the semi-infinite gap shown in Figure 2.5, the left pole piece is bounded by the plane $y = 0$ from $x = -\infty$ to $x = -l/2$ and by the plane $x = -l/2$ from $y = 0$ to $y = \infty$. This type bears close resemblance to practical heads. The flux equation is

$$\phi = \phi' \left(\frac{1-\exp\,(-2\pi d/\lambda)}{2\pi d/\lambda}\right) \exp\,(-2\pi d/\lambda)\, S\left(\frac{\pi l}{\lambda}\right) \tag{17}$$

The gap loss is given by $S\pi l/\lambda$ and is a complicated complex function. It is seen on comparison that the gap-loss function for a head of third type is intermediate between those for types first and second, as could be expected from physical consideration.

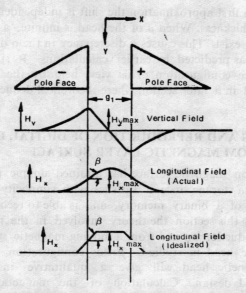

Figure 2.5   Recording with semi-infinite head gap.

Since gap-loss formulae indicated above are in complicated integral form, the simple gap loss expression of Equation (11) is still widely used, especially for rough estimates. In all the cases mentioned above, the assumption has been made that the surface permeability is one, and the head permeability is infinite.

It appears that the methods, based on Schwartz-Christoffel transformation do not apply for solving the case with finite parameters. Dutta Majumder (1963) made field calculations for finite μ and finite surface thickness and the playback process for a pulse pattern. G.J. Fan derived a simplified gap-loss function with arbitrary surface permeability and finite head permeability. His gap-loss function can be written as

$$G_1 = \sin \frac{2\pi}{\lambda} \left(\frac{5 - \lambda^2}{4 - \lambda^2} \right) \tag{18}$$

in the case of infinite permeability. The first approximation to the PB response is,

$$V(\lambda) = \mu_2 \cos \frac{\omega t}{\lambda} \left[\frac{1 - \exp (-2\pi d/\lambda)}{2\pi d/\lambda} \right] \sin \frac{2\pi}{\lambda} \left(\frac{5 - \lambda^2}{4 - \lambda^2} \right) \exp (-2\pi d/\lambda) \tag{19}$$

Qualitatively, shift of the null is due to the fringing field of the semi-infinite gap. When value of μ of the recorded medium is high, there is no effect on separation and thickness-loss of the medium but the gap-loss is changed to

$$G_2 = \sin \frac{2\pi}{\lambda} \left(\frac{6 - \lambda^2}{5 - \lambda^2} \right) \tag{20}$$

It is found that to first approximation the shift is independent of separation loss and surface thickness. When μ of the head is infinite, a low frequency boost is found to exist. This causes a discrepancy in the 6 db/octave rise at long wavelengths as predicted by earlier calculations. It strongly depends on the pole piece configuration. This view held by the present authors will be explained in a later section where theoretical deductions have been presented.

2.7 RECORDING AND REPRODUCTION OF DIGITAL DATA ON AND FROM MAGNETIC LAYER SURFACE

Pulse recording on magnetic surface has attained unique position in the field of digital data storage since it satisfies with simplicity and economy, the requirements of a binary memory, and is able to record two states of a binary digit. In this section the theory involved in the process of pulse recording and production on and from a moving magnetic surface with the help of a magnetic head is studied. Field configuration in and around the gap of magnetic head will give a qualitative insight into the problem of head design. Calculation of the magnetic field in the ferromagnetic layer of the drum in certain cases following the method adopted by Karlqvist (1954), Westmijze (1959) and Dutta Majumder (1963) is presented from which variation of the field components with permeability, layer thickness, airgap and other factors involved in the process are studied briefly. Linear boundary value problem for the two-dimensional static field and the one-dimensional transient field is studied. Pulse frequency has been assumed low enough to neglect eddy current losses in the head and layer that are made of spinel material. The results of these investigations will provide a reasonable balance between conflicting requirements of access time, storage capacity, reliability, size and cost, are analyzed.

The theory involved in the process of magnetic recording in general is rather complicated due to the facts that the particles subjected to recording field are not of uniform sizes and the variations of amplitude of the applied field are different at different depths, thus causing variations in the associated magnetic properties. Further, once the signal is recorded an interaction occurs between places of different magnetization giving rise to a demagnetization field. Also, there exists an intricate interdependence of all these and several other parameters. But in saturation type pulse recording the errors involved in simplifying assumptions made in theoretical deductions are less important, and experimental studies on variation of different parameters involved can be made with sufficient accuracy.

2.7.1 Principles of Magnetic Recording and Reproducing Process

Although the process of recording a '0' or '1' on the magnetic surface may appear straightforward, considerable research efforts has spent into both the development of the recorded patterns used to represent 0's and

1's and the means for determining ' the value recorded. The common interests in this respect are; that the packing density should be made as high as possible which means that each bit should occupy as little space as possible, and second the reading and writing procedure should be sufficiently reliable. Although these two requirements are conflicting, one should have to take proper care for optimizing the whole system for high-density storage of digital data.

In writing information on a magnetic surface, the data is supplied to the recording circuitry, which then codes this information into a pattern and it is then recorded by the writing head. The techniques which are used to write information on a magnetic surface can be divided into two categories, the return-to-zero (RZ) and non-return-to-zero (NRZ) techniques. In the RZ technique, current through the writing head is reduced to zero after recording a '1' or '0' whereas in NRZ type a positive or negative current always flows through the coil. Once again there are two or more methods of RZ and NRZ type of recording. In one class of RZ type recording, a '1' is recorded by sending a positive pulse through coil and '0' by a negative pulse, and between these pulses coil current is zero. In another method of RZ type recording which avoids the need of ac demagnetization, is to send a positive pulse only for recording a '1' so that output occurs only for one signal and no output for zero signal. Similarly, there are various other methods for NRZ type of recording. In the most consistent NRZ type of recording a positive current pulse passes through write head as long as a '1' is to be recorded and a negative current pulse, passes when a '0' is wanted. In the second type most commonly used, and often known as non-return-to-zero inverse (NRZI) recording, a change of the magnetization direction from a negative to a positive represents a '1' and no magnetization change occurs for a '0'. This means that there will be no read out signal for zero information. This type of recording system provides higher packing density. Still there are another NRZ type of recording, usually known as phase encoding (PM). The characteristics of this system is almost similar to NRZI except that a '0' produces a negative pulse in the readout coil. In this system magnetization direction from negative to positive represents a '1' and a change from positive to negative a '0'. This type of recording system requires additional electronic circuitry and reduces the maximum bit density along a track although it provides ease error detection capability. The different recording format and coding scheme that are used in most commercial computers are discussed in subsection 2.11 of this chapter.

2.7.2   Distribution of the Fringing Field of a Semi-Infinite Pole Gap in Ferromagnetic Layer

We intend to determine the nature of field configuration in and around the gap before proceeding with the problem of determining ultimate magnetization of the element in front of the record/read head. From this investigation we shall be in a position to approximate a potential distribution between corners of the recording head. The deduction of the equipotential profiles is important in connection with the design of integrated magnetic heads. We shall discuss the design of integrated heads at the end of this chapter.

Though the problem is non-linear, the linear case gives a first approximation, which in some cases seems satisfactory. Linear boundary value problem for the two dimensional static field and the one dimensional transient field, will be dealt with here. The notations for the physical parameters are:

μ = layer permeability

d = layer thickness

N = half the pole distance

b = head-to-layer distance

B_0 = induction in the pole gap measured in volt-sec per sq meter,

$= \mu_0 \dfrac{V}{N}$

V = magnetic potential of the head

$\mu_0 = 4\pi \times 10^{-7}$ in MKS units

Investigations on the potential between corner of the head treated with conformal mapping shows that the magnetic potential distribution along $y = 0$ can safely be assumed to be linear.

Thus

$$v = -V, \qquad x < -N$$
$$v = V\frac{x}{N}, \qquad -N > x > N$$
$$v = V, \qquad x > N \tag{21}$$

Thus the boundary value problem reduces to finding the magnetic potential $V(x,y)$ is the region $y > 0$, $-\alpha < x < \alpha$ when the potential along $y = 0$ is prescribed. The magnetizing vector is then:

$$H = - \operatorname{grad} v(x, y) \tag{22}$$

The potential satisfies the equation

$$\frac{\partial \mu}{\partial x}\frac{\partial V}{\partial x} + \frac{\partial \mu}{\partial y}\frac{\partial V}{\partial y} = 0 \tag{23}$$

We assume μ, the layer permeability as constant, and we get the Laplace's equation

$$\Delta v = 0, \quad \Delta = \frac{\partial^2}{\partial x^2} + \frac{\partial^2}{\partial y^2} \tag{24}$$

Usually Equation (23) is non-linear.

For *boundary conditions*, we take

v_1 = the potential above the layer
v_2 = the potential in the layer
v_3 = the potential in the layer
v_4 = the potential below the layer

then the boundary conditions along $y = b$ and $y = b + d$ (on the two sides of the layer) are

$$\frac{\partial v_1}{\partial y} = \frac{\partial v_2}{\partial y} \tag{25}$$

$$\mu \frac{\partial v_3}{\partial y} = \frac{\partial v_4}{\partial y} \tag{26}$$

Equations (23 and 24) are elliptic equations. The non-stationary one-dimensional field can be computed from the equation

$$\frac{\partial^2 H}{\partial x^2} = 6\mu \mu_0 \frac{\partial H}{\partial t} \tag{27}$$

where σ is the conductivity of the layer, μ is the permeability of the layer and is assumed constant.

Idealization of problem: The first approximation is to regard the magnetizable surface as plane. The variation of the head to layer distance due to the curvature of the surface is less than 10% for the interval $0 < x < 10N$. The factor b/N is usually between 0.5 and 2. Length of the read/record head is about 100 to 200 times that of the gap width, and therefore for all practical purposes, we can assume the head length as infinite. Width of the head is also about 100 times the gap width, and so our two-dimensional treatment of the problem will be satisfactory. Permeability of the head is very high, and hence lines of force will leave the head surface nearly perpendicular. Magnetic potential of the head is, therefore, assumed constant and is positive on the right half and negative on the left half of the head. However the influences of the pole length on the field in the layer was investigated by Booth; here we shall study the potential between corner of the head.

2.7.3 Solution of Boundary Value Problem

We have to find out the potential $v(x, y)$ for the solution of Laplace's equation, subject to the conditions

$$V = 0 \quad \text{when } y = \infty \tag{28}$$

$$V = f(x) \quad \text{when } y = 0 \tag{29}$$

Fourier's integral solution for this is

$$V = \frac{1}{\pi} \int_0^\infty d\alpha \int_{-\infty}^\infty \exp(\alpha y) f(\lambda) \cos \alpha (\lambda - x) d\lambda \tag{30}$$

Following the same course as in *Byerly* we obtain

$$v(x, y) = \frac{1}{2b} \sin \frac{\pi y}{b} \int_{-\infty}^{\infty} f(\lambda) \frac{d\lambda}{\cosh \frac{\pi}{b}(\lambda - x) - \cos \frac{\pi y}{b}} \qquad (31)$$

When $b = \alpha$, we deduce the formula

$$v(x, y) = \frac{y}{\pi} \int_{-\infty}^{\infty} f(\lambda) \frac{d\lambda}{y^2 + (\lambda - x)^2} \qquad (32)$$

The field for $\mu = \alpha$ is obtained from Equation (31)

$$H_y(x, b) = \frac{H_0}{\pi} \log \frac{\cosh \pi \left(\dfrac{x + N}{2b} \right)}{\cosh \pi \left(\dfrac{x - N}{2b} \right)} \qquad (33)$$

where H_0 is pole gap field intensity.

This is not of much practical use. We get the field for the case $\mu = 1$ from Equation (32) which will be of great practical use. The field is always computed from Equation (22).

$$H_x(x, y) = -\frac{H_0}{\pi} \left[\tan^{-1} \left(\frac{N + x}{y} \right) + \tan^{-1} \left(\frac{N - x}{y} \right) \right] \qquad (34)$$

$$H_y(x, y) = \frac{H_0}{2\pi} \log \left[\frac{y^2 + (N + x)^2}{y^2 + (N - x)^2} \right] \qquad (35)$$

In the above equations we have the field given explicitly as simple functions of x and y and it is easy to compute the actual field. This approximation is satisfactory up to y greater than $0.5\ N$.

The pole gap field intensity H_0 is estimated from a magnetomotive force reluctance relationship, where the reluctance of the head core is piecewise calculated. We have,

$$H_0 = \frac{4\pi n_1 i}{g_1 \left[1 + \dfrac{R_p}{R_{g1}} \right]} \qquad (36)$$

where R_p is the reluctance of the head core, R_{g1} is the reluctance of the head pole gap, n_1 is the number of turns on the write coil, and

$$\frac{R_p}{R_{g1}} = \frac{A_{g1}}{g_1} \left[\frac{g_2}{A_{g2}} + \sum_{i=1}^{T} \frac{l i}{\mu_1 A_{p1}} \right] \qquad (37)$$

Here,

g_1 = length of pole gap in the write/read head (cm)
g_2 = average length of the rear gap (cm)
A_{g1} = area of the pole gap (cm)^2
A_{g2} = area of the rear gap (cm)^2
μ_1 = initial permeability of the head core material at the frequency of operation

Equations (34) and (35) in terms of the above parameters can be written as

$$H_x(x, y) = -\frac{H_o}{\pi}\left\{\tan^{-1}\left[\frac{1 + 2x/g_1}{2y/g_1}\right] + \tan^{-1}\left[\frac{1 - 2x/g_1}{2y/g_1}\right]\right\} \quad (38)$$

$$H_y(x, y) = \frac{H_o}{\pi}\left\{\frac{(2y/g_1)^2 + (1 + 2x/g_1)^2}{(2y/g_1)^2 + (1 - 2x/g_1)^2}\right\} \quad (39)$$

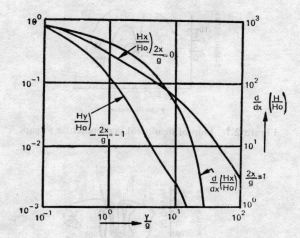

Figure 2.6   Fringing field components and their gradient.

Maximum values of the fringing field components H_x, H_y and the gradient $\partial H_x/\partial y$ at the point of inflexion of the curve are shown in Figure 2.6. The point of inflexion of H_x and the maximum value of H_y are assumed to occur at $x_1 = \pm g_1/2$ for all values of y. The analytical expressions for μ greater than 1 and finite layer thickness can be deduced using Fourier's transform method but for all practical purposes expressions (34) and (35) or (38) and (39) offer very good approximation for ferromagnetic layer of very low permeability such as spinel material. It is seen that at a distance greater than one tenth of the pole gap, the intensity of the longitudinal, component is always greater than the vertical component. For a typical recording head at a distance equal to the pole gap the intensities of longitudinal and vertical field components may be of the order of 1200 and 700 oersteds respectively. The 1200 oersteds field is sufficient to saturate any of the commonly used storage media in the longitudinal direction. Moreover, because of the shearing of the loop in the vertical direction due to adverse demagnetization conditions, the 700 oersted field is insufficient to saturate the medium in the vertical direction. So we take it that the magnetization is predominantly of longitudinal nature. This statement has been demonstrated by mapping the fringing fields of signals stored on oxide and on nickel cobalt plated surfaces with a Hall probe as shown in Figure 2.6. Before going into the more rigorous harmonic analysis and other techniques we would like to show how most of the engineering design conditions can be derived from Equations (34) and (35). We can compute longitudinal and vertical components of magnetic flux vectors in the media from Equations (34) and (35).

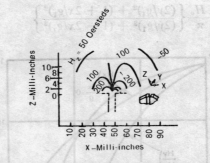

Figure 2.7   Map of head field perpendicular to gap.

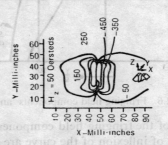

Figure 2.8   Map of head field parallel to head face.

The constant H_x and H_y field contours are circles with centres on the y and x axes respectively, and with the constant H_x circles being tangent to the two gap corners (Figure 2.6). The total constant field $|H|$ contours are ellipses with foci at the gap corners. Considering only the horizontal component and using a linearized model of hysteresis loop of the recording medium, a written transition length l_0 can be obtained from the gradient of the writing head field $(\partial H_x/\partial x)$ and the slope of the hysteresis loop of the recording medium at the coercive field. For a given range of switching fields ΔH it can be seen that the written transition length l_0 increases almost linearly with increasing spacing from the head surface $(b + \delta/2)$, and decreases with increasing coercivity (assuming that the median plane of the medium passes through the centre of the coercive field circle). An estimate of l_0 comes to

$$l_0 = \frac{\Delta H}{H_c}\left(b + \frac{\delta}{2}\right) \tag{40}$$

and can be larger than this predicted value if either the writing head excitation is not near optimum or the thickness of the recording medium is large.

The logitudinal and vertical components of the magnetic flux vector can be deduced from eqns. (34) and (35). The plot of resultant flux vector against the distance is shown in Fig. 2.9.

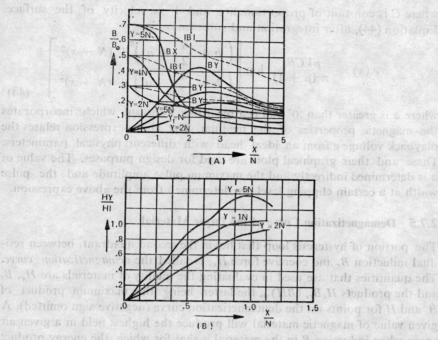

Figure 2.9   Longitudinal and vertical components of magnetic flux vector.

2.7.4   Computation of Playback Voltage Pulse

Considering the idealized playback head to be a semi-infinite block of high permeability material with the flat face at a distance b above the recording surface, playback (PB) signal will be proportional to the rate of change of the X-component of the flux. Using the method of images, the value of flux density in the head can be shown to be the same as though the head filled all the space and the intensity of magnetization in the recording medium were $2\mu/(\mu + 1)$ times the value actually present. Therefore

$$B_x = \frac{2\mu B_0}{\pi (\mu + 1)} \left[\tan^{-1} \frac{N + x}{y} + \tan^{-1} \frac{N - x}{y} \right] \qquad (41)$$

If δ is the thickness of the medium the total flux per unit width will be

$$\phi_x = \int_{b + \delta/2}^{\infty} B_x \, dy \qquad (42)$$

The output voltage will be proportional to the rate of change of ϕ_x, therefore,

$$e(x) = VC \frac{d}{dx} \int_{b + \delta/2}^{\infty} B_x \, dy \tag{43}$$

where C is constant of proportionality and V is velocity of the surface. Equation (44), after integration and substitution is

$$e(x) = \frac{\mu V C B_0}{\pi (\mu + 1)} \log \left[\frac{\left(b + \dfrac{\delta}{2} + a \right)^2 + (N - x)^2}{\left(b + \dfrac{\delta}{2} - a \right)^2 + (N + x)^2} \right] \tag{44}$$

where a is greater than '0' and is a recording constant which incorporates the magnetic properties of the medium. The above expression relates the playback voltage e from an ideal head with different physical parameters. These and their graphical plots are used for design purposes. The value of a is determined indirectly and the maximum pulse amplitude and the pulse width at a certain clipping level are determined from the above expression.

2.7.5   Demagnetization Curve of the Layer Material

The portion of hysteresis loop that lies in the second quadrant, between residual induction B_r and coercive force H_c, is called the *demagnetization curve*. The quantities that are used in evaluating the quality of materials are H_c, B_r and the products $H_c B_r$, $(BH)_m$, the latter being the maximum product of B and H for points on the demagnetization curve (negative sign omitted). A given value of magnetic material will produce the highest field in a given air space when induction B in the material is that for which the energy product BH is a maximum. As an empirical mathematical relation demagnetization curve can be simulated by a rectangular hyperbola (Bozorth), defined by three points $(B_r, H = 0)$, (B_a, H_a) and $(H_c, B = 0)$ as shown in Figure 2.10. The shape of the demagnetization curve between B_r and H_c is fixed by what is often called the fullness factor, defined by

$$\gamma = \frac{(BH)_m}{B_r H_c} \tag{45}$$

and the squareness factor (S) defined by the ratio of retentivity B_r to the asymptotic magnetization predicted by the hyperbola and is given by equation

$$S = \frac{m + h - 1}{mh} \tag{46}$$

where $\qquad m = \dfrac{B_a}{B_r}$ and $h = \dfrac{H_a}{H_c}$.

The squareness factor S is related to fullness factor γ by

$$S = 1 - (\gamma - 1)^2 \tag{47}$$

Using the general expression for a rectangular hyperbola

$$(x - x_0)(y - y_0) = C_0^2 \tag{48}$$

Substituting $y = B$, $x = H$, and $y_0 = 1/b$

$$x_0 = - H_c - \frac{a}{b}, \quad C_0{}^2 = - \frac{a}{b^2}$$

We have

$$\left(H + H_c + \frac{a}{b} \right)\left(B - \frac{1}{b} \right) + \frac{a}{b^2} = 0 \tag{49}$$

From this we can derive

$$\frac{H + H_c}{B} = a + b (H + H_c) \tag{50}$$

which is similar to Frolick-Kenelly relationship

$$\frac{H}{B} = a + bH = \frac{1}{\mu} \tag{51}$$

and differs from it in that the $B-H$ curve is displaced horizontally so that $B = 0$ when $H = - H_c$.

Designating the asymptotes

$$B_s = \frac{1}{b} \quad \text{and} \quad H_s = \frac{a + b H_c}{b} = \frac{H_c B_s}{B_r}$$

the relation may also be written as

$$B = \frac{(H + H_c) B_s}{H + H_s} \tag{52}$$

and making substitutions and simplifications, the second quadrant of the hysteresis loop is given by equation :

$$B = \frac{B_r \left(1 - \dfrac{H}{H_c} \right)}{1 - S \left(\dfrac{H}{H_c} \right)} \tag{53}$$

The reversible permeability μ_2 of the storage medium, considered constant, is defined by the slope of the hyperbola at the point $(0, B_r)$ where

$$\mu_2 = 1 + \tan \theta \tag{54}$$

and

$$\tan \theta = \frac{B_r}{H_c}(1 - S) \tag{55}$$

It is thus seen that the reversible permeability μ_2, is dependent on the squareness factor S. The slope of the hyperbola at the point $(H_c, 0)$ is given by the equation

$$\text{an } \alpha = \frac{B_r}{H_c}\left(\frac{1}{1 - S} \right) \tag{56}$$

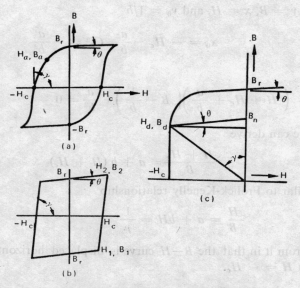

Figure 2.10 Linear approximation of hysteresis loop.

2.7.6 Write Process

For the write process, we linearize the entire hysteresis loop to a parallelogram, then the field intensities at the beginning and end are given by the equations:

$$H_1 = \frac{H_c}{2 - S}, \quad H_2 = \frac{H_c}{S}$$

From the earlier mathematical and physical analysis we assumed the magnetization of the medium as predominantly longitudinal. In NRZ type of recording the longitudinal component of magnetization may be represented by a trapezoid. The transition length of magnetization (Figure 2.5) is equal to the average dynamic transition length with a lower limit imposed by the static transition length. The static transition length is determined by the shape of the hysteresis loop of the layer material and the pattern of the fringing field at the pole gap. The dynamic transition length is determined by the time constant of the write circuitry, the relative velocity of the head and storage medium, and the reluctance of the head core. For the typical array (Figure 2.11) where a succession of ones is separated by p and q bit lengths, the resultant magnetization is described by the Fourier series:

$$B = \sum B_0 \left\{ \frac{p-q}{p+q} + \frac{4}{n\pi} \sin \frac{n\pi}{1 + q/p} \frac{\sin \dfrac{n\pi b}{(p+q) K_0}}{\dfrac{n\pi b}{(p+q) K_0}} \cos \frac{2n\pi x}{(p+q) K_0} \right\}$$

(57)

The corresponding harmonic wavelength and the equivalent harmonic frequency are defined by the equations:

$$\lambda_n = \frac{(p + q) K_0}{n} \tag{58}$$

$$f_n = \frac{nV}{(p + q) K_0} \tag{59}$$

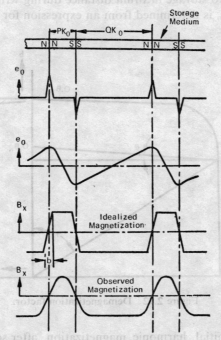

Figure 2.11   Recording a signal array.

2.7.7   Self-Demagnetization of the Recorded Signal

As soon as recording head is removed from the vicinity of the recorded cell, the boundary conditions change resulting in a demagnetizing field H_d and a quiescent magnetization B_d. During reading operation, boundary conditions similar to those of write process are re-established and, ideally atleast, the demagnetizing field is reduced to zero. The resulting magnetization B_n (the initial magnetization considered for the read process) is slightly lower than the retentivity of the storage medium. This is due to nonlinear character of the hysteresis loop and the constancy of the reversible permeability of the medium. It is a standard practice to define a demagnetization factor as

$$D_n = \tan \gamma = -\frac{H_d}{B_d} \tag{60}$$

B_n is then determined by the values of H_d and B_d and the angle defined by the reversible permeability of the storage medium as shown in Figure 2.12.

Assuming the magnetization to be constant throughout the depth, the average demagnetization factor is defined by the equation

$$\overline{D}_n = \int_{b_1}^{b_1 + d} D_n \, dy \Big/ \int_{b_1}^{b_1 + d} dy \tag{61}$$

where b_1 = head to storage medium distance during write process and d = layer thickness; D_n is determined from an expression for H_d and B_d.

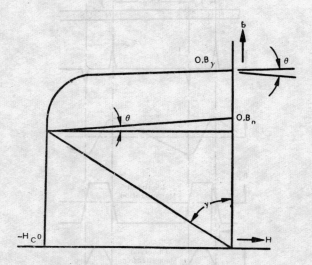

Figure 2.12   Demagnetization factor.

The resultant initial harmonic magnetization after self-demagnetization is given by the equation:

$$B_n = H_c \left\{ \left[\frac{1 + \overline{D}_n (\mu_2 - 1)}{2 S \overline{D}_n} \right] \times \left[1 + \overline{D}_n \frac{B_r}{H_c} \right. \right.$$
$$\left. \left. - \left(1 + \overline{D}_n \frac{B_r}{H_c} \right) \left(2 - 4S + \overline{D}_n \frac{B_r}{H_c} \right)^{\frac{1}{2}} \right] \right\} \tag{62}$$

2.7.8   Process of Playback

The next problem obviously is to determine the total quantity of fringing flux of stored bit in the cell that passes through the read coil when there is a reading operation. Total flux through the head coil can be determined which on differentiation gives the output voltage of the read coil. By considering an equivalent read circuit, loading effect of the amplifier, the line and the stray capacitance of the read coil can be taken account of. Following the above logic, the expression for the head output voltage, for the signal array described by Equation (57) is given by

$$E_0 = \sum X_n Y_n C_n L_n E_n B_n (4 N_2 W V) \sin \frac{n\pi}{1 + q/p} \sin \frac{\pi}{n\lambda}$$

$$\times \left(X + \frac{g_1}{2} \right) \times 10^{-8} \text{ volts} \tag{63}$$

$$X_n = \frac{1}{1 + R_p/R_{g1}} \tag{64}$$

$$Y_n = \frac{\sin \pi g_1/\lambda_n}{\pi g_1/\lambda_n} \tag{65}$$

where R_p = reluctance of the head core

R_{g1} = reluctance of the head pole gap

$$C_n = \frac{1}{n\pi} \left\{ \left[\frac{\tanh \frac{\pi d}{\lambda_n}}{\cosh \frac{\pi b}{\lambda_n}} \right] \frac{1 + \frac{1}{\mu_2} \tanh \frac{\pi d}{2\lambda_n}}{1 + \tanh \frac{\pi b_2}{\lambda_n} + \tanh \frac{\pi d}{\lambda_n} \left[\frac{1}{\mu_2} + \mu_2 \tanh \frac{\pi b}{\lambda_n} \right]} \right\} \tag{66}$$

$$E_n = \frac{\sin \frac{\pi b}{\lambda_n}}{\frac{\pi b}{\lambda_n}} \tag{67}$$

$$L_n = \frac{1}{1 + Z_1/Z_h} \tag{68}$$

where N_2 = number of turns on read coil

W = width of the head at pole tips

V = relative velocity of head and storage medium (cms)

Z_1 = load impedance of the read network (ohm)

Z_h = equivalent impedance of the read head (ohm)

The reluctance ratio R_p/R_{g1} is given in Equation (37), from which X_n is known and the expression for B_n is given by Equation (62). The above equations can be programmed for any electronic computer and can be applied to various head-recording media systems.

2.7.9   Case of One-Dimensional Transient Field

The switching of the state of magnetization of the specified region on the memory drum surface is accomplished by reversing the direction of an electric current in the write coil of magnetic recording head. In order to study the transient field associated with this phenomenon, it can be assumed that polarized electromagnetic wave with the components H_x and E_z comes perpendicular to the ferromagnetic layer. The electromagnetic field must satisfy Maxwell's fundamental equations, and so the corresponding differential equation can be derived from them.

We assume μ = permeability of the layer which is constant

σ = conductivity of the layer

$\mu_0 = 4\pi \times 10^{-7}$ in MKS system

$\mathbf{E}$ = electric intensity

$\mathbf{B}$ = magnetic induction

$\mathbf{D}$ = electric displacement

$\mathbf{H}$ = magnetic intensity

$\mathbf{J}$ = current density

ρ = charge density

Maxwell's equations are:

$$\nabla \times \mathbf{E} = -\frac{\partial \mathbf{B}}{\partial t} \qquad\qquad \nabla . \mathbf{B} = 0$$

$$\nabla \times \mathbf{H} = \mathbf{J} + \frac{\partial \mathbf{D}}{\partial t} \qquad\qquad \nabla . \mathbf{D} = 0 \qquad\qquad (69)$$

In a homogeneous isotropic medium we have the additional relations

$$\mathbf{D} = K\mathbf{E}, \qquad \mathbf{B} = \mu\mathbf{H}, \text{ and } \mathbf{J} = \sigma\mathbf{E}$$

From the above relations we can deduce

$$\frac{\partial^2 \mathbf{H}_x}{\partial y^2} = \sigma \frac{\partial \mathbf{E}_z}{\partial y} = \mu\sigma \frac{\partial \mathbf{H}_x}{\partial t} \qquad\qquad (70)$$

In rationalized MKS system

$$\frac{\partial^2 \mathbf{H}_x}{\partial y^2} = \sigma\mu \mu_0 \frac{\partial \mathbf{H}_x}{\partial t} \qquad\qquad (71)$$

The non-stationary one-dimensional field can be computed from Equation (71) which is a parabolic differential equation and can be solved using Laplace's transforms. Equation (71) is to be solved for infinite layer and for finite layer.

2.7.10   Infinite Layer Thickness

If a wave is applied suddenly at $t = 0$, and the air gap b is assumed to be zero, the initial value problem is

$$H_{(0, t)} = H_0, \ H_{(\alpha, t)} = 0, \ H_{(y, 0)} = 0$$

(X coordinates have been replaced by Y). Laplace transform $f(p)$ of the function $F(t)$ is defined by

$$f(p) = \int_0^\infty e^{-pt} F(t) \, dt \qquad\qquad (72)$$

Then the Laplace transform of Equation (71) can be written as

$$h = \frac{H_0}{p} \exp(-Ky\sqrt{p}), \quad K^2 = \sigma\mu\,\mu_0$$

The corresponding time function is

$$H_{(y,\, t)} = H_0 \operatorname{erfc}\left(y\,\sqrt{\frac{\sigma\mu\,\mu_0}{4t}} \right) \tag{73}$$

where erfc is defined by the equation $\qquad\qquad\qquad$ (74)

$$\operatorname{erf} X = 1 - \operatorname{erfc} X = \frac{1}{\pi} \int_0^X \exp(-t)dt$$

2.7.11   Finite Layer Thickness

While considering this case we have to assume that the Z component of electric intensity E_z is continuous on the other side of the layer, that is, at the point $y = d$, then if σ_1 and σ_2 represent conductivities of the magnetic layer material and base material respectively, we have

$$\lim_{y \to d-0} \sigma_2 \frac{\partial H}{\partial y} = \lim_{y \to d+0} \sigma_1 \frac{\partial H}{\partial y}$$

The conductivity of ferromagnetic layer material σ_1 can be considered as zero in comparison with that of the drum or disk material. We have the Laplace transform

$$h = H_0 \frac{e^{-(y-d)k\sqrt{p}}}{\cosh Kd\sqrt{p}} \tag{75}$$

and the corresponding time function is

$$H_{(d,\, t)} = 2H_0 \sum_{n=0}^{\alpha} (-1)^n \operatorname{erfc}\left[(2n+1)\,d\sqrt{\frac{\sigma\mu\mu_0}{4t}} \right] \tag{76}$$

The graphical plot of magnetic field in transient cases is given in Figure 2.13. From these two cases one can compute the transient time of the layer material and their dependence on μ.

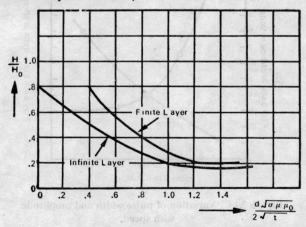

Figure 2.13   Graphical plot of magnetic field in transient cases.

2.7.12   Recording Process Limitations

Several important limitations of recording process are associated with what is known as *record-head trailing effect*. If the field gradient across the record head has no influence on the flux pattern, one would expect the pulse width and amplitude to remain constant after saturation. But it is seen that they are dependent on recording current. The increase in pulse width and decrease in amplitude may be attributed to the record-head trailing effect, and the effect of recording magnetomotive force (MMF). At the moment of flux reversal in the head, all particles under the trailing pole face are magnetized to a varying degree depending on the gradient across the head. The actual field pattern in the coating will depend on the permeability of the material saturated to a constant value at distance from the gap. This record head trailing effect is dependent on the *B-H* characteristics of the medium, recording current, coating thickness, head to medium separation and gap width of the record head. If one plots the experimental results of amplitude versus head to surface gap, it is seen that at higher speeds it tends to become linear and pulse width increases with gap distances, while at lower speed the rate of increase is sharper than at higher speed. If pulse width in microsecond versus rotational speed in rpm is plotted, the curve would seem to approximate rectangular hyperbola. Here also it is seen that the effect of speed variation on playback pulse width is much less at speeds above 8000 rpm and if this variation of amplitude with rotational speed is plotted the amplitude is seen to rise linearly with speed as shown in Figure 2.14.

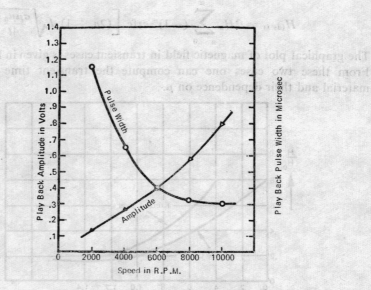

Figure 2.14   Variation of pulse width and amplitude
with speed.

The position of maximum flux gradient at the effective recording point, will depend on the magnetic medium and the recording field strength. We an see it from our theoretical results that the relative distribution of the horizontal and vertical components of the magnetization will depend on the recording field strength and the coating thickness. It is observed experimentally that a current greater than that required to saturate the surface, results in reduction in amplitude and increase in pulse width. It was shown earlier that the longitudinal component is responsible for recording. However, if the recording current is increased beyond the saturation current, the vertical component becomes predominant which results in a shift of the effective recording point farther away from the centre of the gap. This results in increase of the total distance over which the flux is changing and also causes an increase in pulse width and loss of resolution.

The effect of recording head gap width is similar to that of the effect of the trailing field gradient as explained earlier. If the gap width is very small, the field gradient will be greater at the pole face surface which will enable us to use a very thin magnetic coating. This is desirable from many other considerations. For thick coatings, a wider gap will be desirable to set up a sufficiently strong field to saturate those particles that are away from the pole face. In a nutshell, the optimum record head gap will depend on the coating thickness, the B-H characteristics of the layer surface and the separation between the record head and layer surface.

With increase in separation, the layer surface is subject to a diminished recording field gradient, which will widen the flux distribution resulting in loss of resolution. This loss can be minimized by using a coating of magnetic material having near rectangular B-H characteristics, and by designing a record head that gives maximum field gradient for the particular separation being used.

We may also apply the term *self-demagnetization effect* to pulse widening caused by the field within the coating. The field in the coating due to the volume element dv will be $dH = \mathrm{div}\ Idv/r^2$, where I is the intensity of magnetization, div I is the *volume density of magnetic charge* and r is the distance from the volume element to the point (x, y, z) in the coating. The total field at (x, y, z), will be

$$H = \int \frac{\mathrm{div}\ Idv}{r^2} \tag{77}$$

This field within the coating will act on the particles and tend to reorient the particles, thus reducing the resolution. This effect can be reduced by using a coating material with high coercivity to remanence ratio which will minimize reorientation of particles. The demagnetizing field is less with thin coating than with thick coating.

2.7.13   Playback Process Limitations

An expression was derived earlier (Equation 44) showing how the PB signal characteristics depend on coating thickness, head to medium separation and a recording constant along with the expression for head output voltage, for signal array using NRZ recording. A detailed analysis of the playback process limitations from these deductions will not be attempted here, only the salient features will be stated. Theoretical and experimental findings on pulse width and amplitude as a function of separation between PB head and layer surface agree well, the small difference may be attributed to self-demagnetization and record head trailing effects which are dependent on coating thickness.

It can be stated from physical reasonings that the sensitivity contour of the PB head should be wide and sharply defined enough to be able to intercept as much flux as is possible during reading operation. The total flux intercepted by the head will be

$$\phi_x = \int_{x - w/2}^{x + w/2} \phi_x \, dx \tag{78}$$

Therefore,

$$e_x = K \frac{d}{dx} \int_{x - w/2}^{x + w/2} \phi_x \, dx \tag{79}$$

where K is the proportionately constant involving the number of turns in the head, surface speed etc. Using the expression of Leibnitz equation (79) becomes

$$e_x = K \left[\phi_{x + w/2} - \phi_{x - w/2} \right] \tag{80}$$

The maximum signal amplitude is

$$e_{max} = e_0 = K \left[\phi_{w/2} - \phi_{-w/2} \right]$$

But

$$\phi_{w/2} = \phi_{-w/2},$$

hence

$$e_{max} = 2K \phi_{w/2}$$

For pulse width at N per cent of the peak amplitude the following equation must hold

$$0.02 N \phi_{w/2} = \phi_{x_N + w/2} - \phi_{x_N - w/2} \tag{81}$$

where x_N is the head position where the amplitude has dropped to N per cent of the peak value. The solution for x_N will give pulse width as a function of gap width. But the above equation cannot be solved directly as ϕ is a transcendental function. The equation can be solved graphically for particular systems. One point should be marked here is that the effective gap width is not necessarily the physical gap width. The effective gap width is to be determined by measuring the wavelength where the first minima in signal occurred. Therefore, if the pulse width is not to exceed certain limit of an absolute minimum, the effective gap width for the system can be determined. In general, it would be desirable to use the largest gap width consistent with satisfactory performance. If the same head is to be used for both recording and PB operations, the optimum head gap width is to be arrived at in association with the factors discussed in previous section.

2.8 DESIGN CONSIDERATIONS OF HIGH DENSITY MAGNETIC RECORDING SYSTEM

The early history of magnetic recording relates to the application in recording and reproduction of musical and speech sound. Therefore, the theoretical treatment on both sinusoidal and pulse recording such as that attempted by Wallace, Westmijze, Karlguivist and Dutta Majumder is based basically on sinusoidal recording theory. It was, however, recognised that the resolution and signal output are limited by two types of losses, namely, frequency dependent and wavelength dependent losses. *Frequency dependent* losses comprise the eddy current and permeability variation effects in the record/read head, in the layer surfaces and recording current rise time variations with frequency. *Wavelength dependent* losses are related to the geometrical aspects of the record/read system such as head gaps, head to medium spacing, recording medium thickness and demagnetization effects in the recording medium.

There are two methods for the calculation of playback voltages waveform; one is by the well-known reciprocity theorem and other, as was performed by Miyata and Hartel, the method of images. Chapman obtained an estimate of the extent of magnetization transition, demagnetization field in the recording medium equal to the ceorcivity of the medium. Westmijze's classical paper on sinusoidal analysis and the approximate linearity of the response of the playback transducer led different authors to use harmonic analysis to simulate saturation recording, including encoding schemes.

Still there are difficulties in dealing with highly nonlinear recording and demagnetization processes by the above-mentioned theoretical treatments. The iterative method of Iwaski and Suzuki, and of Cusland and Speliotis have claimed to have demonstrated the capability of adequately treating nonlinear recording demagnetization process and predicting ensuing asymmetries in the playback pulse and peak shift that are important at the high packing densities in modern magnetic recording technology. In order to handle these problems the method should include dynamic interaction of the recording-demagnetization process self-consistently and integrally, instead of treating these separately as if they were independent and unrelated. But there is one difficulty in the iterative approach, it needs about ten times more computer time compared with harmonic analysis approach.

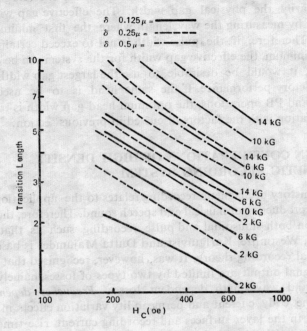

Figure 2.15   Plot of transient length versus coercivity.

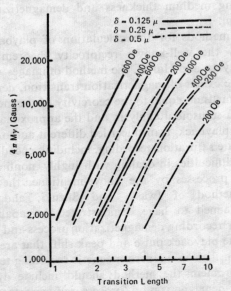

Figure 2.16   Plot of transient length versus remanent induction.

We arrived at an estimate of the written magnetization transition length l_0 as

$$l_0 = \frac{\Delta H}{H_c}\left(b + \frac{\delta}{2}\right) \tag{82}$$

The results for the transition length versus the coercivity of the recording media for three different thicknesses and with remanence as a parameter are shown in Figure 2.15. The results for transition length versus remanent induction of the recording media for three different thicknesses and with coercivity as a parameter are shown in Figure 2.16. Figure 2.17 shows plots of the transition length versus thickness of the recording media for different coercivities with remanence as a parameter. In all the three cases average values of the slopes are constant but they can be higher or lower depending on whether the demagnetization as depicted by the ratio of remanence to coercivity is large or small. Figure 2.18 shows plots of the transitional versus the ratio B_r/H_c with thickness as a parameter.

$H_c = 200$ Oe ————
$H_c = 400$ Oe — — — —
$H_c = 600$ Oe — . — . —

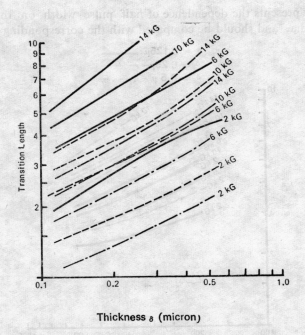

Figure 2.17 Plot of length versus thickness of the recording medium.

We arrived at an estimate of the written magnetization transition length

$$l_0 = $$

$$l_0 = \frac{\Delta H}{M_r}\left(\lambda + \frac{\delta}{2}\right) \tag{82}$$

The results for the transition length versus the coercivity of the recording media for three different thicknesses and with remanence as a parameter are shown in Figure 2.18. These results for transition length versus remanent induction of the recording media for three different thicknesses and with coercivity as a parameter are shown in Figure 2.16. Figure 2.17 shows plots of the transition length versus thickness of the recording media for different coercivities with remanence as a parameter. In all these cases average values of the slope are constant but they can be higher or lower depending on whether the demagnetization is normalized by the ratio of remanence to coercivity is far smaller than ... of the ... and the transitional versus the ratio B_r/H_c ...

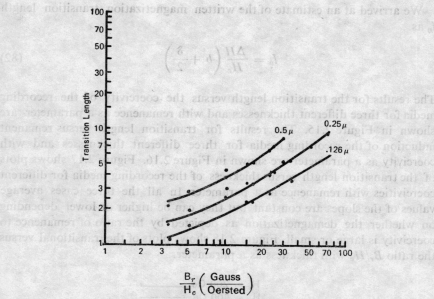

Figure 2.18   Plot of transient length versus B_r/H_c.

Figure 2.19 presents the dependence of half pulse width on the coercivity of the media, and should be compared with the corresponding Figure 2.15

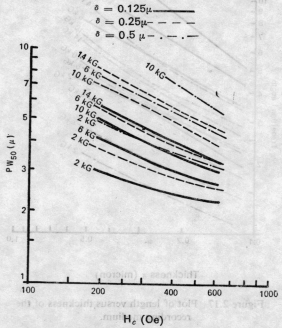

Figure 2.19   Dependence of half pulse width on coercivity.

for transition length. The plots of half pulse width versus remanence are shown in Figure 2.20 and should be compared with the corresponding plots of Figure 2.16. Figure 2.21 shows the dependence of half pulse width on thickness and corresponds to Figure 2.17 for transition length.

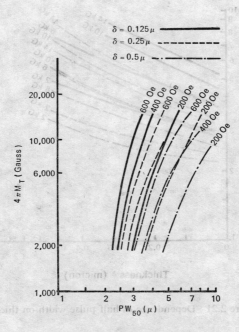

Figure 2.20   Dependence of half pulse width on remanence.

In conclusion it may be said about the digital recording theories that the early simple theories play a very important role in understanding the physical process of magnetic recording and give good results for isolated pulses in very thin media. Harmonic analysis approach is the most powerful available tool for designing digital recording systems, provided that we can correct the serious deficiencies in writing demagnetization side. Further, the self-consistent iterative calculating method offers a great promise for accurate simulation of the nonlinearity interactive high bit density recording. However, a theoretical model which integrally includes all the motions and non-linearities in the system is still an aspiration to be realized. In order to achieve further increase in bit densities, a unified view of digital recording theory with the results of communication theory, as attempted recently by Mallinson, along with the principal ideas concerning pulse response, linear superposition, medium properties, head geometry, channel codes, signal to noise ratio post-equalization and bit densities will have to be undertaken.

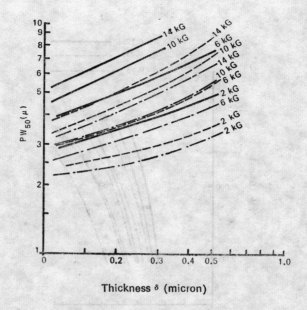

$H_c = 200$ Oe————

$H_c = 400$ Oe— — — —

$H_c = 600$ Oe— . — . —

Thickness δ (micron)

Figure 2.21 Dependence of half pulse width on thickness.

2.9 ROTATING DISKS AND DRUMS AS PERIPHERAL MEMORY IN MODERN COMPUTING SYSTEM

Rotating memories, disks and drums now have capacities ranging from one hundred thousand to four billion bits, access times from 8.7 to 225 milliseconds and costs from 0.5 cents to 0.02 cents per bit. With growing versatility, rotating magnetic memories are more and more displacing magnetic tape as peripheral memories. An important factor in this spur to the growth of rotating memories has been the price drop accompanying higher recording densities and faster data transfer rates made possible by such advances as higher efficiency codes. For applications in sorting and merging of files the need is for much faster access time than is available in tape. Also, for real time applications such as airline reservation system and program swapping the rotating type memory is the only practical peripheral storage medium.

2.9.1 Choice of Head Assembly Design

A crucial choice in rotating magnetic memories is the choice of head assembly design. One aspect of this choice lies in whether one should have in-contact type or flying type. The second aspect is whether one should have movable heads or head per track design. The third factor of importance is the head switching arrangement. Total access time in head per track design depends on the time it takes to switch a head into the read or write mode, which usually takes up to 10 microseconds time plus the latency time. *The latency time may be defined as the time it takes the desired portion of a particular track to rotate into position under a head.*

Whereas in movable type head memories a delay is introduced because of the fact that heads must travel from one track to another, but the movable head memories are less expensive as they use much fewer number of heads in a memory. In late sixties IBM introduced its 2311 rotating removable disk 60 million bits memory which has since become the industry standard. It has only ten heads along a comb-like arm and a one-in-ten selection matrix.

A lower capacity and higher priced memory that stores 20 million bits has been introduced by General Instruments Magne Head Division which has 512 separately mounted flying heads, with a head per track arrangement, giving a total access time of 8.5 milliseconds. Though expensive, head per track memory can improve data processing system and throughput time by a factor as high as 10 to 1 over moving head memories.

In order to arrive at an optimal economy for choosing the head arrangement in a rotating magnetic store to be used as peripheral memories, size of the system and its required capacity is very important. Head per track memories is more economical for capacities under about 10 million bits, because the cost of moving head drives outweighs that of the extra heads. But if the required capacities are of the order of 40 to 50 million bits, the head per track arrangement becomes costly due to a very complicated head switching mechanism. In the commercial time-sharing applications bulk of the market is in the range of 10 to 60 million bits range and the choice in this range is not very clear, the decision in such a case will have to be arrived at from total system cost and other considerations.

2.9.2 Factors Affecting the Choice of Drums and Disks

One of the important effect affecting the memory reliability is known as 'head crash'. When heads smash onto the surfaces of a rotating drum or disk, magnetic material gets scrapped off. The head has to maintain a distance of a few millionth of an inch above the magnetic coating or plating. Usually, dust particles and mechanical instabilities are the chief causes of these crashes. If particles get between the head and the magnetic surface, the aerodynamics of head environment is affected or the particles act as abrasives which scour off the magnetic material.

Since the drum units are sealed and can be kept out of dust, the chances of abrasion and head crashes are much less. On the other hand, the removable disk memories cannot be sealed, but non-removable disk memories can be sealed. There are some disk memories that are kept in helium atmosphere and offer very high reliability.

A major advantage of drums is that they can be rotated at higher speeds up to 24,000 rpm and thus have a faster access time. Disks have one major advantage over drums that they can be removed from the memory and stored. This is highly desirable for applications with alternate programs. If the system permits the use of compatible disk memories, the cost is less and one can choose from a variety of available supplies. Mostly drums are heads per track unit and movable heads are usually used in disk memories.

2.10   METHODS FOR IMPROVING THE RELIABILITY OF DISK STORAGE SYSTEMS

Moving magnetic memories with particulate layer surfaces such as disk, drum and tape, depend on mechanical, electronic and aerodynamic design considerations. By giving high priority to the mechanical and aerodynamic design consideration, highly reliable digital disk recorders with removable disk can be achieved.

Increasing mechanical reliability is a highly precision work which can be achieved by: (i) replacing all major bearing surfaces with air bearings instead of ball bearings, and (ii) controlling the mechanism of the drive system by fluid.

Usually in moving magnetic surface memories the data reliability is affected by abrasion caused by dust particles and mechanical instability. The abrasion and resulting head crashes can be minimized by keeping the disks in sealed cartridges, from where they are loaded into the drive system without being exposed to the dirt of room air. Timing reliability can be improved by controlling the read-write timing with synchronization bits interspersed among the data bits.

Boisvert and Lambert of Digital Information Storage Corporation reported the description of a disk system DDR-1 with large storage capacity, fast access time and increased reliability with air bearings and interspersed synchronization bits. Fast access time is achieved by using a read-write head for every track while air bearings intrinsic property of self-centering permits the disk to be accurately positioned relative to the heads even as it spins at 3600 rpm.

The problem of cross-talk can be largely eliminated by using nickel chromium coating with heads very accurately positioned over tracks rather than iron oxide coating.

In most of the fixed-disk storage units, synchronizing pulses are derived from one of several timing tracks. But at high recording densities, the tolerance in these timing tracks becomes very critical. The disk may seem gyroscopic under even slight external shock. Under certain circumstances, it may also set up a standing wave in the disk. Usually, data and timing heads are mounted on flexible supports to eliminate such disturbances, but they may ride in the opposite direction and upset the phase relationship between the timing and data pulses. These difficulties are obviated in removable disks by incorporating timing pulses into data tracks. The reliability factor is further improved by cushioning all possible external shocks. If there is any change in the rotating masses comprising the disk, the supporting hub, the shaft and the motor rotor as a result of external shock or just ordinary wear and tear, it is compensated automatically by the self-centring effect of the air bearing. The entire disk-loading procedure is to be carried out by pneumatic and fluidic equipment and without any ball bearing anywhere in the business end of the machine.

Ball bearings have serious drawbacks in disk storages as there is both axial and rotational motion in disk memory. Ordinary ball bearings support only rotation, while specialized adaptations would require multiple bearings. Lubrication does not always avert associated problems of ball bearings and the lubricant could pollute the magnetic coating.

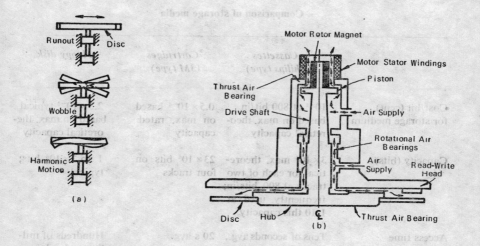

Figure 2.22   Disk rotating mechanisms: (a) with ball bearings;
(b) with air bearings.

Figure 2.22 shows the mechanical design with air bearings, as has been done in Digital Information Storage Corporations DDR-1. The air bearings are intrinsically self-centring, because air's fluid nature tends to equalize the pressure in any given mass of air. The air bearing, unlike the ball bearing inherently permits axial motion. The diagram shows that floating piston, shaft, and hub are cast as a unit. The motor rotor which is a permanent magnet, is press fitted onto the top of the shaft and becomes permanently a rigid part of the coating. After the disk has been mechanically latched onto the hub, air pressure on the piston raises it, together with the disk and the rotor. When the rotor enters the rotating magnetic field of the motor stator the shaft begins to turn; by the time the shaft has reached its uppermost position, it is almost at its maximum speed.

2.11 MAGNETIC TAPE MEMORY SYSTEM

Since the computer's main random access memory is a costly component, its use is economically confined to applications where its characteristic high speed is required. Where speed is less important, inexpensive very high capacity rotating disk and drum or magnetic tape storage are available. The prime virtue of magnetic tape storage is that it can store an enormous amount of data on a small, easily handled reel at very low cost. A comparative statement of cassettes, cartridges and floppy disk is shown in Table 2.3. Apart from feasibility and high capacity, other advantages are ease of

TABLE 2.3

Comparison of storage media

	Cassettes (Philips type)	Cartridges (3M type)	Floppy disk
Cost/bit (cent) for storage medium	10^{-4} at 800 bit/in based on max. theoretical capacity	0.5×10^{-4} based on max. rated capacity	2.5×10^{-4} typical based on max. theoretical capacity
Capacity (bits)	3×10^6 max. theoretical for each of two tracks at 800 bits/in; frequently used at 1/10 this capacity	23×10^6 bits on four tracks	1 to 3×10^6 bits; typical
Access time	Tens of seconds avg., depending on transport search speed	20 s avg.	Hundreds of milliseconds, depending on rotational speed
Transfer rate	10 to 25×10^3 bits/s; typical	48×10^3 bits/s	Hundreds of kilo bits/s

erasure and correction, non-volatility, long-term permanence, high data transfer rates and reliability compatible with modern computer requirements. A major disadvantage that is inherent in its geometry is the slow access time because of the serial nature of tape storage.

As early as 1953, the first successful commercial product of magnetic tape data storage appeared where data could be recorded at a density of 100 bytes per linear inch. Additional forms of successful magnetic tape storage, such as tape cassettes, have been introduced to collect and process data in applications where low performance in terms of density of recording and processing speeds is compatible with low cost, such as point-of-sale terminals and very small data processor. But an amazing thing about half-inch tape is its upward/downward compatibility. Tapes that were generated 20 years ago at 200 bytes/in have the capacity of regenerating data at 6250 bytes/in on the same reel of tape. In this period throughput rates have increased from 15,000 byte/s to 1,250,000 byte/s. Other important disadvantages are high sensitivity to foreign particles, tape wear, sensitivity to high temperature and magnetic fields. The mechanical system of the tape transport mechanism is highly critical in that it must start, stop, and reverse at high speed without introducing error or causing tape damage.

2.11.1 Magnetic Tape Materials

In some earlier sections of this chapter, while dealing with design considerations of the class of ferromagnetic layer surface storage systems, we have described in some detail the general properties of magnetic coating materials. Here we shall deal briefly with the mechanical and magnetic properties of magnetic tapes.

The magnetic tape consists of mechanically strong, but thin and very flexible plastic foil in which the ferromagnetic and ferrimagnetic materials are dispersed (impregnated tape) or on whose surface a film of magnetic material has been deposited (spultered tape). The width of the tape is 12.7 mm or a multiple as composition tapes are not used much nowadays as the concentration of particles attainable in this way is insufficient. As substrate or carrier either cellulose acetate (CA) or polyvinyl chloride (PVC) or polyester (PE) is used. Polyester tapes are more in use because of their excellent qualities. They are of high physical stability between —60°C and +95°C and absorb hardly any moisture.

The magnetizable layer commonly used is the ferrimagnetic material ($v\text{-}Fe_2O_3$) which is a cubic modification of iron oxide and is magnetic. $v\text{-}Fe_2O_3$ is ferrimagnetically and structurally related to magnetite, $FeOFe_2O_3$. Table 2.4 taken from krones gives the mechanical and magnetic properties of various tapes, together with their ranges of tolerance. At a critical particle size of 100-500 mm, H_c of about 40 KA/m can be obtained. By enrichment with cobalt, values up to 120 KA/m and B_r is 0.08 VS/m^2 can be realized.

The use of particles of higher coercivity would only be worthwhile if B_r could be raised at the same time. This could be done by using a higher proportion of Fe_2O_3 in the magnetic layer, but a filling factor of more than 55% by volume makes the tape brittle and less stable. By depositing the particles

TABLE 2.4

Typical, physical, mechanical properties	NiZn	Mn-Zn Type SP-5	Mn-Zn Type SP-8	Single XTAL
Density, g/ml	5.30	5.07	5.07	5.07
Porosity, %	0.2	0.2	0.2	0
Hardness (vickers, 300 g load), kg/mm²	850	800	800	700
Bend strength, polished bar, kg/cm²	1000	3000	3000	800
Magnetic properties				
Initial permeability at, 100 KHz	1600	18000	1200	2800
1 MHz	1200	1600	1200	450
10 MHz	300	400	500	200
Frequency where $Q = 1$, 1 MHz	2.5	5	8	20
Coercive force (dc), oersted	0.12	0.1	0.15	0.1
Saturation flux density, 4π gauss	3200	4250	4650	4700
Curie temperature, °C	145	140	170	265
Resistivity, μohm-cm	10^6	20	30	0.1

from a liquid solution the process can be so controlled that needle-like particles of hydrated iron oxide are formed. Using a suitable heat treatment at 250-300°C, this can be converted into ν-Fe$_2$O$_3$ without changing the external shape of the particles. As a rule the particles have a mean length of 1 μm and mean breadth of 0.1 μm.

By the application of a suitable magnetic field at the time of addition of powder to the carrier, a parallel alignment of particles can be achieved, whereby the remanent flux of tape is suitably increased. The iron oxide dust is suitably and intimately mixed with a special lacquer and applied to the plastic tape to form a layer between 15 μm and 40 μm thick. After it is dry, the magnetic layer adheres firmly to the substrate and shows considerable resistance to abrasion—a property which is clearly necessary to prevent the magnetic material from being rubbed off as the tape passes over the magnetic heads.

Sometimes Fe$_3$O$_4$ (magnetite) is also used as ferrimagnetic material in place of ν-Fe$_2$O$_3$. Chromic oxide (CrO$_2$) to which a few per cent of cobalt has been added, provides a highly coercive ferrimagnetic substance (H_c=48 KA/m) which can be used in the production of magnetic tapes.

Considering the latest experience gained in the study of thin film techniques and also present knowledge as to the production of single domain particles the future use of materials of even higher coercivity cannot be ruled out (Table 2.5).

TABLE 2.5

Basic properties of materials

Material	Sat. magnetization Gauss Rel. Fe_2O_3		Squareness ratio	Coercivity (oersteds)
PARTICLES[1]				
Gamma ferric oxide	1400	—	0.75 typical (orient direction only)	240-300
Modified iron oxides	1400-2000	1.0-1.4	0.75-0.8 (doped oxides can be isotropic)	150-800
Chromium dioxide	1700	1.2	0.8 + (orient direction only)	200-600
Alloy particles	7000	5	0.6-0.7 (orient direction only)	450-800
Iron particles (GE type)	7000	5	High (orient direction only)	High
Colloidal cobalt	5500	4	0.8 + (orient direction only)	400-800
METAL FILMS[2]				
Chemical deposition	18000	15	0.8 + (isotropic in plane)	100-1000+
Electrolytic deposition	18000	15	0.75 (isotropic in plane)	150-1000+
Vacuum deposition	18000	15	0.9 + (in plane of incidence only)	50-1000+

[1]Assuming a volume loading of 33% magnetic/total solids.
[2]Assuming pure cobalt of maximum density.

High energy magnetic powders. In recent years, several new magnetic powders, generally classified as *high energy*, have been commercially introduced. These powders can be roughly divided into two classes: (1) based on metallic cobalt, iron or their alloys, i.e. particles with coercivities above 900 Oe, and (2) based on cobalt substituted iron oxides with coercivities ranging from 300 to 1000 Oe. The first variety generally represents an improvement in recording and playback characteristics of tapes prepared from them, whereas the second variety is basically aimed at matching the performance of chromium dioxide tapes at a lower unit price. In the literature it is stated that the magnetic properties such as saturation, magnetization and coercivity of the cobalt substituted iron oxide are unstable. The instability is believed to be a consequence of the pressure and temperature dependence of the large magnetocrystalline anisotropy of cobalt substituted iron oxide. It has been recently shown by Kaganowiez et al. that by introducing a small amount of zinc into these oxides, they become chemically and magnetically stable. The degree of chemical stability is dependent on the zinc content, and the degree of magnetic stability is dependent not only on the zinc content but also on the zinc to cobalt ratio.

Tape storage—general operational principles. A tape storage system includes the magnetic tape itself and suitable reels, magnetic heads for reading and writing, the tape transport system and the associated electronic circuitry for data preparation and drive control mechanism. There is a control unit that connects the tape transport to computer, and provides a data buffer for synchronizing data transfer, executing processor control commands and reporting back to the computer about tape status.

As the tape is a relatively fragile storage medium, provision of a dust free environment, with controlled temperature and relative humidity is very important to ensure increased number of error free passes. A dusty environment will increase errors, since particles on the tape surface introduce a gap to the magnetic head, and may cause permanent damage to the tape. The tapes magnetic surfaces should not be touched by hand.

Tape damage may also result from imperfections caused by tape misalignment and variable tape tension, particularly during acceleration and deceleration. Imperfect mechanical transport characteristics set practical limits to storage capacity as expressed by the maximum bits per inch and the maximum number of parallel tracks.

An important mechanical requirement of parallel recording is alignment and uniformity of separate sections of the multi-track magnetic head consistent with recording density. Timing deviations among separate tracks result from misalignment of individual gaps, and from misorientation of entire head assembly. These deviations in high density recording constitute the skew error. Skew error may also be found as a result of tape motion irregularity. These timing errors limit data storage density.

Considerable design effort has gone into minimizing the skew error. In high performance tape systems, electronic relays may be introduced in each track to compensate for the non-uniform timing resulting from mechanical misalignment. But other skew errors may vary between tape transports and cannot be similarly corrected.

Tape transport and drive architecture. Digital tape transports by the requirements that start, stop and reverse must occur within a relatively few milliseconds under computer control. Figure 2.23 shows the typical tape path area of a 200 in/s half-inch magnetic tape unit. Source data tape reel is on the right side that is initiated in the computer, the hub expands automatically to grip the reel. The reel then rotates in the clockwise direction and the tape moves toward the left reel and is supported by air jets located in the right threading channel. It drops into a channel as it passes the read/ write head and is then lifted by air jets on the left threading channel and carried through to the machine reel. The hub of the left reel has vacuum applied which attracts the tape. Clockwise motion of the reel wraps the tape several revolutions until enough tape is taken up so that vacuum on the reel can be discontinued. At that instant the left reel stops clockwise rotation and starts a counter-clockwise rotation. The right reel keeps on turning clockwise, which provides a slack condition of tape between the two reels.

The application of vacuum at that time pulls the tape into columns. Once the tape reaches the middle of each of the two columns, the capstan is activated to move the beginning-of-tape reflective marker to a position above the beginning-of-tape/end-of-tape sensor.

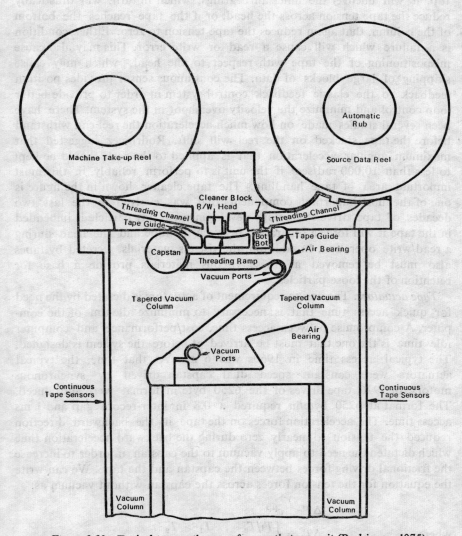

Figure 2.23   Typical tape path area of magnetic tape unit (Rodriguez, 1975).

The machine is now ready for use. In this design vacuum column acts as the air-cushion buffer between the acceleration requirements of the capstan and the acceleration limits of the tape reel and reel motor. In Figure 2.23 the oxide coated surface touches only two points, namely, the read/write head and the tape cleaner. The automatic hub engagement and disengagement was introduced in 1970. The column walls as shown in the figure contain a sensor as part of the reel control system. The reel control system prevents the tape loop from going beyond the top of the column, or going to the bottom of the column during normal operation. If the tape goes beyond the top, it will uncover the inner air bearings, which in turn, will drastically reduce the tape tension across the head; or if the tape reaches the bottom of the column, that again reduces the tape tension to zero. Either condition is a failure which will cause a read or write error. This may also cause mispositioning of the tape with respect to the head, which may cause skipping of large blocks of data. The continuous sensor provides position feedback to the classic feedback control system in order to provide better loop control and minimize the velocity overshoot in the system. There have been several studies made on how much acceleration the reel can withstand before the tape stacked on the reel will shift. Rodriguez suggested that maximum angular acceleration that is applied to the reels should be kept to less than 10,000 rad/sec^2 if the unit is to perform reliably in this most important area of tape handling. The tape cleaner shown in the figure is one of the most important components that was evolved in the last two decades of tape drive technology development. If any particle is imbedded in the tape it will force a separation between the tape and the head during a read/write operation. In addition, the viscous materials secreted by tapes also must be removed as these viscous materials provide a base for retention of the loose particles.

Tape actuators. The design requirement of actuators is dictated by the need for quick access time that is necessary to minimize idle time of the computer. A compromise between access time, cost/performance and computer idle time is the one that must be arrived at before the system is designed. The typical access time in 1960s was 6 ms. At that time, the typical actuators were constant speed dual capstan driven by synchronous motors. In 1976, tape drives of the 6250 byte/in format were introduced. The format at 6250 byte/in required a 0.3 in inter-record gap and 1 ms access time. The acceleration forces on the tape in the backward direction reduced the tension to nearly zero during the backward acceleration time which dictated the need to apply vacuum to the capstan in order to increase the frictional driving forces between the capstan and the tape. We can write the equation for the tension forces across the capstan without vacuum as:

$$\Delta T \leqslant e^{\mu \beta}$$

where
$$\Delta T = \begin{cases} T_1/T_2 & , \quad T_1 > T_2 \\ T_2/T_1 & , \quad T_2 > T_1 \end{cases}$$

where T_1 and T_2 are the tensional forces on both ends of the tape across the capstan, μ is the coefficient of friction between the tape and capstan, and is the warp angle across the capstan. The inequality indicates that if the value of ΔT is greater than that of the write side, the equation is no longer valid and slip will occur between the tape and the capstan.

Typically $\beta = \pi$ rad, and the value of μ varies from 0.3 to 1. Hence $e^{\mu\beta}$ varies from 2.5 to 23. Under this condition T_1/T_2 will certainly exceed the maximum value of $e^{\mu\beta}$.

The expression is modified on the application of the vacuum to:

$$\frac{T_1 + T_v}{T_2 + T_v} \leqslant e^{\mu\beta}$$

where $T_v = 2\,T_1$ (under steady state conditions).

Figure 2.24.

If $T_2 \to 0$ and T_1 approaches twice its steady state value and the ratio will now be 2, which is less than the minimum value of $e^{\mu\beta}$.

Digital cassette recorders. In the previous section we have discussed about latest trends in large tape drive and transport architecture. In smaller tape transports notably those used with cassettes and cartridges, direct reel-to-reel drive as shown in Figure 2.25 is feasible and provides good performance in simple and reliable manner. A practical configuration uses two opposed rotating capstans that are belt-driven by a constant speed motor. Each capstan supports a high inertia flywheel to reduce short term speed fluctuations. Since maximum data storage density occurs when linear velocity is minimum, density is reduced to 40% of maximum at peak linear velocity, reducing overall tape capacity by about 40% due to the varying diameter of the drive reel over the length of the tape unless suitably compensated. Various methods are used to keep storage tape speed more or less constant so as to maintain uniform density. The most obvious method is to use a pre-recorded clock track. During operation, the clock track's output frequency is compared with the reference frequency and the deviations are employed to correct drive motor speed.

The above method has serious disadvantages—both economic and technical. The other method as shown in Figure 2.26 in which individual motors'

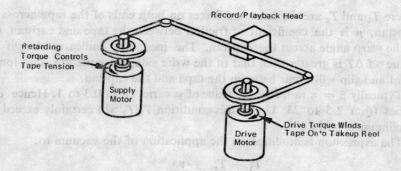

Figure 2.25 Configuration of a reel-to-reel tape transport (Davis, 1974).

velocities as measured by their counter emfs are used in a servo system to maintain a uniform linear velocity. Reel motors can form both speed and tension.

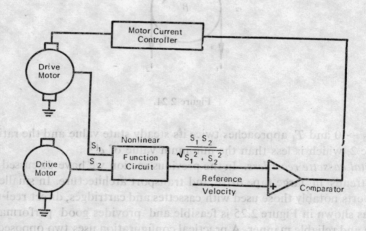

Figure 2.26 Block diagram of a servo system used to hold tape velocity constant.

An alternate method is to use the sum of the velocities of separate motors in a velocity feedback loop to maintain uniform linear velocity over the length of the tape to about ± 5%. In conclusion, it may be remarked that no matter how carefully designed or how thoroughly tested, elements such as clutches, solenoids, belt, and pulleys contribute heavily to sytem mean-time-between-failure (MTBF). Units having the fewest moving parts tend to show improved MTBF though exceptions are obvious.

Magnetic tape cartridges.   Magnetic tape cartridges have been extensively described in trade journals as they appeared in the market. We shall briefly describe here some of their notable variations. It seems 3M cartridge has received widespread acceptance as evidenced by the number of manufacturers introducing compatible tape transports. As shown in Figure 2.27, these transports are appreciably simpler than cassette transports because of the cartridge design. The cartridge uses a unique drive based on an elastic belt which moves the tape and maintains the tensions. The transport itself must include drive motor with suitable friction wheel, necessary drive electronics and magnetic head.

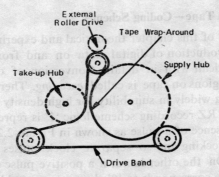

Figure 2.27   Configuration of the 3M cartridge (Davis, 1974).

Although the cartridge costs two to three times as much as a cassette, its per-stored-bit price is considerably less, since its capacity is four to eight times higher. Depending on whether the cassette uses one or two independent recording tracks, it is inherently faster, and has a much high data rate, longer life, and higher reliability.

Another very interesting variation of cartridges was introduced by one of the manufacturer is shown in Figure 2.28 with coaxial tape reels and coiled springs between them to maintain tension. This arrangement required no power for tension control. This is claimed to be the smallest and highest of all such devices.

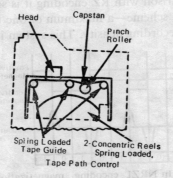

Figure 2.28   Configuration of the Iomec transport.

Floppy disks, digital carsettes and cartridges. A comparative statement showing the performance of cassettes, cartridges and floppy disks is presented in Table 2.3 while Table 2.6 shows the specifications of 3M cartridge as updated by Sidney Davis. Disks offer much lower access time and higher reliability. On the other hand, tape cassettes and cartridges are very low in cost and provide more storage capacity than the floppy disks. So user will choose tape if his applications do not call for faster access time.

2.11.2 Recording on Tape—Coding Schemes

In previous sections of this chapter theoretical and experimental analyses of recording and reproduction of digital data on and from magnetic layer surfaces have been dealt with in detail. Conversion of digital input data into magnetized regions on tape is called *encoding*. There are many encoding formats differing widely in suitability for high density storage.

RZ encoding. In RZ recording scheme logic '1' is represented by a pulse, and logic '0' by absence of a pulse as shown in Figure 2.29. This encoding format is not self-clocking and so separate clock pulses are required for timing purposes. On the other hand, if a positive pulse corresponds to '1' and a negative pulse corresponds to '0' the system could be self-clocking. Since the tape is not magnetized between the binary digit pulses, this is described as return to zero or RZ.

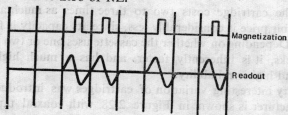

Figure 2.29 RZ recording.

NRZI encoding. In nonreturn to zero inverted (NRZI) scheme, magnetization is reversed for logic '1' and unchanged for logic '0' as is shown in Figure 2.30. In comparison with RZ encoding it is seen that there are fewer flux reversals in this scheme—a maximum of one transition per bit which permits higher pulse recording density. This system is also not self-clocking.

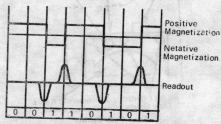

Figure 2.30 In NRZI encoding, magnetization is reversed for logic '1' and remains unchanged for logic '0'.

Phase encoding. In phase encoding (PE), the information is conveyed by the direction of flux transition. A flux reversal from positive to negative represents a logic '0' and from negative to positive represents a logic '1' as shown in Figure 2.31. The transition at the centre of the bit cell is called data transition. The advantage of this type of encoding scheme over NRZI is that there is at least one transition per bit cell as a result of which the system can be self-clocking. The disadvantage of this scheme over NRZI is that for a certain bit density, the system must have the capability to record at twice the transition density of NRZI. From the nature of PE scheme, it can be seen that a single bit error will lead to error in succeeding bits unless provision is made for resynchronization. A phase-locked oscillator is often used to carry out this resynchronizm function.

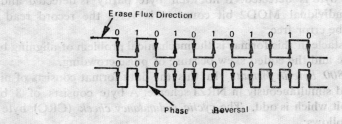

Figure 2.31   Phase encoding (Davis, 1974).

Group-coded recording scheme. This encoding scheme offers a compromise between the maximum flux transition requirements of NRZI and the self-clocking capabilities of PE scheme. This scheme takes 4 data bits and converts them into 5 recorded bits. A recorded bit is defined as in NRZI.

The limitation on the 5 recorded bits is such that there shall be no more than 2 recorded NRZI zeros in a row. The 4 and 5 data bits have 16 and 32 possible combinations. Out of the 32, there are 24 combinations that obey the basic rule of no more than 2 consecutive recorded NRZI zeros. By placing a further restriction that there shall be no more than 1 zero at a boundary of a 5-recorded bit group, the number of 5 recorded bit combination, 16 can be chosen to be equivalent to the 16 data-bit group, the number of combinations that can be recorded. This scheme adds to NRZI a self-clocking capability by providing a minimum of 2 out of every 5 possible recording transitions, while reducing the transition density requirements of PE by 37.5 per cent. The limits of detection are same as NRZI.

2.11.3 Magnetic Tape Recording Format Schemes

Several formats are in use and others are in the process of development, depending on the requirements of higher pulse packing density and better error correction capability.

Seven-track 200 byte/in format. In this format there are seven tracks recorded simultaneously using NRZI codings cheme on tape, six of which are data and the seventh is a parity (odd) track. A byte here is defined as 6 parallel data bits and a parity bit. An additional byte, called the *Longitudinal redundancy check* (LRC) byte is also recorded which serves two purposes: (a) to return the track to the polarity of the interblock gap, and (b) to provide a means of error detection. This format has very little error correction capability.

As the parity track contains odd parity, number of transitions in a byte is odd. The first bit in a byte will open a gate whose typical duration is half of a bit cell. Any transition that occurs in other six tracks while the gate is open will be ones. When the gate is closed the byte is assembled and odd parity is checked and a MOD2 bit count is kept on every track until the LRC byte is detected. If no even byte parity is detected and if every one of individual MOD2 bit counters is zero, the record read is considered to be error free.

A major obstacle in this format is the mechanical problem of aligning bits within the byte and the coded skew because of pulse crowding.

Nine-track 800 byte/in format. In this the data format consists of nine tracks recorded simultaneously in NRZI scheme. A byte consists of 8 bits and a parity bit which is odd. The *cyclic redundancy check* (CRC) byte is generated as follows:

$$G_1 = X^0 + X^3 + X^4 + X^5 + X^6 + X^9$$

C is computed from data polynomials M_1 through M_n according to the following relationship:

$$C = (X^n M_1 + X^{n-1} M_2 + \dots + X^2 M_{n-1} + X^1 M_n) \text{ Modulo } G_1$$

All arithmetic operations are Modulo 2.

The calculated CRC character is modified by the polynomial $1 + X + X^2 + X^4 + X^6 + X^7 + X^8$. Exclusive OR ed with C in the corresponding bit positions; the resultant is the CRC character. The last byte is an LRC byte similar to that in 200 byte/in. The CRC byte has the characteristic that it can detect the track that is in error as long as the error is not cyclic every 9 bits. On identifying the track in error, the system attempts a re-read to correct the track previously identified in error. On detection of parity error the CRC character is regenerated in the error correction operation. If it matches with that recorded on tape and the LRC byte is matched, the record is considered to be successfully corrected. In all other respects, this format contains all the advantages and disadvantages of the 200 byte/in in format.

Nine-track 1600 byte/in format. This system contains 9 tracks recorded simultaneously in PE scheme. A byte is 8 bits plus an odd parity bit. Each track starts with a 40-zero preamble followed by a 'one'. The

40 zeros are used for synchronizing clocks, the one to detect the beginning of data. The last data byte is followed by a postamble consisting of a 'one' followed by 40 zeros.

This format has a great advantage over 800 byte/in in that through electronic circuits the skew problems are solved. Since each track is self-clocking and each track is detected independently of every other track, its relative position to any other track is rather immaterial, at least in concept. Aligning of the bits in byte is done electronically through the use of skew buffers. The first '1' in the format identifies the beginning of data; thereafter each bit is assigned sequentially to a byte, and when all the bits in a byte are received, the byte is transferred out.

Nine-track 6250 byte/in format. Here also a byte consists of 8 data bits and an odd parity bit, but each track is recorded in the group-coded recording code. Every eighth byte in this system is an *error correcting code* (ECC) byte.

The ECC byte is generated as follows: the data byte is D_1 D_2 D_3 D_4 D_5 D_6 D_7, where D_1 through D_7 are coefficients of polynomials respectively and have the following assignments:

Polynomial position. X^1 X^4 $X^7 - X^3$ X^6 X^0 X^2 X^5 corresponds to track numbers 1 2 3 4 5 6 7 8 9. Track number 4 contains odd parity bit P and is not a part of the ECC character. ECC byte E is an 8 byte character and are coefficients of polynomial E with same track assignments. Track number 4 contains odd parity on the 4 byte bit E.

The generator polynomial G is given by:

$$G = X^0 + X^3 + X^4 + X^5 + X^8.$$

The polynomial E is given by:

$$E = (X^7 D_1 + X^6 D_2 + X^5 D_3 + X^4 D_4 + X^3 D_5 + X^2 D_6 + X^1 D_7) \text{ Modulo } G$$

All arithmetic operations are Modulo 2.

This system can detect and correct all single track errors and with a priori pointers, correct all double track errors.

Some comments on magnetic tape storage. In the presentday state of the art, magnetic tape may be considered as a nearly ideal means of storing large quantities of digital data for long periods of time at a low cost and in compact package. For the last two and a half decades, it has occupied a place of pride in the storage hierarchy as an auxiliary storage device. In the recent years, expanding use of mini-computers and microcomputers has accelerated the growth of tape systems which offer reduced performance and capacity at a greatly reduced price. Cassettes and cartridges will have a definite usage in the spectrum of storage systems.

In 1972, the American National Standards Institute (ANSI) and European Computer Manufacturers' Association (ECMA) agreed on an international standard governing cassettes and data recording means to assure interchangeability of cassettes for writing and reading purposes. Although this is first step towards standardization, it is oriented primarily to online computer peripheral applications which are only a function of digital cassette applications. Hence, new ANSI standards were proposed in 1973. Those who are interested should study them.

As mentioned above, over the past seven to eight years, different forms of magnetic tape storage have been developed to fulfil the diverse types of needs in the data processing industry. These are the magnetic strip credit card, the tape cassette, the floppy disk, and the IBM 3851 tape cartridge.

If one analyzed the cost/performance curve it would be seen that each of them filled a different need at a different optimum point. (This comment can be expanded for the 25 years to include the earlier ferromagnetic layer surface storage systems such as magnetic drums and disks.)

It is true that the magnetic strip card is a low performance system, but it can strive in hazardous environment where other systems may not survive.

2.12   STUDIES ON THE DESIGN OF MAGNETIC HEAD FOR DIGITAL DATA RECORDING AND REPRODUCTION

It has been discussed earlier that in digital recording and reproduction, information is handled in binary form, requiring a discrimination in two states corresponding to two opposite senses of saturation. The design of magnetic heads for the purpose, even at the present time, is largely an empirical subject. Generally speaking, the heads used must have a wider bandwidth than the heads used in sound recording on account of the very short pulses which must be recorded and reproduced. The distinctive features of the digital recording and reproduction in comparison with magnetic sound recording, may be enumerated as follows:

(i)   Two-level saturation recording on the magnetic surface.
(ii)   The fundamental frequency of operation is higher and is in relation to the bit rate.
(iii)   Necessity for reliability is much more stringent in digital data recording.
(iv)   The surface velocity is much higher in this case.

The merit of magnetic drum and disk storage system may be measured by the ratio of capacity to access time as it is advantageous to increase the capacity and decrease the access time or both. We have

$$C/A = V/S = p$$

where

C = capacity of track in bits
A = inherent access time
V = surface velocity
S = cell length
p = information transfer rate, bits/time

A minimum separation between the head and the surface allows an increase in the orders of magnitude of the surface velocity over permissible contact values, more than overcoming the loss in resolution (increase in the maximum value for S). We have earlier discussed in detail the mechanical problems of increasing the surface velocity and the associated aerodynamic defects, bearing problems, etc. Hence, it appears from those discussions that the problem is reduced to effecting reduction in cell length for certain surface velocity. A similar argument is valid in case of magnetic tape storage system.

The desirable characteristics for a magnetic recording/reproducing head for computer use may be enumerated in short as follows:

(a) High efficiency
(b) Uniform electrical characteristics
(c) Constructional complexity
(d) Overall reliability
(e) Facilities of simple shielding and accurate positioning of gaps
(f) Low writing current
(g) Large reading voltage

The design of recording and reproducing heads for digital work, even at the present time, is largely an empirical subject.

There have been some practical experimentations in the earlier years using the electrolytic tank and also some discussion on the optimum design of magnetic record/reproduce heads to be used in conjuction with magnetic storage units. Implications of two well-known problems in potential theory in the designing of magnetic heads were indicated by Booth in 1952. The first problem is the edge effect in a parallel plate condenser, first treated by Helmholtz and the solution given by Jeans. The second problem is the study of field configuration in the space surrounding the boundary of the condenser gap which in the ideal case is the same as recording gap boundary.

The solutions to these problems are obtained by Schwarz-Christoffel transformation and we have discussed them earlier in this chapter. Though the treatment is for electrostatic cases, the results are equally applicable for magnetostatic cases in which the conductors are replaced by a magnetic circuit whose permeability can be assumed to be infinite compared with that of air ($\mu = 1$). The assumption can be easily approximated as the permeability of the materials used for the construction of the magnetic heads, is very high and it is not used near the saturation region. Assuming that there is no other magnetic substance in the vicinity to disturb the magnetic fields, the equipotential surface (discussed in the appendix) can be considered to represent a set of head profiles such that each produces an identical external field distribution.

In the following sections we enunciate the design considerations of: (i) conventional magnetic heads, (ii) modern ferrite transducers, and (iii) integrated magnetic film heads. Of course, the design considerations of conventional heads and ferrite heads are all mutually applicable. We have included separately the ferrite head designs because of the trend in usage. Integrated film heads discussed with briefly, as still these are being experimented with.

2.12.1 General Design Considerations of Conventional Heads

The problem of head design is effectively reduced to an engineering proposition of generating suitable profiles which satisfy the desirable characteristics mentioned earlier in this section. The experimental optimization of record reproduce head structures is difficult, as the dimensions involved in the pulse recording and reproduction processes are extremely small, and their fabrication involves many special techniques. The effects of different parameters in recording/reproduction process (viz. recording MMF, separation between record head and layer surface, characteristics of the coating material, record/PB head gap width, etc.) have been discussed earlier.

Several useful methods of developing qualitative design concepts in the evaluation of magnetic head structure and in their design for high density storages, have been published by different authors.

The results of our investigation with regard to the important factors contributing in the conventional magnetic head design may be summarized as follows:

(1) The demand for low writing current and large reading voltage requires that the reluctance of the magnetic path in the head should be small, a short path, a large cross-section, and a material of high permeability are therefore desirable.

(2) Also, in the interest of low writing and large reading voltage there should be a large number of turns on the respective coils. But during the process of writing, if the inductance of the coil is large it may require unduly large voltages for turning the current on and off in the time available. These considerations along with simplicity of construction and the permissible size determine the optimum number of turns.

(3) The *gap spacing* should be small to provide for a close packing of information, and a small gap also produces a large voltage output during

reading, because the flux change occurs over a shorter distance and there-fore over a shorter period of time. There is a limit to the amount of voltage increase by reducing the gap spacing, as the total number of flux lines which can pass from the interior of the magnetic surface is severely limited for very small gaps.

(4) Another parameter which can be varied to increase the voltage output is the *width* of the head and the gap. The amount of flux intercepted is directly proportional to the dimension in this direction; the compromise in this case is with the number of parallel tracks per inch. *Track density* can be increased by designing heads as thin as posssible, but it reduces the signal to noise ratio. The skew of head or the surface is also an important consideration.

(5) The geometry of the *pole tips* should be designed so that there is as much fringing as possible of the magnetic flux lines in the direction perpendicular to the magnetic surface, but this fringing should be limited as closely as possible to the region of the gap. This requires that the pole tips must not become saturated during writing.

(6) The magnetic head with its windings and associated circuits should have wide-band frequency response; also it is necessary to guard against unexpected resonance. It is desirable to eliminate eddy currents to improve the response of the core and to reduce the power loss. For this reason laminated sections of ferrite materials are used.

(7) There should be minimum residual magnetization in the head.

Binary Coding Techniques

There are different classes of binary coding techniques. The overall storage transfer process involved in the magnetic recording of binary information is

$$i(t) \rightarrow \left[M(x) - \phi_h(x) \right] \rightarrow \frac{vN \, d\phi_h}{dx} = e_0(vt)$$

where

$M(x)$ = distribution of magnetization on the surface
$\phi_h(x)$ = reading-coil flux as a function of the angular position
e_0 = open-circuit readback output voltage
N = number of reading turns
v = surface velocity
t = time

Hence $e_0(vt)$ is a pulse-like signal for a step change in $i(t)$, and the surface velocity appears as a scaling factor in both time and amplitude for the output signal. For an arbitrary input pattern consisting of sequences of alternating step-like changes in writing current, the magnetic field presented during readback is extremely weak, and so the magnetic head will behave very nearly as a linear element. Writing definition, corresponding to the width of the saturation transition region, is much less than the corresponding reading resolution because of the non-linear surface saturation characteristic. Therefore, even a considerable pulse crowding will not affect the adjacent surface changes. Due to these considerations, Hoagland applied the principle of superposition, and reciprocity theorem and developed a powerful tool for the exploration of high-density recording. In this method actual factors causing perturbations of the recording system may be included and the overall detection characteristics can then be examined.

Let us consider NRZI version of digital recording where the current is switched in direction each time for recording a '1'. An output pulse is then associated with each recorded '1'. There are two types of sensing techniques, *amplitude sensing* and *peak sensing*, enjoying considerable popularity as well as providing an illustration of the approach for two conceptually different methods to information detection.

Amplitude Sensing

With this method of detection, in NRZI recording a '1' is indicated by the presence of a pulse and a '0' by the absence of a pulse. If e_T is a present discrimination level, $e(0)$ and $e(1)$ are outputs for '0' and '1' respectively, then an error will result, when at sample time, $|e(0)| > e_T$ or $e(1) < e_T$. Let ρ represent the pulse width from the pulse peak to the point on either side at which the pulse amplitude is equal to $1/3$ the magnitude of the pulse peak. Consider the case of a '1' surrounded by '0's. At density equal to $1/\rho$, the adjacent '0's will provide a sample pulse signal equal to $1/3$, where the maximum signal amplitude of the waveform is considered normalized to '1'. This is the worst case that pertains to the detection of a '0' among all possible binary patterns. Consider the case of three consecutive '1's surrounded by '0's, the pulse corresponding to the outer '1' is then subtracted from the central pulse. At the density $1/\rho$ the signal level at sample time for the central bit is equal to $1 - 2(1/3) = 1/3$. This is again the worst case for detection of '1'. Thus at a density equal to $1/\rho$ we are at the limit of amplitude discrimination detection and hence $1/\rho$ is the maximum possible density that could be expected with amplitude sensing. For a triangular pulse of base width λ:

$$\rho = \frac{1}{\lambda} \tag{83}$$

And the maximum theoretical storage density is equal to

$$(bp_i)_{max} = \frac{3}{\lambda} \tag{84}$$

Peak Sensing

The peak of a recorded step response, being centrally located, possesses the greatest degree of isolation (among all the sections comprising the waveform) with respect to inter-symbol interference. Therefore, the technique which intuitively seems obvious as a means to extend density in the face of pulse crowding is peak sensing. Inherently, this method provides insensitivity to amplitude variation since it does not directly exploit this waveform feature. In peak sensing, the detection problems are somewhat different as it is necessary to determine if a signal peak of proper character occurred within a prescribed bit interval. Thus the readback waveform must be examined throughout the entire bit interval for the presence of such a signal peak.

Clock Timing

One operating condition that limits high density is clock timing. All systems must tolerate a certain degree of clocking inaccuracy. When an external or fixed clock reference is used, some sacrifice in bit density must be accepted in order to tolerate timing variations; if the timing inaccuracy is potentially extreme, one is forced to employ self-clocking. In the next sections we shall deal with some important characteristics of recording head and its adjustments.

Effect of Residual Magnetism of Recording Head

One other effect that may cause pulse widening and decrease in amplitude is that of residual magnetism of recording head. Since a comparatively large mmf is utilized in saturation type recording, the residual magnetization in a poorly designed magnetic recording head may be great enough to cause deterioration of the recorded signal after several passes. When the magnetized particles in the coating pass through the residual field of the record head, they are reoriented to a degree dependent on the direction and strength of this field. The effect of this field can be shown graphically. Figure 2.32 represents rectangular and non-rectangular B-H loop characteristics of the coating materials. Let us consider a flux pattern as shown by curve of Figure (2.33b). All points on this curve correspond to some B_r of Figure 2.32. Passage of the residual magnetizing field over the coating is the same as the application of a bias field ΔH to all points of curve (a) of Figure 2.33c. This bias field will give a new value for the remanence B_{r1} in the curve of Figure 2.32. If the residual magnetization in the record head is now reversed, the bias field $-\Delta H$ will give the distribution as shown in curve (c) corresponding to B_{r2} (Figure 2.33a). Since the playback voltage is approximately proportional to the derivative of the flux, one can see that the residual magnetization in the record head results in a decrease in signal amplitude and an increase in pulse width. The pulse amplitude may decrease by 50 to 60 per cent in a poorly designed head. In a system using fixed level amplitude discriminators, this variation in amplitude may lead to erratic performance. The residual magnetization may be reduced by increasing in backgap or by using a core material with lower remanence.

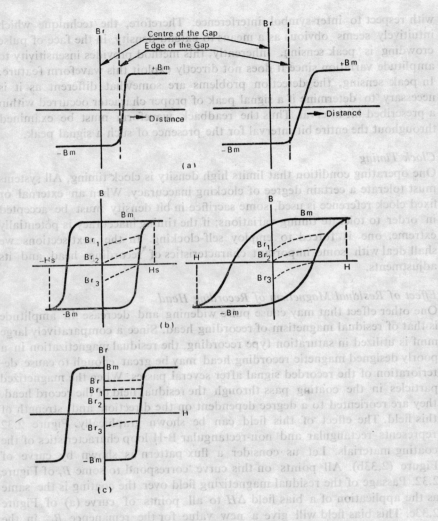

Figure 2.32 Flux distribution characteristics of rectangular and non rectangular loop coating material.

2.12.2 Design Considerations of Ferrite Transducers

There has been extensive treatment in literature about the design of magnetic recording head. We have dealt with the theoretical perspective of magnetic record/reproduce transducer design in an earlier section. From the engineering point of view the gap length is dictated by the shortest wavelength to be recorded, the track width by the signal to noise ratio, azimuth sensitivity and the desired information packing density while the gap depth is selected for the minimum value that will yield an acceptable mechanical strength.

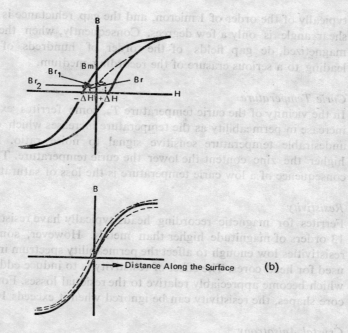

Figure 2.33   (a) Effect of residual magnetization on record/read head characteristics; (b) Effect of (a) on record signal.

From the point of view of magnetic circuit design, only the permeability spectrum and the saturation induction are of primary interest. However, a large number of other factors enter into the choice of the proper material from the mechanical point of view.

Permeability Spectrum

The permeability spectrum is related to grain size, resistivity, crystal anisotropy, magnetostriction and many other properties.

Saturation Induction

Since in many ferrite head applications the same head is used for reading and writing, for this reason, the saturation induction B_s is of primary importance, and kept around 2500 to 5500. For out-of-contact recording, the saturation induction becomes the single most important parameter in selecting a high frequency ferrite as the field falls roughly inversely with the distance from the gap.

Coercivity

The coercivity of high frequency ferrite ranges usually from 0.1 to 0.5 for frequencies up to 10 MHz, and for very fine grain particles, it is almost 1 oersted at 20 MHz. However, ferrite heads, are highly susceptible to becoming magnetized, and in high resolution heads gap length are very small, typically of the order of 1 micron, and the gap reluctance is so low that the shear angle is only a few degrees. Consequently, when the head becomes magnetized, dc gap fields of the order of hundreds of oersted result, leading to a serious erasure of the recording medium.

Curie Temperature

In the vicinity of the curie temperature T_c, some ferrites exhibit a marked increase in permeability as the temperature increases which can result in an undesirable temperature sensitive signal to noise ratio. In general, the higher the zinc content the lower the curie temperature. The most serious consequence of a low curie temperature is the loss of saturation induction.

Resistivity

Ferrites for magnetic recording heads typically have resistivities from 5 to 13 orders of magnitude higher than metals. However, some ferrites have resistivities low enough to affect the permeability spectrum in the dimensions used for head cores. The effect of resistivity is to induce eddy current losses, which become appreciably relative to the residual losses. For most practical core shapes, the resistivity can be ignored when it exceeds 100 Ωcm.

Crystal Anisotropy

The anisotropy constant is the energy density associated with magnetizing a crystal along a given axis. It is highly dependent on the temperature and influences the permeability to a high degree.

Of the three classef of ferrites namely, polycrystalline, single crystal,and magnetoplumbite (hexagonal), used or considered for magnetic head materials, only the polycrystalline materials are isotropic in their permeability spectra. The single crystals will have to be oriented since the permeability differs in each axis due to anisotropy. Magnetoplumbite has extremely high anisotropy along the C axis. In general, the lower the anisotropy constant average over a plane, the higher will be the permeability in that plane.

Dimensional Resonance

Since ferrites have a high permeability, the velocity of propagation is very low, with the result that magnetic standing waves can be set up in the material if the smallest transverse core dimension approaches one half wavelength.

Magnetostriction

The magnetostriction constant λ is a strain energy tensor that effects the permeability and should be as low as possible to prevent mechanical noise from generating signals in the core.

Disaccommodation

An imbalance in Fe^{++} level can cause migration of cations and vacancies within the lattice after a mechanical or magnetic disturbance, with a resultant temporary change in permeability.

Strain
A major cause of failure in ferrites at contact surfaces and in gap areas relates to internal strain in the material. Generally strains are caused by the ferrite due to the presence of grains with differing compositions. It is by far the most difficult property to control in the fabrication of a high frequency ferrite.

Porosity
Pores permit Lorentz fields to exist within the ferrites which reduce its permeability, and have a deleterious effect on glass bonding, since they permit infusion of the glass within the pole face and can even cause crystallites to become dislodged in the gap. Pores on the contact surface of tape heads can even damage the tape and fill with binder debris from the tape, thereby introducing spacing losses.

Choice of Ferrites
Most heads are fabricated either of nickel zinc ferrite, which is usually isostatically pressed prior to sintering, or manganese zinc ferrite, which is used in a hot pressed form and as single crystals. These materials have been selected over other ferrites because of their low coercivity, high saturation induction and high permeability. It has generally been considered that nickel-zinc is the preferred ferrite for high frequency applications above 2 MHz. Manganese-zinc-ferrites are used primarily for low frequency applications.

Fabrication of Head Gaps
The most successful method for fabricating gaps in ferrite head cores has been glass bonding, both from the viewpoint of noncontact operations and abrasion resistance in contact applications. Single crystal heads exhibit a relatively high noise level, which may be caused by microcleavage planes due to the gap strain, or possibly by magnetostriction. The major cause of gap deterioration is erosion of the gap edge for which nickel-zinc isostatic ferrites have been unsucessful for contact applications. With proper control of grain boundaries hot pressed manganese-zincs have held well in contact.

Wear Rate of Ferrite Heads
The major factors determining wear rate are: (i) head-to-tape speed, (ii) head-to-tape contact, (iii) head material properties, (iv) humidity, and (v) head type and heads previous history. Wear rate of heads against abrasive tapes is determined primarily by the head material and is only very approximately related to the surface hardness. Some authors have pointed the effect non-

stoichiometry on wear of ferrite recording heads which are of considerable interest.

2.12.3 Integrated Magnetic Film Heads

Integrated circuit technology has also pervaded the realm of ferromagnetism. Miniaturized recording heads fabricated by techniques similar to those used in integrated circuit technology, namely, evaporation, sputtering, plating and photoetching, were first proposed by Gregg, Barton and Stockel, and Barcaro and associates in early sixties. But the theoretical and experimental work dealing with feasibility and performance of such devices was not published until early seventies

Basically, two types of such heads namely *vertical* and *horizontal*, were proposed. In the vertical head the two films forming the magnetic circuit are perpendicular to the plane of recording medium and the gap is formed by a conductive or insulating layer sandwitched between magnetic films. In the horizontal head the two magnetic films are parallel to the plane of the medium and the film that is nearer the medium contains the gap.

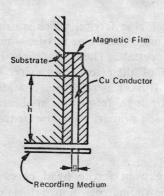

Figure 2.34 Vertical integrated recording head.

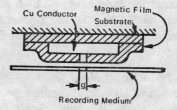

Figure 2.35 Horizontal integrated recording head.

Figures 2.34 and 2.35 are schematic representations of single-turn heads. Different versions of single-turn and multi-turn integrated heads are possible. The dimension W determines the track width. In writing, the conductor carries a current I, so that the magnetic material is magnetized circumferentially and a fringing field is established across the gap. In reading, a small change in the circumferential magnetization takes place in the magnetic head whenever the moving recording medium passes the gap, thus generating a voltage pulse in the conductor. Highest efficiency is achieved if the magnetic circuit is closed except for the gap. Both the vertical and horizontal heads have their advantages and disadvantages. The gap in horizontal head is produced by photolithographic methods whereas in the vertical head it is produced by lapping or polishing.

Single turn heads require high write currents and generate low read signals. Therefore, several versions of integrated multi-turn heads (Figure 2.36) have been proposed for which one should study the important references on the subject attached to this chapter.

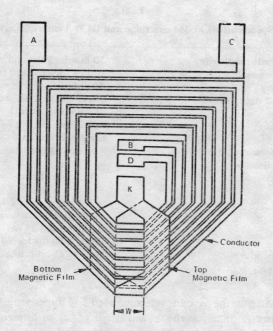

Figure 2.36 Integrated multi-turn head.

Another attractive feature of magnetic-film heads is their shape which, especially in the case of vertical heads, results in higher resolution. On the basis of a Schwarz-Christoffel transformation, Elabd, Potter and their co-workers have computed the X and Y components of the gap field generated by the vertical head and investigated the read back properties.

A number of interesting papers have been published in the recent past and it is hoped that a substantial amount of experimental work with integrated recording heads will be available in the near future.

Some Comments on Future Trends in Magnetic Recording Technology
In computing systems of modern architecture peripheral memories are rapidly becoming as important as the central memory. It is expected that in future peripheral memories will have the same characteristics as the main memory at peripheral memory cost per bit. Main limitation of peripheral memory, however, is the access time. The extended core concept has developed as a peripheral memory with access and transfer time equivalent to a main memory. But the cost per bit for extended core is about 10 times that of an equivalent capacity rotating memory.

The peripheral memory market is dominated by rotating memories and tape memories commonly known as file technology. The main limitation to file memory systems of today is their low access time due to their mechanical movements.

TABLE 2.6

Specifications of 3M cartridge and DCD-3 cartridge drive

Operating speeds read/write	30 in/s forward and reverse
Fast forward, rewind,	90 in/s forward and reverse
Packing density	3200 bpi
Recommended data format	Phase encoded bit serial; 1600 bits/in
Transfer rate	48 kilobits/s max
Inter-record gap	1.33 in typical; 1.2 in min as per ANSI standard
Maximum recommended start/stop rate	3 operations/s without forced air cooling
Total speed variation	$\pm$ 4% max
Interface logic	TTL compatible
Power	5 Vdc $\pm$ 5%, 0.9 A max; $\pm$ 18 Vdc $\pm$ 5%, 1.4 A, 3.6 A surge during acceleration/ deceleration; 18 ms for 30 in/s; 60 ms for 80 in/s
Ambient temperature	5 to 45°C operating
Maximum weight	11 1b

The following methods can be suggested for improving the performance of files systems: (i) increase the aerial density; (ii) minimize the mechanical movement; and (iii) develop a new technology. One area of development is in relation to the decrease in mechanical movement, with the help of novel electronic scanning methods for writing and reading information. New technology based on laser and electron beams is the ultimate solution. Another direction of development is the aerial density with emphasis on media. The primary reason for the quest of new materials is that gamma ferric oxide is considered barely sufficient for current system requirements. Most tape and equipment manufacturers have development program on magnetic recording materials other than gamma ferric oxide. The most important of these materials are chromium dioxide (CrO_2), alloy particles (Fe-Ni-Co) and cobalt phosphorous thin films (Co-P). Morrison made an extensive study on particulate materials versus thin films as recording media. The list of various tape materials used in commercial tapes and the different manufacturers marketing these tapes are shown in Table 2.7.

Due to the combined improvement in magnetic and physical parameters, particulate media have improved more than two orders of magnitude in storage density over the last two decades. Technology has progressed from 4 tracks/inch to 100 tracks/inch and the corresponding speed from 2.5 kc/s to 20 kc/s. At present the ferromagnetic oxide CrO_2 is getting attention because it promises a higher bit density although at slightly higher cost.

TABLE 2.7

List of materials and firms with experience in them

Materials	Tape manufacturer	OEMs (Orig. Eqip. Manuf.)	Others
PARTICLES			
Modified iron oxide[1]	3M, Agfa, EMI, BASF Sony RCA	IBM, Lockheed, Philips, Bell	Pfizer, TDK, Hercules, Magnetronics, Orrox, Wright Ind.,
Chromium dioxide Alloy particles	Dupont, RCA, Sony, EMI, Agfa Memorex, Graham Magnetics	IBM	Tohoku Univ., Pfizer
Iron particles Colloidal cobalt	Fuji, Ampex, Memorex	GE, Bell & Howell	Cal. Research
METAL FILMS			
Chemical deposition	Lash Laboratories	NCR, IBM, Honeywell, ICT Sperry Rand	
Electrolytic deposition	3M, Ampex, Data Disc	IBM, Burroughs Honeywell ICT	Wilhelm, Mel. Dyke
Vacuum deposition	3M, EMI, Memorex Ampex	IBM, NCR, ICT	Temescal
Other types[2]		Lockheed	

[1]For example, magnetite, cobalt doped (cubic and acidcular) particles, various ferrites.
[2]For example, sputtered films, extruded metal.

APPENDIX I

Field Configuration in and Around the Gap of the Magnetic Head

To determine the nature of the field configuration in and around the gap, it is assumed that the permeability μ of the head is infinity and that of the layer material is unity. We approximate a practical head such that its left pole piece is bounded by the plane $y = 0$ from $x = -\infty$ to $x = -l/2$

and by the plane $x = -l/2$. The right pole piece is symmetrical with respect to the plane $x = 0$. This is the case of semi-infinite gap and bears close resemblance to practical heads, but the calculations are rather difficult to carry out. The other two models, that of infinite gap and thin gap are not of much practical use, and hence will not be treated here. Looking normal to the gap surface, the gap is infinitely extended in the positive direction. The assumption that μ of the head material is infinite can easily be approximated as the permeability of the head materials ranges from 10,000 to 100,000 (radiometal, mumetal, permalloy, etc.) and they are not used near the saturation region. The pole surface may then be said to represent a set of magnetic equipotentials.

Supposing there is a one turn coil in the head, and a current I is passed through it, then there will be a magnetic potential difference I between the pole pieces. Therefore, the potential function $V(x, y)$ has to satisfy the boundary condition $V = I/2$ and $-I/2$ respectively for the two pole pieces. It is clear from the symmetry that $V(x, y) = 0$ at $x = 0$. We shall apply Schwarz-Christoffel transformation in solving the problem and shall present all the consecutive steps as an example for students, and then shall numerically compute the equipotential profiles and the lines of forces, that gives a physical insight into the problems of head design.

We now picture the head on the positive side of the axis in the z-plane with magnetic pole potential $\phi = \pm I/2 = \pm V$. Application of the Schwarz-Christoffel transformation gives us the relation from which the transformation of the contour ABCDEF in Z-plane into the W-plane (Figure 1A.1). Let length of the head gap be $2a$. Then

$$\frac{\partial \phi}{\partial x} = \frac{V}{a} = \frac{\partial \psi}{\partial y}$$

Hence
$$\psi = \frac{V}{a} y + k$$

Let $\psi = 0$ at B and E. From Z-plane consideration, Figure 1A.1, we have

$$\frac{dz}{dt} = A(t + 1)^{1/2}(t-0)(t-1)^{1/2}$$

$$\frac{dz}{dt} = A\left[\frac{\sqrt{t^2-1}}{t}\right] \tag{2.1.1}$$

Again, from W-plane considerations, we have

$$\frac{dW}{dt} = B(t + 1)t^{-1}(t-1) = \frac{B}{t}$$

Therefore, $W = B \log t + C$ $\qquad\qquad$ (2.1.2)

At the point E, $t = 1$, $\qquad W = V, C = V$

At the point B, $t = -1$, $\qquad W = -V$, and hence

$$B = \pm \frac{2V}{i\pi}$$

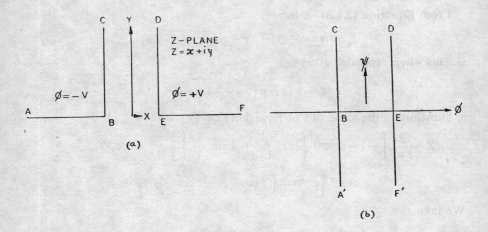

Figure 1A.1. Z- and W-plane diagram.

We take

$$W = \frac{2V}{i\pi} \log t + V$$

$$= -\frac{2iV}{\pi} \log t + V \qquad (2.1.3)$$

Since this satisfies the conditions,

$$t \to 0, \quad \text{(along real axis) } \psi \to \infty$$
$$t \to \pm \infty \text{ (along real axis) } \psi \to \infty$$

From Equation (2.1.1)

$$Z = A \int \frac{\sqrt{t^2 - 1}}{t} \, dt + D$$

which on integration yields

$$Z = A\left[\sqrt{t^2 - 1} - \cos^{-1} \frac{1}{t} \right] + D$$

We have

$$Z = +a \text{ at } t = +1, \text{ so } D = a$$

and

$$Z = -a \text{ at } t = -1 \text{ so } -a = A\{\cos^{-1}(-1) + a\}$$

Hence

$$A = \pm \frac{2a}{\pi}$$

Now we have

$$Z = \frac{2a}{\pi}\left[\sqrt{t^2 - 1} - \cos^{-1} \frac{1}{t} \right] + a \qquad (2.1.4)$$

(valid for $x \to 0$)

From Equation (2.1.3) we have

$$t = e^{-\pi(W/V-1)/2i}$$

This when expanded gives

$$t = -i \exp\left(-\frac{\pi\psi}{2V}\right)\left[\cos\frac{\pi\phi}{2V} + i \sin\frac{\pi\phi}{2V}\right]$$

Substituting the value of t in Equation (2.1.4)

$$Z = \frac{2a}{\pi}\left[-1-e^{-\pi\psi/V}\left\{\cos\frac{\pi\phi}{V} + i \sin\frac{\pi\phi}{V}\right\}\right]^{1/2}$$

$$-\cos^{-1}\left\{e^{-\pi\psi/2V}\left(i\cos\frac{\pi\phi}{2V} + \sin\frac{\pi\phi}{2V}\right)\right\} + a \qquad (2.1.5)$$

We take

$$\cos^{-1}\left\{\exp\left(\frac{\pi\psi}{2V}\right)\sin\frac{\pi\phi}{2V} + i\exp\left(\frac{\pi\psi}{2V}\right)\cos\frac{\pi\phi}{2V}\right\} = C-iD$$

This on solution leads to

$$C = \cos^{-1}\left[\frac{1}{2}\left\{\left(\exp\left(\frac{\pi\psi}{V}\right)+1\right)-\exp\left(\frac{\pi\psi}{2V}\right)\left(\exp\left(\frac{\pi\psi}{V}\right)+\right.\right.\right.$$
$$\left.\left.\left.\exp\left(-\frac{\pi\psi}{V}\right)-2\cos\frac{\pi\phi}{V}\right)^{1/2}\right\}\right]^{1/2}$$

and

$$D = \cos^{-1}\left[\frac{1}{2}\left\{\left(\exp\left(\frac{\pi\psi}{V}\right)+1\right)+\exp\left(\frac{\pi\psi}{2V}\right)\left(\exp\left(\frac{\pi\psi}{V}\right)\right.\right.\right.$$
$$\left.\left.\left.+\exp\left(-\frac{\pi\psi}{V}\right)+2\cos\frac{\pi\phi}{V}\right)^{1/2}\right\}\right]^{1/2}$$

Now we take

$$-1-\exp\left(-\frac{\pi\psi}{V}\right)\left\{\cos\frac{\pi\phi}{V} + i \sin\frac{\pi\phi}{V}\right\} = A'-iB' = R\exp(i\theta)$$

Therefore

$$A' = R\cos\theta + B' = R\sin\theta$$

$$R = e^{-\pi\psi/2V}\{e^{\pi\psi/V} + e^{-\pi\psi/V} + 2\cos^{\pi\phi/V}\} \qquad (2.1.6)$$

and

$$\tan\theta = -\frac{e^{-\pi\psi/V}\sin\frac{\pi\phi}{V}}{1 + e^{-\pi\psi/V}\cos\frac{\pi\phi}{V}} \qquad (2.1.7)$$

Equation (2.1.5) can now be written as

$$Z = x + iy$$

$$= \frac{2a}{\pi}\left[\sqrt{Re^{-i\theta}} - \left(C-iD\right)\right] + a$$

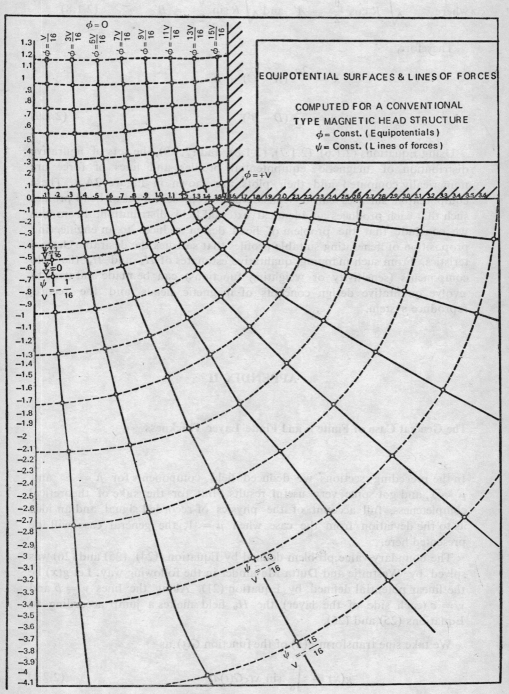

Figure 2A.1

where $\qquad \sqrt{R \cos \dfrac{\theta}{2}} = A'$ and $\sqrt{R \sin \dfrac{\theta}{2}} = B'$ $\qquad$ (2.1.8)

Therefore

$$x = \frac{2a}{\pi} \, (A' - C) + a$$

$$y = \frac{2a}{\pi} \, (D - B')$$ $\qquad$ (2.1.9)

Using Equations (2.1.6), (2.1.7), (2.1.8), and (2.1.9), the sets of figurative distribution of magnetic equipotential profiles and lines of force are numerically computed and their plots are shown in Figure 2A.1. These equipotential surfaces can be considered to represent a set of head profiles such that each produces an identical external field distribution. From this we conclude that the problem of head design reduces to an engineering proposition of generating suitable profiles that satisfies the desirable characteristics. From such mapping, qualitative estimates of H_x and H_y the field components (sensitivity or weighting functions) can be made and used to evolve qualitative design concepts of magnetic heads and the record/reproduce system.

APPENDIX II

The General Case of Finite μ and Finite Layer Thickness

In the preceding sections we deduced field components for $\mu = \infty$ and $\mu = 1$, and got some very useful results. But for the sake of theoretical completeness, full account of the physics of recorded signal, and an idea as to the deviation from the case when $\mu = 1$, the general case will be presented here.

The boundary value problem defined by Equations (24), (25) and (26) was solved by Westmije and Dutta Majumder in the following way. Let $g(x)$ be the linear potential defined by Equation (21). Along the lines $y = b$ and $y = c$ (each side of the layer) the H_y field makes a jump according to Equations (25) and (26).

We take sine transform $g(x)$ of the function $G(t)$ as

$$g(x) = \int_0^\infty \sin xt \cdot G(t) dt$$ $\qquad$ (2.2.1)

and its inverse as

$$G(t) = \frac{2}{\pi} \int_0^\infty \sin xt \cdot g(x) dx = \frac{2V \sin Nt}{\pi Nt^2} \qquad (2.2.2)$$

We want to determine the field components in layer at the lines $y = 0$, $y = b$ and $y = c$, each with boundary value potentials $f_1(x)$, $f_2(x)$ and $f_3(x)$. Their potentials should be equal to the function $v(x, y)$.

Let

$$f_1(x) = \int_0^\infty F_1(t) \sin xt \cdot dt \qquad (2.2.3)$$

$$f_2(x) = \int_0^\infty F_2(t) \sin xt \cdot dt \qquad (2.2.4)$$

$$f_3(x) = \int_0^\infty F_3(t) \sin xt \cdot dt \qquad (2.2.5)$$

and

$$v(x, y) = \int_0^\infty V(t, y) \sin xt \cdot dt \qquad (2.2.6)$$

Now we consider the function $U(x, y)$ defined by

$$U(x, y) = \int_0^\infty e^{-t[y]} \sin xt\, F_1(t)\, dt \qquad (2.2.7)$$

This function satisfies Laplace's equation

$$\Delta U = 0 \qquad (2.2.8)$$

This shows that a layer with a boundary potential $f_1(x)$ at the line $y = 0$ gives a potential that is the sine transform of

$$e^{-t[y]} F_1(t)$$

and similarly for F_2 and F_3. Therefore, we have

$$V(t, y) = F_1(t)\, e^{-t[y]} + F_2(t)\, e^{-t\,|b-y|} + F_3(t)\, e^{-t\,|c-y|} \qquad (2.2.9)$$

Now we express the boundary for the transform, which gives a linear system with three equations. Solving this system,

$$F_1(t) = \left\{ r^2 - e^{-2t(c-b)} \right\} \frac{G}{D} \qquad (2.2.10)$$

$$F_2(t) = \left\{ e^{-t(2c-b)} - re^{-tb} \right\} \frac{G}{D} \qquad (2.2.11)$$

$$F_3(t) = e^{-tc}\left(r - 1 \right) \frac{G}{D} \qquad (2.2.12)$$

where

$$r = \frac{\mu - 1}{\mu + 1}$$

and
$$D = r^2 - r \left\{ e^{-2tb} - e^{-2tc} \right\} e^{-2t(c-b)} \tag{2.2.13}$$

The various derivatives of $v(x, y)$ can now be formed, and the *field* components computed as given by the following equations:

$$B_{2x} = -B_0 \frac{4\mu}{\pi} \int_0^\infty \frac{dt}{t.k} \cos \frac{tx}{b} \sin \frac{tN}{b} \left[\sinh \frac{td}{b} + \mu \cosh \frac{td}{b} \right] \tag{2.2.14}$$

$$B_{2y} = B_0 \frac{4\mu}{\pi} \int_0^\infty \frac{dt}{t.k} \sin \frac{tx}{b} \sin \frac{tN}{b} \left[\mu \sinh \frac{td}{b} + \cosh \frac{td}{b} \right] \tag{2.2.15}$$

where B_{2x} and B_{2y} are the fields at $y = b + 0$, that is, the fields inside the layer. Further

$$B_{3x} = -B_0 \frac{4\mu^2}{\pi} \int_0^\infty \frac{1}{t \cdot k} \cos \frac{tx}{b} \sin \frac{tN}{b} dt \tag{2.2.16}$$

$$B_{3y} = B_0 \frac{4\mu}{\pi} \int_0^\infty \frac{1}{t \cdot k} \sin \frac{tx}{b} \sin \frac{tN}{b} dt \tag{2.2.17}$$

where B_{3x} and B_{3y} are the fields at other side of the layer at $y = b + d - 0$. The function K in the above equations is defined by:

$$k = (\mu + 1) \sinh t \left(1 + \frac{d}{b} \right) + (\mu - 1) \sinh t \left(1 - \frac{d}{b} \right) + \mu(\mu + 1)$$

$$\cosh t \left(1 + \frac{d}{b} \right) - \mu(\mu - 1) \cosh t \left(1 - \frac{d}{b} \right) \tag{2.2.18}$$

The asymtotic expansions of these expressions are found as follows. The integral

$$f(x) = \int_0^\infty F(t) \sin xt \cdot dt \tag{2.2.19}$$

can be expanded by repeated partial integrations in a series of $1/x$ given by:

$$f(x) = \frac{F(0)}{x} - \frac{F''(0)}{x^3} + \dots \tag{2.2.20}$$

Following the same method, the integral of Equation (2.2.16) can be expanded:

$$g(x) = \int_0^\infty G(t) \cos xt \cdot dt \tag{2.2.21}$$

$$g(x) = - \frac{G'(0)}{x^2} + \frac{G'''(0)}{x^4} - \dots \tag{2.2.22}$$

In our case the series are divergent for all values of x. The derivatives are computed recurrently, and the first two terms in the expressions for Equations (2.2.14), (2.2.15) and (2.2.17) are given by:

$$B_{2x} = -B_0\left[\frac{2bN\mu}{\pi x^2} + \frac{2b^3N\mu}{\pi x^4}\left(2\mu q + p^2 - 1 + 6q^2 - \frac{6q(2\mu + r)}{\mu^2} + \dots\right]$$

(2.2.23)

$$B_{2y} = B_0\left[\frac{2N}{\pi x} - \frac{2b^2N}{\pi x^3\mu^2}\left(\mu^2 + 4q\mu - 2q^2\mu^2 - \frac{p^2\mu^2}{3} - 4q\mu^3 + 2q^2\right) + \dots\right]$$

(2.2.24)

$$B_{3x} = -B_0\left[\frac{2bN(\mu + q)}{\pi x^2} + \frac{4b^4\mu}{\pi x^4}G'''(0) + \dots\right]$$ (2.2.25)

$$B_{3y} = B_0\left[\frac{2N}{\pi x} - \frac{2b^2N}{3\pi x^3\mu^2}\left(3\mu^2 - p^2\mu^2 + 12q\mu + 6q^2 - 3q^2\mu^2 - 6q\mu^3\right) + \dots\right]$$

(2.2.26)

where

$$p = \frac{N}{b}, \quad q = \frac{d}{b}.$$

$$G'''(0) = \frac{p}{2\mu^4}\left[12\mu^4 q + 15q^2\mu^3 + (p^2 - 1)\mu^3 + p^2\mu^2 q - 5q^3\mu^2\right.$$

$$\left. - 15q\mu^2 - 189\mu - 6q^3 - \dots\right]$$ (2.2.27)

The fields when plotted for $b/N = 1$, $d/N = 1$, and $\mu = 2$, and compared with Figure 2.9, it is seen that the deviation with the case when $\mu = 1$ is not very large.

Both the equations for B_{2y} (2.15) and B_{3y} (2.17) show that the field is almost independent of μ but depends on x/N only. Naturally, this conclusion applies for the whole layer.

The linear case where μ is a constant can be used as a first approximation of the nonlinear case. The hysteresis loop for the material is shown in Figure 2A.2. We see that in the initial magnetizing curve the values vary from 1.1 at the origin to 2 at $x = \pm 4N$.

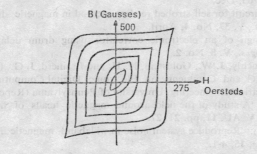

Figure 2A.2 An approximate hysteresis loop for layer material.

References

Aharoni, A. and Fisher, R.D. (1965): 'Dependence of packing density on coercivity and thickness of recording tapes', *Proc. INTERMAG Conf.* 12.3.1-12.3.5.

Aharoni, A. (1966): 'Theory of NRZ recording, *IEEE Trans. Magnetics*, V. MAG-2, pp. 100-109.

Axon, P.E. (1952): 'An investigation into the mechanism of magnetic tape recording.' *Proc IEE* 99 [III] (59), pp. 109-26, May.

Barcaro, E.B., Best, D.T. and Zajaczkowski, J.S. (1967): 'A new magnetic read-only memory, *Int. Solid State Circuits Conf. Dig. Tech.* papers, V. 10, pp. 80-81.

Barkouki, M.F. and Stein, I. (1963): 'Theoretical and experimental evaluation of RZ and NRZ recording characteristics', *IEEE Trans. Electronic Comp.* V. EC-12 pp. 92-100.

Barton, J.C. and Stockel, C.T. (1964): 'A novel type of magnetic recording head', *Radio and Electronic Engineering*, V. 26, pp. 11-18.

Began, S.J. (1954): 'A survey of magnetic recording,' *E. I. Engg.*, V. 73, pp. 1115-1118, Dec.

Bloch, F. (1936): 'Theory of the exchange problem and of residual ferromagnetism', *Z. Physik*, V. 52, pp. 555-600.

Bonyhard, P.I., Davies, A.V. (1966): 'A theory of digital magnetic recording on metallic films', *IEEE Trans. Magnetics*, V. MAG-2, pp. 1-5.

Booth, A.D. (1952) : 'On two problems in potential theory and their application to the design of magnetic recording heads for digital computers,' *Brit. J. Appl. Phys.*, V. 3, No. 2.

Booth, A.D. (1960): 'Truck switching systems for serial type memory', *Electronic Engineering*, V. 79, p. 264.

Bozorth, R. M. (1951) : 'Ferromagnetism', Bell System Laboratories Series. Bryant Gage and Spindle Division : Brochure, Springfield, Vermont.

Chapman, D.W. (1962): 'A study of the writing and reading process in digital recording process', *IBM Corp. Rept.*, San Jose, Calfornia.

Davis, S. (1974): 'Update on Magnetic Memories Computer Design', pp. 127-33 August.

Dutta Majumder, D. (1963): 'Studies on the Design of Magnetic Drum Stores for use in Electronic Computer', Ph.D Thesis, Calcutta University.

——(1961): 'Design of an Electronic Correlator using Magnetic Drum Delay System', *J. Inst. of Telecomm. Engrs.*, V. 8, No. 2, pp. 83-92.

——(1958): 'A track switching system for a serial type memory', *Electronic Engineering*, V. 76, pp. 702-05, Dec.

——(1963): 'A circuit for self strobed reading method in magnetic drum digital stores', *Indian J. Phys.*, V. 37, No. 4, April.

——(1962): 'Design of an electronic correlator using drum delay system', *J. Inst. of Telecomm. Engrs.*, V. 8, No. 2.

Eckert, J. P., Mauchly, J. W., Goldstein, H. H. and Brainerd, J. G. (1948): 'Description of the ENIAC and Comments on Electronic Digital Computing Machines', Moor School of Electrical Engineering, University of Pennsylvania (Report).

Elabd, I. (1963): 'A study of the field around magnetic heads of finite length', *IEEE Trans. Audio*, V. AU. 11, pp. 21. 27.

Emaller, P. (1964): 'Reproduce system noise in wideband magnetic recording, systems', *Intermag. Proc*, 15, 4-1.

Fan, J.G.J. (1961): 'A study of the payback process of a magnetic ring head', *IBM J. Res. and Dev.*, V. 5, pp. 321-325.

Greeg, D. P. (1967): 'Deposited film transducing apparatus and method of producing the apparatus', US Patent-3, 344, 237.

Harvard University Computation Laboratory (1946): 'A manual of operation for the automatic sequence controlled calculator.' *Annals of the computation Laboratory* (Harvard University) **VI.**

Hartree, D.R. (1946): 'The ENIAC and Electronic Computing Machine', *Nature*, V. **158**, p. 500.

Herbert, J.R. and Patterson, D.W. (1965): 'A computer simulation of the magnetic recording process', *IEE Trans. Magnetics*, V. **MAG-1**, pp. 352-357.

Hoagland, A. S. (1956): 'Magnetic data recording theory head design', *Trans. AIEE Communication and Electronics*, V. **75**, pp. 506.

——(1963): 'Digital magnetic recording,' J. Wiley & Sons, New York, N.Y.

Iwasaki, S. and Suzuki, T. (1968): 'Dynamical interpretation of magnetic recording process', *IEEE Trans. Magnetics*, V. **MAG-4**, pp. 269-276.

Iwasaki, S. (1972): 'An analysis on the state of AC Bias recording', *Advance in Magnetic Recording* (Annals of the New York Academy of Sciences) V. **189**, January.

Karlquist, O. (1954) : 'Magnetic field components in the ferromagnetic layer', *Trans. Royal Inst. of Tech.* (Sweden), V. **86**, pp.1-27.

Kostyshyn, B. (1962); 'A [harmonic analysis of saturation recording in a magnetic medium', *IRE Trans. Electronic Computers*, V. **EC-11**, pp. 253.

Landau, L and Lifshitz, E. (1948): 'Theory of dispersion of magnetic permeability in ferromagnetic bodies', *Physik, Z. Sowjetunion*, V.8., pp. 153-69.

Lazzari, J.P. and Melinck, I. (1970): 'Recording Integrated Magnetic Heads', *IEEE Trans. on Magnetics*, V. **MAG-6**, pp. 601-602.

Lemke, J.U. (1972): 'Ferrite Transducer'. (Annals on New York Academy of Sciences), *Advances in Magnetic Recording*, V. **189**, pp. 171-190.

Lee, J.E. (1970): 'Calculation of the output pulse shape for digital recording process', *IEEE Trans. Magnetics*, V. **MAG-6**, pp. 652.

Mallinson, J.C. (1975): 'A unified view of high density digital recording theory', *IEEE Trans, on Magnetics*, V. **MAG-11**, No. 5.

Monson, J. E., Olson, D. J. and Valstyn, E. P. (1975): 'Scale-Modelling the read process for a film head', *IEEE Trans. on Magnetics*, V. **MAG-11**, No. 5, September.

Morrison, J.R. (1972): 'Particulate Materials versus Thin Film—A System Overview', Advances in Magnetic Recording, (*Annals of the New York Academy of Sciences*), V. **189**, p. 146.

Morrison, J.R. and Speliotis, D.E. (1967): 'Study of peak shift in thin recording surfaces', *IEEE Trans. Magnetics*, V. **MAG-3**, pp. 208-211.

Potter, R.I., Schmulian, R.J. and Hartman, K. (1971): 'Fringe field and read back voltage computations for finite pole-tip length recording heads', *Intermag, Conf. Paper*, No. 24.7.

Richards, R.K. (1964): 'Digital Computer Components and Circuits', Von Nostrand Company, New York.

Rodriguez, J.A. (1975): 'An Analysis of Tape Drive Technology', *Proc. IEEE*, 63, 8, pp. 1153-159, August.

Speliotis, D.E. (1972): 'Digital Recording Theory', *Advances in Magnetic Recording* (Annals of New York Academy of Sciences), V. **189**, pp. 110.

Suguya, H. (1968): *IEEE Trans. on Magnetics*, V. **MAG-4**(3), pp. 295-307.

Toshiro, Yamada, et al. (1975) : *IEEE Trans. on Magnetics*, V. **MAG-11**, No. 5, September, pp. 1227-229.

Valstyn, E.P. (1972): 'Integrated head developments', *Advances in Magnetic Recording* (Annals of New York Academy of Sciences), V. **180**, pp. 191-205.

Wallace, R.L. Jr. (1951): 'The reproduction of magnetically recorded signals', *Bell Syst. Tech. J.* V. **30**, pp. 1146-1173.

Watanabe, Y.S. Matsumoto and Yajima, N. (1969) : 'Fabrication of Grouped Magnetic Heads', *IEEE Trans. on Magnetics*, V. Mag-5, pp. 918-920.

Westmijze, W. K. (1953): 'Studies on Magnetic Recording', Philips Research Report, V. 8, pp., 245.

Williams, F.C. and Lolburn, T. et al. (1952): Universal high speed digital computers—a magnetic store', *Proc. IRE.*, V. 99, Part-II, p. 94.

3. MAGNETIC CORE MEMORY SYSTEMS

As memory is the central part of all data processors and any improvement in it has determining influences on the performance of the whole system, the search for faster, larger, cheaper and more versatile memory is as old as the computer technology itself. Among the well known devices employed for this purpose, a large percentage of modern digital computers use the magnetic core digital storage systems as *main store*, *intermediate store* or *buffer store* and *auxiliary store*, depending on the class of computer and the type of use.

The technical variables involved in the design of a magnetic core storage system may be listed as: core output voltage, basic magnetic properties of the core material and size of the core, access time and propagation delay, limitations on drive currents, noise voltage and temperature sensitivity of the core material. Due to the complex inter-relationship between these parameters, their nonlinear characteristic of variations and conflicting requirements of speed, reliability and cost, render the design procedure somewhat difficult. In this chapter some studies on the design parameters of magnetic cores as computer storage elements have been presented. Also, the performance of magnetic core memory systems have been discussed here. The possibilities and limitations of magnetic core stores are discussed and the extent to which the design can be optimized for different types of computer is indicated.

3.1 WORKING PRINCIPLE OF A MAGNETIC CORE MEMORY SYSTEM

The basic requirements of a storage device for memory system of any of the information processing systems are:

   (i) Physical stability of the stored data.
   (ii) Sufficiently large capacity to store the informations.
  (iii) Combination of physical properties of nonvolatility and alterability.
   (iv) Small access time for read-write operations.

Small ferrite cores, possessing nearly rectangular hysteresis loops and satisfying all the above requirements found wide use as storage elements in digital computers. These cores make it possible to design memories that have the combined features of high speed, large capacity, and relatively low power consumption characteristics.

The internal memory system of a digital computer consists of the basic storage devices, address and information registers, timing and control circuits, and the interface logic with the registers. In addition, necessary circuitry is provided for sensing and driving currents for the read-write operations. All programs and data, moved into the computer from the peripheral devices, are stored in the memory. The memory holds all the programs to be executed, the data which is to be operated upon, the intermediate results of computations and the final result to be transmitted to the output peripheral devices.

A simplified block diagram of a magnetic core storage system is shown in Figure 3.1 and the associated memory timing diagram in Figure 3.2. Four wires, namely, a X-selection wire, a Y-selection wire, a readout wire and an inhibit or digit wire, are passing through the centre of each of the cores. The information in a particular core is read out or sensed by applying coincident half currents to the X and Y lines threading the core. Since the sensing operation destroys the information in the selected core, provision must be made for inserting either the same or new information back into the core. During the write operation, coincident half currents are applied to the selected X and Y lines in a direction to switch the core into the 'one' state. However, if the information to be inserted is a 'zero', an inhibiting current is applied to the digit line and the 'zero' state is preserved.

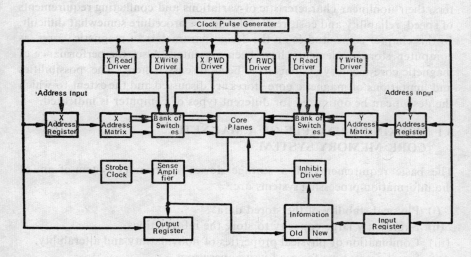

Figure 3.1   Simplified block diagram of a magnetic core memory system.

Referring to Figure 3.1 the address input from the control circuit is fed into X and Y address registers, and is then decoded by the address matrix. The selected X and Y matrix lines, through the associated switches, permit the current from the read and write drivers to flow through the selected row and column in the core plane.

The output from the selected core is detected by the sense winding. The noise from the half selected cores is also coupled into the sense amplifier along with the signal from the selected core. As the peak value of noise and signal voltages do not occur at the same time, these can be distinguished from each other by sampling the output of the amplifier at a time when the signal-to-noise ratio is most favourable, that is, at the strobing time. The strobe output from the sense amplifier sets up the output register.

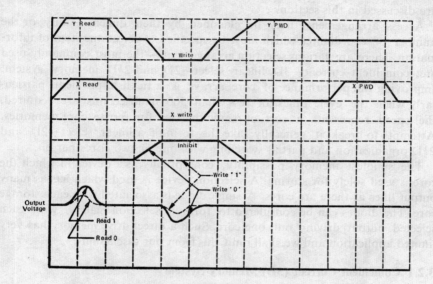

Figure 3.2   Timing diagram of one memory cycle.

The timing cycle for one address time is shown in Figure 3.2. The requirement in the inhibit current is that it must overlap the write current, as shown in the figure and has a small rise and fall time to keep the induced back voltage minimum. Just before the start of the memory cycle, the address registers receive an address change clock pulse and transmit the new address to the address matrix. To write a '1' into the core, the currents in the X and Y wires are reversed and the core is switched to the remanent state corresponding to a stored '1'. When a '0' is to be written into the selected core, the inhibit driver turns on slightly before the write drivers. Hence the write current is cancelled and the selected core remains in the '0' state.

The *post write disturb* pulse (PWD) which follows the write operation, is used to reduce the noise in the memory plane. As the name implies, this is a pulse which is applied to all the cores in the plane after the writing operation. The PWD pulse ensures that all the cores in the plane are subjected to the same polarity, so that the noise output is reduced to its half value. The disadvantage of this method is that it needs to extend the store cycle long enough to allow the pulse to be applied.

3.2 MEMORY ADDRESS SELECTION CONFIGURATION

Different schemes have been developed for packaging the magnetic core memories depending upon the class of computers and type of their use. Novel and indigenous mechanical design techniques have evolved from efforts to develop compact plug-in memory units and to simplify the fabrication and maintenance of these units. The characteristics of various memory selection techniques and their organizations, together with their merits and demerits are discussed in this section.

Access arrangements may be classified by their dimensionality or the number of coordinates which must be specified to select one item of information. There are various selection arrangements—the most commonly used are: coincident current—3D, linear select—2D and $2\frac{1}{2}$D memory system. Improving the performance of core arrays is a ticklish problem, particularly when the cycle times of less than 500 nanoseconds are required; the speed represents a sort of sonic barrier for ferrite core memories. Attempts to break it generally take the form of a linear select—2D and $2\frac{1}{2}$D organization and partial switching with one or two cores per bit.

The simplest memory possibility, conceptually, is a device in which the core is used solely for storing. A selection device is used which has as many output lines as there are cores. A single diode is associated with each storage core. The diodes can be considered to form a selection matrix, with each selected output driving only one core. Such a direct drive memory has very limited application and we shall omit this from our discussions.

3.2.1 Coincident Current (3D) Memory System

For moderate storage capacities, the most economical configuaration is the coincident current or the three dimensional (3D) organization. A coincident current memory is a random access magnetic memory in which all cores in an address are read out by a coincident action of a pair of currents. This arrangement is generally used in the great majority of core memories. It is inexpensive because it requires the minimum number of drivers and decoders. Other organizations can provide more speed than 3D system but they are always expensive.

The variety of geometrical configurations possible with the 3D system is limited because of the addressing technique used. The memory cores in 3D system are arranged in a set of bit planes, each plane contains one bit of all words. A sense amplifier and an inhibit driver are associated with each bit plane; memory register receives signals from the sense amplifiers and controls the inhibit drivers.

The wiring arrangement of a typical coincident current memory plane with diagonal sense winding is shown in Figure 3.3. The plane (an 8×8) contains four sets of wires; 8X and 8Y selection wires, each threading 8 cores in a given row and column; an inhibit wire threading all cores in the same phase as X and Y wires, and a sense wire threading half the cores in phase with the inhibit winding and the other half in the opposite phase to the inhibit wire.

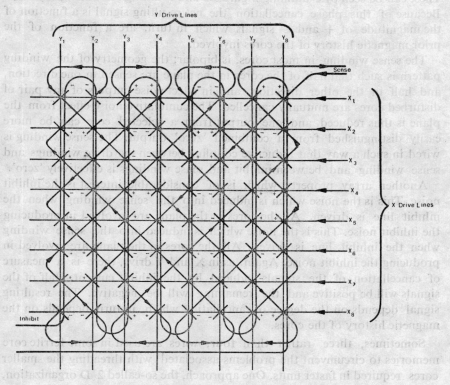

Figure 3.3   3D-four wire memory plane.

The X wire carries half-select 'read' or 'write' current pulse that equals to one half of the current required to switch the core. The Y wire also carries a half-select 'read' or 'write' current pulse. The inhibit wire threads all the cores of a memory plane. During the write operation, when a 1 is to be written, X and Y half-select current pulses are passed, so that they add at the core location and cause a change in the polarity of the core. When a 0 is to be written, the X and Y half-select current pulses are passed again, and in addition to these, another half-select current pulse is simultaneously passed down the inhibit wire. The direction of this additional current pulse is such that it opposes and, therefore, cancels out a X or Y half-select current pulse. Consequenty, there is only one half-select pulse to act on the core. Since a half-select pulse is not sufficient to switch the core, the net result is that a 0 is written.

For a memory with N total bits and M bits per word, there are N/M words. There are $\sqrt{N/M}$ x wires, and $\sqrt{N/M}$ y wires. Address selection is achieved by energizing 2 out of 2 $\sqrt{N/M}$ wires. For any array with dimensions $\sqrt{N/M} \times \sqrt{N/M}$ there are $2\sqrt{(N/M)} - 2$ half-selected cores, of these

$\sqrt{N/M}$ cores are in one phase and $\sqrt{N/M} - 2$ cores are in the opposite phase. These can be seen by examining Figure 3.3 and counting cores along any lines. Because of this phase cancellation the net resulting signal is a function of the magnitude of $+$ and $-$ signals which in turn, are a function of the prior magnetic history of the cores involved.

The sense winding, in most cores, is bipolar; the geometry of the winding pattern is such that half of the cores in the plane are sensed in one direction, and half in the other direction, and in effect noise outputs of any pair of disturbed cores are mutually cancelled. The cumulative noise effect from the plane is thus reduced, and 'one' output from a selected core can be more easily distinguished from a combined 'zero' output. The sense winding is wired in such a way that inductive coupling between the drive windings and sense winding and between inhibit and sense windings is effectively 'zero'.

Another array property which is of considerable interest is the inhibit noise. This is the noise which is induced into the sense winding when the inhibit line is driven. All the cores in the plane are involved in producing the inhibit noise. This is the noise which is induced into the sense winding when the inhibit line is driven. All the cores in the plane are involved in producing the inhibit noise. Again, as in X and Y drive, there is a measure of cancellation of the signals induced by the inhibit current. Half of the signals will be positive and the remaining will be negative. The resulting signal depends on the degree of cancellation which, in turn, depends on the magnetic history of the cores.

Sometimes, three, rather than four, wires are used in some ferrite core memories to circumvent the problems associated with threading the smaller cores required in faster units. One approach, the so-called $2\frac{1}{2}$D organization, though popular, requires considerable amount of peripheral electronic circuits and is expensive. An alternative method employs the redundancy of one of the four wires in the standard three dimensional array. Since the sense wire is used only during cycle's read portion, and the inhibit wire only during the write portion, both functions can be combined on a single wire.

One of the basic requirements of core memories which are in common use is that the core's hysteresis loop must be square so that the core is fully switched by currents carried in the same direction by two selection wires passing through it, and it is undisturbed by either one of the currents alone. With this coincident current scheme the core array itself performs part of the address decoding, thus minimizing circuit costs. Instead of locating a specific core in a plane external decoder locate two lines of core matrix that intersect at the address. A single set of drive circuits steers current through all cores in the data word, which are strung on a single selection wire.

The three-wire approach does not require substantially more expensive peripheral circuitry than the standard four-wire array, and it permits smaller cores with faster switching speeds to be used. Among the factors that require attention in the design of a three-wire array are reflections in the line during a sense operation. There are also noise problems that must be compensated differently than in a four-wire array. But once these factors are understood, a three-wire design with a given speed can yield a faster and a cleaner design than the corresponding four-wire design.

Current drivers specifications for the coincident current memories are based on core switching characteristics and memory timing requirements. The determination of current tolerances and ratios for 3D system is based on the criteria, such as the effective writing of 'one', the effective writing of 'zero', the limitation of the inhibit current to a value less than the switching threshold current and the pair of write currents. In designing 3D system, therefore, strict tolerances must be imposed on all drive currents, the squareness ratio of core, the switching time of the core to ensure '1' and '0' output voltage which are consistently distinguishable both from each other and from worst case noise signals. Partial switching mechanism which gives faster operation of memory cores is not practical in coincident current design because it creates enough delta noise to swamp the lower output signal. The delta noise, the difference in output voltage between a half selected 'zero' and a half selected 'one' can be quite large even in a fully switched coincident current memory. Because the outputs of half selected cores would be more unequal if they were partially switched, the delta noise would increase to an unacceptable level.

Sometimes higher selection ratios rather than the conventional 2 : 1 are used to increase the speed of memory system. This ratio can be increased to 3 : 1 by using 2/3 of the nominal drive on the selected row and column and 1/3 of the drive in the inhibiting winding. Then the selected core is subject to a current equal to full drive current while the unselected cores on the selected coordinates are subjected to 1/3 of the full drive current. The result is that the noise due to partial select current is reduced. But the price which has to be paid for this increase in selection ratio is increased complexity of the driving system and some practical disadvantages of increased threading complexity. However, the principal advantages and disadvantages of coincident current system are as follows.

Advantages
  (i) Less expensive selection system.
  (ii) Memories up to a few million bits can be realized easily.

Disadvantages
  (i) Upper limits for all drive currents are predetermined.
  (ii) Limited temperature range in fast memories due to inhibit current dissipation.

3.2.2   Linear Select (2D) Memory System

Conceptually, the simplest organization of a random access memory consists of completely separating the address selection function from the storing function. Such memories are variously known as *word-organized, linear select* or 2D *memory*. The memory elements are in a rectangular array with each row line corresponding to a word and each column line to a bit. Basically this is a random access memory in which each word stored is addressed by an individual word selection element. The 2D system differs from the 3D in that the memory element storing a given word in a 2D system is read by a single full select current, rather than by coincidence of two half-select currents.

A simplified diagram of one core per bit 2D system is shown in Figure 3.4a. In most word-organized magnetic core memories each memory core is threaded by a drive winding and a bit plane winding. The bit plane winding links all the cores in each plane. To keep the number of windings to a minimum, the plane winding can combine the functions of sensing and of information driving. Here the application of read current in one word wire selects all the cores in the word and again the information is read out in parallel on the digit line. The major advantage of this selection method is the elimination of all half current disturbances from the system during reading, since only the cores in the selected word are subjected to full write current. In this system the reading operation does not require current coincidence while the writing operation does require coincidence of currents applied to a word and digit lines. From this it can be seen that on reading, the storage element has only one function, that of storage. On writing, both the storage and selection properties of the core are used.

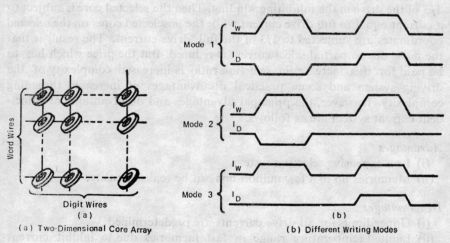

Figure 3.4   Word-organized memory plane.

(a) Two-Dimensional Core Array

(b) Different Writing Modes

To read one word in the system of Figure 3.4a, a read current in the selected wire switches all the cores in the word to the 'zero' state, causing a large voltage to appear on the digit wires threading those cores which had contained 'one'. Writing operation can be performed in three ways as shown in Figure 3.4b. It is assumed that all cores in an addressed word are in the 'zero' state just prior to writing operation.

In the first mode, a full select word current tends to switch all cores in the word to 'one' state, but it is offset by a half select digit current through those cores that should remain 'zero', while it is aided by a half select digit current in a reverse direction through cores to be switched to 'one'. In the second mode of writing, a full select word current as above switches all cores to 'one' except when it is opposed by a half select digit current. In the third mode, a full select word current switches only those cores where it is aided by a half-select digit current, the other cores remain in the 'zero' state.

Of these three modes of writing the first two modes require very close tolerances on their currents. A core heavily saturated in one direction can tolerate a larger opposing current than a core that has partially switched in that direction. The third mode of writing offers faster speed than the other modes because the word write current does not have to be overlapped as in cancelling schemes. In this case the digit currents always reinforce the partially set state and oppose only the fully reset state.

The determination of drive current tolerances for 2D memory are based on the criteria that the effective writing of 'ones', the effective writing of 'zeros' and the effective limitations of the information current to a value less than switching threshold current. With linear selection, there are no half selected cores to place an upper limit on the read current pulse while the lower limit is established by the need to fully reset all the cores on a selected wire from 1 to 0. With the partially switching linear select array, not only there is no upper limit established by disturb restrictions, but also the lower limit is even lower because the read current pulse does not have to switch as much material. On the other hand, this smaller amount of changing flux generates a smaller output signal. In any case, however, significant noise signal can be produced at write time. The digit current links all the cores in the sense line normally half in one phase, and half in the opposite phase. If the cores in one phase have 'ones' stored and in the other 'zeros', a large noise signal will be produced in the trailing edge of the digit pulse.

In read operation there is no output from the half selected cores, the flux change in the core does depend on the number of digit current augments the word current, all the disturbances are in the write direction and, therefore, only cores on the digit line which are storing 'zero' are affected. In the inhibiting case, all the disturbances are in the read direction and only affect core storing 'one'. The worst discrimination is in the first case between an undisturbed 'one' and a many times write disturbed 'zero', while in the second, between many times disturbed 'one' and an undisturbed 'zero'. If the core characteristics are such that its remanent state is changed appreciably by disturb pulses after the first, the effect of disturbance can be reduced by employing unequal word and digit currents. These noises will be the major factor in determining the minimum cycle which can be achieved in the system.

Partial switching is a method of writing in a core so that some of the available flux is reversed. The switching that occurs in a core by the application of an external applied field is characterized by a process which starts from its interior and gradually extends to its circumference. If, however, the applied field ended prematurely, only the in ner part of the core would contain reversed flux.

Partially switched cores dissipate less power and require lower drive currents. In case of one-core-per-bit designs, a partially switched core output signal is much smaller, then a fully switched core and hence it is difficult to distinguish it from a 0. Theoretically, a 0 output is characterized by absence of signal, but noise is always present because the hysteresis loop is never perfectly square. To obtain a reasonable difference between the 1 signal and 0 noise the core must be almost fully switched. This switching problem can be overcome by using two cores to store one bit of information.

All two-core-per-bit systems are of the word-organized type. One core is set to 1 for a stored 'one', while the other is set to 1 for a stored 'zero'. As a result, read 'zero' can be indicated not by the absence of a signal but by the presence of a signal equal in amplitude to that of a 'one' but in opposite polarity. The absence of a sensed signal in any bit plane during read can thus be detected as an error, and not assumed to be a zero. The technique doubles the required number of memory cores for a given word capacity, but permits greatly relaxed current tolerances and more reliable operation than is possible with other memory system.

The read/write method in two-core-per-bit is shown in Figure 3.4c. Application of either read pulse I_r or write pulse I_w alone switches both

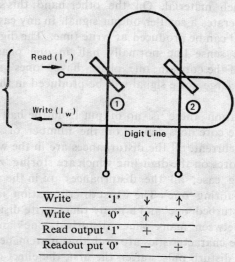

Write	'1'	↓	↑
Write	'0'	↑	↓
Read output '1'	+	—
Readout put '0'	—	+

Figure 3.4c Two-core-per-bit system.

the cores to similar amount and there will be no voltage output as the cores digit windings are connected in series opposition. If, however, at the same time as I_w, occurs, a digit current I_d is applied which flows up the right-hand wire and down the left then it will reduce the amount by which the core 1 switches by inhibiting and augmenting I_w in those cores respectively. Now if I_r is applied, more flux will change in core 1 than in core 2 and the left terminal of the digit wire will go positive with respect to right say, a positive output '1'. If a digit current of $-I_d$ is applied a negative output '0' will be obtained.

The flux change in the core depends on the time integral of the applied field in excess of the critical field which just starts switching the core. Hence the duration of the current pulse is as important as its amplitude. The flux change in the cores can, therefore, be limited by controlling the duration of write current with two cores for every bit position, one is always in the 'zero' state and connected to the sense circuits in such a way that its noise cancels the noise from the switching core. But wiring up such an array is as complex as wiring a $2\frac{1}{2}$D array. However, the merits of the two-core-per-bit-storage system can be summarized as:

(i)   It is faster than one core per bit system.
(ii) Cores specifications are not stringent.
(iii) The system is a balanced one and, therefore, always presents the same load to both the word and digit drive circuits.
(iv) Discrimination between 1 and 0 is much easier.

3.2.3 $2\frac{1}{2}$D Memory System

The core array selection methods which we have so far been considering, namely, coincident current selection and linear selection, are not the only methods which may be used, but they represent two practical extremes of organization. Between these two extremes, there is another method which is known as $2\frac{1}{2}$D system. This is a three wire hybrid of the 2D and 3D memory system.

The $2\frac{1}{2}$ method consists of three wire system which preserved the decoding advantage of a coincident current system, but has the cost advantage of planer linear select system. The primary advantage of the system lies in the elimination of the inhibit circuit and thereby no inhibit noise in the sense wire. The overall system has the coincident current read cycle and a linear select write cycle.

In the $2\frac{1}{2}$D memory array, the cores are arranged in a pattern which is similar to, but different from, that used in 3D array. Figure 3.5 shows the wiring of a typical 4×16 plane. The core plane is not square but rectangular $(H \times L)$ and there is no inhibit wire. The sense wire is strung to give maximum cancellation of the half select signal along both the X and Y dimensions. As shown, the sense wire is usually an orthogonal one parallel to the Y wire. Reading of information conforms to the 3D system and

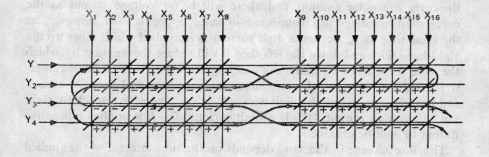

Figure 3.5 $2\frac{1}{2}$D-3-wire memory plane (arrows show +ve current flow).

the writing conforms to the 2D system. Thus, for writing a 'one' two coincident partial currents are needed, and for writing 'zero' the only one drive wire is energized.

In any read operation in a plane which has dimensions of W by L, there will be $W + L - 2$ cores half selected and one core fully selected. As in 3D array, the degree of cancellation of the half select signals depends on the magnetic history of the cores. On write, since there is no inhibit wire, the maximum number of half select signals is the same as on read if a 'one' is being written. If a 'zero' is being written only W half selects are seen.

The $2\frac{1}{2}$D system has many advantages, there is no inhibit recovery problem, since there is no inhibit current. Another important advantage of this system is that the drive lines are much shorter than the drive lines in a comparable 3D or 2D system. Therefore, all system resonances are significantly higher than the frequency spectrum of a core switching. This simplifies the sensing problem. The short drive lines also allow fast rise time on the current pulses, with relatively low drive voltage.

The drive circuits in a $2\frac{1}{2}$D memory require lower voltage than do those in a 3D memory, so that large scale integration will be easier to apply in $2\frac{1}{2}$D systems. Regarding the consumption of power it has been found that the bit drive system accounts for the largest part of the power used in a memory system. In case of $2\frac{1}{2}$D system, since the bit line is shorter by a factor of four or eight than a linear select or a coincident current memory, the power requirement is lower and minimum. The dissipation in the $2\frac{1}{2}$D system will occur, however in external resistors, and therefore, stack heating problems will be minimized.

Although the mass memories and the smaller high speed main memory both use a $2\frac{1}{2}$D structure, there is a significant difference in the array used. The small main memories use a 3 wires plane configuration. A separate sense wire is used which is wound to give an optimum noise cancellation characteristics. The sense amplifier circuits for this system would be similar to those used in a comparable 3D memory. On the other hand, mass memory uses a 2 wire core array in which the read signals are sensed on the Y drive wire. This requires some tricky circuitry and the noise cancellation techniques to achieve satisfactory signal-to-noise ratio. The elimination of third wire results in a significant cost saving which more than compensates for the increased sensing problem.

The sense line of the system is strung to achieve cancellation of the half selected signals, similar to the 3D array inhibit-sense cancellation. The degree of cancellation is determined also by the core secondary characteristics and its magnetic history. Since the system resonances are high, a wide band sense amplifier may be used effectively to achieve time discrimination. The lack of large inhibit noise and the larger output signals from the core permit a less expensive sense amplifier.

3.3 TESTING MECHANISMS OF MEMORY CORES AND PLANES

Nearly all modern computers employ high speed memories, consisting of square loop ferrite toroids. The recent history of development of computers is, thus, strongly dependent on the magnetic properties and the economics of square loop ferrite cores. A large variety of toroidal cores varying in size, speed and cost are now commercially available to satisfy the requirements of different types of memory. In the previous section we have presented the working principles involved in magnetic core storage system and their different organizational structures along with the study of factors affecting the choice of cores. In this section we shall study some testing methods of memory cores and memory planes along with the design, development, construction and performance of an automatic testing equipment. After testing of individual cores, memory matrix is constructed with those cores that conform to the chosen characteristics. Then the matrix should be tested to determine whether it is done correctly or not, as also its ability to work under worst conditions that may arise in the machine.

Memory core testing technology consists in some levels of hierarchy. At the first level is the testing of individual core. Elements that pass the above test are assembled into arrays or planes which are then subjected to higher level of testing, known as plane testing. Then the drive and sense circuits, memory address, data, and timing logic are put into a final test, known as the *system test*. During this test, the memory is operated under normal and extreme conditions and environment.

Generally, the best test of a memory system is a functional test. Worst-case patterns, which depend on the wiring configuration of the memory, determine the degree to which inherent noise affects the stored data in the memory. This noise is either generated in half selected cores, or capacitively coupled from drive to sense lines. When the noise is too large, the discriminator may detect it and erroneously indicate the presence of a 'one' in place of a 'zero' and vice-versa.

3.3.1 Underlying Principle of Testing of Memory Cores

A toroidal ferrite core, used for memory applications, along with a typical hysteresis loop, is shown in Figure 3.6. A core is normally considered to have only two stable states of magnetization. But this is only partly true. An examination of core hysteresis loop presented in Figure 3.6 shows that within the two major states 'one' and 'zero', there are minor variations in magnetization which are determined by the sequence of partial current pulses to which the core is subjected.

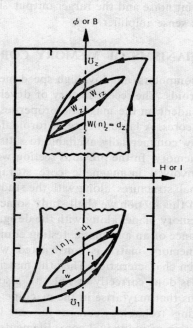

Figure 3.6   Memory core disturb states.
Note: Read $u1$ and uz for υ_1 and υ_z respectively in the figure.

Referring to the two stable states of Figure 3.6, the remanent point zero (uz) represents a clockwise magnetization of the core, and the second remanent point 'one' ($u1$) represents an anticlockwise magnetization of the core. By the application of full read pulse, the core which is initially at the remanent point $u1$, travels to the positive saturation point and comes back to the remanent point zero (uz). If the core was initially at remanent point uz, the application of read pulse will cause a small change in flux. The states $d1$ and dz are called the maximally disturbed states for a given amplitude of partial current. These states are reached by subjecting the core (first set to the $u1$ or uz state) to a long burst of disturbing pulses in the direction to switch flux in the core. The other disturb states are reached by subjecting a core (in the $u1$ or uz state) to a series of $\pm$ partial current pairs. The core will stabilize on minor loop and shuttle back and forth between the $r1$ and $rw1$ or wrz and wz states.

A half read current pulse, applied to the core at the 'zero' or 'one' remanent state, cannot take it round the 'knee'. This pulse simply takes the core back along the minor loop almost to its original state. But in actual practice, due to deviations of the magnetic characteristics from the ideal ones, the application of the current pulses bring the core to a state, slightly different from the undisturbed zero or one state. However, the deviation from the rectangularity of the B-H loop for most of the cores creates several engineering problems in core memory operations.

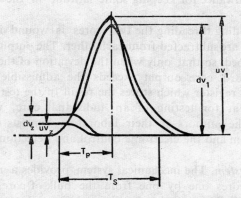

Figure 3.7   Core output signal characteristics.

Memory cores are more commonly described and specified by means of voltage response curves. Figure 3.7 shows the core output signals and their characteristics. The disturbed signals dV_1 and dV_z are the outputs corresponding to the $d1$ and dz states. The difference between $u1$ and $d1$ or the uz and dz gives us a test for the quality of the core. The smaller the difference, better is the performance of the core. Similarly, the tests for the switching time and peaking time are fairly straightforward and are not much affected by the magnetic history of the core.

3.3.2 Core Testing Procedure and Equipment

From the previous analysis it can be summarized that for memory operations, the factors which need careful consideration are: (a) the output voltage when the core is switched from the state 'one' to the state 'zero', and the corresponding switching time; (b) the noise voltage when the core is switched from disturbed 'zero' state to undisturbed 'zero' state or the output voltage from the disturbed 'one' to undisturbed 'zero' state; and (c) the peaking time—the time required for the output to reach its peak value.

For the purpose of testing, there are two different approaches, namely, (i) the direct measurement of core characteristics and (ii) comparison of these characteristics with those of a previously tested and selected core. The second method is quite easy from the point of fabrication of the instrument. A repetitive sequence of pulses, containing read/write pulses and a number of disturbed 'zero' pulses corresponding to half amplitude are used for this purpose.

In order to simulate the worst case marginal condition of operations arising from the variation of selection currents, the read/write current pulses are set to have a full amplitude which is 90 per cent of the nominal value and disturb half pulses are set to 55 per cent of the nominal full value specified for the particular type of core, thus giving a disturb ratio of 0.61. This gives enough allowance for keeping some latitude in the design of driving amplifiers.

The sense winding threading the two cores is wound in such a fashion that the outputs are subtracted from each other. The output of sense amplifier is suitably clamped, so that only when the deviation of the test core output from the standard core output exceeds the admissible limit, a pulse is transmitted to a register which stores the result of the test.

The equipment for testing of an individual core, which have been developed by the authors at their laboratory, consists of two parts—the mechanical system and the electronic control and detection system. These are discussed below.

Mechanical system. The mechanical system provides a mechanical means of taking the cores one by one from the bulk of cores. The system then brings the individual core to the checking position where testing of core is done automatically. Then it removes the tested core either to the 'reject' or 'select' pocket, according to the test results. Testing of the core is done by passing a sequence of test pulses through the core at the checking position and then comparing the output of the core with that of standard core.

The above objective can be realized in two processes. First, the testing pin itself is used for picking up the individual core from the bulk and then transporting it to the checking station, and second, a separate transporting medium is used. Equipment of the first variety is shown schematically in Figure 3.8a. In both the cases, the cores are separated from each other with the help of a vibrating bunker ('A' in Figure 3.8a). This is indispensable because the cores used in modern memories are extremely small in size. The vibrating bunker consists of a cylindrical container with a helical channel (along its inner wall), starting from its floor and ending in a delivery spout at the top. The container is given a helical vibration by an ac operated electromagnet. A suitably bent sensing pin p, attached to the wheel W, picks up the cores from the delivery spout one by one. The wheel is rotated intermittently by a geneva mechanism. At the testing station, a pair of electrical contacts are pressed against the pin to drive the test pulses and to receive outputs from the core. In the next station, these cores are dropped into a chate C, with bifurcated channels ending in the select and reject pockets. The passage to the right pocket (select) is controlled by an electromagnetically operated flap. The rate of testing is rather slow, usually of the order of 60 cores per minute.

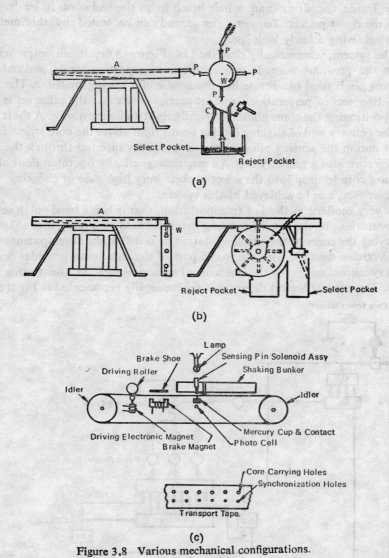

Select Pocket

Reject Pocket

(a)

Reject Pocket   Select Pocket

(b)

Lamp

Brake Shoe   Sensing Pin Solenoid Assy

Driving Roller   Shaking Bunker

Idler   Idler

Driving Electronic Magnet   Mercury Cup & Contact
Brake Magnet   Photo Cell

Core Carrying Holes
Synchronization Holes

Transport Tape.

(c)

Figure 3.8   Various mechanical configurations.

Figure 3.8b represents an improved system. Here the transporting media is a drum with counter-bored seats for carrying cores. I neach seat, there are two fine bores through which sensing pin comes out as the cores leave the receiving station. In the checking station each of the two pins comes out totally and the core rides on the top half of the pins. The up and down movement of the pin is achieved by a cam inside the drum. Magnetically operated contacts press upon the pins in the checking station that is midway between the vertical receiving position and the horizontal 'select-core' position. A good core is magnetically picked out. After this, the pins submerge fully inside the drum and a hair brush helps the bad cores to be dropped into the reject pocket. Ten cores per second can be tested by this method, thus achieving a fairly high speed.

The system, schematically described in Figure 3.8c, is an improvement over the previous ones. It uses a tape as transporting media, and only one sensing pin is used to operate like the needle of a sewing machine. The tape has two sets of perforations, one set carries cores, and the other set is used for positioning the cores photoelectrically right under the needle. A short tube at the delivery end of shaking bunker opens right above the core track. In the next station the sensing pin is electromagnetically inserted through the hole in the core into a mercury cup. An electromagnetically operated door allows a good core to drop into the select pocket. Very high rate of checking, 10 to 25 cores/sec, can be achieved by this system.

A very modern method of transportation, that is being tried out in several laboratories, is the use of rotating magnetic field of a particular shape for carrying the cores to the checking station. It is still in the development stage.

Electronic system. The electronic part of the core tester provides control and synchronization for the mechanical system as well as the testing process. The general logical diagram is schematically represented in Figure 3.9,

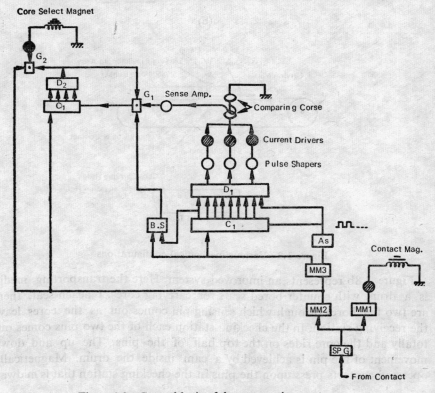

Figure 3.9   General logic of the automatic core tester.

although the details of the control and synchronization logic depend on the particular mechanical system chosen. The necessary sequence of test pulses and the sequence of control pulses, are shown in Figure 3.10.

A suitable contact along with its associated circuit generates a single pulse, known as synchronizing pulse, at the stationary state of the core. The synchronizing pulse triggers the monostable multivibrators MM_1 and MM_2. The output of MM_1 drives a power amplifier for operating the contact system or the sensing pin, as the case may be, MM_2 provides the delay necessary for setting the contacts. The trailing edge of MM_2 controls the astable multivibrator AS, which generates the clock pulses. The clock pulses are fed into the counter C_1. The output of the counter is decoded D_1 to generate the three different sequences of pulses which would combine, after the pulse shapers, and current amplifiers, to produce the sequence of test pulses as shown in Figure 3.10b. The spillover pulse from the counter C_1 sets the flip-flop BS. The trailing edge of MM_3 resets the counter C_1 and the flip-flop BS.

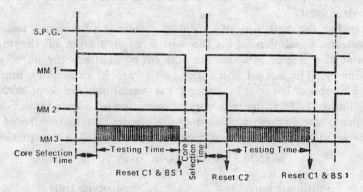

Figure 3.10 Time sequence of control pulses.

The output windings of the standard core and the test core are so arrang-ed that the outputs are subtracted. The resultant output is then amplified in the sense amplifier. The output from the sense amplifier is then gated through the gate G_1 to the counter C_1 which keeps record of the number of times the output of the sense amplifier crosses the preset threshold value. The gate G_1 is an AND gate which permits the sense amplifier output to pass only when BS is set. The output of the decoder D_2 is high. The coun-ter C_2 is reset by the trailing edge of MM_2. The gate G_1 blocks or allows the output of the sense amplifier during the first sequence of test pulses, depending on the condition of C_2. The decoder D_2 has a single low output when the counter registers a preset number.

The output of the sense amplifier crosses the threshold value only when the deviation of the test core from the standard one (in respect of the signal voltage, the noise voltage) exceeds the specified tolerance limit. Each core is tested 60 to 70 times. To minimize the probability of rejection of a good core due to some stray signals picked up by the sense amplifier, the logic incorporates a counter. This counts the number of times the sense amplifier gives an output and when this number reaches the specified number, the decoder output is low and the gate G_1 is closed.

The gate G_2 permits the pulse from MM_2 to drive the power amplifier for operating the magnet for selection of good cores for which the output line of D_2 is high.

3.3.3 Plane Testing Mechanism

Memory core testing technology consists of some levels of hierarchy. At the first level is the testing of individual storage elements as discussed in an earlier section. Elements that pass the individual tests are assembled into arrays or planes which are then subjected to a higher level of testing, known as plane testing. Then the drive and sense circuits, memory address, data, and timing logic are put to a final test, known as the *system test*. During this test, memory is operated under normal and extreme conditions and environment.

Generally, the best test of a memory system is a functional test. Worst case patterns, which depend on the wiring configuration of the memory, determine the degree to which the inherent noise affects the stored data in the memory. The actual condition under which a memory unit works inside a computer is variable, though the variations are kept within the design limits. In fact, the reliability of operation of a core matrix depends upon the following factors. Assuming the physical characteristics of all the cores to be more or less the same, we can write the reliability quotient as

$$Q = f[I_c, I_{in}, \tau_1, \tau_2, \tau_3, \beta, \gamma, T]$$

where

I_c = co-ordinate currents	τ_2 = strobing time
I_{in} = inhibit current	τ_3 = duration of stroble pulse
τ_1 = risetime of the read current	β = sensitivity of read amplifier
γ = distribution of information in the matrix	T = ambient temperature

The current conditions, distribution of information in the matrix and the ambient temperature influence the switching of the matrix itself and may, therefore, be treated as inherent characteristics of the matrix operation. The time parameters and the sensitivity of the read amplifier affect the reliability of the read channel and hence, are actually external characteristics. The reliability quotient can, thus, be broken up as the sum of two separate reliability quotients Q_1 and Q_2, Q_1 being the inherent reliability quotient of the matrix, and Q_2 being the read reliability quotient. We may thus break the above equation into two parts as

$$Q_1 = f_1(I_c, I_{in}, \gamma, T)$$
$$Q_2 = f_2(\tau_1, \tau_2, \tau_3, \beta)$$

Optimum condition for both the functions may be calculated exclusively from the theoretical point of view. The study of the matrix operation is done separately for the quotients Q_1 and Q_2. The distribution of information, magnetic and electrostatic pickup from the row and column windings in the matrix, influence the noise parameters. Depending on the geometrical orientation of the sense winding with respect to the directions of co-ordinate currents, every plane has a particular distribution of information which gives the heaviest noise. If the same information is put in all the locations, the noise is the least. For the purposes of finding the reliable working area of the matrix, only heaviest noise code needs consideration. Thus γ, for the moment, may be taken as constant, and if we work at a particular temperature T, then the reliability quotient Q_1 is only a function of I_c and I_{in}.

First keeping T constant along with the factors relating to read channel and with the heavy code put into the matrix, vary I_c and I_{in} in turn till error occurs in matrix operation. The points representing the starting of error form a closed curve in the $I_c - I_{in}$ plane (Figure 3.11). The enclosed area represents the reliable working area of the matrix for a particular temperature T. If the area is too small, it may be due to some of the cores given faulty operation. This may be checked by observing the unstrobed output of the sense amplifier by continuously switching the cores.

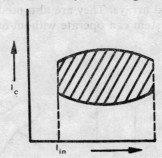

Figure 3.11   Workable area of a memory matrix.

The upper limit of working in Figure 3.11 corresponds to the value of co-ordinate currents when they start to disturb the states of the unselected cores, whereas the lower limit is reached when the signal output falls below the value sufficient for the read channel to give correct reading. The left limit is reached when the value of inhibit current is too low to inhibit one of the coordinate currents properly, while the right limit indicates that the inhibit current is large enough to disturb the 'one' condition of the unselected cores.

For each matrix, such areas are experimentally determined for different temperatures within the working range. The intersection of these areas gives the working area for the matrix regarding the factors influencing the function f_1.

In order to determine the influence of factor f_2, we shall assume sensitivity of the amplifier to be constant. Taking one of three variables, say, τ_1 constant and varying successively the other two parameters, we can determine the points when errors begin to appear. As before, we can plot a curve in the $\tau_2 - \tau_3$ plane. This curve will also be closed curve enclosing the area of reliable operation. For different values τ_1, such areas are obtained and the intersection of these areas, again, gives the working area of the matrix. Optimum values of τ_1, τ_2 and τ_3, with the tolerance limits can then be easily determined.

For operation of all the matrices in the memory stack, the intersection of working areas of individual matrices in relation to the function f_2 is first obtained. The nominal values of the parameters τ_1, τ_2 and τ_3 are then determined and the tolerance limits are set carefully so that the working point always remains well within the intersecting area.

Characterization tests for memory arrays defining operating margins, presented graphically, are called Schmoo plot. Theoretically, they should be polygons in two dimensions or prisms in three dimensions, depending on the number of independent variables. But since the inherent noise tends to round off the corners, whose shapes explain their name—the Schmoo was originally a curvy little comic-strip character as shown in Figure 3.12. Schmoo plot is one of the methods of defining the acceptance limits for subsequent manufactured arrays. They are also used for defining the operating range over which system can operate without any disturbances.

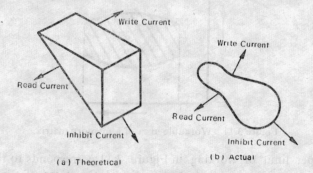

Figure 3.12   Evaluation of the typical Schmoo: (a) Theoretical
maximum variation of various currents; (b) Noise and other
parasities round off the sharp corners.

3.3.4 Block Diagram of the Plane Testing Equipment

The equipment for automatic testing of memory planes is designed for testing of the matrices as well as for studying the influences of different memory parameters on the overall operation of the matrices. The checking of the matrices is done after putting the matrix on the test table and fixing the necessary connections with electronic system through special connectors. With the help of control switches and press buttons provided for in the console, the working regime and the mode of operation can be set up. The whole matrix can be displayed on the screen of the oscilloscope with the help of a special scanning system incorporated in the design, with bright dots, for 'one' and blanks for 'zero'. During the testing of the matrix, the error location is shown in the display panel and the testing stops whenever an error occurs. For the convenience of explanation, the logical design may be divided into three blocks, namely, (a) control block, (b) addressing and decoding block, and (c) read-write check block as shown in Figure 3.13.

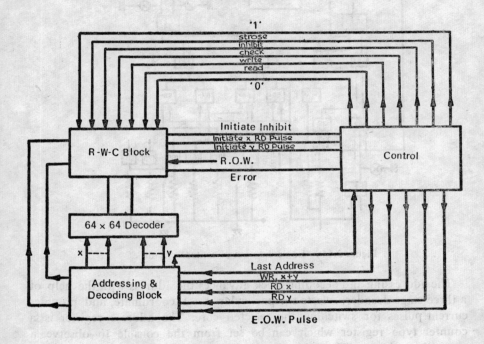

Figure 3.13   Block diagram of plane testing equipment.

The control block produces the start-stop pulses, the error signals and provides the other blocks with necessary control pulses. By pressing the start button, a single pulse is generated, which then generates the sequence of test pulses with appropriate duration. The logical block diagram of control unit and the timing diagram are shown in Figure 3.14. The pulses are generated by the variable delay lines, so that the memory unit of cycle time 4 to 8 microsecond can be tested by this instrument. The mode of checking is first established and then the checking of the matrix is done according to this mode. The result of the testing is then compared and if any error occurs, the error signal will be generated at once, which will stop the further process of checking.

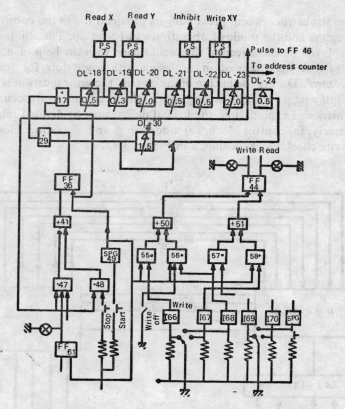

Figure 3.14a   Logic diagram of control circuit.

The addressing and decoding block advances the address with the help of a three stage decoder, selects the particular $X-Y$ coordinate, and provides current pulses for switching the selected core. The address register is a counter type register which can be set from the console to observe a particular address. The address register is divided into two parts, X and Y register, each having six bits storage capacity. Each of the X and Y register is decoded into eight lines, which then drives the eight current drivers. Once again, the provision is made here for testing the various types of memory units requiring various drive currents, ranging typically from 400 to 800mA. The outputs of the current drivers are again decoded by diode decoder into 64 lines to drive the 64×64 memory matrix.

The read-write check block is used for reading and writing of 'ones' or 'zeros' or the 'heavy code pattern', and also for checking the results by comparing with the written information. There are two flip-flops—one is controlled by the output voltage from the matrix and the other is controlled by the information written into the matrix. The states of these two flip-flops are then compared amongst themselves and if they do not agree, a signal will be generated which will stop the checking process further.

The timing diagram of the working logic is shown in Figure 3.14. Signal from the start switch when pressed, goes to the single pulse generator (SPG-49) which then gives out a single start control pulse. This pulse, in turn, feeds the sequence generator circuits and at the same time, sets the start flip-flop [FF-36]. The sequence generator circuits produce the sequence of control pulses. After one cycle, the end pulse is recirculated if the start flip-flop remains in set position. The condition of the start flip-flop depends upon whether there was an error in the previous cycle or not. Whenever an error occurs, the error flip-flop is set and the start flip-flop is reset by the fourth control pulse via the 'AND' gate.

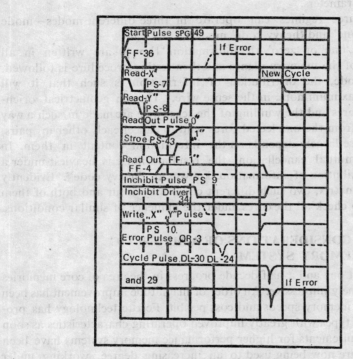

Figure 3.14b   Timing chart.

The start pulse, apart from setting the start flip-flop, also sets or resets the read-write flip-flop [FF-41], depending on the position of switch. When the switch is in the check position, this read-write flip flop will be set in the 'write' condition first and after 4096 cycles, it will reset to the 'read' condition by the spillover pulse from the address counter via the 'AND' gate [48].

The testing and study of the matrix can be carried out in three different regimes, namely, write regime, read regime, and check regime. The write regime may be used for studying output signals from the sense amplifier on an oscilloscope screen. These signals may be observed during the continuous writing of any information. The nature of operation of the memory matrix may be understood from the broadening of patterns due to superimposition of different signals in the oscilloscope screen. By changing the current amplitude, the sharpness of the pulse pattern may be controlled. The read regime may be used for general observation of the working area of the matrix on the oscilloscope screen via a special scanning system. This regime may also be used for the testing operation of the matrix. The check regime is used for automatic detection and location of error during the determination of working area of the matrix. The switches for the selection of modes and regimes are provided on the console. The console further contains the address display panel and the various controls including those for the variation of parameters.

All these three regimes can operate in three different modes—mode 'zero', mode 'one' and 'heavy code' mode.

In the mode 'one' or 'zero', the information '1' or '0' are written in all the location of the memory planes and then testing procedure is followed. In the other mode, the distribution of information is such that it will produce the maximum noise in the sense wire. Though geometrical orientation of the cores and the winding of the sense wire are made in such a way that the noise from the unselected cores tend to cancel each other in pairs, the overall noise largely depends on the information content in them. In spite of the mutual cancellation, the resultant noise is heaviest under a particular distribution of information, known as "heavy code". Evidently for a memory matrix, two such different codes may occur and both of them may be used to check all the cores under the influence of similar conditions.

3.4   DESIGN CONSIDERATIONS OF A MAGNETIC CORE MEMORY SYSTEM

During the past one and a half decade progress in the area of core memories has been extremely impressive. An order of magnitude improvement has been made in both memory speeds and cost per bit. Ferrite technology has provided new core types with greatly improved operating characteristics as soon as the real requirements for higher performance memory systems have been defined. They are now being used to an increasing degree, working under extreme environmental conditions, which generally must be transportable. It is, therefore, necessary to provide memory stacks of the smallest possible dimensions and weight which can withstand rough handling. At the same time, they must remain operatable over a wide temperature range ensuring utmost reliability.

A memory stack manufactured according to conventional methods will meet these requirements, at best, only in part. In order to assess the performance of a square loop ferrite device as a storage element, important properties, such as squareness ratio, threshold speed, the magnitude of 'one' and 'zero' signals, temperature sensitivity and pulse responses of the driving and sensing circuits must be studied. The deviation from perfect squareness of the so-called square loop ferrite core, presents a significant problem in the design of coincident current memory. The noise output of a single core disturbed by a half select current is small, but the uncompensated accumulation of many such outputs in a single bit plane, in the worst cases, can create a difficult discrimination problem for the associated sense amplifier. Also, the memory capacity, speed of operation and the cost of memory require considerable attention for the design of memory system.

3.4.1 Memory Array Design

Significant advances in the state of the art of random access storage have occurred in the past few years. These advances have followed developments in ferrite material technology, in ferrite core utilization techniques, and in associated driving and sensing circuitry. Ferrite core memory planes cause many problems, especially if a more stringent environment and mobility are specified. These stacks are customarily assembled from a number of individual planes; each plane consists essentially of a wire threaded core array, a supporting plate, and a frame. All threading wires are terminated on the frame enclosing the matrix field. During stack assembly all X and Y terminals must be interconnected properly so as to yield a set of continuous conducting paths. To this end one or two additional terminals are required for each wire, depending on the frame design. The total weight and outer dimensions of the memory stack in this case are determined mainly by the supporting plates and frames as well as various other supporting parts. A considerable reduction in weight and size can be achieved by folding a long plane because the frame can be eliminated. Different techniques such as, extrusion, stapelblock, etc. have been evolved to arrive at highly reliable ferrite core storages of low weight, small dimensions, and high mechanical strength under dynamic loads. However, in all these methods a certain degree of redundancy must be provided by adding a few rows of cores in each plane. If any cores are damaged, the corresponding X or Y wires have to be disconnected and the redundancy rows are used.

In a conventional coincident current memory, in addition to X and Y drive windings, a sense winding and an inhibit winding, each linking all the cores in one bit plane, are used. The sense winding functions during 'read', and the inhibit winding functions during 'write' operation. They can, however, be time shared on a single winding, if necessary. The inhibit winding carries unipolar pulses in the same direction as read pulses. The sense winding, in most cases, carries bipolar pulses. The geometry of winding pattern is such that one half of the cores in the plane are sensed in one direction and the other half in the opposite direction. Consequently, noise outputs from any pair to distributed cores are mutually cancelled. The array size, its configuration, and the core type suitable for the performance objectives of the systems can be determined with computer program. Access time and the signal level at the sense amplifier input are the two major criteria by which a given array configuration is judged.

Coincident current designs take full advantage of the inherent selection capability of square loop ferrite cores. The principle of coincident current selection, using X and Y coordinates for word selection and the Z coordinate for data storage and interrogation, requires significantly fewer word drive $(X=Y)$ circuits than other memory organizations typically used to realize high performance. The reduction of the number of active devices is a major consideration in design for low cost and high reliability. The minimization of driving circuits and the resulting influence on packaging are key factors in the decision to concentrate on coincident current memory design approach. There are other approaches to memory wiring technique. One approach known as $2\frac{1}{2}$D system, though popular, requires lots of peripheral electronic circuits and is expensive. The three wire system requires special attention of the reflection in the line during sense operation. There are also noise problems that must be compensated differently than in a four system. But once these factors are considered, a three wire system can yield a faster and a cleaner design than the corresponding four wire system. Moreover, the three wire system is much less affected by temperature gradient than four wire because its sense-inhibit wire dissipates less power.

For high speed core memories with pulse repetition rate of 10 MHz and above, the interconnecting method has a dominant role in the overall performance. The electrical behaviour of pulse propagation in memories can be predicted by the transmission line model. Different core planes behave like a transmission line with distributed circuit parameters (L, R, C) per unit length. Each toroidal core can be replaced by their equivalent inductance and resistance. The overall effects of attenuation, distortion and cross coupling are such that these are superimposed on the sense signal. The transmission characteristics of the array lines are not only frequency dependent but also information sensitive because the resistance and inductance of the storage device change with the information state of the memory. However, we have considered it later in this section.

Lastly the energy losses must be considered in high speed memory stacks. The resulting heat is more readily dissipated if metal core supporting plates are chosen. In case of small number of planes however, heat conduction can be directed perpendicular to matrix planes onto a metal plate, the spacing between even the outmost plane and the heat sink is short in a flat stack. Heat dissipation can be further improved by filling free space between the core supporting plates with a suitable sealing compound.

3.4.2 Memory Cycle Time

One of the most significant characteristics of a storage system is the speed with which data can be read out from or written into the memory. The total time for reading or writing may be regarded as having two components, namely, the *latency time* and *reading-writing time*. For most of the random access systems, the latency time is very small and the only significant time is the read-write time.

The most conventional 3D system has two types of operating cycles—the *store* cycle in which new information is entered in, and the *fetch* cycle in which information is obtained from a selected address or location of the memory. In a store cycle, it is normally necessary first to 'clear' the previously stored information, and then to 'write' the information to be stored. Therefore, a store cycle is composed of a 'clear' followed by a 'write' sequence. In some cases, 'clear' operation may be accomplished during a previous cycle of operation. This is termed as *split cycle* operation. In a fetch cycle, the information is 'read' from the memory, and then because of the 'destructive-read' characteristics, the information is to be restored or regenerated. In some cases, the regenerate operation is omitted and the content of the address is left in the cleared state which again falls into split cycle category.

The various factors that limit the access time and cycle time of any random access store are the transmission delays in the system, the gain bandwidth product of the active elements in the access and digit circuits, and the switching time of the storage element itself.

3.4.3 Transmission Line Model of Memory Plane

The terminal characteristics of a magnetic core can be studied by replacing the toroidal cores by their equivalent circuits, as shown in Figure 3.15. The basic magnetic properties are described by the hysteresis curve, but the relationships between the magnetomotive force and the switching flux are more important in practice. The slope of the curve, drawn between the magnetomotive force versus the switching flux, will provide an estimate of the inductance per turn of the core below the saturation level. However, below saturation level, the equivalent inductance and resistance a toroidal core is related to the dimensions of the core by the relations:

$$\frac{L_2}{N^2} \simeq \frac{\mu_r A}{l_m} \tag{1}$$

and

$$\frac{R_2}{N^2} \simeq \frac{K_1 A}{l_m} \tag{2}$$

such that

$$\frac{L_2}{R_2} = \frac{\mu_r}{K_1} \tag{3}$$

where μ_r is the average permeability in the region of remanence, A is the core cross-sectional area, l_m is the mean magnetic path length and K_1 is a constant for the core material. The time constant, L/R of the equivalent circuit is dependent on the intrinsic properties of the core material and is independent of the core dimension as shown by Equation (3).

Analysis of the behaviour of the rectangular loop core when switching from one remanent state to other was considered by various workers.

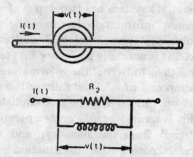

Figure 3.15   Equivalent circuit of a magnetic core.

Assuming that at a time t, the state of the core material is $B(t)$ and the applied field is $H(t)$, we may write

$$\left.\begin{array}{l} \dfrac{dB}{dt} = 0, \text{ when } H(t) < H_0 \\[2mm] \dfrac{dB}{dt} = f(B)[H(t)-H_0], \text{ when } H(t) \geqslant H_0 \end{array}\right\} \tag{4}$$

and

where H_0 is called the threshold field and is a constant for the material.

The relationship between the switched magnetic flux ϕ and the half select current I can be written as:

$$\phi \simeq \phi_0 + L_2 I; \quad \text{for } |I| \leqslant I_0/2$$

where $|I_0|$ is the magnitude of the current required to switch the core from one remanent state to the other and L_2 can be interpreted as core-inductance which is not constant and is a function of drive current. But for our analysis, we are taking L_2 as a constant. During the process of disturbance some energy is dissipated in the core in the form of heat. The energy loses can be accounted for by the introduction of a resistor. Hence the simplest representation of a half selected core involves atleast an inductor and a resistor, as shown in Figure 3.15 and the equivalent impedance presented by parallel circuit is

$$Z = \frac{jwL_2R_2}{R_2 + jwL_2} \tag{5}$$

The back emf induced in the wire by the core due to current $I(t)$ is

$$v(t) = R_2 \int_{-\infty}^{t} \exp\left[-\frac{R_2}{L_2}(t-t')\right]\frac{dI(t')}{dt'}\,dt' \tag{6}$$

Equations (5) and (6) are the basic equations for constructing magnetic memory plane.

Having established the equivalent circuit of toroidal core we are now in a position to develop the transmission line model of the memory plane. The transmission line model for toroidal cores has been studied by various authors Week, Dutta Majumder and Das, and others and is extremely important for the considerations of interference and noise effect in the memory systems.

In constructing the mathematical model for the simplest memory organization (linear selection), it is necessary to consider the interaction of the crossed wires with each other. Since the bit lines and the word lines are at right angles and are in close proximity, the couplings are mainly capacitive. The bit line without the storage element and word line, have their own distributed inductance and resistance which are again coupled to the rest of the arrary by distributed shunt capacitance and possibly shunt conductance. Let,

$$L_1 = \text{inductance/length}, \quad R_1 = \text{resistance/length}$$
$$C_1 = \text{capacitance/length}, \quad G_1 = \text{conductance/length}$$

and $\quad X = $ the distance between two consecutive bit storage devices

Then, the equivalent circuits of a bit line in the absence and in the presence of a bit storage element, are shown in Figures 3.16a, 3.16b respectively.

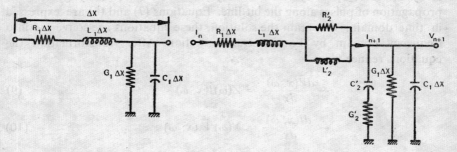

Figure 3.16a Section of a bit line in the absence of a core.

Figure 3.16b Section of a bit line in the presence of a core and intersections with a word line.

In Figure 3.16b, C'_2 and G'_2 are respectively, the equivalent capacitance and conductance of a bit line arising due to the coupling between bit and word lines. For the entire memory array, there will be a series combination of above circuits, and the voltage difference between the two successive nodes can be written as

$$V_n - V_{n+1} = R_1 \Delta x I_n + L_1 \Delta x \frac{dI_n}{dt} + R_2 \Delta x \int_{-\infty}^{t} \exp\left[-\frac{R_2}{L_2}(t-t')\right]\frac{dI_n(t')}{dt'}dt'$$

or

$$\frac{V_n - V_{n+1}}{\Delta x} = R_1 I_n + L_1 \frac{dI_n}{dt} + R_2 \int_{-\infty}^{t} \exp\left[-\frac{R_2}{L_2}(t-t')\right]\frac{dI_n(t')}{dt'}dt'$$

Writing in terms of partial derivatives with respect to X and replacing the variable X_n by the continuous variable X, the above equation reduces to

$$\frac{\partial V(x, t)}{\partial x} = R_1 I(x, t) + L_1 \frac{\partial I(x, t)}{\partial t} + R_2 \int_{-\infty}^{t} \exp\left[-\frac{R_2}{L_2}(t-t')\right]\frac{\partial I(x, t)}{\partial t'}dt'$$

(7)

Similarly, we can write the expression for the shunt current from the bit line at any node to ground as

$$-\frac{\partial I(x, t)}{\partial x} = G_1 V(x, t) + C_1 \frac{\partial V(x, t)}{\partial t} + G_2 \int_{-\infty}^{t} \exp\left[-\frac{G_2}{C_2}(t-t')\right]\frac{\partial V(x, t)}{\partial t'}dt'$$

(8)

Equations (7) and (8) are the two fundamental equations of the mathematical model for pulse propagation along the bit line of a ferrite core array as developed by Dutta Majumder and Das. They govern the propagation of pulses along the bit line. Equations (7) and (8) are expressed in time domain. To obtain the solution, these equations are converted into frequency domain by Fourier transformation. After transformation the equations reduce to

$$-\frac{d\bar{V}(x, \omega)}{dx} = Z(\omega)\bar{I}(x, \omega)$$

(9)

$$-\frac{d\bar{I}(x, \omega)}{dx} = Y(\omega)\bar{V}(x, \omega)$$

(10)

where

$$Z(\omega) = R_1 + j\omega L_1 + \frac{j\omega L_2 R_2}{R_2 + j\omega L_2}$$

and

$$Y(\omega) = G_1 + j\omega C_1 + \frac{j\omega C_2 G_2}{G_2 + j\omega C_2}$$

$Z(\omega)$ and $Y(\omega)$ are respectively the series impedance and shunt admittance per unit length of the bit line. The solutions of Equations (5) and (6) are well known from transmission line theory and the most general solution is

$$\bar{I}(x, \omega) = A(\omega) \exp\left[-\gamma(\omega) X + B(\omega) \exp\left[\gamma(\omega)X\right]\right.$$

(11)

and

$$\bar{V}(x, \omega) = Z_0(\omega) \{A(\omega) \exp\left[-\gamma(\omega)X\right] - B(\omega) \exp\left[\gamma(\omega)X\right]\}$$

(12)

where, $A(\omega)$ and $B(\omega)$ are arbitrary functions of ω. The quantities $\gamma(\omega)$ and $Z_0(\omega)$ are called respectively the propagation constant and characteristic impedance of the bit line. The transmission of pulses may be viewed from three points, namely, the attenuation which varies with the frequency, the degradation of the rising edges of the signal, and lastly, the increased delay. The expressions for these factors are standard and have been discussed in any textbook on transmission line.

However, the sense signal of a magnetic core memory system sustains various losses in the course of travel along the sense line. The losses are, attenuation in magnitude, distortion in phase due to reflection caused by interconnection of sense lines and deterioration of waveform due to cross coupling of word lines. The multiple reflections and deterioration can be expressed as a temporary sequence of travelling waves.

3.4.4 Effect of Cross Coupling and Memory Noise

In the design of core memory wiring, whenever two interconnections are near one another, it is possible for electric and magnetic coupling to give rise to spurious signals, known as *crosstalk*, causing malfunctioning of the system as a whole. After selection of the logic element to be used in the system, the degree of coupling and the length over which the two lines may run in proximity may be controlled to keep crosstalk below the appropriate level for that logic.

The capacitance between orthogonal lines in a memory array may be considered as an additional loading on the line, affecting characteristic impedance, wave velocity and attenuation of the line. Stray capacitance, due to the cross coupling of the sense and word lines, acts as drainage path of the electrostatic energy contained in the sense signal. It deteriorates the waveform, while delaying the pulse at the same time. In a large capacity memory, the sense line crosses numerous word lines. The capacitors, shunting the sense line, are shown schematically in Figure 3.17. The shunting branch has an impedance of $[(1/pC) + (Z_w/2)]$, where Z_w is the impedance of word line, which is quite low ($<50\ \Omega$). On the other hand, the term $1/pC$ has a value of the order of 10-1000 kilo-ohms for a 20 nsec rise time of the signal. Under these conditions and because of discontinuity, one can write the expression for transmission coefficient as

$$T = \frac{\dfrac{2}{\left\{\dfrac{1}{pC_c}+\dfrac{1}{Z_0}\right\}}}{\dfrac{Z_0+1}{\left\{\dfrac{1}{pC}+\dfrac{1}{Z_0}\right\}}} \simeq \frac{2/Z_0C_c}{p+2/Z_0C_c} \simeq \frac{a}{p+a} \tag{13}$$

where $a = \dfrac{2}{Z_0C}$.

The signal voltage at point b (Figure 3.17) due to discontinuities only is

$$V_b(p) = V_a(p)T^3 = V_a(p) \left(\frac{a}{p+a}\right)^3 \tag{14}$$

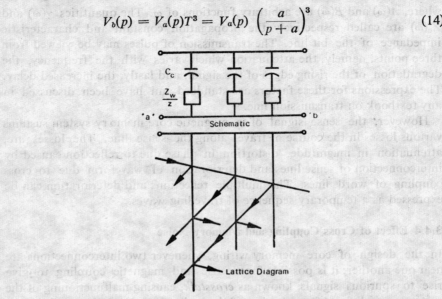

Schematic

Lattice Diagram

Figure 3.17 Equivalent representation of capacitive couplings shunting the sense line.

The reflections of second order and above are negligible. If there are crossing of n word lines, we have then

$$T^n = \left(\frac{a}{p+a}\right)^n \tag{15}$$

This factor should be included in calculating the waveform of the sense signal at the preamplifier.

For large scale memories, the value of cross coupling capacitor must be reduced. Due to this, the waveform is degraded approximately by a factor proportional to $C_c\sqrt{n}$. The value of this capacitance is equal to the product of dielectric constant and area/separation. The area cannot be reduced to a greater extent, because it is governed by the requirements of the line parameters. Therefore, a thick insulating layer between the word and sense line is often preferred.

The noise problem has been studied extensively by various authors and can be attributed largely to the departure of a core's hysteresis loop from the ideal rectangularity. During interrogation of a core in a $n \times n$ array, apart from the selected core, other $2n-2$ cores are also disturbed and produce half selected signals. Of these, n cores produce noise signal of one polarity while $(n-2)$ cores produce noise outputs of the opposite polarity. Grouped together, they comprise $(n-2)$ cancelling pairs, plus one noncancelling pair. For any one cancelling pair, the average difference in the half selected outputs is called *delta noise* voltage V_δ, and the outputs of the two cores of the noncancelling pair are called *half select noise voltage* and designated as V_{hs}. The delta noise and half select noise together comprise the disturbing noise in coincident current memory system. The effect of this noise on the selected output signal can be represented by

$$V_{\text{out}} = V_s - 2V_{hs} \pm (n-2) V_\delta \tag{16}$$

Apart from the above two sources, noise from magnetic and electrostatic pick-up from the row and column windings are also present. These noise signals include the emf induced in the s nse line by the drive windings and the voltage excursions due to capacitive couplings between the wires in the memory plane.

Considering the simplest linear select arrangement of the memory, the bit current passing through the core induces a back voltage $E(t)$ in the word line at the junction of a bit line and a word line. Thus, the core acts like a voltage generator, with output $E(t)$ in series with the word lines. Furthermore, at the intersection of the bit line with a word line, the bit and the word lines act like two plates of a capacitor and some shunt current $J(t)$ leaves the bit line and enters the word line. Thus the interaction acts like a current generator with output $J(t)$ placed in shunt with the word line. Thus, the transfer of noise from bit line to word line can be simulated by placing a voltage generator with output $J(t)$ in shunt with the word line. as shown in Figure 3.18.

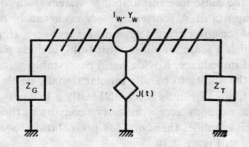

Figure 3.18   Noise transfer from bit to word line.

However, owing to different paths by which this coupling may take place, both amplitude and time of occurrence of these signals may vary, resulting in a differential output between the ends of the sense wire. This differential output may be reduced by suitable choice of winding arrangements for the cores in the array.

Ideally, this noise should be eliminated from the signal before amplification by putting the read strobe before the input to the sense amplifier. Discrimination between the '1' and '0' signals depends upon the peak amplitude and their time of occurrence. The variation in amplifier gain increases the amplitude range, and the variation in delay through the amplifier increases the uncertainty of timing. Although the time, when the output from an element storing a '1' is maximum, may be well defined, the limits are bound to be extended by the variation of the delay of the signals in the storage array.

3.4.5 Sense Amplifier Design Considerations

The function that the sense amplifier is to amplify the signals received by the sense winding, to an energy level suitable for detection of whether a 'one' or 'zero' datum state has been read. It must also drive the information control logic. Usually, the information is determined by amplitude-discrimination techniques—a 'one' signal being large and a 'zero' signal being small in amplitude. Frequently, the shorter time duration of the 'zero' signal is used to enhance the discrimination. There are two standard techniques that are employed individually or in combination to take advantage of this time difference. One is to strobe or gate the amplifier into operation after the 'zero' signal occurs. The other is to use an amplifier that has less amplification for predominant frequencies of the zero signals.

Although the sense amplifier may initially appear to be a straightforward circuit design problem, the designer usually faces many difficulties in reaching a satisfactory performance of the sense amplifier. In practice, the recovery time of the sense line and amplifier system from digit interference is even more important. A shorter memory cycle can be made possible by reducing the total sensing circuit delay and bit recovery times. The general requirements, which a sense amplifier must fulfil, include pattern sensitivity, controllable input impedance, a wide band pass, stable gain, high common mode rejection, the ability to handle bipolar signals, stable reference levels, a fast comparator, low threshold level, and lastly a low cost. A sense amplifier for use in a random access memory, consists of the sense line and a preamplifier which amplifies the signal for presentation to a discrimination element, as shown in Figure 3.19.

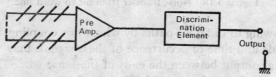

Figure 3.19   Block diagram of a typical sensing system.

The impedance that the amplifier presents to the sense winding must match the characteristic impedance in order to avoid reflections. This impedance is normally of the order 100-200 ohms. Also, the frequency response of the amplifier must be determined by the consideration of allowed signal delay and the distortion of the amplifier. Due to the amplifier delay, the input waveform attenuates and spreads, the extent of which is a function of the upper frequency response of the amplifier. Since the amplified signal is only concerned when the SNR of the amplifier is maximum, any amplifier delay will manifest itself in the overall memory timing cycle, i.e. the stored information will not be available to the buffer flip-flop until the delay Δt after the peaking time of the core has elapesd. Assuming the disturbed 'one' output of the memory core is equivalent to a half $(\sin)^2$ pulse, whose amplitude is equal to the amplitude of disturbed 'one' and whose width is equal to the width of the disturbed 'one' output measured at 10 per cent amplitude, Goldstick has calculated the signal delay through the amplifier which is a function of amplifier cut off frequency for a given pulse width of π/ω as

$$2\left(\frac{\omega}{\omega_c}\right)\exp[-\omega(\pi/2+\omega\Delta t)/\omega_c] + 2\frac{\omega}{\omega_c}\cos 2\omega\Delta t - \sin 2\omega\Delta t = 0 \quad (17)$$

The solution of the above equation is presented in normalized form in Figure 3.20.

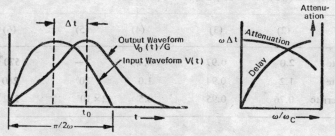

Figure 3.20   Pulse delay and attenuation as a function of amplifier cut-off frequency.

3.4.6   Temperature Effect

The dominant position of the ferrite core as a static memory device is due to its outstanding reliability and cost performance record. The essential requirements of a good magnetic material for fast, reliable, random access core memories are good squareness ratio and good thermal stability. The temperature problem in a ferrite core memories arises due to the energy that is applied for switching the cores. With the increase in temperature, the thermal motion of magnetic domains increases and this disturbs the alignment achieved by the exchange forces. This causes the domains to deviate from their direction of easy magnetization.

The stability of certain ferrite properties above the range of ambient temperature is of importance in computer memory operation. The temperature sensitivity of ferrite core has an inverse relationship to curie temperature which varies almost linearly with ferrite composition. The essential properties of memory cores are initial permeability, saturation magnetization, coercive force, switching coefficient and resistivity of the material. The resistivity of the magnetic material is primarily determined by the ion concentration and falls with rising temperature. These parameters are shown in Table 3.1 for various ferrite core materials. The switching constants given by the equation $S_w = \tau (H - H_0)$. The temperature coefficient of the threshold H_0, which is used as a measure of the temperature sensitivity of a ferrite composition, is defined as the average percentage change in the threshold per degree change in temperature between -50 and $100°C$. The variation of switching coefficient with temperature is shown in Figure 3.21. However, these parameters should be optimized before the ferrite material is used in memory applications.

TABLE 3.1

Various Ferrite Core Characteristics

Composition	Coercive force (Oe)	Squareness ratio B_r/B_m	Switching coefficient μsec-Oe	Resistivity ohm-cm	Curie temperature °C
(1)	(2)	(3)	(4)	(5)	(6)
Lithium ferrite	2.0	0.97	0.4	—	570
Mg-Mn ferrite	1.2	0.94	1.0	10^8	280
Zn-Mg-Mn ferrite	0.76	0.95	0.5	2×10^7	262

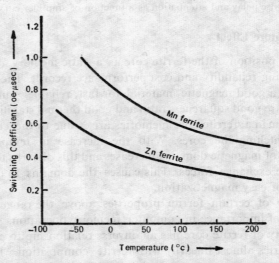

Figure 3.21   Switching coefficient as a function of temperature.

The internal heating of the core material causes a gradual decrease in magnetic properties of the core. This deterioration of magnetic properties increases the selection line impedance of the core memory and the transmission delay of the sense signal. The changes in magnetic properties are more prominent near the curie temperature of the core material.

The magnetic cores that are normally used in fast access memories are usually nickel ferrites and lithium ferrites having high curie temperatures approximately 600°C. The operating condition of such digital data handling devices is not temperature regulated, that is, in most cases there is no provision for temperature compensation of the driving currents. This might cause erroneous data transfer when sensing the memory. Usually the current tolerance limit of the coincident current memories is based on the following criteria:

(i)   Effective writing of ones.
(ii) Effective writing of zeros.
(iii) The limitation of inhibit current to a value less than the switching threshold current.
(iv) Similar limitation on the pair of read currents and on the pair of write currents.

These criteria, once again, depend on the disturb ratio. The temperature coefficient of disturb ratio is defined as the percentage change in drive current required to maintain a constant disturb ratio. Usually this varies from 0.45 to 0.65, depending on the material of the core and is a function of temperature and drive current, as shown in curves of Figure 3.22. Normally, for a ferrite core memory, the value of disturb ratio for a constant drive decreases with increasing temperature. This effect can be thought of, as if the minimum threshold current for switching decreases with increasing temperature. Under these circumstances, unless the drive currents are reduced to compensate the threshold current, the half selecting currents will result in more disturbing voltage from both the half selection of 'ones' and full selection of 'zeros'. This will affect the normal operation of the memory unit.

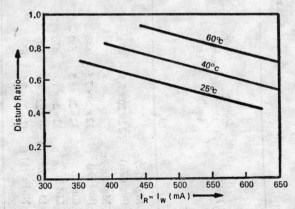

Figure 3.22   Disturb characteristic versus drive current at several temperatures.

TABLE 3.2

Summary of Memory Core Characteristics ($t_r = 0.1$ µsec and $t_d = 1.0$ µsec)

Ferrite	Dimensions (mil)	Drive current (mA)	'One' output voltage uV_1 (mV)	'Zero' output voltage dV_z (mV)	Peaking time t_p (µsec)	Switching time (µsec)	Disturb ratio	Temp. coeff. of disturb ratio %	Temp. coeff. of output voltage %	Stress sensitivity
Mg-Mn-Zn (high Zn)	32 × 20 × 7.5	450	40	5.0	0.25	0.50	0.62	0.68	0.36	Low
Mg-Mn-Zn (low Zn)	32 × 20 × 7.5	640	41	5.0	0.21	0.41	0.63	0.60	0.37	Low
Cu-Mn	32 × 20 × 6.5	650	43	5.0	0.22	0.38	0.64	0.63	0.42	Med
Li-Mn	32 × 20 × 10	630	43	6.5	0.29	0.53	0.63	0.11	0.11	Low
Li-Ni-Zn-Mn	30 × 22 × 7.5	550	50	4.5	0.27	0.49	0.64	0.45	0.23	High
Ni-Fe^{2+}+Mn	32 × 20 × 7.5	650	41.0	6.5	0.23	0.45	0.63	0.43	0.31	High

Data regarding the temperature sensitivity characteristics of ferrite materials usually include 'one' and 'zero' output voltages and the associated switching and peaking times, all these parameters varying as a function of temperature and are presented in Table 3.2. The temperature coefficient for output voltage is defined as the percentages in drive current required to maintain a constant uV_1 and is calculated to be 0.4. At room temperature the value of coercive force falls at rates from 0.3 to 3.0% per °C, depending on the ferrite material. In such cases, a 10 to 20°C rise is often sufficient to impair the discrimination in a large store owing to subsequent reduction in coercive force value which increases the flux change in cores subjected to half drive pulses.

The duration of the read/write pulses is so chosen as to be enough to cover the full switching time of the core materials. It is usually taken to be 1.5 times the nominal switching time of the core materials and further decreases with increasing temperature. Hence, for optimum S/N ratio, the sense amplifier requires further adjustment due to fluctuation of temperature.

Hence for successful operation of magnetic core memories either the operation of memory at higher temperature is avoided or compensation by the addition of a temperature sensitive element to the current driving circuits is provided, and this element should be located in the same environment as the storage core. Sometimes high efficiency cooling method is devised, based on total immersion of the memory in an inert fluorochemical substance. Heat is transferred from the flourochemical liquid to the outside environment by a watercooled head exchanger.

3.4.7 Properties and Choice of Cores

Earlier work in the development of miniature ferrite core had been directed toward very high performance partial switching devices for word oriented memory. The emphasis was then placed on material development of square loop toroids having switching time of approximately 50 nsec when operated in a three dimensional mode. The requirements for smaller faster cores presented great challenges to the ferrite industry since core specifications have become more critical and higher coercivity materials are required to achieve these objectives. These challenges have been met but generally at the cost of a lower yield.

The commercial cores that are now available in the market can be classified into two broad groups: (i) temperature insensitive but slow switching time like Li, and Li-Ni ferrites, and (ii) fast switching but temperature sensitive cores like Cu-Mn and Mg-Mn ferrites. The properties of these cores are functions of their: (i) material composition, (ii) polycrystalline structure, and (iii) porosity and the pore structure. The manufacture of ferrite is rather straightforward in principle. Using conventional core manufacturing technique, granulated ferrite powder mixed with binder is pressed into a grain core, which after a subsequent firing treatment obtains its memory core characteristics. Points (ii) and (iii) require a very consistent high grain density throughout each core. Particularly for smaller cores this consistency is difficult to obtain in high volume production. Rigorous core grading assures the required quality but at the cost of decreased yield.

Although chemical principles described above are not so difficult, there are several complicating factors, such as atmosphere of the furnace, course of the reaction, etc. The course of the reaction will be influenced by particle size, intimacy of mixture, percentage and nature of impurities, and the way in which heating is carried out. Table 3.3 indicates the effect of the firing temparature on magnetic properties. The switching coefficient does not apparently change appreciably with firing temperature but the threshold field, coercive force, and switching time depend largely on the firing temperature.

TABLE 3.3

The Effect of Firing Temperature on Magnetic Properties

Firing tempe- rature (°C)	Switching coeffi- cient S_w (Oe-μsec)	Threshold field H_0 (Oe)	Coercive force H_c (Oe)	Drive current (mA)	Peak output voltage uV_1 (mV)	Peak disturb voltage dV_z (mV)	Peaking time t_p (μsec)	Switch- ing time (μsec)
1125	0.42	2.60	2.70	505	52	7	0.20	0.40
1180	0.45	2.24	2.46	485	52	6	0.21	0.43
1250	0.40	2.10	2.06	355	34	5	0.31	0.66
1320	0.42	1.55	1.43	280	26	4	0.39	0.88

The most desirable feature in a square-loop ferrite, however, is high saturation magnetization, small coercive force, and a value of squareness ratio as near to unity as possible. A high saturation magnetization gives a large separation between the two magnetization states. With a small value of coercive force, a correspondingly small drive current is needed for read/ write operation. High squareness ratio is required to define the state of magnetization with a fair degree of accuracy. Another characteristic of the ferrites responsible for high speed storage applications is its resistivity. The value of resistivity is of the order of 10^5 ohm-cm, as a result of which the eddy current losses remain negligible. At present lithium and lithium-manganese cores seem to be the best compromise for most of the digital computer applications. Also, the crystalline structure of lithium ferrite is such that it gives stable magnetic properties over a wide range of tempera-ture. But the major disadvantage of presentday lithium ferrites is an increase in the value of coercive force over those of manganese-magnesium ferrites which leads to a higher drive requirements.

Advances in manufacturing techniques have made it possible to produce ferrite memory cores having wide range of sizes and switching time requirements. The selection of cores for computer memory application requires consideration of several factors. The first factor is the switching time of the core material. It helps the core to switch fast enough to allow the required cycle time. The ratio of core switching time to the total cycle time depends on the memory size and its organization. Usually the ratios 1/4 to 1/6 are suitably used in 3D systems and 1/3 for $2\frac{1}{2}$D system.

The other important considerations in selecting the core are drive currents and voltages and signal-to-noise ratio. These factors are all interdependent, and the limitations fixed for them are strongly influenced by the size of the memory. The signal-to-noise ratio is determined by the 'one' signal amplitude and the 'delta noise'. *The delta noise is also a function of the core plane and the core characteristics.* For selecting a core for high speed large capacity storage, the entire memory stack should be treated as a transmission line rather than a lumped inductance. The current itself then becomes the dominant factor. The temperature sensitivity of the core material is also an important factor, because with increase in temperature both the saturation flux density and the coercive force decrease. Normally the use of a material exhibiting a low rate of change of coercive force with temperature will be an advantage.

When a core type has been tentatively selected, it is desirable to compare the manufacturer's recommended operating conditions against the measured core characteristics. The nomograph of Figure 3.23 has been suitably used to select the cores along with their characteristics for a particular memory design.

The curves show the core switching time versus the recommended full drive currents of the various core materials. When two of the variables are

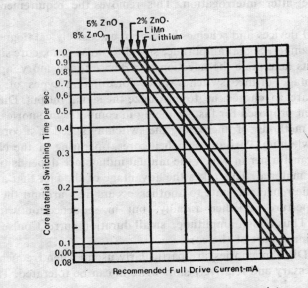

Figure 3.23   Core characteristics for different material composition.

known or chosen, the third can be determined from the graph by use of straight edge. Conceptually, the method of making modern memories faster is to select smaller cores. Signal-to-noise ratio does not deteriorate when core size is reduced, because delta noise, which is produced by half selected cores, can be reduced in proportion to signal output, and lower drive voltages and the line delays reduce spurious couplings thus generating less noise.

3.5 NONDESTRUCTIVE READOUT TECHNIQUES

The advantages of high speed nondestructive readout (NDRO) memories in present day computer system prompted studies to determine the potential of ferrite technology for such an application. Ferrite memory cores are used in computer memory in both destructive (DRO) and nondestructive (NDRO) readout mode of operation. Usually in DRO mode, the readout is accomplished by a clear or reset pulse, while in the NDRO mode, the readout of information is carried out by an interrogating pulse. Most ferrite core memories are of DRO type, and hence they require a subsequent write operation to restore the original information. In NDRO mode the data are not destroyed during readout, with the subsequent advantage that the write portion of memory cycle is not necessary.

Two types of nondestructive readout memories are available. In the first type, called read-only (ROM), the information is mechanically written by threading wires, punching holes, or cutting wires by some relatively permanent means. In the second type, electronically alterable, the information is written into the memory in a manner similar to the DRO memory. Reading is also performed as in the DRO case, but the magnetic disturbance produced by the read current is self-reversible, that is, the element returns to its initial state after interrogation. This removes the requirement of a restore cycle.

Ferrite NDRO devices and schemes have been extensively catalogued and analyzed by Holzinger. Signal amplitude, signal-to-noise ratio, core size and drive requirements determine the selection of a device for memory application. The percentage of flux switches varies for different types of cores. Drive currents are so chosen as to maximize the signal output. Different schemes have been proposed for fast switching in computer memories. One of the simplest methods of increasing the switching speed of a core is to employ partial switching. Partially switched cores, operating in the NDRO mode, act as transformer in which the mutual inductance depends on flux state of the core material. This takes the advantage of the fact that a core-switching from one remanent state to another occurs first around the inner surface of its aperture and then rapidly, but in sequence outward, in concentric rings. Thus a high amplitude, small duration current pulse may switch only the inner part of the core.

In general, NDRO memories are particularly useful when frequent and rapid read is necessary and relatively slow write-in can be tolerated. This is the case in a number of applications ranging from data processors, in which the ratio of readouts to write-in may be typically 4 or 5, to applications which are essentially read only. This is the case, for example, for an airborne memory to be set on the ground and frequently readout on flight. A brief outline of different techniques employed for NDRO scheme is presented in this section.

3.5.1 Mechanism of Core Switching

To discuss the topic of flux reversal, it is convenient to consider the hysteresis loop of the toroid. We will limit the discussion here to *thin walled* toroid, so that the applied field is effectively uniform over the toroid. The dynamic behaviour of the magnetic toroid is observed by subjecting the toroid to current pulses of alternate polarity. The plot of the reciprocal of switching time against the applied field, as shown in Figure 3.24, often shows three distinguished regions, in each of which an approximately linear relation applies, i.e., the curve of $1/\tau$ against H can be divided into three nearly linear segments. The division is not always very clearly defined. It appears to be best demonstrated by plotting the switching coefficient against the field on a logarithmic scale, as in Figure 3.24b for a number of ferrites. The regions are designated as I, II and III in order of increasing fields, and are attributed due to the effect of wall motion, nonuniform rotation and uniform rotation phenomena.

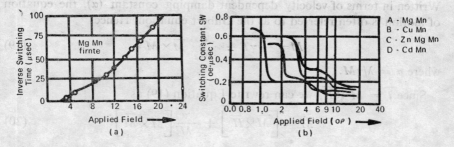

Figure 3.24 Plot of switching time against the applied field showing three distinct values.

Manyuk and Goodenough formulated the domain wall motion model of flux reversal which occurs when drive field is slightly larger than the coercive force of the material. The domain walls are usually of the bloch type and the energy required to form the domain walls can be broken into three parts namely:

(i) Exchange energy associated with the misalignment of the spins against exchange forces.

(ii) Anisotropy energy resulting from the rotation of the spins against the anisotropy fields and the magnetoelastic fields.

(iii) Demagnetizing field energy resulting from the additional field energy caused by divergence of the magnetization of the wall.

The second threshold appears at some value of drive field from two to five times the wall motion threshold. In this intermediate drive region, a non-uniform rotational model was proposed by Gyorgy for the flux reversal in magnetic cores which allowed the magnetization to rotate in such a manner that the effects of the boundary can be neglected. For the third linear portion of switching curve, a reversal mechanism of coherent rotational model, suggesetd by Conger and Essig and later by Kikuchi, provides the best explanation of the experimental observations.

A theory of dynamic behavior of magnetization vectors requires introduction of equation of motion. The first such equation was given by Landau and Lifshits and is given by

$$\bar{M} = -\lambda \bar{T} - \frac{\lambda}{M_s^2} \cdot \bar{M} \times \bar{T} \tag{18}$$

where λ is the phenomenological damping constant with dimensions $\sec^{-1}$ and $\bar{M}$ is the magnetization vector. For small damping, the torque is approximately $T = -[1/\gamma]\bar{M}$. The gyromagnetic ratio γ is very nearly equal to the value for free electrons 1.76×10^7 (Oe sec)$^{-1}$. Thus, the damping term is approximately equal to

$$\left\{ \frac{\lambda}{\gamma M^2} \right\} \cdot \bar{M} \times \bar{M}$$

Written in terms of velocity dependent damping constant (α), the equation of motion is often referred to as the Gilbert equation. Hence

$$\bar{M} = -\gamma \bar{T} + \frac{\alpha}{M_s} \bar{M} \times \bar{M} \tag{19}$$

where $\alpha = \lambda/\gamma M$.

Since $\bar{T} = \bar{M} \times \bar{H}$, we can rewrite Equation (19) as

$$\bar{M} = \left[\bar{M} \times \bar{H} \right] + \frac{\alpha}{M_s} \left[\bar{M} \times \bar{M} \right] \tag{20}$$

where $\bar{H}$ is the total magnetic field acting on the magnetization vector. Here we have neglected the crystalline anisotropy fields, strain fields and the field arising from imperfections in magnetic materials. The term α is the damping constant and is a measure of the rate of energy dissipation.

Equation (20) is solved to predict the various flux reversal processes. At low drive fields, imperfections and crystalline boundaries play an important part in the flux reversal process and the magnetic field arising from these effect should be included in Equation (20).

In the incoherent rotation model, it is assumed that magnetization rotates uniformly and as a result, the surface poles arising from the discontinuity at the boundary would give rise to a large demagnetizing effect. The surface poles form a helical pattern with a spacing of λ. In fact, the threshold field for this type of rotation is about 10^3 Oe, three orders of magnitude higher than the threshold fields usually encountered experimentally.

For high speed operation, the most desirable remagnetization process is uniform or coherent rotation. This process, to a good approximation, can be described in terms of the phenomenological theory proposed by Landau and Lifshitz and modified by Gilbert.

The interaction of demagnetizing fields has been suggested by Shevel and Gyorgy for the third region of switching curve. The ferrite toroids have been approximated to hollow cylinders of decreasing radii and of infinite length. The flux configuration is helical with a small radial component. The magnetization in each cylinder is independent of magnetization in the other cylinders. This helical mode of flux is an approximate solution of the equation of motion.

Returning back to the domain wall motion model, the reversal time is approximately equal to the average distance through which a wall must move before colliding with neighbouring wall divided by the average wall velocity. The velocity of the walls depends linearly on the applied field, and the model, suggested by Menyuk and Goodenough, leads to a linear relationship between the reciprocal of switching time and applied field. They assumed that the number of walls nucleated was independent of the applied field, for fields larger than the threshold for switching. Using the general equation of motion, they obtained the expression for switching time as

$$\tau = \frac{<d>}{v} = \frac{\alpha <d>}{2\gamma H_a < \cos\theta >} \cdot \left(\frac{K}{A}\right)^{1/2} \tag{21}$$

where v is the average domain wall velocity; $<d>$ is the average distance through which a wall moves before colliding with another wall and $< \cos\theta >$ represents average of cosine of the angle between the applied field and the initial magnetization. However, as shown by Goodenough, the average distance $<d>$ is approximately equal to the average grain size of the material. A variation of grain size of ferrites from 2×10^{-4} cm to 1.5×10^{-1} cm only produced a variation in switching coefficient from 0.3 to 0.7 Oe-μsec.

In the second region of the switching curve, the important experimental observation is that the switching coefficient is relatively independent of the material under consideration. Ferrites of a wide selection of chemical compositions, garnets and permalloy tapes have switching coefficients of about 0.2 Oe-μsec. The expression for switching coefficient according to incoherent rotational model is

$$\tau H_a = \frac{\alpha^2 + 1}{\alpha\gamma} \ln\frac{1+f}{1-f} = S_w \tag{22}$$

with the condition that $M_z/M_s = f$, at $t = 0$ and $M_z/M_s = -f$ at $t = \tau$. The exact value of switching coefficient depends on the value of f which is determined by the initial conditions. However, under normal experimental conditions, the logarithmic factor in Equation (22) is about 2, and the minimum value of S_w, as predicted by this nonuniform model is 0.2 Oe-μsec which is in favourable agreement with experimental value observed in this region.

But the equation for switching time in a nonuniform rotational model does not specify the threshold field for such switching. This discrepancy is, perhaps, the result of neglecting the crystalline anisotropy of the individual grains. For ferrite toroid having a small cross-sectional radius, the value of exchange field is small and can be neglected. Thus, putting the value of applied field and damagnetizing field in Equation (20), we can arrive at the equation of motion of the helical mode which is identical to the equation of motion derived by Kikuchi for the case of isotropic thin film. For smaller value of damping, the switching coefficient in this coherent rotational mode can be written as

$$S_w = \frac{\alpha}{\gamma} \ln \frac{1+f}{1-f} \tag{23}$$

The lowest value of S_w reported in this third region of the switching curve is 0.04 Oe-μsec and the corresponding value of the damping parameter is 0.35. This uniform rotational model gives a relatively satisfactory explanation for the existence of high speed switching.

3.5.2 Various Classes of NDRO Scheme

The different types of NDRO stores for various applications that have been reported so far can be grouped in two broad classes, namely, those which can only have their information content changed by mechanical means and those which can have the information altered by electrical means. The second category can again be divided into two subgroups, viz. those which retain their information when the power is interrupted, and those which lose their data when the power is interrupted. The NDRO stores of the former class are all based on magnetic principles, while those of the latter class use bistable circuits with active devices. In the present discussion we are interested in the first kind of NDRO stores, that is, one which is based on magnetic principle.

3.5.2.1 QUADRATURE FIELD METHOD

One class of nondestructive readout method uses a magnetic field at right angles to the direction of the flux that stores the information, as shown in Figure 3.25a. A field of this nature will cause a change in direction of magnetization without switching the core irreversibly. The effect of this quadrature field is simply to rotate the direction of magnetization without causing appreciable change in the magnitude of the flux. The component of flux along the principal axis of the core is thus reduced. The polarity of this flux change will indicate the nature of stored information. Thus, an output winding coupled to this principal field will produce either a small positive voltage or a small negative voltage, depending upon the stored information. The mechanism of flux change in this method does not involve domain wall movement which is practicable. Thus, for fast rise time the outputs may be quite large in amplitude.

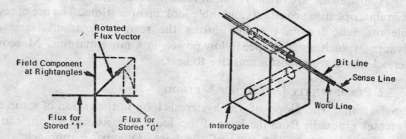

Figure 3.25a   Effect of quadrature field.   Figure 3.25b   Biax store element.

The difficult problem in this method is the generation of the interrogating or quadrature field. The method works when the core is mounted in the gap of an electromagnet, but this is hardly practicable for large memories. Other methods which are suggested include a hollow toroid inside which lies an interrogation winding and a block of ferrite containing holes at right angles.

Biax memory element, as shown in Figure 3.25b, was first proposed by Wanless in 1959. These memories provide truly nondestructive readout which significantly enhances system performance and reliability. The memory element consists of a block of pressed square loop ferrite material having two orthogonal nonintersecting holes. Of the two holes, the one hole called storage hole, acts like normal toroid to store '1' or '0' by clockwise or anticlockwise direction of magnetization and information is written into the storage hole by normal coincident technique. The readout characteristics of the element are derived from flux interference in the common volume of magnetic material located between the two orthogonal holes as shown in Figure 3.25b. Writing into the memory element is accomplished by passing current pulses through the large hole, while the binary state of the element is determined by the polarity of the remanent flux around the storage hole. This stored information can be detected by the interaction between this stored flux and a changing flux around the other hole. The reversible interaction of these two interfering flux paths is utilized in the biax memory element to produce a true NDRO capability.

During the read operation flux shuttling action results in a temporary reorientation of the magnetic domains within the shared magnetic material in such a way that the domains favour the interrogate flux path at the expense of the information storage flux. This increase in the interrogate flux causes a corresponding decrease in the magnitude of the flux around the storage hole. The decrease of the storage hole flux is absolute in magnitude and is independent of flux polarity. Therefore, the induced voltage in the sense line is positive for one polarity of storage flux and negative for the other polarity. This positive or negative polarity of the induced voltage indicates the binary state of the stored information.

Biax memories are ideally suited for the storage of subroutines, microprograms, operating constants and table look up operations. The use of reversible magnetic domain rotation during the read mode results in several advantages such as high speed, low power, low noise margins. Moreover, these elements are almost insensitive to heat.

3.5.2.2 Permeability Difference Method

The fact, that the slope of the hysteresis loop in the region of saturation decreases gradually from the knee of the loop towards saturation, can be utilized to determine the state of the core. One basic approach was to apply read field in the direction that would ordinarily switch the core to the zero state, but restrict the amplitude to an amount that would cause only reversible flux changes. Information could be sensed owing to the nonlinear and asymmetric characteristics of the upper and lower relatively horizontal regions of the hysteresis loop. One of the first contributions by Harrison and others using this scheme, made use of cores as a frequency mixing device where two drive frequencies are mixed by the nonlinear characteristics, and the phase of the difference frequency would be either 0 or 180 degrees, depending on the information state of the core.

The above scheme is not very practical owing to the need for elaborate drive and output circuits in addition to the normal pulse drive circuits. Another method suggested by Perry and Widrow using pulse drives rather than sine waves, appears to be more promising. In this method they used a pair of cores for each digit stored, because the direct discrimination of the core state by comparison of outputs resulting from small drives towards saturation and towards the knee of the loop is not feasible. When reading nondestructively, a read pulse of insufficient amplitude to cause significant irreversible flux change, is applied in the same direction as the read pulse in the conventional reading system. In this case, however, the difference of the reversible flux changes in the two cores will appear on the output wire. These flux changes are comparatively small, but an output voltage of a few millivolts can be obtained from a read pulse with a fast rise time.

The NDRO with conventional square loop toroid can be accomplished with permeability sensing. This technique recognizes that permeability for reversible flux changes in the core is higher for the partially switched state than for the fully switched states.

Partially switched cores operating in the NDRO mode act as transformers in which the mutual inductance depends on the flux state of the core material. Writing to this partially switched state is accomplished with conventional coincident techniques where the drive amplitude and duration must be controlled to achieve the desired degree of switching. The low permeability state is the zero remanent state. Nondestructive read is accomplished with a current pulse that is below the switching threshold of the device. It generates an output signal that is proportional to permeability. Signal-to-noise ratios of three to one have been predicted and ratios of two to one are realized in practice.

This one core per bit organization offers a poor signal to noise ratio, moreover, the pulse width and amplitude tolerances of the drivers affect the percentage of flux switched and can, therefore, cause the high permeability state to be less than maximum. Manufacturing tolerances on device size and threshold are another source of 'one' and 'zero' signal variation. These drawbacks to some extent can be removed by using a two core per bit technique. When reading the storage cell, each core develops an output signal proportional to its permeability state. The drive current may be bipolar or unipolar. For unipolar digit drives, the 'one' signal is the difference between the partially switched and the remanent state output voltage, while the 'zero' signal is determined by the unbalance between the remanent states. For bipolar digit drives, bipolar 'one' and 'zero' sense voltages result.

The NDRO sense voltage from a two core per bit cell is dependent on, among other things, the clear pulse amplitude. The optimum clear pulse amplitude is dependent upon whether the cancellation core has been partially switched in a previous store cycle as is the case with a bipolar digit drive.

References

Agajanian, A.H. (1970): 'Li-Mn ferrites for high speed computer memory applications', *IEEE Trans. on Magnetics*, V. MAG-6, No. 1, pp. 90-95.

Ahemiya, H. et al. (1964): 'A 10^5 bit high speed ferrite core memory system design and operation', *AFIPS Conf. Proc.*, V. 25.

Baba, P.D. (1965): 'Non-magnetic inclusions in ferrites for high speed switching', *J. American Ceramic Soc.*, V. 48, pp. 305-309.

Benda, O. and Slama, J. (1968): 'A contribution to partially switching of square loop ferrite cores', *IEEE Trans. on Magnetics*, V. MAG-4, Sept. p. 586.

Betts, R. and Bishop, G. (1961): 'Ferrite toroid core circuit analysis', *IRE Trans. on Electronic Computers*, V. EC-10, March, pp. 51-55.

Brown, D.A.H. (1959): 'Approximate methods for calculating the behavior of square loop magnetic cores in circuits', *Electronic Engineering*, V. 31, p. 408.

Chapman, F.W., et al. (1964): 'Variation with temperature of the magnetocrystalline anisotropy of several nickel iron ferrites', *J. Appl. Phys.*, V. 35, No. 3, p. 1063.

Chen, T.C. and Papoulis. A. (1961): 'Terminal properties of magnetic cores', *Proc. IRE*, V. 46, No. 5, pp. 839-849.

Ching, S.W.F. and Stram, O.B. (1968): 'Nonlinear analysis of ferrite core circuits', *Proc. IEEE.*, V. 56, No. 12.

Connolly, J.B. (1966): 'Cross coupling in a high speed digital system', *IEEE Trans. on Electronic Computers*, V. EC-15, No. 3, p. 323.

Cooke, P. and Dillistone, D.C. (1962): 'The measurement and reduction of noise in coincident current core memories', *Proc. IEE.*, V. 109, pp. 383-389.

Eggenberger, J.S. (1960): 'Distributed parameter aspects of core memory wiring', *Proc. of the Conf. on Nonlinear Magnetics*, October.

Forrester, J.W. (1951): 'Digital information storage in three dimensions using magnetic cores', *J. Appl. Phys.*, V. 22, pp. 44-48.

Freeman, J.R. (1954): 'Pulse response of ferrite core memories', *IRE WESCON Convention Record*, pp. 50-61.

Galt, J.K. (1954): 'Motion of individual domain walls in a nickel iron ferrites', *Bell System Tech. J.*, V. 33, September, pp. 1023-1054.

Greene, F.S. Jr. (1966): 'An automatic ferrite core tester', *Computer Design*, April.

Gilligan, T.J. (1965): 'High speed ferrite $2\frac{1}{2}$D memory system', *Fall Joint Computer Conf.*, pp. 1011-1021.

Gilligan, T.J. (1966): '$2\frac{1}{2}$D high speed memory systems—past, present and future', *IEEE Trans. on Electronic Computer*, V. EC-13, No. 4, p. 475.

Geisselhardt, W. (1970): 'History effect of ferrite cores as analog storage element', *IEEE Trans. on Magnetics*, V. MAG-6, No. 3, September.

Gogos, B. and Zagursky, J.J. (1967): 'Ferrite device characteristics and coincident current store performance', *IEEE Trans. on Magnetics*, V. MAG-3, September, pp. 307-310.

Gogos, B. and Probst, R.E. (1968): 'An investigation of delta noise in square loop ferrites', *IEEE Trans. on Magnetics*, V. MAG-4, No. 3, September.

Gray, J.H. (1976): *High speed digital memories and circuits* (Advances in Modern Engineering Series), Addison—Wesley, New York.

Gyorgy, E.M. (1958): 'Modified rotational model of flux reversal', *J. Appl. Phys.*, V. 29, p. 1710.

Haynes, M.K. (1957): 'A model for nonlinear flux reversals of square loop polycrystalline magnetic cores', *AIEE Conf. on Magnetism and Magnetic Materials* (Washington DC.) November.

Hesterman, V.W (1965): 'Switching properties of a partially set square loop ferrite cores', *IEEE Trans. on Magnetics*. V. MAG-1, December, pp. 309-314.

Im, H.B. (1974): 'A note on the magnetistrictives ringing in core memory system', *IEEE Trans. on Magnetics.*, V. MAG-10, No. 1, p. 93.

Im, H.B. and Wickham, D.G. (1972): 'Memory core characteristics of cobalt substituted lithium ferrite', *IEEE Trans. on Magnetics.*, V. MAG-8, No. 4, p. 765.

Im, H.B. and Wickham D.G. (1973): 'Magnetostrictive ringing in substituted lithium ferrite memory cores', *1973 INTERMAG Conf.* (Paper 28.7).

Kittel, C. and Galt, J.K. (1956): 'Ferromagnetic domain theory' in *Solid State Physics*, Series III, Academic Press, New York, pp. 483.

Kiseda, J.R., et al. (1961): 'A magnetic associative memory', *IBM J. Res. and Devol.*, V.5, No. 2, April.

Kmetz, A.R. and Barkar, R.C. (1968): 'Threshold switching delayed response in ferrite memory cores', *IEEE Trans. on Magnetics*, V.MAG-4, No. 3, September.

Kobayashi, S. and Torri, M. (1966): '12 mils ferrite cores for computer memories', *IEEE Trans. on Magnetics*, V. MAG-2, pp. 608-610.

Koehler, H.F. and Covaleski, J.F. (1967): 'Speed capabilities of ferrite cores in NDRO operation', *IEEE Trans. on Magnetics*, V.MAG-3, September, pp. 311-315.

Koppel, R.L. (1958): 'A transistor driven magnetic core memory using non-coincident current technique', National Symposium on Telemetering.

Lindsey, C.H. (1959): ' The square loop ferrite core as a circuit element', *Proc. IEEE*, V. 106C, February, p. 117.

Macmahon, R.E. (1958): 'Linear selection, core memory techniques using transistors', Digest of Tech. Papers, Transistors and Solid State Circuit Conf., 1958.

Maiwald, W. (1970): 'The stapelblock—a novel technique of manufacturing highly reliable ferrite core memory stack', *IEEE Trans. on Magnetics*, V. MAG-6, No. 3.

Mckay, R.W. (1959): 'Reversible component of magnetisation', *J. Appl. Phys.*, V.30, pp. 56-57.

Mckay, R.W. and Smith, K.C. (1960): 'Effect of previous history on switching rate in ferrites', *J. Appl. Phys.*, V.31S, pp. 311-314.

McNamara, F. (1957): 'The noise problem in a coincident current core memory', *IRE Trans. on Instrumentation*, V.6, June, pp. 153-156.

McQuillan, J.P.R. (1962): 'The design problems of a Megabit storage matrix for use in a high speed computer', *IRE Trans. on Electronic Computers*, V.EC-11, pp. 390.

Menyuk, N. and Goodenough, J. (1956): 'Magnetic materials for digital computer components—I. A theory of flux reversal in polycrystalline ferrites', *J. Appl. Phys.*, V.26, pp. 8-18.

Meyerhoff, A.J. (1960): Digital application of magnetic devices, New York, John Wiley.

Moore, D.W. (1966): 'A cost/performance analysis of integrated circuit core memories" *AFIPS Conf. Proc.*, V. 29, (Fall Joint Com. Conf.) p. 267.

Neeteson, P. (1964): 'Square loop core ferrite switching', Philips Tech. Library.

Neeteson, P. (1961): 'Analysis of ferrite core switching for practical application', *Electronic Applications*, V.20, February, pp. 135-152.

Nitzan, D. (1963): 'Flux switching in overdriven multipath cores', *J. Appl. Phys.*, V.34, No. 4, April.

Nitzan, D. and Hesterman, V.W. (1967): 'Elastic flux switching properties of a thin ferrite core', *J. Appl. Phys.*, V.38, No. 3, March.

Papian, W.N. (1952): 'A coincident current magnetic memory cell for the storage of digital information', *Proc. IRE*, V.40, pp. 475-478.

Peloschek, H.P. (1962): 'Square loop ferrites and their applications', *Progress in dielectrics*, V. 5, pp. 39.

Petschauer, R.J. (1965): 'Large capacity low cost core memory', IFIP Congress, New York.

Quartly, C.J. (1959): 'A high speed ferrite storage system', *Electronic Engineering*, December, p. 756.

Rajchman, J.A. (1961): 'Computer memories—A survey of the state of the art', *Proc. IRE*, V.49, pp. 104-127.

Reese Brown, J. (1966): 'First and second order ferrite memory core characteristics and their relationship to system performance, *IEEE Trans. on Electronic Computers*, V. EC-15, No. 4, pp. 485-501.

Reichard, R.W. and Jordan J.F. Jr. (1968): 'A compact economical core memory with all monolithic electronics', *Spring Joint Comp. Conf.*, V.32, p. 253.

Rhodes, W.H. and Russell, L.A. et al., (1961): 'A 0.7 microsecond ferrite core memory', *IBM J. Res. and Devol.*, V.5, p. 174.

Riley, W.B. (1971): *Electronic computer memory technology*, New York, McGraw-Hill.

Sacks, I.J. (1969): 'Thermal hysteresis in ferrite memory cores', *IEEE Trans. on Magnetics*, V. MAG-5, No. 2, June.

Schwabe, E.A, and Campbell, D.A. (1963): 'Influence of grain size on square loop pro - perties of lithium ferrite', *J. Appl. Phys.*, V.34, pp. 1251.

Shahan, V.T. and Gutwin, D.A. (1962): 'Threshold properties of partially switched ferrite cores', *J. Appl. Phys.*, V.33, pp. 1049-1050.

Shevel, W.L. (1966): 'Ferrite core memory—a status report', *IEEE Trans. on Magnetics*, V.MAG-2, pp. 608.

Smit, J. and Wijn, H.P.J. (1959): *Ferrites*, New York, John Wiley.

Stacey, F.D. (1959): 'Thermal activation of ferromagnetic domains', *Proc. Phys. Society* (London), V.73, p. 136.

Stoughton, A.M. (1968): 'Computer controlled memory testing', *Modern Data System*, August.

Sweet, M.E. (1963): 'Temperature dependence of domain wall creep', *Proc. 9th. Conf. on Magnetism and Magnetic Materials*, p. 814.

Tancrell, R.H. (1960): 'Impulse selection for core logic', *Conf. on Magnetism and Magnetic Materials*, November.

Tencrell, R.H. and McMahon, R.E. (1960): 'Studies in partial switching of ferrite cores', *J. Appl. Phys.*, V.31, May, p. 762.

Tabble, R.S. and Craik, D.J. (1969): *Magnetic Materials*, New York, John Wiley.

Tusi, F.S. (1962): 'Improving the performance of sense amplifier circuit through preamplification strobing and noise matched clipping', *IEEE Trans. on Electronic Comp.*, V.EC-11, October, pp. 677-683.

Wanlass, C.L. and Wanlass, S.D. (1959): 'Biam high speed magnetic computer elements', *IRE WESCON Conv. Rec.*, pt. 4, p. 54.

Weber, G.H. (1970): 'Advanced methods of producing ferrite memory cores', *IEEE Trans. on Magnetics*, V.MaG-6, No. 3, September.

Weeks, W.T. (1963): 'Computer simulation of the electrical properties of memory arrays, *IEEE Trans. on Elect, Computers*, V.EC-12, December, pp. 874-887.

Weiss, R.S. and Brown, D.L. (1960): 'Square loop properties of copper manganese ferrites', *J. Appl. Phys.*, V.31, p. 2695.

Wiechec, W. (1968): 'New technologies for production of ferrite cores', *IEEE Trans. on Magnetics*, V.MAG-4, September, pp. 465-467.

Werner, G.E. and Whalen, R.M. (1966): 'A 110 nsec ferrite core memory', *IEEE Trans. on Magnetics*, V.MAG-2 September, p. 440.

Werner, G.E. and Whalen, R.M. (1965): 'A 375 nsec main memory system utilising 7 mils cores', *AFIPS Conf. Proc.*, V.27, Part I, p. 985.

Womack, C.P. (1965): 'Schmco plot analysis of coincident current memory systems', *IEEE Trans. on Electronic Computer*, E.VC-14, February, pp. 36-44.

Yao, F.C. (1966): 'Propagation of sense signals in large scale magnetic thin film memory', *IEEE Trans. on Electronic Computer*, V.EC-15, No. 4, p. 468.

4. SPECIAL FERRITE DEVICES

As a random access storage element the advantages of square loop ferrites over the other known devices are well-known. The driving of a core memory by magnetic switch was shown to be based on transfer of flux from the switch core to the memory cores by means of electrical flux linkages. This concept can be generalized to direct geometrical transfer of magnetic flux between branches of cores having multiple flux paths. In fact, the possibility of simplifying ferrite core logic circuitry by using complex flux patterns in multiaperture geometries resulted in the development of a number of new magnetic circuit elements. Cores with more than one aperture have been called by various names: the multiaperture cores, MADs, multileg cores, multipath cores. These devices have broad utility for many switching and storing functions. All the characteristics of the multiaperture devices are not be presented here; only some of their applications in memories and logic circuits are discussed.

These multiaperture geometries which provide several distinct flux paths within one device generally fall, more or less, into two classes or types: *transfluxors* and *laddics*. One of the most important properties of the transfluxor is its ability to store a level of control established by a single electric pulse. An array of transfluxors can be used as a random access memory with so called nondestructive readout (NDRO) mode of operation. Moreover, the possibility of simultaneous reading and writing in two unrelated addresses of a transfluxor store provides a higher speed of operation and simplifies the logic of some types of computing machines. The other geometrical structures, called laddics, provide a simple means of generating the elementary Boolean functions. The attractive features of logic ultilizing these elements are its low cost and the convenience of design from the point of view of fabrication.

Once again, the arrays of individual ferrite cores, although provide the best solution to selective access high speed memories, are expensive to construct. A significant cost reduction for the whole memory system is possible by using integrated magnetic structures with elements having closed magnetic flux paths, such as, aperture ferrite plates and the laminated ferrite devices. A plate with regular array of holes is moulded from a square loop ferrite material. Their assembly and wiring into memories are relatively simple. Also, these elements with closed magnetic flux paths can provide a relatively high ratio of sense voltage to drive current than an open flux memory element. Then there are no limitations to geometrical shapes due to demagnetizing effects and there are no fringing fields limiting packing density.

4.1   THE TRANSFLUXOR

One of the earliest devices using more complex core shape is known as transfluxor (Rajchman and Lo, 1955) in which a single small aperture was added to a simple toroidal core. This new device, shown in Figure 4.1, operates by the controlled transfer of flux from leg to leg in the magnetic circuit by means of input signals on windings linking different parts of the element. The standard transfluxor is a versatile circuit element which may be wired in a variety of ways to generate logical functions. The advantage of transfluxor-stores, when compared with normal core memories, is that once the required information has been written in, this information is permanently available without recourse to a rewrite cycle. Consequently, they may be used in semi-permanent memory applications. However, proceeding further into the memory operation, a brief explanation of the operation of these devices with reference to simple toroid core may be useful.

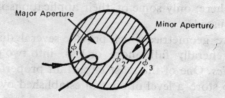

Figure 4.1   Two aperture transfluxor.

4.1.1   Principles of Transfluxor Operation

A two aperture transfluxor (Figure 4.1) performs simple operations but it illustrates the principles used in all other transfluxors. This simple two aperture transfluxor forms a useful type of switch for both memory and gating functions. Consider a core made of magnetic material which has a fairly rectangular hysteresis loop. Let, there be two apertures of unequal diameter which form two distinct flux paths $\phi_1-\phi_2$ and $\phi_1-\phi_3$ enclosing the major aperture. The areas of cross section of the leg 1 is equal to or greater than the sum of those of legs 2 and 3. The two flux paths are additive, i.e. the total flux capacity of legs 2 and 3 equals the flux capacity of leg 1. When a core has thick walls the decrease of magnetic field H with radius has to be taken into account. Thus, we have

$$r = \frac{2NI}{H_c}$$

where r is the outer radius of the area of material with threshold field H_c and the associated flux is reversed in it by a current I flowing in N turns.

For a wire carrying current through major aperture of the device, there is a specific value of current that will only reverse the flux about the path $\phi_1 - \phi_2$ and there is another larger value of current that will reverse the flux about both paths, i.e. $\phi_1 - \phi_2$ and $\phi_1 - \phi_3$. Representing one unit of flux capacity by an arrow, Figure 4.2a shows the blocked or clear state in which the two flux paths have been saturated in the same direction; this state being defined as the 'zero' state.

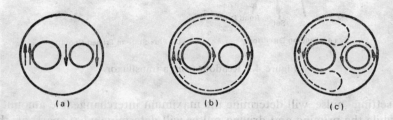

Figure 4.2 State of a transfluxor: (a) blocked or clear; (b) and (c) unblocked or set.

If now a current pulse is applied to the same winding as the blocking pulse, but in opposite direction to the latter, we have the condition shown in Figure 4.2b, the set or 'one' condition. The pulse amplitude is arranged to produce a field exceeding the coercive force of the material in the path $\phi_1 - \phi_2$ but less than the coercive force in the path through legs 1 and 3. But this method of setting is rather indefinite since the set current must never exceed the threshold of the outer path. An alternative set state may be obtained by passing current through the winding in the minor aperture. This method utilizes flux switching around the path ϕ_1 and ϕ_3, as shown in Figure 4.2c, to give a double loop pattern since flux lines cannot cross.

A readout method may be obtained by using the set and clear state of the transfluxor to represent the stored information. For nondestructive readout operation three more windings are passed through the minor aperture: the sense, 'prime' and read winding as shown in Figure 4.3. A current, applied to prime wire in the direction shown, will cause the flux around the minor aperture to reverse as shown in Figure 4.2b. The subsequent application of a pulse to read drive wire in the direction shown will then reverse the flux, again leaving the device in the set condition. If the device is blocked there can be no flux change on reading.

There will obviously be a voltage induced in the sense winding whenever the flux around the minor aperture is reversed and the voltage induced at either of the two reversals, i.e. primed to read or read to primed, may be amplified as the 'one' output. The drive current amplitude should be sufficient to exceed the coercive force of the material in the path around the minor aperture. The amount of flux, which is interchanged between legs 2 and 3 for a given setting by priming and driving pulses, determines the output from the transfluxor and will be referred to as the output flux.

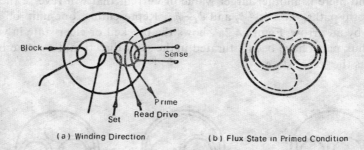

Block

Sense

Prime
Read Drive
Set

(a) Winding Direction

(b) Flux State in Primed Condition

Figure 4.3 Readout from a transfluxor.

The setting pulse will determine the maximum interchangeable amount of flux while the priming and driving pulses will determine what part of that flux is actually interchanged. Figure 4.4 shows the general form of curve relating the setting pulse amplitude to the output obtained for a given drive. In some on-off applications of the transfluxor, it is convenient to set on leg 2 rather than leg 1 to avoid the possibility of oversetting. In this case the setting pulse is not critical, provided that the maximum output is desired, since a winding on leg 2 cannot reverse more than half of the total flux around the major aperture. The drawback of the system is that sometimes the output of the circuit is loaded by the impedance of the setting winding. It can also be seen that if after priming, the device is blocked by applying a blocking current, a 'one' output is obtained destructively.

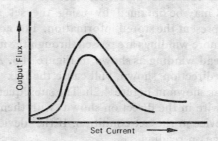

Output Flux

Set Current

Figure 4.4 Setting characteristic (Rajchman et al., 1956).

In fact the transfluxor operates like a pulse transformer, and the relation which exists between the primary and secondary circuits of the pulse transformer holds equally good to the output circuit of the transfluxor. In this case proper account should be taken of the definite set cross-sectional area of the equivalent core and the properties of the material of the core. These include the shape of the hysteresis loops and the intrinsic possible rates of flux reversal. In many cases they are used as an adjustable transformer with a primary winding energized by a current generator and secondary winding carrying the load.

The two aperture transfluxor discussed so far illustrate the general principle of operation of the device in one of its simplest forms. The use of more than two aperatures creates many new modes of flux transfer and can be used in many novel applications. In the case of more than one minor aperture, one will get several outputs nondestructively and these are independent in that the reading of one output does not affect the others. Also, the device may be set from any one of these apertures. This property of independence of the apertures makes it possible to construct shift registers and logic circuits using only the transfluxors and the connecting wire.

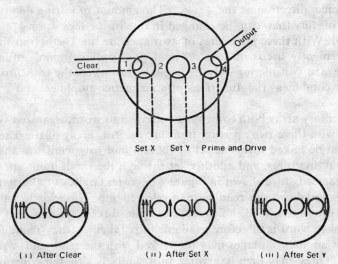

Figure 4.5 Transfluxor sequential gate with three apertures.

A transfluxor with three apertures in a row, as shown in Figure 4.5, can be used as a two input sequential gate. An output is obtained if the two inputs X and Y are applied to it in the order XY, and no output is produced if either input is absent or if the two inputs are applied in the order YX. The operation is illustrated symbolically in Figures 4.5 (i), (ii) and (iii). It can be appreciated that the operation of three aperture device is the same as of the two aperture device except that when the output is obtained there is no flux change around the input aperture and thus no voltage is induced in the input winding, i.e. there is isolation between input and output.

There are other applications of transfluxor in computing circuitry. The two aperture transfluxor may be used to form a nondestructive readout memory in which the addressing of individual cores is done by the coincident current technique. This will be considered in the subsequent section. The channel selection is another application of transfluxor. For this purpose one transfluxor is connected to each output channel. All transfluxors are blocked except the one which is set and which determines the selected channel.

4.1.2 Transfluxor Memory System

The two aperture transfluxor, sometimes called Theta transfluxor, is made from ferrite material which has good square loop hysteresis properties. The cross-sectional areas of the material at ϕ_1, ϕ_2 and ϕ_3 are governed by normal transfluxor requirement that ϕ_1 is greater than $\phi_2 + \phi_3$. The two memory states are the blocked and unblocked remanent conditions of the transfluxor. The transfluxor is blocked when the legs ϕ_2 and ϕ_3 are saturated in the same direction as the leg ϕ_1. The amount of setting determines the amount of flux that can be changed in one of the legs ϕ_2 or ϕ_3 before it is saturated. With these properties of two aperture or Theta transfluxor, one can conveniently use them to store analog as well as digital informations. Here we are considering only the digital store where the transfluxor array basically combines the functions of a magnetic amplifier and a memory core.

As a memory array both coincident current and word organized system can be made with these two aperture transfluxors. An array of the Theta transfluxors can be linked with one set of column and row windings through the large input apertures, and another set through the small input apertures. In word organized store shown in Figure 4.6, current pulses of alternate polarities are passed down the 'read' wire of selected line. This switches any available flux round the 'read' holes of all the transfluxors on this read wire and the complete word is therefore available in parallel on the 'readout' wires. Usually a number of planes may be stacked with the read and write wires in series. 'Ones' may then be written into similarly situated cores in all the planes, whilst the block winding itself may be used to inhibit those planes where a 'zero' is required.

Coincident current setting of the transfluxors is possible because a threshold of current is required to produce setting around the larger aperture. Similarly, coincident readout can be obtained because a threshold of current is required to switch the flux around the smaller aperture. In coincident current memory plane, selection of a particular core is made by sending half currents down each of the mutually perpendicular 'write' wires. These currents add to exceed the switching threshold in the selected core. Thus a 'one' may be written into any of the transfluxors in the plane. A nondestructive coincident current random access memory can be made by

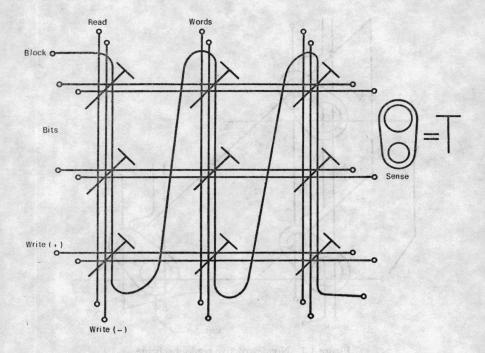

Figure 4.6 Word organized system.

providing digit write and digit sense windings through the larger and smaller apertures. In this type of memory, readout operation is usually much faster than the conventional core memories with destructive readout.

Several nondestructive readout schemes are possible with these transfluxor arrays. The NDRO operation depends on switching back and forth of the nonelastic flux set successively in legs 2 and 3. An arrangement of transfluxor nondestructive readout memory is shown in Figure 4.7. The set and blocked states of the transfluxor are used to represent the stored binary information. A coincident current matrix wired through larger aperture is used for writing and a separate matrix wired through the smaller aperture is used for reading. The addressing of individual transfluxor is done by coincident current techniques. The fact that neither the prime current nor the read drive current affect the transfluxor, storing a 'zero' means that it is unnecessary to have the inhibit winding required for the conventional rewrite operation. Also, the principle of elastic switching in toroidal cores is sometimes used in the nondestructive readout operation of a transfluxor system. The nondestructive memory system is, however, complicated because the separate addressing circuits for write-in and readout are necessary. For this reason the simpler destructive readout memories are used more commonly.

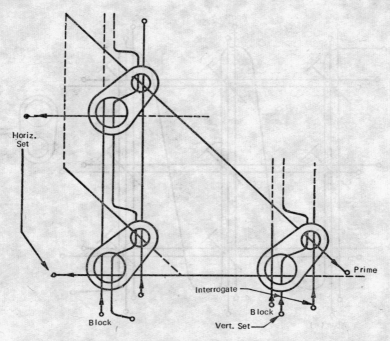

Figure 4.7 Nondestructive readout scheme.

4.2 THE LADDIC

The laddic storage methods which are special cases of a general system of logic are used in typical systems where the output function is not required frequently. They are widely used in logical applications. The basic structure of a laddic *ladder logic element* shown in Figure 4.8 is sufficient for most applications although particular advantages may be obtained in certain cases by using modified structure. The main merits of the laddic appear to be its low cost, versatility and compatibility with existing core circuits and the convenience of its design from the point of view of fabrication.

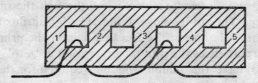

Figure 4.8 Typical laddic structure.

The laddic structure, shown in Figure 4.8, has the property that if a reversal field is applied to one of the legs then the magnetic flux is returned almost entirely by the shortest available path. A symmetrical pattern of flux is chosen as the initial pattern which is established by saturating the even numbered legs in one direction and the odd numbered legs in opposite direction. A current is passed through the reset winding and this disturbs the existing flux patterns in different legs. The operating principle of the laddic element is rather simple. The flux pattern, which is initially set in the structure, changes according to other fixed patterns by application of driving pulses. When a driving pulse that is limited in magnitude only by the minimum value corresponding to the switching threshold, is applied in leg 1, flux changes in leg 1 and it completes the flux closure by the shortest available path through leg 2. If in any case leg 2 is held in saturation and is not available as a return path for the flux reversed in leg 1, then leg 3 will provide the next shortest return path. Obviously, the switching speed for a given input drive depends on the length of the path in which the flux change takes place. Short, large amplitude pulses are generally applied to get the faster operation from the laddic. The wiring schemes for these multi-aperture devices have been proposed by Tuttle (1963) and later on were modified by Rabbi and Ricci for content addressable memories (CAM) using these multi-aperture devices (MADs). Dettann (1969) has reported a feasibility study of a 10 megabit, 1 μsec access, 6 μsec cycle MAD CAM with magnetic word selection.

4.2.1. Laddic Logic Circuit

A block of ferrite of the type shown in Figure 4.9 can be used for a large variety of logical operations by making suitable external connections. These laddic logic elements occupy relatively smaller volume. The standard AND/OR gate using laddic is shown in Figure 4.9. The input to this gate is applied in the hold windings. Apart from the hold windings, three other windings reset, drive and output are also present for the gate shown in Figure 4.9. A voltage is induced in the output winding if, and only if, the current pulses are present at the same time in hold and drive windings. The sense output under such condition will be the Boolean function $F = X \cdot Y$.

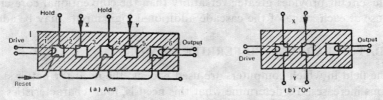

Figure 4.9   Two input logic gates: (a) 'AND' and (b) 'OR'.

In these logic structures where more than one input is present, these pulses must overlap for a sufficient period for the complete switching. The input winding is generally wound on even number of legs. A large number of inputs can be applied in the simple laddic structure through their hold windings. The maximum limiting factor for each hold current is the acceptable signal to noise level. The basic laddic structure is sufficient for most applications, but sometimes particular advantages may be obtained by using modified structure. As an example, consider the function $F = (X + Y) \cdot (Y + Z) \cdot (X + Z) = X \cdot Y + Y \cdot Z + X \cdot Z$. This logic function can be realized by the wiring pattern shown in Figure 4.10.

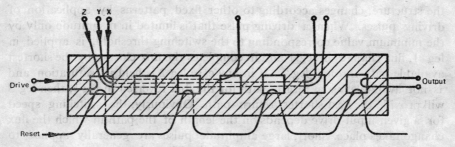

Figure 4.10   Generation of the function $F = (X + Y) \cdot (Y + Z) \cdot (X + Z)$.

This function, as can be seen from the figure, is generated by holding leg 'two' with input X or Y, leg 'four' with X or Z and leg 'six' with Y or Z. Thus an output is obtained only if the condition $(X + Y) \cdot (Y + Z) \cdot (X + Z) = 1$ is satisfied.

In this logic gate the different hold currents must be equal in magnitude. The final logic structure will be the compromise between wiring complexity, number of laddics and the acceptable signal to noise level. For specific logic applications, a reduction in size of the laddic and the number of windings can be obtained by using a more complicated, less general laddic. In constructing different laddic structures from a single ferrite sheet, it is necessary to separate these basic structures from each other, otherwise interactions between adjacent laddics might take place. Similarly, in cascading different logic gates some kind of isolating elements, such as diode or transistor circuit are required. This is also true for core logic circuits where isolating media is placed between input-output coupling loop. The cascaded laddic circuit provides greater versatility than the conventional core circuit, because at each stage of the cascade additional logic inputs may be added.

4.3 BATCH FABRICATED FERRITE MEMORY

As the field in which computers are used widens, the need for better storage systems increases. To determine what this need is, four characteristics of a store must be considered in relation to its use. These characteristics are speed, size, cost, and reliability and are in general related to each other. Any means of fabrication which improves one of these characteristics is of importance, but if several aspects can be affected simultaneously, the benefit is significantly increased.

The question of obtaining large storage capacities at any electronic speed is mostly one of economy in fabrication. The size and capacity of a memory system is so related that in general, the maximum attainable capacity decreases with increasing speeds. Also, the characteristic cost is of very great importance and it is here that the greatest gain can be made. To reduce the cost of a store, a batch fabrication process is essential for the storage elements themselves. But there must also be a reduction in the peripheral electronics if any significant decrease in the total cost of a store is to be achieved. Several attempts have been made to batch fabricate memory arrays using ferrites. An early example of manufacturing on a production basis was the aperture ferrite plate. Their assembly and wiring into memories is considerably simpler. The other monolithic ferrite memory technique called the *laminated ferrite memory* is the only advanced memory of this type that has been carried to production status. These monolithic memories have been proposed for NDRO, scratchpad, main internal memory, and aerospace applications. In this section we shall consider some of the features of these memory techniques.

4.3.1 Ferrite Aperture Plate Memory

For large storage capacities, the fabrication, the testing, and the assembly of separately made individual cores becomes prohibitive. For this reason investigations were carried out in different organizations to fabricate a large memory arrays as units, rather than assembly of large number of discrete elements. The memory function is particularly adaptable to batch fabrication techniques, since it consists of large numbers of similar elements and hence is highly repetitive. The Rajchman's idea of moulding a plate with an array of holes out of ferrite material having a square hysteresis loop, will provide many storage sites inherent in the continuous medium and yet preserve the distinctiveness of the cells. In fact, batch fabrication of logical and memory circuitry and of arrays of storage cells will be the key factor making possible more versatile and sophisticated computers with greater reliability, lower cost, and smaller size, weight and power requirements.

4.3.1.1 CONSTRUCTION AND CHARACTERISTIC OF APERTURE PLATE

Aperture ferrite plates are proposed for building high speed random access memories. They provide a simple means to fabricate large numbers of discrete storage cells in convenient packages which can be easily assembled into large memory systems. A square ferrite plate is moulded with the arrays of holes. The direction of remanent magnetization around each aperture stores one bit of information. Typical hole diameter d is 25 mils, plate thickness is 7 mils, and the separation between the successive holes D is 50 mils as shown in Figure 4.11. The ratio of hole diameter (d/D) to hole spacing is approximately one-half. This ratio is a compromise between discrimination improvement and interaction between holes.

Memory arrays of $16 \times 16 = 256$ and higher capacities have been developed. Squareness of the hysteresis loop and switching characteristics are comparable to those of individual cores made of same material. The firing

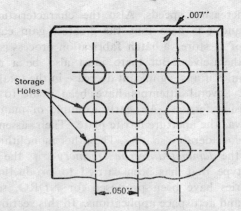

Figure 4.11   Section of aperture plate.

of the aperture plate is somewhat more critical than the firing of individual cores. As the ferrite itself is an insulator, conducting layers can be printed on the ferrite surface to link [the holes. These layers can then be used as combined digit and output wire. These plates are also suitable for external word addressing system, because the switch can be made of plates identical to those used for the memory. The switches can be operated in a number of ways such as set-a-line system, and the dc bias system.

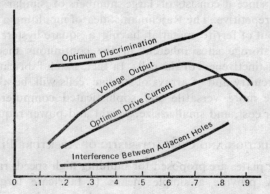

Figure 4.12 Typical characteristics of aperture plate
arrays (Rajchman and Lo, 1956).

The flux change in the storage plates is limited to that taking place in the switch. Also, the signal interaction becomes significant only when the hole peripheries are less than the radii of the holes. The general behaviour of signal output, interaction, and the signal discrimination properties of aperture plate as the function of the geometry of the array is shown in Figure 4.12. The current producing optimum discrimination increases linearly with hole size except for slight deviation from linearity for large holes. The resulting output voltage cu rve starts rising with hole size and reaches a maximum value after which it decreases as the available cross-section area between the adjacent holes diminishes. Similarly, the curve for maximum discrimination ratio rises, first slowly, then more rapidly. This is because of the fact that the region where the flux reverses between the aperture and its nearest neighbours becomes thinner; therefore, the hysteresis loop, which is an average of the elementary zonal hysteresis loop, is square as the averaging extends over a smaller radial spread.

4.3.1.2 STORAGE SYSTEMS USING APERTURE PLATE

The proposal of Rajchman for driving the memory plates by a switch made from the plate itself, makes it possible to construct large storage capacities, readout signals free from disturbances, fast access and large tolerances in the amplitude of the driving currents. The plates, stacked with all holes in register, are threaded in a single operation which does not need to be repeated separately for each plane as is necessary for the memory core planes. For cancellation of unwanted output signals, sometimes a pair of holes is used for storing one bit of information. A complete stack of Rajchman plates may be operated in either a coincidence or direct selection system. Also, the two holes per bit are advantageous in direct selection systems.

In direct selection system the requirements of uniform properties of the holes are not so critical. Straight wires may be threaded through both the store and switch plates. The drive pulses are provided by the switch matrix stacked at the end of the store. During writing operation, only one of these holes is switched. Similarly, the coincidence method of address selection can also be achieved with these plates. In coincident current operation, the holes of stack of plates are threaded back and forth by row and column windings. The wiring of different plates is made similar to that of two cores per bit system because the disturb signals from the half selected holes in the energized row and column in a particular plate do not cancel each other. The plates are arranged in a square and are connected in series diagonally in pairs. The two diagonal pairs are connected in opposite series and the midpoint is grounded. For writing operation or rewriting, the inhibit signal is sent into both branches of the common winding, positive in one and negative in the other branch. Similarly, in reading operation the two ungrounded terminals of the diagonally connected plates generate output voltages, the difference of which is sensed by sense amplifier. This type of winding arrangement offers a very good discrimination due to the lack of any appreciable air coupling.

4.3.2 Laminated Memory System

A laminated ferrite memory array, originated by J.A. Rajchman and R. Shahbender, is a monolithic sheet of a ferrite with an embedded matrix of conductors. In these memories, the magnetic cores are replaced by ferrite memory sheets, so that the cores are all processed together and need not be handled individually. For this reason reduced equivalent dimensions and, therefore, smaller circuits than in the case of conventional ferrite cores are possible. The laminate technology permits a great flexibility of geometries of the windings. This technique has been developed to take advantage of integrated circuit principles, i.e. the simultaneous fabrication of large number of memory elements. As the laminate ferrite offers a simple way of fabricating, what amounts to very small magnetic 'cores', all properly interconnected, it is possible to use drive currents which are very low compared with those used for conventional cores. These memories have performance characteristics in terms of capacity and speed which anticipate the needs of future computers. These needs are expressed in terms of a hierarchy of memories having cycle times in the range of 0.1 to 5 μ sec and corresponding capacities of 10^5 to 10^8 bits. However, the ferrite composition and their inherent characteristics should be evaluated before they are used in such memory applications.

4.3.2.1 FERRITE COMPOSITION AND CHARACTERISTICS

In addition to the normal requirements for a good magnetic material for core memories (fast switching, good squareness and good thermal stability) as discussed earlier, the low power laminated memory imposes three additional requirements: (i) small grain structure to ensure uniformity of the storage elements, (ii) high resistivity of the ferrite material which acts as insulator between the orthogonal windings, and (iii) coercive forces values of less than one oersted so that the memory array operating characteristics are compatible with integrated semiconductor drive circuits.

The flux density, remanence ratio, curie temperature, and switching coefficient parameters, are the normal requirements for memory applications. The limitation on the coercivity for this application is imposed by the low drive currents. The curie temperature value is established to ensure adequate thermal stability. The need for a grain size restriction beco mes clear when it is recalled that the laminate conductor planes are separated by a ferrite spacer that is approximately 10 to 15 microns thick. The grain size must be restricted to less than the memory cell size, and when the grain size is comparable to memory cell size, nonuniform operations of the memory plane result. Small grains result in a large number of walls si multaneously participating in switching operation. Thus, the small grain size required for signal uniformity contributes to fast switching. These ferrite characteristics just discussed, a re interrelated and it is not possible to simultaneously optimize all the desired properties in any given material.

Attempts have been made to develop special ferrite composition for laminated ferrite memories. Laminate made from two ferrite compositions, MgMnZn and MgMn were extensively tested to determine their high speed operating characteristics. The first composition is used for high speed cores while the MgMn composition yields better results for laminated memory materials. Table 1 summarizes the properties of these compositions for high speed operations.

TABLE 1

Properties of some Laminates

	Ferrite Composition	
	MgMnZn	MgMn
Coercive force (oersteds)	1.5	2.5
Curie temperature (°C)	205	2.70
Peak read current (mA)	600	700
Bit back voltage (mV)	250	250
Digit current (mA)	25	35
Sense signal RZ type (mV)	7.5	7.2
Sense signal NRZ type (mV)	10.5	12
Propagation delay for 1K word memory (nsec)	32	20
Typical switching time (nsec)	150	100

4.3.2.2 PLANE FABRICATION

The basic operations involved in the fabrication of a laminated memory array are *doctor blading, laminating and sintering,* and *conductor screening.* The doctor blading (DB) technique for fabricating sheets of ferrites consists of preparing a slurry of desired ferrite powder and appropriate organic binders. The slurry is spread in an even layer on a glass substrate by the sweeping action of a blade, called the doctor blade, held at a fixed distance above the glass surface. The height of the blade regulates the thickness of the ferrite slurry applied to the substrate. During drying, the adherence of the slurry to the substrate must be sufficient to prevent lateral shrinkage. All shrinkages should be vertical. The sheet is air dried and peeled off the glass surface. Sheets thicker than 10 mils are not feasible due to the difficulty in drying the film slowly and uniformly.

Conductive lines are then placed in the ferrite by different techniques, such as (i) to embed a solid wire, (ii) to sequeeze a conductive paste through the mask on to a flat substrate and then to use doctor blade over the conductor pattern, and (iii) to form grooves in the ferrite (embossing) and then fill with a conductive paste or powder. The material used for conductors must withstand ferrite firing temperatures and atmospheres. In most cases, this requires that platinum, palladium, rhodium, iridium or osmium be used.

Thicker sheets can be made by laminating as many thin sheets as desired. Three sheets are laminated together (two sheets containing conductors and one sheet serving as an insulator) to form a ferrite wafer. The wafer, which is in the unfired state, is conventionally sintered to yield the square loop

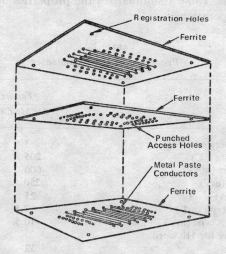

Figure 4.13 Getails of a laminate (Shahbender et al., 1963).

properties. The pressure sintering technique is more advantageous as it eliminates some of the drawbacks of standard fabrication procedure of laminated ferrite memory arrays. The standard pressure sintering process consists of applying pressure to the material in a suitable die that is simultaneously heated to some optimum temperature for densification. After sintering, the ends of the palladium conductors are exposed and photoetched copper conductor combs are manually soldered to the ends of exposed conductors on all four edges of laminate.

The laminated ferrite array is word organized (linear select), i.e. the word lines carry full read and write currents and the digit lines carry sense signals and digit currents. The array can be operated in a one-crossover-per-bit or two-crossovers-per-bit mode at low power levels. To store a binary zero in a cell, a positive digit current is applied in the time coincidence with the write current, and a negative current is applied to store a binary one. A test program incorporating digit disturbs in combination with prewrite pulses, which tends to minimize the stored flux, is used for testing.

A number of experimental arrays of different dimensions were made and tested successfully. Each wafer contained 16×16 or 64×64 intersections and is encapsulated in a semi-hermetic package. The planes can be usually operated with low word read write currents and with a read current rise time of 0.2 μsec the typical disturb sense signal peaks at $\pm$ 2 mV for binary 1 and 0, respectively. The word back voltage peaks at approximately 20 mV per crossover (40 mV per bit). In low power operation, the limitation of word current amplitude causes the ferrite switching time to be more dependent on current amplitude than on rise time. The maximum number of bits that can be incorporated in a laminated array is a function of delay, attenuation and matching of the line impedance by the terminations. The characteristic impedance of laminated ferrite plane can be measured by using impedance bridge on the basis of the impedance measurements. The attenuation and memory delay can also be computed.

4.3.2.3 SYSTEM ORGANISATION AND ITS OPERATIONS

Feasibility of the modular memory depends on the development of LSI techniques to maintain bit costs at an economic level. The design of laminated ferrite memory module exploits the potential of LSI of semiconductor elements for reducing the ratio of semiconductor costs to magnetic stack costs in memory systems while utilizing relatively greater number of semiconductor components. As the drive currents are very low, MOS transistor switches can be used for routing word current, digit current, and address selection. The bi-directional characteristics of MOS transistors make certain simplification in the driving circuits possible. Thus by distributing the magnetics and semiconductors in modules throughout the system, faster operation, improved signal-to-noise ratio, lower digit power and wider operating margins are obtained.

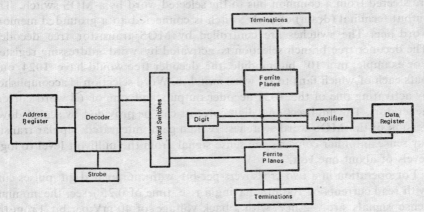

Figure 4.14 Block diagram of a memory system.

The memory system organization is shown in Figure 4.14. The matrix of conductors provides necessary wires for a two wire linear select memory system in which the wires in the word oriented direction are used as read and write drive lines and the wires in the perpendicular direction are used as sense lines and digit drive lines. Each of the different components of the memory systems (laminated ferrite array, word driver strip, digit driver strip, etc.) is mounted on an insulating frame with connection tabs coming out through the sides of the frame. The metal connection tabs are fabricated in strips by *photoresist* techniques from 0.001 inch thick copper. The write current generates a closed flux path in a plane perpendicular to the the plane of the read-write drive wire. At the same time, the current through the digit wire rotates the magnetic vector slightly, resulting in a component of magnetization perpendicular to the bit sense wire. The direction of this component is determined by the information to be stored. A subsequent word-oriented read current destroys this component and the resulting flux change produces the readout signal.

The memory system is operated in a unipolar digit, two-crossover-per-bit mode in which the adjacent digit lines are used to store one bit of information. The sense signal is the differential voltage between the two lines, resulting in cancellation of common inductive and capacitive noise. Operation using one-crossover-per-bit is also possible. In this mode a negative digit current writes a binary 1 and a positive digit current writes a 0.

The system orgnization shown in Figure 4.14 is operated in a linear select mode as it offers higher speed in a memory system. The larger number of circuits required in the linear select mode will be offset by lower costs resulting from less critical tolerance requirements. The magnetic storage is divided into two parts to minimize the digit sense electronics and the propagation delay and attenuation. MOS transistors have been used for memory address selection and for word and digit current switches. Word read-write currents are steered from a common bus to the selected word by a MOS switch. The output terminal (drain) of each switch is connected to a grounded memory word line. The switches are controlled by MOS transistor tree decoder. The decoder tree branch selection is activated by word addressing register. For example, in a 10^7 bit module, the decoder tree would have 1024 outputs each of which fans to 64 word switches. Word selection is accomplished by activating one of the 1024 decoder outputs and one of 64 word current generators. The unidirectional digit currents can be provided by scaled-down version of the MOS word switches. A high gain integrated bipolar transistor sense amplifier converts the sense signal from the millivolt level to logic levels of about one volt.

For operation in a two-crossovers-per-bit with unipolar digit pulses and with read currents of 100 mA having a rise time of 0.25 μsec, the nominal sense signals are ± 2 mV, with a back voltage of 40 mV per bit. From the measurements on the propagation characteristics of the sense digit winding, it can be estimated that a cycle time of 3.5 μsec can be realized for a system in which the sense amplifier/digit driver circuit services 8,000 bits and a cycle time of 1.5 μsec can be realized with the circuit servicing 2,000 bits. These cycle times are determined mostly by the recovery of the sense winding following digit transition. Normal sensing is differential in that the output sense voltage obtained during read is the difference between the two voltages induced along the digit sense windings linking the two crossovers of a bit. Different polarities of voltage correspond to the two binary states. The differential amplifier which is the basic building block for the sense amplifier lends itself particularly well to monolithic fabrication since its peformance characteristics (gain, temperature stabiltiy, etc.) are primarily dependent on resistance ratios, device matching, tracking, etc. that can be readily achieved in monolithic form. There exist a number of techniques for the design of an integrated, high gain (60 db), high sensitivity (1 mV) sense amplifier.

The laminates offer advantages for realizing large capacity systems with respect to either plated wire or $2\frac{1}{2}D$ two-wire core system. Economic feasibility of the above system hinges on the economic feasibility of integrated circuits at low production volume. For memory systems operating at 0.5 μsec cycle time, laminated memories offer no economic advantages over the core systems for commercial application. However, for space-born and military applications, the laminates with their high packing density, smaller volume, and lower operating power may be of use.

References

Abbott, H. W. and Surran, J. J. (1957): 'Multihole ferrite core configuration and applications', *Proc IRE*. V. 45, August, pp. 1081-1093.

Abeyta, I., Kaufman, M and Lawrence, P. (1965): 'Monolithic ferrite memories', *Proc. Fall Joint Computer Conf.*, pp. 995-1010.

Amemiya, H., Lemaire, H.P., et al. (1962): 'High speed ferrite memories', *Proc. Fall Joint Computer Conference*, p. 184.

Baldwin, J.A. et al. (1959): 'Inhibited flux—a new mode of operation of three hole memory core', *J. Appl. Phys.*, V. 30, No. 4, pp. 585-595.

Bardidge, V.V., Larin, E.M. et al (1970): 'The Physical analysis of laminated ferrite wafer individual storage element', *IEEE Trans. on Magnetics*, V. MAG-6, No. 3, September.

Bartkus, E. Browlow, J. et al. (1964): 'An approach towards batch fabricated ferrite memory planes', *IBM J. Ros. and Devel*, V. 8, pp. 170-176.

Briggs, G.R. and Tuska, J.W. (1963): 'Design and operating characteristics of a high bit density permalloy sheet transfluxor memory stack', *Proc. INTERMAG, Conf.* April, paper 3-4-2.

Briggs, G.R., Grabowski, J.T. and Tuska, J.W. (1968): 'Laminated ferrite modular memory for 150-250 nsec cycle operation' (Abstract), *INTERMAC Conf.*, April.

Dehann, H.J.M. (1969): 'Themis—three hole element memory with integrated selection', *IEEE Trans. on Magnetics*, V. MAG-5, No. 3, pp. 403-407.

Gianola, U.F. and Crowley, T.H. (1959): 'The laddic—a magnetic device for performing logic', *Bell Syst. Tech. J.*, V. 38, p. 45.

Gordon, I. et al. (1968): 'A MOS transistor driven laminated ferrite memory', *RCA Review*, V. 29, No. 2, June.

Haneman, W.J. and Lehman, J. (1958): 'Aperture plate memory, operation and analysis', *IRE National Conv. Rec.*, pt. 4, pp. 254-262.

Harvey, R.L., Gordon, I., and Robbi, A.D. (1966): 'Laminated ferrite memory—phase II', *RCA Laboratory*, Princeton, Final Tech. Rept., August.

Kaufman, M.M. and Newhouse, W.L. (1958): 'Operating range of a memory using two ferrite plate apertures per bit', *J. Appl. Phys.*, V. 29, pp. 487-488.

Li, K. (1968): 'High speed characteristics of laminated ferrite memory planes' (Abstract), *INTERMAG Conf.*, April.

Lockhart, N.F. (1958): 'Logic by ordered flux changes in multipath ferrite cores', *IRE Nat. Conv. Rec.*, Pt. 4, pp. 298.

Meinkin, R.H. (1960): 'The ferrite sheet memory', *Proc., Electronic Components Conf.* (Washington DC.), May, p. 105.

Prywes, N.S. (1958): 'Diodeless magnetic shift registers utilizing transfluxors', *IRE Trans. on Electronic Computers*, V. EC-7, pp. 316.

Rajchman, J.A. (1957): 'Ferrite apertured plate for random access memory', *Proc. IRE*, V. 45, pp. 325-34.

Rajchman, J. (1956): 'The transfluxor', *Proc IRE*, V. 44, pp. 321.

Ricci, R.C. and Truscello, P.J. (1966): 'A monolithic ferrite space memory', *Proc. Nat. Electronics Conf.*, Chicago, p. 758.

Riddler, D.S. and Grimmond, R. (1957): 'The magnetic cell—a new circuit element', *Proc. IEE* (London), V. 104B, Suppl. No. 7, p. 445.

Robbi, A.D. and Tuska, J.W. (1967): 'Integrated MOS transistor—laminated ferrite memory' (Abstract), *IEEE Trans. on Magnetics.*, V. MAG-3, pp. 329.

Robbi, A.D. and Ricci, E. (1964): 'Transfluxor content addressable memory', *Intern. Conf. on Nonlinear Magn. Proc.*, papers 8-3-1 to 8-3-7.

Rumble, W.G. (1958): 'Coincident current applications of ferrite aperture plates', *IRE Wescon Conv. Rec.*, Pt. 4, pp. 62-65.

Shahbender, R., Wentworth, C. (1963): 'Laminated ferrite memory', *RCA REVIEW*, V. 24, December, p. 705.

Shahbender, R., Wentworth, C., Li, K., Rajchman, J.A., et al. (1965): 'Laminated ferrite memory', *AFIPS Conf. Proc.*, pp. 77-90.

Shahbender, R. (1968): 'Laminated ferrite memories—review and evaluation', *RCA Review*, V. 29, pp. 180-188.

Shahbender, R., et al. (1964): 'Laminated ferrite memory', *Proc. INTERMAG Conf.*, April, paper 5-6-1.

Tuttle, G.T. (1963): 'Now to quiz a whole memory at once', *Electronics*, V. 36, p. 44.

Warren, C.S. (1959): 'Ferrite aperture plate memories', *Digest of Tech. Papers*, Intern. Solid State Circuit Conf., Philadelphia, Pa., February, pp. 18.

5. MAGNETIC THIN FILM MEMORY SYSTEMS

Magnetic films were first proposed as high speed main memory elements by Blois in 1955. The films, when deposited in the presence of a magnetic field, exhibit square hysteresis loops in the field direction and possess several properties suitable for computer storage. In spite of these inherent advantages, development of the thin film memories has remained 'around the corner' for almost ten years. The difficulties encountered were in respect of circuits and material problems. First, many unanticipated effects made achieving the required reproducibility and uniformity over large areas (hundred to thousand of bits) a laborious and time consuming task. Secondly, the cancellation of spurious signals and issue of open versus closed magnetic structure, are typical circuit problems.

The first commercial application of a film memory attempted to avoid these problems by exploiting their natural performance advantage (inherent higher speed) in a small scratch pad; but the much heralded semiconductor memories rapidly eroded this opportunity. Even with these difficulties, which required over a decade to surmount, magnetic film memories have been and are being designed into commercial computer systems. They are emerging as the dominant technology in areas where nonvolatility, low power, NDRO, or some combination of these are important in system design. Thin film memory element is characterized by such parameters as output signal, minimun and maximun drive currents, and the distrub sensitivity which, in turn, depends on such physical parameters as saturation magnetization film composition, film thickness, coercive force and anisotropy field. Before going further into the principle of thin film memory operation, a brief discussion of the above parameters characterizing a memory element and the physical phenomenon occurring in thin films will be made in the subsequent sections. Films and film properties which are not relevant to thin film memories are avoided in the discussion.

5.1 PHYSICAL PROPERTIES OF MAGNETIC THIN FILM ELEMENTS

Properties of ferromagnetic films are investigated first in an attempt to seek those factors which tend to produce the most suitable films for memory applications. The dominant film material used for high speed random access memories is the zero magnetostrictive alloy of 81.5 per cent nickel and 18.5 per cent iron. This particular permalloy is used for high speed applications because of its low dynamic losses, low coercive force and low anisotropy constant. For film materials such as permalloy it is found that if the films are formed in magnetic field, these films will possess a uniaxial axis of anisotropy. The films are usually highly polycrystalline with very small crystal size so that the effects of cubic symmetry of the single crystal anisotropy are not observed. The axis normally lies in the plane of the film. The magnetostriction of permalloy films also varies with composition. In fact 80 per cent nickel, 20 per cent iron composition which is normally used, has very low magnetostriction. Straining or bending of the specimens has very little effect on the magnetic properties. Depending on the specific requirement, other alloys besides permalloys may be found to be more desirable. Sometimes some other alloys have been added to meet a wide range design specifications, and these have been summarized by Freeman (1969). As an example, addition of cobalt increases saturation magnetization (B_s) and thus the signal output. It raises coercivity (H_c), thus reducing creep, and also raises anisotropy field (H_k) thereby reducing demagnetizing effects. The use of these materials in computer memory depends on the two stable magnetic states of remanence in zero applied field, as shown in Figure 5.1. The stability of magnetization in each state is of prime concern, since the integrity of the stored information depends on this. Much work has been done in understanding how to obtain films and design film arrays which resist demagnetization from various stray field effects.

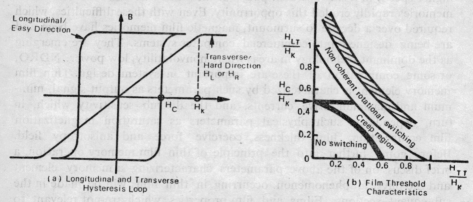

(a) Longitudinal and Transverse
Hysteresis Loop

(b) Film Threshold
Characteristics

Figure 5.1 Magnetic thin film characteristics.

Very often the problem of depositing the film of an alloy rather than of a pure element, presents unusual difficulties. A considerable number of preparation variables are known to be important in determining the structure and switching behaviour, namely: (1) composition, (2) substrate temperature, (3) thickness, (4) rate of deposition, (5) residual gases present during evaporation, (6) type of substrate, and (7) angle of incidence between the incident vapour beam and the substrate. Many methods are available for forming surface films, such as, sputtering, electroplating, thermochemical deposition, chemical deposition and vapour deposition in vacuum. It is convenient to classify thin films by their methods of deposition, realizing that other ordering systems are also possible and useful. It will be seen that within each general type of film deposition method there is a wide range of materials, properties and applications.

Usually in the construction of magnetic thin films for storage purpose, the following steps are generally adopted:

(i) Surface preparation of the substrate.
(ii) Heating of the substrate in vacuum to the correct temperature.
(iii) Evaporation of the Ni-Fe in a magnetic field through a mask, to deposit as memory array to the correct thickness and composition.
(iv) Cooling of the substrate before removal of magnetic field.

The two distinct magnetic states of these materials are the natural states which require no external energy to be maintained. Uniaxial anisotropy in the magnetic film is established by an orienting field during the formation of the element or in a subsequent anneal. Anisotropy can also be established through evaporation at an oblique angle. The material acquires an easy direction of magnetization along the direction in which the hysteresis loop is square and a hard direction at right angle to the easy direction along which there is a straight characteristic and practically no hysteresis. The film is characterized by a coercive force H_C, along the easy or longitudinal direction and an anisotropy field H_K along the hard or transverse direction as shown in Figure 5.1. At remanence, the film is magnetized longitudinally in one direction or other. Magnetization reversal can occur either by domain wall motion or by rotation, or by both depending on the nature and geometry of the film and the nature of the drive. The switching threshold and switching time depend on both the value of the longitudinal field H_L and the transverse field H_T. Typical dependence is depicted in Figure 5.1b.

5.2 THEORY OF THIN FILMS WITCHING

Magnetization reversal in these films can occur in three different modes: domain wall movement, incoherent rotation, and coherent rotation. The way in which a particular sample undergoes magnetization reversal depends on the properties of the particular film and the experimental conditions during switching. If switching occurs by wall motion, then switching time depends on the average distance a wall has to move. In fact, in film materials, wall motion switching characterises the slowest switching process. It is, therefore, reasonable to suppose that minimum switching time will occur if all spins rotate uniformly in space and coherently in time. Spin rotation during reversal by the familiar domain wall motion is clearly not uniform, but instead sequential in both space and time, and in fact would appear to be the slowest possible switching mode. However, uniform switching will not be fast unless the precessional response of a free spin to an applied field can be modified. Owing to the demagnetizing effects, geometry is a key factor in any magnetic switching problem. In addition to the uniform mode of film switching, it is known that nonuniform or quasi-static modes can also occur. The most familiar of these is the nucleation of a reverse domain and subsequent domain growth by parallel wall motion.

The sense signal is inversely proportional to the time in which the magnetization rotates from easy to hard direction. The time taken to rotate is approximately 1 nsec for a field which is applied in hard direction and which is about twice the anisotropy field H_K. Switching of this order were predicted by Smith. In order to calculate the switching time of the magnetic film, one has to start with the equation of motion as proposed by Gilbert

$$\bar{M} = \gamma \left[\bar{M} \times \bar{H} \right] + \frac{\alpha}{\gamma} \left[\bar{M} \times \bar{M} \right]$$

where γ is the gyromagnetic ratio and α is the damping constant. According to this equation, in the case of a magnetic sphere, the first term means a fast precession of $\bar{M}$ around the field vector $\bar{H}$. This precession would last for ever if the second term, representing damping effects, did not exist. As a result of this term the magnetization spirals around the field axis until $\bar{M}$ and $\bar{H}$ are parallel. A relatively long time is required for this spiralling switching process. In case of thin film the situation is much more favourable. Again, as a result of the first term the magnetization starts to precess around $\bar{H}$ but as soon as it turns out of the plane of the film a large demagnetizing field originates, normal to the plane of the film and much larger than the applied field. The magnetization starts to precess quickly around this demagnetizing field and slows down when it becomes parallel to hard direction field.

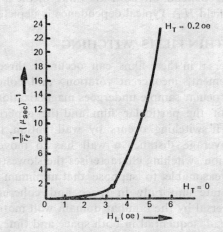

Figure 5.2 Inverse of switching time as a function of applied field H_L.

Experimentally, the relative importance of the three flux reversal mechanisms is most easily shown by plotting the reciprocal of switching time as a function of applied field (Figure 5.2). To obtain magnetization curves the material is first placed at a reproducible remanent point by a large pulse. The flux is then reversed by a second pulse. During this reversal the switching time is measured. Experimental plots similar to those shown in Figure 5.2 were first reported by Olson and Pohm who made a systematic study of rapid flux reversal in thin films. It can be seen in this diagram that there are three regions separated by definite breaks in the curve for the three modes of switching mechanisms. For very high slope (fast) and for very low slope (slow) regions, reversal mechanisms are generally considered to be coherent and domain wall motion respectively, while in the intermediate slope region, where the switching time is 0.1 μsec, 0.5 usec, the flux reversal is by noncoherent rotation. However, in practical cases, the application of transverse field causes an abrupt increase in the slope of the switching curves when the longitudinal field exceeds a certain value. Below this value of longitudinal field, the switching curves approximate to those with no transverse field.

Permalloy film when prepared in the presence of a magnetic field exhibits a uniaxial magnetic anisotropy. If we assume that the magnetization in the whole film is always pointing in the same direction, i.e. like a single domain, then anisotropy energy of the film will be

$$E = K \sin^2 \theta \tag{1}$$

where θ is the angle that the magnetization makes with the easy axis, torque and energy calculations give the ideal static and dynamic magnetization characteristic of the film. For a combination of applied transverse H_T and longitudinal H_L fields, the total energy per unit volume will be

$$E = -MH_L \cos \theta - MH_T \sin \theta + K \sin^2 \theta \tag{2}$$

For a given applied field the angle θ is stable for which $\partial E/\partial \theta = 0$, $\partial^2 E/\partial \theta^2 > 0$.
That is,

$$\frac{\partial E}{\partial \theta} = MH_L \sin \theta - M H_T \cos \theta + 2K \sin \theta \cos \theta = 0 \tag{3}$$

and

$$\frac{\partial^2 E}{\partial \theta^2} = MH_L \cos \theta + MH_T \sin \theta + 2K (\cos^2 \theta - \sin^2 \theta) > 0 \tag{4}$$

Transitions from unstable to stable states will occur at critical field for which $\partial^2 E/\partial \theta^2 = 0$. Eliminating θ in the above equations, we find, for the critical value

$$H_T^{2/3} + H_L^{2/3} = \left(\frac{2K}{M}\right)^{2/3} \tag{5}$$

which is a hypocycloid, usually called astroid, the vertices of which are at $(\pm 2k/M, 0)$ and $(0, \pm 2k/M)$. The astroid can be used to determine the magnetization direction graphically for any given field.

When a field equal to H_k is applied in the hard direction the magnetization is also parallel to this direction. In order to store information in a film element, positive or a negative bit field is applied in easy direction and the word field is switched off. Figure 5.3 shows how the magnetization rotates back to the easy axis. Depending on the polarity of the bit field, 0 or 1 is stored in the film element. To a first order, the values of H_k and H_c will specify the operating currents. The field needed for rotational switching vary directly with H_k while the maximum longitudinal field which can be applied without causing wall motion is H_c.

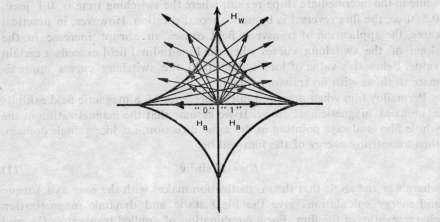

Figure 5.3 Writing the binary '0' and '1' by means of a bit field (bipolar operation).

On most films, if measurements are made, it is found that switching occurs for longitudinal fields considerably lower than predicted by the rotational threshold curve for cases in which $H_T \ll H_k$. This merely reflects that the rotational and wall motion processes are competitive and wall motion can occur first in many cases. Consequently, the wall motion threshold H_c/H_k is marked on Figure 5.3. The ratio of coercive force to anisotropy field and the nature of creep threshold obviously vary with material thickness and the fabrication process. Wall coercive force for an infinite planar film is found to vary inversely with the thickness of the film according to t^{-n}, where n usually varies between $1/2$ and $3/2$ depending upon the substrate surface and the method of film preparation. The film is deposited on a locally smooth surface such as fire polished glass or mica. To provide uniform surface, the substrate is normally cleaned ultrasonically, placed in a bell jar and a layer of SiO evaporated just prior to the permalloy. During film deposition the temperature of the substrate is maintained at 350°C. This tends to drive gases from the substrate and provides an anneal which generally results in a lower value of anisotropy field. Also, the rate of deposition is controlled since higher evaporation rates produce more uniform films. The pressure during the evaporation is maintained typically at 10^{-5} mm of mercury.

Not all films can be used as memory elements, and a film proposed for such use must be tested to determine whether it is sufficiently homogeneous and meets the specifications with respect to sense signal, drive currents, etc. The selection fields for switching can be applied in different directions with respect to easy direction of the material giving rise to different performance characteristics and material requirements for satisfactory memory operation. In word organized memory system, the word line provides the transverse field. In this system the material requirements are low and the material is normally capable of extremely high speed operation. Another conventional class of memory organization is known as bit organized system, which means that the information in one element can be changed without destroying the information in the other elements. In practice a distinction is also made between destructive readout (DRO) elements and nondestructive readout (NDRO) elements. All these are discussed in subsequent sections.

5.3 CLASSIFICATION OF MAGNETIC THIN FILM MEMORIES

Computer memories can be characterized by their capacity and speed, and the future development will tend to increase both to the highest possible degrees. Although the ferrite cores have offered the best compromise from the point of view of speed, cost and reliability, but the developments in magnetic thin film elements and integrated circuits promise fast speed, low cost and easy fabrication. For fast memories magnetic thin films are, due to their nanosecond switching time, the most promising memory elements. High speed memory units using planar magnetic thin films have been built. In addition to planar films, cylindrical magnetic thin films are now commercially available. Difficulties in obtaining the uniformity of the characteristics of these films led to further research into electrodeposited films, rather than evaporation, which resulted in the successful production of the plated wire memory elements.

Also, when a pair of thin film memory elements are placed face to face, sandwitching striplines, the magnetic film lines of individual magnetic fields are almost wholly contained in magnetic material. This forms another class of magnetic film, known as *coupled films*. These films, therefore, operate with large disturb margins and produce relatively large output signal but require only small input current. We shall briefly discuss below the important classes of magnetic film memories and their salient features obtained by the different techniques.

5.3.1 Planar Magnetic Thin Film Memories

Planar magnetic thin film memories represent one of the most established approaches to batch fabrication of storage arrays. Thin film memories use a smaller array of discrete elements fabricated by vacuum deposition process on a substrate, such as glass or aluminium. The NiFe alloy in a crucible evaporates and a thin film condenses on a heated substrate (25 to 400°C) mounted about 30 cm above the crucible. A well cleaned glass or metal, such as, Ag, Al, or Cu is used as substrate. The pressure during evaporation is held between 10^{-5} and 10^{-6} mm of Hg, and a magnetic field is applied in the plane of the film to align the easy axis of magnetization. The easy axis of magnetization is normally chosen parallel to the longest side of the element. Each element is typically about 1000 angstroms thick and is approximately 25×50 mils in area. Three sheets of mylar, with conductors are mounted on the top of the memory plane. The conductors parallel to easy axis are called word lines. The broad conductors normal to easy axis are called bit lines and the narrow conductors normal to easy axis are known as sense lines. Figure 5.4 shows a typical memory plane with associated drive lines.

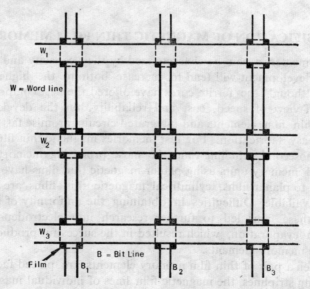

Figure 5.4 Schematic illustration of a memory plane
with word and bit lines.

Other classes of developments use either a continuous sheet or narrow strips of thin magnetic film, vacuum deposited on the same substrate with appropriate insulation between them. In some cases drive and sense lines are fabricated on separate substrate which are then mechanically superimposed over the one containing the magnetic elements. Registration problems are less severe for the strip and the continuous sheet arrays.

In conventional planar thin film memory, the word lines run parallel to easy axis of magnetization creating a field pattern in hard direction. The digit and sense lines run parallel to hard axis of magnetization, creating a field pattern in easy direction. A word line rotates all bit positions of a word in the hard direction, but they tend to flip back, when released. A relatively small digit signal pushes them into the one state or back to the zero state, as desired. In both planar and cylindrical thin film memories, a word field and a digit field are applied at right angle to one another in such a way that they combine at one and only one memory element. This arrangement permits a fairly large tolerance in drive currents. It permits each field to be somewhat greater than its nominal value without causing spurious switching, while permitting both fields to be somewhat less than nominal and still cause switching where they combine.

Since planar magnetic thin film memories are basically open flux device, the sense signal is small. The flux is only rotated rather than switched, and this results in a smaller sense signal and a tendency to creep or demagnetize along the outer edges of the bit spot. Due to later effect, a large number of disturb signals may tend to destroy the information stored in the bit position. To avoid the creep problem, the film is made thinner. The thicker the film, the greater is the tendency to demagnetization and creep; on the other hand, the thinner the film, the less is the sense signal. Hence, a compromise must be made between the desired sense signal and minimum creep in choosing the thickness of the film.

Thin film memories are usually operated in a linear select or word-oriented mode rather than a coincident current mode, because of the inherent magnetic properties of planar films. Most planar thin film memories operate in destructive readout mode. The speed advantage of magnetic thin films is tempered by the need to write back the original information immediately after reading. On the other hand, most cylindrical thin films, particularly, plated wires, use nondestructive readout (NDRO) principle, the magnetization is rotated only slightly, giving a much smaller readout signal, but permitting a large memory to operate with smaller number of electronic circuits that are shared among different parts of the memory.

However, to get the successful operation with magnetic thin film one should carefully design, and control the memory's external circuits and also the film's deposition processes. During deposition, it is necessary to optimize anisotropy and to minimize skew. Regarding the stability of magnetic thin films, Ni-Fe films are not very stable, and time dependent changes of their properties are observed even at room temperature. High temperature exposure may cause gross metallurgical changes. At lower temperature, changes in properties are caused by magnetization controlled reorientation of original field induced anisotropy. In the memory, the failure rate is determined by the loss in operating margins of the site as the material characteristics change. Thus the increase in bit failure or error rate over the life of the memory depends on the memory design as well as on the material parameters. Additional development work has been going on in the area of multilayer planar thin film structures which offer the possibility of extremely high density. The problem of uniformity, yield, and high density interconnections of such large batch fabricated arrays make this still appear to be a high risk approach.

5.3.2 Cylindrical Thin Film Memories

Cylindrical thin magnetic films plated on wires with axially oriented storage states, find wide applications in modern high performance computer memories. There are two versions of cylindrical thin film memories which are generally used in commercial computers, namely, the magnetic 'Rod', and the 'Plated wire'. These two types of film memories offer a number of advantages over planar films in that the closed flux path and the close physical coupling between the film and the wire substrate require smaller digit currents and produce a large sense signal. Use of wire substrate as either the digit or word conductor reduces the mechanical registration problems in the fabrication of the memory.

Magnetic rods, which are organized in arrays like cores, have been used in many experimental and commercial memories. The rods used in NCR's 315 RMC processor are made from a continuous length of beryllium-copper wire 10 mils in diameter. This wire is passed at a constant speed of 15 feet per minute through a series of bath containing an alloy of Ni and Fe. When the wire emerges from the last bath it is immediately and continuously tested, helically wound with a copper ribbon, and cut into pieces seven inches long.

In this rod memory, a 4000 Å cylindrical film of magnetic material is deposited. The axial switching mode produces an open flux path element. A multiple turn winding is placed over the plated rod for each bit position. The plating material is essentially isotropic and have high coercive force, so that proper operation of the memory does not depend on anisotropy in the material. The use of high coercive material, tight coupling and multiple turn winding has the advantage of fast switching of the memory element and large output signal.

In another type of plated wire memory which has the advantage over the planar thin films and cylindrical magnetic rod memories, the direction of magnetization of the cylindrical elements is circumferential to the plated wire, providing closed flux paths and renders less liable to creep effect. The closed flux path offers significant advantages over the open path devices, that the film thickness is not dictated by consideration of self-demagnetization, with no gaps in the path, the minimum bit current is obtained for a given material and path length.

A nickel iron film (80% Ni and 20% Fe) of the order of 1 micron thickness, is plated on a specially cleaned and prepared beryllium copper wire 2 to 5 mils in diameter. During plating a current passes through the wire to generate a magnetic field which induces a circumferential anisotropy in the film as the electrodeposition proceeds. This anisotropy implies that the film has a preferred or an easy direction of magnetization around the wire circumference. The word drive conductors consist of flat metal strips placed over the parallel digit wires. The word drive strips are either returned under the digit wires or terminated in a ground plane beneath the digit wires. The digit wires are placed on 15 mils centres and the word drive straps on 45 mils centres. A typical crosspoint geometry of plated wire memory is shown in Figure 5.5. The storage elements are formed at the intersection of plated digit wires and the word strap lines. Typical bit density is about 1500 bits per square inch. This memory uses low level signal switching and selection prior to the sense amplifier.

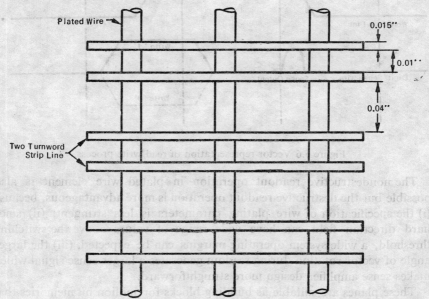

Figure 5.5 Crosspoint geometry of plated wire memory system.

Binary data are stored in the two stable states of clockwise and anticlockwise easy direction remanence. Figure 5.6 shows the vector representation of the read/write process. To read the content of the elements, a hard direction field is applied and the film magnetization vector rotates towards the hard axis, inducing a signal in the substrate wire of a polarity corresponding to the stored bit. For destructive readout operation the hard direction field is of sufficient magnitude to exceed the anisotropy field of the element. On removal of this field, the magnetic vector would fall back arbitrarily to one or other of the circumferential remanence conditions bearing the element demagnetized. To control either regeneration or writing in of a new data before removal of word current, a small digit current of a polarity corresponding to the required direction of vector rotation is applied.

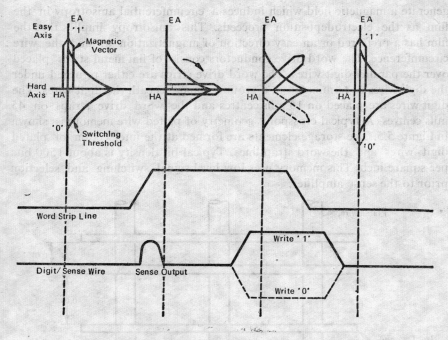

Figure 5.6 Vector representation of read/write process.

The nondestructive readout operation in plated wire element is also possible but the destructive readout operation is more advantageous, because (i) the specification of wire plating parameters is less stringent; (ii) since hard direction field can have wide range of values above the switching threshold, a wide system operating margins can be expected; (iii) the larger angle of vector rotation during readout generates a larger sense signal which makes sense amplifier design more straightforward.

These planes are suitable as building blocks for million bit memories that cycle in less than 100 nsec, and can be operated with a word current of 60 mA and a bit current of 30 mA, the output signal is approximately 150 microvolts and readout mode is nondestructive. These memories operate at or near a limit imposed by thermal noise in the amplifier, indicating that further development in detection techniques should be incorporated to keep pace with other magnetic memories. The electronic circuits and the memory planes containing the plated wires are undergoing evolutionary changes, most of them representing attempts to improve the signal-to-noise ratio. They include a new low gain preamplifier stage, layout changes in sense amplifier and signal strobe circuits, and improved low level switching circuits.

There is still another form of plated wire memory which is very similar but uses a weaving process to fabricate the plane. The plated wire, which acts as both the storage media and digit drive line, is woven into a matrix at right angles to the insulated word drive lines. This provides a tighter magnetic coupling than in ordinary plated wire memory, but the major difference lies in the fabrication techniques.

Plated wire memories have been designed or proposed for mass memory, internal memory, aerospace memory, and read only memory application.

5 3.3 Coupled Film and Other Types of Memory

The advantages of magnetostatically coupled films over the thin film approach were shown by Chang, Suits and Pugh et al. These include: (i) smaller memory cells as a result of reduced demagnetizing field, (ii) larger output signal, and (iii) low input current. Moreover, these films have the same advantages as the thin film memory performances so far as the speed, capacity and cost are concerned. In such a coupled film memory, an additional layer of magnetic material is placed between the two conductors of flat film configuration. The static magnetic properties of additional layers, however, depend on the material in the previous layers as well as the thickness and deposition temperature of those layers. The characteristics of the lower magnetic layer are, in general, not dependent on the post-evaporated layers, except when it is exposed to a temperature high enough to cause recrystallization or diffusion between layers.

Depending upon the direction of applied dc magnetic field during the evaporation process, two versions of coupled film are possible. In one type, the flux is magnetostatically coupled in the easy direction of the film. The easy axis of the film is horizontal, and the two films are magnetostatically coupled around the bit sense line. This is shown in Figure 5.7. In the other version the easy axis of the film is along the lines (into the paper in Figure 5.7) and is termed as *closed hard axis configuration*. Both the structures are physically alike, and there is essentially no difference in the fabrication process.

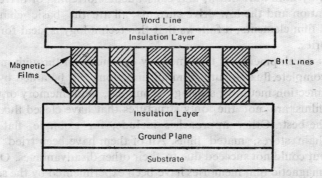

Figure 5.7 Cross-sectional view of a typical closed easy axis memory plane.

Two layers of permalloy films are deposited on both sides of a thin copper bit line. In the structure shown in Figure 5.7 the ground plane is used to provide the return paths for the currents sent through the bit sense lines and the word lines. Thus the two insulation layers are required. The flux closure is no longer held during the read operation, since both films have their magnetization drive in the hard direction. Typical thickness of layers are 6-12 μ for an evaporated ground plane and for insulation, and 1000 Å for permalloy films and 1 to 6 μ for strip lines. All the dimensions can vary over a considerable range; different working models have been built with different dimensions.

In the design of the film, the choice of materials and dimensions is determined largely by electromagnetic requirements and material compatibility. The desired range of magnetic properties determines the choice of alloy composition for magnetic films as well as the deposition temperature, and the film thickness. The material and the thickness of conductor layer are determined by system design, being chosen to give minimum attenuation of drive currents and sense signals. Since the magnetostatically coupling of the two magnetic films require a small separation, high conductivity metals are desirable. The insulation between the bit lines and word lines is thinner, to minimize the magnetic reluctance in the hard direction, but not so thin that capacitive loading between the two sets of conductors would be a problem.

In order to obtain the flux property during read operation, a magnetic keeper may be placed over the word line. This ferrite keeper is the best way to limit current spreading in the ground plane, but it does not work very well at high frequencies because its permeability decreases as frequency increases.

Both plated wires and coupled films obtain complete flux closure around only one conductor. Partial closure around the other conductor is achieved by a ferrite keeper. Coupled film elements permit greater miniaturization than other magnetic film elements; their storage density can be made large. Also, the signal transmission delays in the drive and sense lines are obviously reduced by miniaturization, and consequent shortening of drive lines. As miniaturization and the low drive currents, all are the basic characteristics of coupled film elements, it follows that this technology is ideal for large and fast memories.

Further development of film memory optimization through miniaturization and complete flux closure from all directions will be aided by advances in interconnection methods, sensing techniques, and memory organization. Coupled films are not the only structures that have closed flux paths but they are the best. Other approaches include, for example, flat film with keepers, chain stores, mated films. All of them have been tried by manufacturers but could not succeed due to their other disadvantages. Other forms of hybrid magnetic film memories have been experimented by the scientists in different laboratories. Of these hybrid technology—the post and film memory technique shows some positive results. This technique comprises either one or two continuous films on the top of a ferrite wafer which has two sets of closely spaced grooves cut into it at right angles. The system, thus, creates an array of square posts that provides a path for flux closure, thereby preventing creep effect. Word wires are in the grooves parallel to the film's easy axis of magnetization, digit wires are in the orthogonal grooves. Flux closure in this case is through the ferrite rather than air. This design offers high reliability, wide operating tolerances, low noise, and very low power dissipation—as a result of which the drive and sense circuits can be built with monolithic integrated circuits.

Lastly, another very promising batch fabricated, high packing density memory is known as *waffel-iron memory*. The system uses square wafers of ferrite which is grooved to make an array of posts. The word and digit lines pass through these grooves at right angles to each other. The storage film is electroplated on a metal substrate, and as the film is thick and isotropic, the plating requirement is less stringent in this case than in the other thin film memories. On these substrates, the ferrite wafer is placed and they are maintained in position with the associated word and digit lines by a spring clamp. This has the added advantage of repairing or inspecting, either the film or the ferrite unit.

A hybrid technology which gives the designer the advantages of thin films over the core, such as batch fabrication, high speed, wide temperature range, NDRO capability and low noise, but at the same time, it overcomes the thin films disadvantages, such as close tolerances on drive currents and tendency to creep. The packing density is about ten times that of plated wire memories, the signal output is about two times and the capacitivecoupling is much less than plated wire memory system.

5.4 THIN FILM MEMORY PLANE CHARACTERISTICS

The reasons of research and development towards ferromagnetic thin film memories are well-known. Apart from their higher speeds, they possess other basic properties which significantly enlarge their (for both flat sheets and thin cylinder) potential memory use beyond that attainable in ferrite toroidal core memory. First, magnetically effective fields may be applied simply in either of the perpendicular directions because of the small demagnetizing factors in the plane of the film. Secondly, a single storage element may be composed of two or more layers of magnetic material to achieve unusual and desirable memory properties. Lastly, thin geometry lends itself to etched wiring strip line techniques.

Although it has been for long known that thin Ni-Fe film memory elements can be switched in a very few nanoseconds, the extent to which their potential can be exploited is limited by the electrical and mechanical characteristics of the total memory system. Such limits are imposed, for example, by array noise, signal amplification and consequent delay, transistor driver capabilities and the organization of regeneration loop.

5.4.1 Substrate Selection

The major decision that should be taken at an early stage, is that whether to use magnetic films deposited on metallic ground planes or to use films deposited on glass or mica. If the substrates are conductors, the return lines can be eliminated by shorting bit and word lines to the substrate. Return paths for current flow are then provided by substrate or ground plane. In addition to reducing the number of strip lines in the memory, the scheme also reduces line impedance and stray fields since the thickness of the substrate does not intervene between the drive lines and its electrical return path. Also during the film deposition, as the metallic substrates are good thermal conductor, greater uniformity of bit properties can be obtained during film deposition. Glasses are sometimes used as substrate because of their surface smoothness, and also glass yields films with lowest rotational coercive force field (magnetic anisotropy field). Also, the lower susceptibility to stresses of the thicker glass is important for many characteristics in early film evaluation. Using glass substrate, the bit spacing is limited by the substrate thickness, since the fields generated by currents in the drive conductors are spread with respect to increasing the substrate thickness.

Major disadvantages of metallic substrate include current spreading in the ground plane, which effectively reduces drive margins, and the trapping of magnetic flux of the bit which increases the bit field required to switch the film. However, these ground plane eddy current problems can be reduced to some extent by using magnetic keeper and by careful design of electronic circuits.

5.4.2 Operational Mode

Since the selection fields for switching the magnetic film elements can be applied in different directions with respect to easy, axis, various performance characteristics are possible in magnetic film memories. The basic requirements for a magnetic film memory device can be understood by referring to idealized critical curve for single domain rotational switching and to internal creep threshold curve shown in Figure 5.18. Rotational switching is possible when the sum of applied fields exceeds the critical curve. In practical films, single domain behaviour does not occur for all of the field configuration implied in Figure 5.1b. Various reversal processes have been adequately discussed in literature.

However, to avoid the loss of stored information the film must be stable against all fields which may be applied between the time information is stored and the time it is finally read. If one of the memory selection fields is parallel to the easy direction (H_x) and one is perpendicular to easy direction, a number of different modes of memory operation are possible. With this field arrangement and coincident current selection, moderately high speed, relatively small destructive readout memories can be made requiring good material uniformity. The magnitude of transverse field (H_y)

is limited by creep threshold and the unwanted signal, and hence it is desirable to keep this field as small as possible. But this imposes the restriction of relatively high ration of H_c/H_k. The optimum choice of H_a and H_y will be determined by the shape of the creep threshold, simply rotational threshold, and attainable value of H_c/H_k.

In a word organized system, the orthogonal drive scheme offers high speed nearly coherent device switching, as opposed to the much slower wall motion switching associated with parallel drive scheme. In addition, this mode offered relaxed tolerances on drive currents and film properties. The size and speed of this type of memory is determined primarily by the electronics of the system. Delays in the sense and inhibit windings along with the necessity of turning on the inhibit driver to rewrite information limit the speed of operation. The full select or half select currents from the word select gates also impose a limit on size. Small memories with cycle time of less than 100 nsec is feasible with this type of operation.

5.4.3 Testing of Memory Arrays

Magnetic films are typically made in batches on flat substrates or wires. Evaluation of the performance of fully assembled memory planes is necessary before they are used in memory operations. Magnetic film memories undergo a pulse test which subject each bit to transverse and longitudinal disturb fields. Films are more susceptible to transverse disturbance than to longitudinal disturbance. The characteristics of individual elements, specially those in a continuous sheet, are highly dependent on environmental conditions, e.g. on the geometric structure, dimension of the array, presence of magnetic material around the individual storage areas, and presence of metallic substrate on which the film is deposited.

For satisfactory operation of memory, the fields applied to half selected elements from all sources must lie within the stable operating region, and the fields applied to a fully selected element must be adequate to ensure switching under the worst conditions. All the sources of spurious fields on the memory elements must be taken into account to ensure adequate operation. This, in general, will depend on the type of element construction which is used. Specifically the factors which must be taken into account are: (a) demagnetizing fields, (b) misalignment of easy axis, (c) effective element dispersion, and (d) worst pattern of stored information.

However, the worst case pattern which includes all effects known to be deleterious to device performance, is shown in Figure 5.8. This consists of five parts—precycle, pump and set, write, disturb and read. Before the start of each pulse test, the magnetic material around the individual storage locations was set antiparallel to the magnetization of the area under test by an external magnetic field in order to simulate worst case condition.

During precycle, the bit (W_i, B_j) is saturated with 10^3 write operations, of incident word and bit pulses, in a direction opposite to the desired informa-

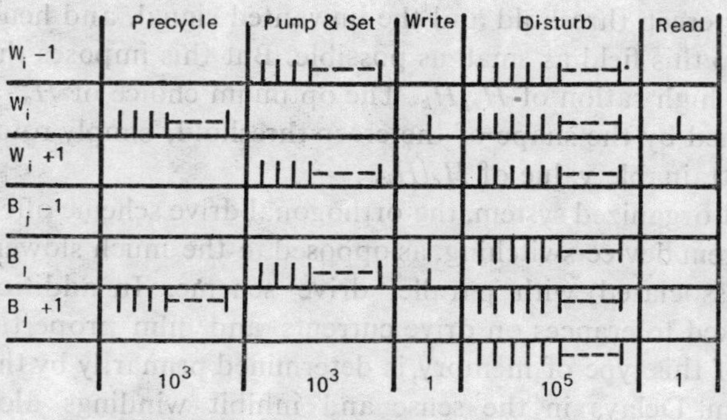

Figure 5.8 Worst case pulse pattern.

tion state. This is done to ensure maximum bit spreading. The pump and set sequence consists of a series of 10^3 bit pulses and coincident adjacent word line pulses. The write pulse follows the last pump and set pulse by a time no greater than would occur in the memory cycle to realize the effects of the pumped up ground plane current. A bit pulse is simultaneously sent down the adjacent bit lines of such polarity that their stray field will oppose the writing bit field. The net bit field acting on the bit at write time will be the field from the bit pulse minus the field from the pumped up ground plane current, the stray fields from the adjacent bits, and the demagnetizing field from its own lines of flux which remain trapped in the ground plane during switching. The disturb portion of the cycle is designed to destroy the write information by domain wall creep. Lastly, the read pulse is preceded by a pause long enough for the various transient effects to subside so that the circuit noise will be minimized. After the pause, a single read pulse is applied to word line W_t. The pulse is designed to simulate the most seriously degraded word pulse in the array. The response of the element is tested by measuring the voltage time integral of the sense signal induced in the sense line by the element under test during the read operation. Sensing (in the tester) is done on a short loop terminated for minimum reflection at its output end. The detected signals must be sufficiently large than specifications to account for all uncertainties of calibration, tester noise, etc.

5.5 ORGANIZATION OF THIN FILM MEMORIES

The principal field of application of planar magnetic thin film memory lies in computer main memories having capacities of about one million bit or greater with short cycle times. For small capacity stores, semiconductor memories have an advantage in cost and system flexibility, while for slower memories, core memories are likely to remain competitive. The high speed capabilities of planar thin film stores have been limited to scratch pad applications. Although it is obvious that magnetic film element can be switched to approximately 1.0 nsec, the speed of magnetic film memories that have been reported by several researchers lies in the range of 100 nsec. The big gap between the element switching time and memory speed is partly due to the spatial extension of memory array with its unavoidable delays. This is mainly due to the big drive currents and the weak signals which require gains of several order of magnitude. The delays in the circuit and their recovery time, therefore, determine the speed to a great extent.

Magnetic films are used for information processing machine architecture in two main areas, namely, random access high speed memory and serial access lower speed memory. These films are made in batches on flat substrates or wires. A number of element geometries have been used to build these memories. For example, two strip lines wraped around a single film element, or a single element placed against a ground plane that provides return path may be used to build these memories. Sometimes, use of two wire strip lines with coated wire or a flat film with a high permeability keeper to prevent undesirable effects are used for this purpose. Each of the various element geometries may have certain constructional or performance behaviour. Before going further into the organized behaviour of a magnetic thin film memory we shall briefly discuss the film material properties that are important in design specifications of memory system.

5.5.1 Material and Array Characteristics

Magnetic memory planes are usually made by evaporation. Other well investigated processes like electrodeposition, vapour reaction (including thermal decomposition) and sputtering technique have found their place in the list of useful process, each having its inherent advantages for some applications. In the preparation of films for computer application it is desirable to use a material that is insensitive to stress introduced during packaging or handling which require materials having zero magnetostriction. Similarly, low magnetocrystalline anisotropy is desirable to minimize grain orientation effects. Thus, a material having both zero magnetostriction and zero magnetocrystalline anisotropy with an easily variable uniaxial anisotropy is desired ideally. Normally all these parameters varying the degrees of dependence on film composition, require a compromise to achieve usable films. For the permalloy material, these considerations have led the investigators to concentrate on the 81.5% Ni and 18.5% Fe alloy, which has zero magnetostriction and low magnetocrystalline anisotropy.

The use of thin film in a memory depends on the two stable magnetic states of high remanence in zero applied field as shown earlier. The reliability of stored information depends on this, much work has gone into understanding how to obtain films, and design film arrays, which resist demagnetization from various stray field effects. External fields may be avoided by means of shielding but the internally generated fields due to adjacent 'bit' of information, or from induced or capacitive sneak currents, or from currents used to read or write operation possess some difficulties. The major stack design problem has been the reduction of capacitively induced interference from the word to sense line. The demagnetizing field which occurs by wall motion to some extent can be controlled by increasing the wall motion threshold, i.e. by increasing the coercive force H_c.

The array characteristics are highly dependent on the properties of magnetic materials used for memory application. Word drive is controlled to a first order by the anisotropy and demagnetizing fields, bit drive by angular dispersion and anisotropy field, and the signal output by the film thickness. The basic array properties can be summarized as in Table 5.1. This is only an approximate one but provides a guidance for memory materials and design development. The material properties to some extent can be modified by adding cobalt to cover a wide range of specifications.

TABLE 5.1
Basic Array Characteristics

Parameter	Physical mechanism involved	Controlling factor
Signal flux	Magnetization rotation	Volt-time integral signal
Word current	Field Interaction (applied demagnetization anisotropy)	Signal amplitude, H_k, etc.
Current cell area product	Field interactions	Signal amplitude, H_k, etc.
Maximum bit current (disturb)	Wall motion	Drive field, H_k and H_c
NDRO capability	High anisotropy components in H_k distribution coupled to low anisotropy components	Composition, grain size, substrate thickness and roughness
Coercive force	Wall motion threshold	Grain size, strain, thickness, crystal texture
Anisotropy field	Ordering of Fe atom	Composition, annealing temperature strain

The addition to cobalt increases the saturation flux density and hence the signal output. It also increases the coercive force and thereby reducing the creep effect; and lastly, it raises the anisotropy field reducing the demagnetizing effect.

The memory planes are usually made by evaporation and are built on typical silver copper alloy substrate on which successive pumpdowns are used to etch the NiFe film into a pattern of rectangular spots. The films can be deposited on glass or mica. The word, sense and compensation lines are laminated on mylar foils. The magnetostatic parameters of different NiFe films should be identical, typical values being $H_c = 2.6$ Oe, $H_k = 6$ Oe, and skew and dispersion are $\pm 1.5°$. The pressure during evaporation is maintained at 10^{-5} to 10^{-6} mmHg and a magnetic field is applied in the plane of the film to align the easy axis. The substrate temperature is a very important parameter in deciding the film properties. The heating of the substrate at higher temperature drives gases from the substrate and provides an anneal which generally results in substantially lower anisotropy value for films at lower temperature. The other properties of substrate that are important in this context include their composition and chemical stability, microstructure and surface structure, thermal and different mechanical characteristics. The main drawback of metal substrate is the current spreading in the ground plane which effectively reduces the drive margins.

The most important engineering problem in memory plane is to achieve the optimum combination of capacity and speed attainable within the limitations imposed by transmission delays, cross-talk and circuit bandwidth. The size of thin film spot is another factor in determining memory performance. Input drive currents, signal output are almost proportional to spot size. Various attempts are made to reduce the spot size and thereby to reduce transmission delays. A variety of different techniques, such as selective etch, optical and infrared spectroscopy are used in evaluating the films. The tests include various measurements of physical parameters as well as insulation effectiveness as measured by passivation of microelectronic devices. In optical method, the refractive index and film thickness are measured by a specially constructed interference microscope. The refractive index of a film is influenced by its density, composition, and its oxygen deficiency. In the other techniques, known as infrared spectroscopy, the band position, half widths, and intensities, information on the composition and structure of the glass is obtained.

5.5.2 Memory Configuration

A number of experimental magnetic film memory systems have been built and their achievements reported. These differ from ferrite memory elements in two important ways. The nickel-iron alloy used for thin films is deposited under conditions that cause a magnetic anisotropy and the film thickness and geometry are chosen to permit coherent rotational switching. The magnetic anisotropy makes possible the simple operating mode that is widely used, in which coherent rotational switching of the magnetization can be completed in several nanoseconds. Subject to minimum word length requirements, the store may be easily organized internally with word lengths that are binary multiple of the system word length. Various schemes are suggested by logic designers to best utilize the multiple word address. Typical large memories are divided into smaller substrates which are then connected in a row to increase the number of bits and a number of such rows increase the number of words in a memory plane. A number of such planes constitute the total capacity of the memory unit.

The typical organization of memory plane having 32 words and 36 bits per word in shown in Figure 5.9. The system is organized in a conventional word organized rotational switching mode, since the requirements for film uniformity are less stringent. There are 32 word drivers, one for each word line, with the associated decoder and address registers. The address is decoded at the input of every word driver. The word field applied parallel to film's hard direction, rotates the magnetization vectors from their easy direction into the hard direction. In this method one word pulse per cycle is used, the leading edge of which performs reading by including bipolar read signals into the sense line. The input/output registers are connected to the sense-bit loop circuits by means of 'enabled read' gates for controlling the read signals and the 'write' gates for controlling the write signals. Writing and rewriting is performed at the end of the word pulse in conjunction with an overlapping bipolar bit pulse. Furthermore, a gate driver circuit is shown that is common to all 36 bit sense loop circuits to detect the read and write signals.

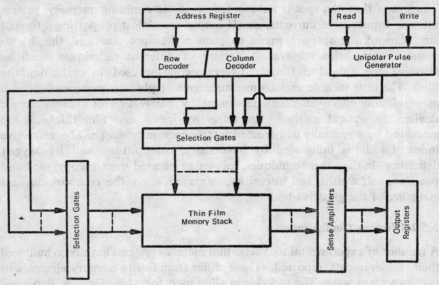

Figure 5.9 Block diagram of a thin film memory organization.

The main function of word selection circuitry is that it should be capable of delivering a word pulse of up to 800 mA amplitude with very small rise and fall times into a terminated word line. The choice of selection circuit is greatly dependent on the size of the memory. In a small memory (say up to a few hundred words), a straightforward approach of one driver per line with high level matrix decoding is used. A system like this has the merits of its simplicity and ease of design. However, in a larger system (4096 words) the number of drivers required makes this scheme impractical. A diode matrix scheme is used. Similarly, the drivers and sense amplifiers for magnetic film memories must be designed according to certain basic criteria such as, maximum gain bandwidth product, and minimum propagation delay. The rise time of the drive pulses must be small enough to achieve reasonable sense signals. The requirement of minimum propagation delay for fast access time means that the transistors must be operated in their active region and not be driven into saturation or cut off. This is in contradiction to the requirement for having minimum standby power, and a compromise has to be made. For high speed memories the drivers must be decoupled to avoid level shift and they must be carefully designed with respect to heat dissipation.

The memory cycle is initiated by a 'start' pulse which turns on both the gate driver circuit and one of the word driver, the output current pulse of which induces read signal in all sense lines, with the polarity of the signals depending on the stored information. The polarity of the read signals is detected in the sense bit loop circuits which in turn supply readout information and bit pulses of the proper polarity for rewriting. The start pulse is also accompanied by a 'write pulse' for inserting new informations into the memory. The write pulse transfers the new information via the write gates into the sense bit loop circuits before the read signals arrive. The memory timing diagram is shown in Figure 5.10.

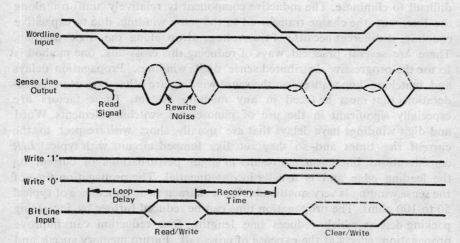

Figure 5.10 Timing diagram of a read/write cycle.

Transmission line principle is generally used for high speed current pulses which are transmitted through long conductors to prevent ringing in these lines. The sense amplifier is the most difficult part in the film memory circuitry. The sense and digit lines are closely coupled and although a first order cancellation of the interference takes place, the peak amplitude of the digit noise may be more than hundred times the signal amplitude. This must have delayed to a level that is small compared with the signal at read time, and the time taken for this interference to decay is likely to be the ultimate limit to cycle time in large thin film stores. Although the signal output from a film element is high, the common mode noise on the balanced sense line caused by the word current changing and the uncommon mode noise caused by the digit current changing could be large enough. Rejection of the former and rapid recovery from the latter are essential to the operation of the sense amplifier. For high speed operation the period between read and write is necessarily short. For 200 nsec cycle time memory, the tolerable sense amplifier delay can be only about 10 nsec. The current gain required can be defined as

$$A = I_d/I_s$$

where I_d is digit current for restore, I_s is sense winding current during read, A is the required current gain. Unfortunately, I_s varies greatly due to sense winding length as well as from losses and integrating effects. There are various approaches for rejecting the common mode noise and the most common one is to carry the signal in two separate channels followed by a difference amplifier.

Limitations on memory speeds and sizes (bits per common sense and digit circuit), neglecting the elements switching time, are determined primarily by the cross-talk sense amplifier delay and propagation time. Memory noise is both inductive and capacitive in nature, the capacitive noise is more difficult to eliminate. The inductive component is relatively uniform along the line, but the charge transferred to the sense winding, due to capacitive coupling, is different because of the voltage drop along the digit winding. There are several practical ways of reducing this cross-talk, one method is to use the progressive distributed sense digit windings. Propagation delays and matching impedances on the sense winding are other important considerations that must be faced in any memory system. These factors are especially significant in the use of nanosecond switching elements. Word and digit windings have delays that are usually short with respect to the current rise times and so they act like lumped circuits with typical L/R considerations, line mismatch results in slight perturbations of current on the leading edge and is usually inconsequential. The propagation time of the sense winding is very small and it has a characteristic impedance of typical 50 to 100 ohms. The propagation time can be reduced further by increasing packing density which reduces line lengths. Size reduction can improve propagation effects at the expense of cross-talk. Future memory speeds and sizes will be determined by optimizing switching current, line voltage drops, and winding organization to take advantage of nanosecond switching properties of thin film elements.

5.5.3 Magnetic Thin Film NDRO Memory

Aerospace processors and other digital equipment have obvious requirements for electrically alterable NDRO memories. The aerospace systems, in particular, have need for NDRO memories which are not only very reliable, but also consume very little power and are of very small volume. The simple uniaxial thin film is itself a poor NDRO element, and two or more different magnetic films (or different areas in the same film) are used for NDRO operation. These films rotate by different amounts under the influence of hard direction read pulse. The NDRO property is then based on magnetostatic or exchange coupling between the different regions which allows the less switched region to control the direction of fall back to the easy axis of the region.

The film's switching behaviour is best explained with the help of Stoner-Wohlfarth diagram, although this diagram is much complex with the introduction of biaxial anisotropy. The magnetic films in the NDRO memory possess mixed anisotropy, the uniaxial component of energy is:

$$E_1 = K_1 \sin^2\theta$$

while the biaxial component is given by

$$E_2 = K_2 \sin^2\theta \cos^2\theta \qquad (6)$$

where K_1 and K_2 are respectively the uniaxial and biaxial anisotropy constants of the material. When an external field is applied to the film, the total energy is given by

$$E = -H_x M \cos\theta - H_y M \sin\theta + \tfrac{1}{4} K_2 \sin^2 2\theta + K_1 \sin^2\theta \qquad (7)$$

Setting the first and second derivatives of E to zero yields parametric expressions for the two fields, H_x and H_y, as follows:

$$H_x = \frac{2K_2}{M} \left[\frac{1}{4} \sin\theta \sin4\theta + \cos\theta \cos4\theta + \frac{K_1}{K_2} \cos^3\theta \right] \qquad (8)$$

$$H_y = \frac{2K_2}{M} \left[\frac{1}{4} \cos\theta \sin4\theta - \sin\theta \cos4\theta + \frac{K_1}{K_2} \sin^3\theta \right] \qquad (9)$$

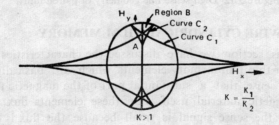

Figure 5.11 Switching curve for mixed biaxial and uniaxial anisotropy.

The critical threshold curve is shown in Figure 5.11. The direction of magnetization vector is given by the tangent drawn from the point of the applied field to the critical curve. For a field applied in the hard direction reversible switching occurs as long as the field does not exceed the threshold curve C_1. When the applied field crosses threshold curve C_1, the film operates in an intermediate state (region B), remaining in this state as long as the applied field is maintained within the C_2 curve. When the field is reduced to a magnitude smaller than point A, film's state becomes uncertain and the magnetization breaks up into components parallel to the direction. However, writing of a film state occurs when the point of the two applied fields (word and digit) falls outside of curves C_1 and C_2.

Thin magnetic films with characteristic suitable for NDRO operation, are now readily available. The typical memory contains array of flat magnetic films as shown in Figure 5.12. Each storage cell comprises a pair of coupled film spots, the spots being separated by the words sense and digit lines. Separation between the coupled film spots is about 4 to 6 mils and this magnetic coupling reduces the film's shape anisotropy by about

50 per cent. Three or multilayer NDRO coupled film devices have also been proposed in which the film thickness and film anisotropies can be adjusted. Such a device has a coupled easy axis (CEA) structure with two permalloy layers beneath the bit line and one above. The thicknesses are in the ratio 1 : 1 : 2, and the anisotropies are in the ratio 1 : 4 : 2. Such coupled films have the properties that the net easy direction demagnetizing field of the element remaining near zero throughout the readout cycle and only magnetostatic coupling of the elements is utilized.

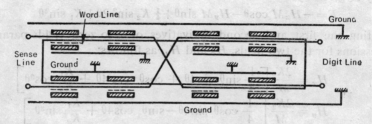

Figure 5.12 Digit sense line geometry of paired films.

5.6 PLATED WIRE CYLINDRICAL FILM MEMORY

In the previous section we have discussed the characteristics and organization of planar thin film memory elements which are basically open flux devices in the sense that a substantial part of the magnetic flux lines lies outside the magnetic material itself. For these elements flux path is not closed. Hence, the sense signal is small because the flux is only rotated rather than switched. These elements sustain an internal demagnetizing field opposing their magnetization. Due to this effect, a large number of disturb signals may tend to destroy the information stored in the bit position. Also, these miniaturized memory elements always generate smaller output signals and, therefore, require more sophisticated detector and amplifier designs. In the search for a memory device which combines the advantages of oriented magnetic flux devices with larger signals obtainable from ferrite cores, one looks for geometries which allow magnetic flux closure in both word and bit directions.

In closed flux devices, the magnetic fields are almost wholly contained in magnetic material itself, and the film thickness is not dictated by considerations of self-demagnetization. These elements usually operate with large disturb margins and produce relatively large output signals but require only small input currents. There are various approaches of closed flux devices such as, flat films with keepers, chain stores, mated films, coupled films, and plated wires.

The cylindrical film device which is used in the orthogonal mode, offers a more flexible approach to the utilization of fast rotational switching characteristics of metallic film than do the flat, open flux devices. In this device the hard axis of magnetization lies along the axis of cylinder while the easy axis is around the circumference of the cylinder. The magnetization theory discussed earlier, applies to this device also except that there is an additional contribution to the anisotropy by the geometry of the device. In practical condition some problems arise which should be taken into account in the final design phase of the memory system. One of the problem called *end effects*, arises due to nonuniformity of the hard direction field along the length of the cylinder. Since word drive line is narrow with respect to the length of the cylinder, there will be regions near the ends of the cylinder which do not switch. As a result, the signal output contributed by the ends during read may either add to or substract from the signal produced from the central portion of the cylinder. Regarding the length of the cylinder, it is clear from the memory point of view that the shorter the storage element the better is its performance, since drive line delay and attenuation are direct functions of the element length. However, the developments in fabrication techniques of cylindrical film, particularly plated wire technology, appears promising. Plated wire memories have been designed for a variety of applications, such as, mass memory, internal memory, read-only memory and associative memory systems.

The magnetic wire memory element developed in different organizations has a number of special properties that are particularly interesting when compared with those of the conventional ferrite cores and planar thin films. It has the potential for several major improvements in the cost performance index. Presently available 2 mil diameter plated wire permits a memory bit to be packaged within 3×10^{-6} cubic inch volume. This also allows for the exclusive use of medium scale integrated circuits in both the word digit and sense dimension in order to enhance the system reliability, reduce package complexity and power requirements and to lower the cost of plated wire memory systems.

5.6.1. Plated Wire Memory Element Preparation

Two basic approaches for plated wire memories, the strip line and the woven wire techniques are now commercially used. In the first technique, the word driver consists of flat metal strips placed over the digit wires. These word drive strips are either returned under the digit wires or terminated in a ground plane beneath the digit wires. Typical distances of digit lines are 30 mil centres and word strips are 50 mil centres, thus giving a packing density of 700 bits/in². The second type makes use of a weaving process to fabricate the memory planes. The plated wire is woven into a matrix at right angles to insulated word drive lines by means of a large automatic loom. The rest of the process is very similar to the strip line technique. The woven wire provides a tighter magnetic coupling than in the strip line approach and also enables easier implementation of multiple turns in order to reduce the drive currents.

Plated wire is a specially cleaned prepared beryllium copper wire, 2 to 5 mil in diameter, that is electroplated with a layer of 80 per cent Ni, 20 per cent Fe alloy material. Thickness of the permalloy films is of the order of one micron. Wire specimens are pre-annealed for six minutes immediately after plating in a nitrogen atmosphere at 250°C. The wires are then tested. The testing is implemented on the plating line and is in continuous operation by using a package identical in physical characteristics to the one in which it will be subsequently inserted. The testing operations measure four quantities—intrinsic amplitude of the readout pulse from the wire, effect of disturb currents in both the word and bit directions, and effect on a particular bit cell of repeated reading and writing operations in adjacent cells. These measurements are usually made immediately after the last step in the plating process. During plating a current is passed through the wire to generate a magnetic field which induces a circumferential anisotropy in the film as the electrodeposition proceeds. This anisotropy implies that the film has a preferred or easy direction of magnetization around the wire circumference. This circumferential magnetization allows for a combination of high speed rotational switching of magnetic films and the noise immunity of a closed flux path. This easy direction of magnetization of the closed flux path can be oriented either clockwise or counter-clockwise around the wire, and leads to the applications of the element as an efficient magnetic storage device for binary information.

However, the new frontier of plated wire technology is the *fabrication technique*. The different approaches have in common the fact that the plated wire comes into close contact with a keeper which completes the essential magnetic path. Such a magnetic configuration provides two important advantages. First, the required word current for a single turn or half turn word strap comes down to the 300-400 mA region. This permits the effective use of integrated edge circuits along the word dimension. Second, the inter-bit interference is reduced, allowing the bits to operate at higher density along the wire. Densities typically 50 bits per inch can easily be achieved.

5.6.2 Memory Design Objectives

Array design. The memory array is formed by means of simple orthogonal arrangement of plated wires and an overlay copper straps. Size of the memory stack depends on how close the bits are positioned, while size of the individual bit cells along the wire depends on the uniformity of the material and the hard direction threshold value. Also, the configuration and dimensions of word lines are important in determining bit density along the wire, because the word field on the adjacent bit depends on the word line configuration. The typical dimensions of word line in a memory system is shown in Figure 5.13. The mechanical construction of memory stack employs a digit line of double-sided printed circuit which is made on mylar. The flat wires are 10 mil copper dummy wires etched on both sides of the mylar. Similarly, the distance between digit lines depends on difficulties of positioning the wires and on limitations due to inductive and capacitive coupling. In the configuration shown in Figure 5.13, the word noise is cancelled between dummy and plated wire. Digit noise cancellation is obtained between the two halves of the stack. The positioning and holding of wires before soldering is a critical problem. After the wires are positioned, the printed circuit is folded and a sandwich of few planes is made with a possible distance between planes of less than 50 mils. Plexiglass or other insulating medium is used to separate the planes.

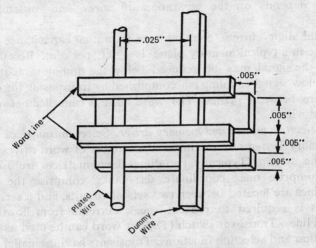

Figure 5.13 Details of a plated wire memory cell.

The behaviour of word line can be represented by transmission line model. For shorter line the reflected voltage is a function of several parameters such as rise time and amplitude of word current, length of transmission line (L), speed of propagation (v) on the word line, etc. The delay introduced in the word line can be represented by

$$T_D = L/v$$

while the current coupling is induced by the mutual inductance and capacitance between the digit lines. The approximate expression for the capacitance between two wires at an equal distance from ground plane is given by

$$C = \frac{0.12L}{\log_{10}\left(\dfrac{2D}{d}\right)}$$

where C is in pf, d is the diameter and D is the distance between the wires. In this case we have assumed that the separation between the wires is very small compared with their distance from the ground plane. The value of this capacitance for four adjacent lines ($2D/d = 10$) is approximately 10 pf.

Similarly the expression for mutual inductance (M) in μH between two wires is given by

$$M = 0.002L \left[2.3 \log_{10} \frac{2L}{d} - 1 + \frac{D}{L} \right]$$

Typical value of mutual inductance of four adjacent lines is of the order of 0.12 μH. Over and above to this value, there will be mutual inductance between the different memory planes. This value of mutual inductance obviously depends on the separation of wires and different memory planes.

The total digit current coupling due to mutual capacitance and mutual inductance in a typical memory plane is $\pm$ 11 per cent. Because of signal coupling, the signal may be reduced below the minimum required value. However, low signal coupling is accomplished by transposing the dummy and plated wire between planes. The word noise is cancelled between dummy and plated wire.

Word selection matrix and memory driver. Selection matrices are used in large memory systems to minimize the number of word drives required to operate the system. Typically, two dimensional matrices are used. Current sources comprise one coordinate set; sinks comprise the other. The memory lines are located between two sets of circuits, and a series of isolating diodes is required to prevent sneak currents from flowing through unselected lines. Transistor switch (TS) per word can be used as it performs both isolation and selection functions. Transistors having smaller collector to base capacitance are used, they must be designed so as to minimize the voltage swing of the base driver. The TS system offers low noise which is necessary for better performance of the memory unit. Another alternate approach for large memory system is to use diode-steered transformer matrix (DTS) for word selection. Diodes with less junction capacity are used here. The comparison between these two methods is summarized as follows.

In DTS system the characteristic impedance of the bus line must be as low as possible to minimize the voltage shift of the bus line and also the voltage swing must be greater than the peak amplitude of the back voltage on the word line. While in TS system the characteristic impedance of the bus line can be made higher, and the voltage swing which is a function of transistor parameter is generally smaller than the peak amplitude of the back voltages on the word line. A damping resistor is usually added in TS system only while the transformer in DTS system prevents common mode current.

Separate drivers for the read and write operation are generally provided for fast access memories. Individual read driver for each word generates the read currents, while the write currents emerge from the transistor matrix.

Sometimes bipolar currents are used for writing information into the memory systems. The obvious advantages of bipolar drive in a system are:

(i) Signal output will be large.

(ii) There will be no dc level shift on the digit line and this allows dc coupling of a sense amplifier to digit lines.

(iii) In digit drive circuit, one can use a transformer to reduce the memory cost.

(iv) As mentioned in (i), the threshold of digit current beyond which the wall creeping occurs, can be increased.

Moreover, if two phases of timing are provided for word current (as shown in Figure 5.14), one for the even planes and the other for the odd planes, it will become unnecessary to invert the polarity of readout signals or digit currents according to the plane of the selected word.

Reading and writing. There are two standard methods of reading—the easy axis and hard axis read. The easy axis read of a conventional plated wire memory depends on the voltage induced on the plated wire by the change of easy axis flux linkage while the hard axis read relies on the voltage induced on the straps by the change of the hard axis flux linkage. The relation of strap and wire currents is shown in Figure 5.14.

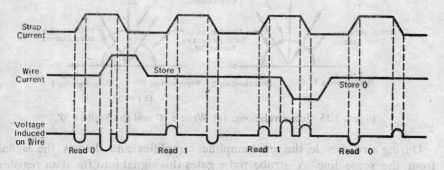

Figure 5.14 Timing diagram of strap and wire currents.

In hard axis read mode, a strap current is applied which rotates the stored magnetization representing 1 or 0 towards the hard axis. This movement decreases the flux linking the plated wire and at the same time creates new flux linking the strap. The resulting flux change induces a voltage of one polarity for a stored 1 and of the opposite polarity for a stored 0. This voltage which is induced on a plated wire, is generally sensed at the ends of the wire. However, it is also possible to detect the induced voltage on a strap. If the amplitude of the hard axis field is limited, the magnetization vector will turn to its original rest position when the driving field is turned off, and the readout is nondestructive.

If the strap and the plated wire are exactly orthogonal and there is absolutely no skew in the magnetic flux around the plated wire, then there will be no hard axis flux linkage. Under these assumptions there should be no detectable hard axis read signal when a small current flows through the plated wire. To overcome this difficulty, a bias current is sometimes fed into the strap. This bias current produces a small hard axis field which rotates the magnetic vectors away from their easy axis.

To write an information into a bit location, a strap current is first passed. This tilts the magnetization vector beneath the strap towards the hard axis direction. Then a wire current is passed which steers the termination of the current. Typical relation between the strap current, the wire current, and the voltage induced on the plated wire are shown in Figure 5.14. In this timing diagram, the wire current pulse is wide enough to overlap the trailing edge of the strap current. However, when the amplitude of the wire current is large enough, this overlap during the trailing edge of the strap current is not necessary. A bit can be written by applying a wire current over a short period in the presence of the strap current and then turning this wire current off prior to the trailing edge of the strap current. Figure 5.15 shows the magnetization vector relations of this form of write action. This form of write operation, however, alleviates the critical timing problem.

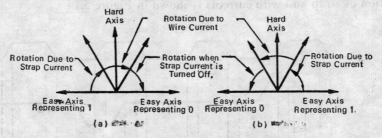

Figure 5.15 Vector relations: (a) Write a '1' and (b) Write a '0'.

During a read cycle, the sense amplifier amplifies and detects the signal from the sense line. A strobe pulse gates this signal into the data register so that a '1' signal emerging from the sense line setst hese flip-flops. The data register then contains the information previously stored at the selected memory address, and this information is available at the flip-flop outputs. The information is rewritten into the memory. In write cycle the strobe pulse is not present and so the signal from the sense line does not enter the data register.

There is another constraint on array design, namely, adequate signal-to-noise ratio. This is brought about by the finite gain of the sense amplifier. The reduction of word noise which occurs during read time is sometimes achieved by the antiparallel connection of two adjacent active sense lines. The antiparallel connection is preferred because it provides the shortest sense line delay. The thermal noise is assumed to determine the smallest signal which can readily be detected. Read noise and write noise may have larger rms amplitudes than thermal noise, but since they arise from deterministic processes (the operation of the memory), they can, in theory, be completely cancelled. Thermal noise, being a random process, cannot be eliminated in the same way. The rms thermal noise voltage σ at the output of the sense line is given by

$$\sigma = \sqrt{4kTR_N\Delta f}$$

where k is Boltzmann's constant, T is temperature in $°K$, Δf is effective bandwidth, and R_N is effective noise resistance which is given by

$$R_N = R_A + Re[Z_{in}]$$

where R_A is the amplifier input resistance and Z_{in} is the impedance looking into the sense line terminals. This noise is related to the dimensions of the device and array. In fact, noise resistance decreases monotonically as the line width increases.

5.6.3 Temperature and Aging Characteristics

The military environment requires electronic equipment to operate reliably within very wide ranges of temperature, humidity, vibration, and shock. Plated wire possesses a good parameter stability over a wide temperature range. This is evident from the curves shown in Figure 5.16. The changes in operating characteristics are shown at three temperatures. The curve indicating the maximum value of digit disturb current utilizes a unipolar digit current to give the effect of maximum disturb. From the curve it is clear that the plated wire element temperature stability allows for operation within the military temperature range (-45 to $85°C$) without the use of expensive current compensation technique.

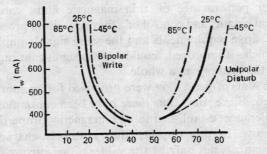

Figure 5.16 Operating window as a function of temperature.

Although plated wire technology has many potential advantages, it is not without problems. The major problem is an aging effect, where it is found that the NDRO properties of the plated wire deteriorate over a period of time. Therefore, the reliability and the aging properties of plated wire elements should be evaluated before they are used in the memory unit.

Lifetime or aging of plated wire may be defined as a small percentage change in its magnetic parameters (such as skew) measured against time-temperature relationship. These magnetic changes associated with aging follow a rate process equation. The plated wires are subjected to accelerated aging tests at several elevated temperatures under a hard axis magnetic field and the NDRO mode are traced. It has been clear that the stabilizing anneal after the plating extends the lifetime of the wire markedly and is positively necessary in the wire fabrication process. The aging phenomena can be divided into two categories. The first category comprises the rapid ordering processes observable at relatively low temperature and thus cause skewing of the easy direction of magnetization in the presence of hard direction magnetic field. They are desirable by magnetic annealing theory and are associated with the directional ordering of mobile impurities and imperfections. Apart from these fast ordering processes, there remain irreversible physical processes such as intrinsic diffusion, and grain growth which require higher temperatures for convenient observation and these must also be considered in magnetic aging phenomenon. A thorough comparison of pulse shape, rise time, memory cell geometry, pulse pattern, etc. of plated wire from various sources has been made by Luborsky et al.

5.7 SYSTEM DESIGN CONSIDERATIONS AND LIMITATIONS

Thin magnetic films have recently drawn considerable interest mainly because of their potential application as fast memory elements for computers. Each memory element is characterized by such parameters as output signals, maximum and minimum drive currents and disturb sensitivity which, in turn, depend on such physical parameters as saturation magnetization, film composition, film thickness, coercive force and film anisotropy constant. To obtain better performance of thin magnetic films, careful design of memory's external circuits and control of a film deposition process is required. Creep resistance, drive requirements and the sense signal amplitude are the three factors which, if improved, could lead to significant improvements in the efficiency of the memory as a whole.

Thin magnetic films of permalloy were proposed for memory application several years ago. Since that time there have been continuing changes and more rigorous tolerances established in the magnetic properties needed to implement such use. In this respect, films have been characterized in low frequency measurements not only by the values of anisotropy field and wall coercive force, but also by skew and dispersion of anisotropy field. These problems are very serious so far as the packing density and the speed of the memory are concerned. The full characterization of these parameters is of interest in quick estimating creep, disturb sensitivity, and memory drive requirements.

It is technically and economically advantageous to use the highest possible packing density for the storage cell. The packing density is, however, limited in practice by the interconnections between the adjacent cells. These interconnection effect can occur in continuous film and is attributed to domain propagation during writing operation, resulting in variable demagnetizing fields. Also, as the flux path is not closed, it gives rise to a smaller sense signal and a tendency to creep or demagnetize along the outer edges of the bit spot. To alleviate the creep problem the film is made thinner which further reduces the sense signal. On the other hand, the thicker the film, the greater is the tendency to demagnetization and creep. Hence a compromise should be made between the desired sense signal and minimum creep in choosing thickness of the film.

5.7.1 Memory Noise

In the design of the memory array standard transmission line characteristics are normally considered. During propagation of sense signal along the sense lines, they suffer various losses, such as attenuation of magnitude, distortion in phase, reflection caused by interconnection of sense lines and deterioration in waveform due to cross coupling of word lines. Generally speaking, the design objective is to minimize all these effects. High array impedance is usually a source of noise within the array. The higher voltage excursions which occur when these lines are excited, aggravate capacitive coupled noise, in addition to placing a burden on the voltage and power requirements of associated circuitry. Memory array delays add to excess cycle time. They also cause the difficulty of sense amplifier strobing. The key limiting factors are the resistance of lines and the capacitance of line interconnections.

In magnetic memories, generally, there are two sources of noise, namely, electromagnetic and electrostatic coupling. The former presents more serious noise problem. Inductive noise is merely the '0' output of the selected bit and is most apparent during write time, when the bit current flows. In a typical memory plane, transposition of the sense and bit lines keeps the bit noise to a few millivolts. Also, when a sense line crosses over a word line, a capacitance is created at the intersection. This acts as a drain for the energy contained in the sense signal. It deteriorates the waveform while delaying the pulse at the same time.

The major stack design problem is the reduction of capacitively induced interference from word to sense lines. A first order balance may be achieved by means of dummy cancellation line, but maintenance of good worst-case signal-to-noise ratio requires proper initial design of the transmission line geometry. The memory array model can be represented by a two dimensional partial differential equation, the general solution of which is then matched with the specific boundary conditions, namely, the array termination of eigen-functions. However, the effect of these couplings generate two categories of noise, namely, Read and Write.

When a given word line is selected, the resulting voltage transient causes a displacement current to flow in the sense line. This displacement current produces a voltage at the sense amplifier which has the slope of di/dt and is referred to as Read noise. This is induced by the leading edge of the word pulse and has the same polarity as the word pulse transition. This is superimposed on the information signal and, therefore, can introduce a high degree of asymmetry between the '1' and '0' signals, thereby increasing the complexity of the detection circuits. A number of schemes might be utilized to cancel this noise. For fast signals one might use a dummy sense line for each active sense line, and the difference mode signal between the active and dummy sense lines correspond to the device signal alone. The degree of cancellation of read noise is limited primarily by variations in word sense coupling capacitance and variations in line impedance. Sometimes, in cases where the propagation delay of the word line is much less than the rise time of the word pulses, the read noise can be reduced significantly by terminating the word lines in short circuits. This possibility arises from the fact that the reflected leading edge of the word pulse cancels the incident wave at the position of the crossover after a time equal to twice the electrical length of the word line between crossover and short circuit.

Minimization of Write noise is also an important requirement in magnetic memories. It occurs at the end of rewrite cycle and lengthens recovery time of the sense amplifier. This prevents squeezing of the cycle time due to interference with the next readout. The bit lines and sense lines are parallel to each other and the coupling is due to both electric and magnetic fields. Common bit sense amplifier circuits for memories with cycle time of more than 100 nsec were described by Kaufman and Hammond. With separate bit and sense lines, directional coupling may be applied to reduce the noise in memory circuits. This requires the lines to be accurately terminated and the bit driver and sense amplifier to be located at opposite ends of the array. The value of terminating impedance is determined by the electromagnetic characteristics of the bit-sense line structure. This provides excellent write noise cancellation except for two cases: (i) the magnetic characteristics of the keeper and the finite conductivity of ground plane prevent the full benefit of the directional coupling, and (ii) stray fields from adjacent bit lines couple the sense line, giving a noise signal whose polarity is dependent on the information being written into the adjacent bits. The magnitude of the coupling due to the second effect falls off rapidly with distance and can, therefore, be reduced by increasing the bit line spacing.

The measure of efficiency of any sense bit combination is the degree of coupling between the film and the windings. This varies with the spacing between the conductors and is limited by the thickness of the film substrate. A rough measure of the efficiency of this coupling is the ratio of signal current to bit current and this increases with the increase in the switching speed. Additional source of noise in the array can be the reactive and resistive discontinuities in the array line and in the ground plane. In strip line transmission of fast risetime currents, there arises the problem of shield grounding. To counter this problem, the strip line shields are grounded at a single point near the current driver.

Mechanical design of the array and its supporting structure should be directed towards minimizing these effects. The strip lines are tapered with wide, low-impedance end near the driver and narrower, high-impedance end at the matrix to improve drive current rise time in memory unit.

5.7.2 Magnetic Keepers

Magnetic flux keeper first proposed by Pohm and others is widely used in computer memories with planar or cylindrical thin magnetic films. Although analytical and numerical methods of calculating magnetic field distributions can often help memory designer to understand how the field spreads and, therefore, how the cell size for a given overall configuration is limited, they are based on ideal films. Therefore, such methods should be complemented with experimental measurements before attempting to make a final design. In memory cell with suitable localized fields, the area interrogated during a read operation should be as large a portion of area switched when writing as possible. This condition is best achieved with a magnetic field whose cross-section is as nearly rectangular as possible. There are two ways to approximate such a distribution with multiple turn word straps and with magnetic keepers.

To ensure satisfactory operation of the memory unit, all the sources of spurious fields on the memory elements should be taken into account. This, in general, will depend on the type of element construction which is used. When the permalloy fields are used for computer storage, a magnetic keeper can improve performance by reducing the demagnetizing effects, worst-case ground plane currents, trapped flux, and line to line interconnections. The important functions of magnetic keeper are:

(i) Dimunition of field at a bit from an adjacent strip line.
(ii) Reduction of flux from the bit that is trapped in the ground plane during switching.
(iii) Reduction in the effect of ground plane current spreading.

In flat film memory, use of a thick metallic substrate for ground return path possess two important problems. First, the flux from bit trapped in the ground plane will introduce an adverse bias field during switching for a read '1' write '0' or a read '0' write '1' sequence. Also, the current in the ground plane, which spreads when the word line crosses over the bit under consideration, is selected repeatedly and accordingly has an appropriate dc component. This reduces the field available for switching. The other factors which are also very important in flat film memory system are the disturbing fields from adjacent bits and disturbing fields from adjacent lines. These factors are referred to as *worst-case effects*.

The primary effect of flux keeper is to reduce the magnetic stray fields of the storage elements and drive lines. The stray field of the storage elements is affected only by the permeability distribution. In magnetic thin-film memory both permeability and permittivity are distributed discontinuously. The distribution affects the transmission and coupling properties of the drive lines. The keeper reduces the inductive part and enhances the capacitive part. The keeper materials may be either ferrite or metallic, having very high permeability value and is placed over the word lines as shown in Figure 5.17(a). The properties of various keeper samples are shown in Table 5.2. When such a high permeability material is placed over the

TABLE 5.2

Characteristics of some Keeper Materials

Material	μ_r	ε_r		$\rho \times 10^{-10}$
	(1 mHz)	(30 KHz)	(RF)	($\Omega . cm$)
Ni-Zn ferrite	10	4	3	65
Ni-Zn-Cu ferrite	12	8	4	1.1
Mn-Zn ferrite	13	22	10	0.2
Carbonyl iron	7	24	15	160

word lines, both applied and demagnetizing fields tend to enter and exit the keeper at a 90° angle to its surface—so much as if identical word lines and magnetic film elements were behind the keeper surface—at the position of a mirror image. These image currents and image magnetic charges reduce the demagnetizing field and tend to localize the resultant field. The ferrite keeper is the best way to limit current spreading, but it does not work very well at high frequencies because its permeability decreases as frequency increases. A permalloy keeper is good at all frequencies, but it is effective only when the width of the word lines is much greater than the word bit line separation. However, in all cases, the role of conductivity of the keeper material at high frequency should be taken into account.

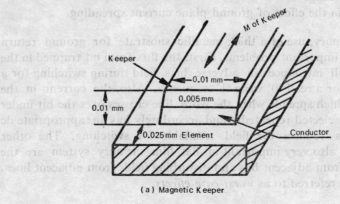

(a) Magnetic Keeper

Figure 5.17(a)

The flat film memory systems are basically open flux devices, and hence there exists demagnetizing field. This field is kept less than the coercive force of the material to prevent excessive clearing of the hysteresis loop. The demagnetizing field which can be computed in terms of the divergence of the magnetization, can be reduced by reducing the thickness of the film. But this lowers the signal level. It can be reduced by providing a semicomplete magnetic path either by use of a pair of elements or by a keeper, or by increasing element size. Trapped flux and stray field effects are reduced in a straightforward manner by providing a low reluctance path for flux lines through the keeper. Also the dc component gains by the word current during repeated selection of a particular word line, spreads throughout the ground plane and the field from the ground plane image at the bit is reduced. With a keeper the effect of ground plane current spreading can be diminished. Due to the keeper, the field is distributed so that the field on top of the conductor is very small. Essentially, a low reluctance path is provided which keeps the internal field immediately below the conductor near its original value.

The efficiency of a keeper (η) in reducing each of the deleterious effects can be defined as:

$$\eta = \frac{\Delta I_0 - \Delta I_K}{\Delta I^0}$$

where ΔI_0 is the equivalent bit current associated with a given effect without a keeper and ΔI_K is the same current with a keeper. Although the permeability of a permalloy keeper is sufficiently high, its efficiency is not so high as that of a nonconductor. This is due to the fact that its conductivity prevents adequate penetration of magnetic flux lines at high frequencies, which is a requisite of a good keeper action. The investigation of the keeper efficiency as carried out by Ravi and Koerber is shown in Table 5.3. This shows that a keeper improves the performance of thin film memories considerably, and for this purpose ferrite materials perform more effectively than the metallic keepers. The gap between keeper and magnetic devices (determined by the thickness of the word and bit sense strip lines) is one of the fundamental determinants of keeper efficiency. Figure 5.17(b)

TABLE 5.3
Worst-case Effects and Keeper Efficiency

Worst-case effects	Metallic keeper	Non-metallic keeper
Trapped flux effect	40	64
Ground plane current spreading effect	55	73
Stray field from adjacent bit lines	67	75
Stray field from adjacent bits	80	100
Overall efficiency	56	73

shows how keeper efficiency varies with the distance. For this reason, it is desirable to keep the distance occupied by the word and bit/sense strip lines as small as mechanically possible.

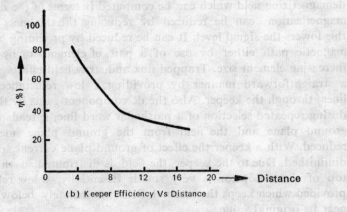

(b) Keeper Efficiency Vs Distance

Figure 5.17(b)

However, keepers do have some disadvantages,. Even though a high demagnetizing effect requires higher drive currents and puts a lower limit on packing density, it tends to wash out non-uniformities in film properties and dimensions. For example, in the presence of large demagnetizing field, the variation in drive line width affects the resultant field only slightly, whereas with a keeper, and consequently with a small demagnetizing field, the resultant field is inversely proportional to the drive line width.

5.7.3 Skewness

The minimum bit field necessary for complete magnetization rotation of whole film element to the desired easy direction is composed of three parts: (i) to overcome the influence of skew effect; (ii) related to the intrinsic angular dispersion of hard axis owing to strong exchange and magnetostatic coupling; and (iii) to prevent demagnetization during rotation of magnetization from the hard to easy direction. In fact, in the practical memory systems the third effect easily overrides the others. In such cases a strong dependence of angular dispersion on the magnitude of the demagnetizing field in easy direction has been found.

The idealized critical curves shown earlier (Figure 5.16) are, however, complicated in practical applications by many factors, among which the very important are skew (β) and dispersion (α). If the easy axis of a film is rotated by β degrees from the word line, we say it has a skew of β. Skewness is defined as the angle between the word field and the hard axis. It is, however, very often found that the field and hard direction are not parallel, and zero sense signal occurs only when a certain bit field is applied. In the absence of skew, the word field and digit field are mutually perpendicular along the two coordinate axis. But skew causes one or the other of these fields to effectively appear at a slight angle to its axis, and thus to bring the sum of magnetization plus word field components closer to the threshold value of the creep region. The minimum positive and negative skew in an array may be represented by the rotations of two critical curves in Figure 5.18.

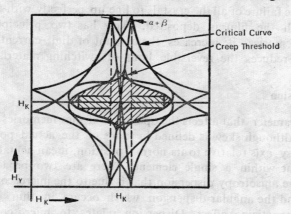

Figure 5.18 Critical curve showing the creep threshold
value (Pugh et al., 1967).

If the field produced for compensating this misalignment by the bit current is H_b, the skewness may be calculated as:

$$\text{arc sin } H_b/H_k$$

where H_k is the anisotropy field. The easy axis of all films fabricated on the same substrate will not be exactly parallel. So skew is an unavoidable problem. However, the real troublesome factor in thin film arrays is neither skew nor dispersion but magnetostriction. Magnetostriction causes the skew to increase greatly when a small mechanical strain appears in the element. Strain is almost impossible to avoid completely. To avoid this problem, the composition of alloy is chosen such that magnetostriction is as small as possible. Skewness is also caused by such factors as misalignment of the substrate with respect to the magnetic field during evaporation, insufficient magnetic field, spurious magnetic fields from the heating furnace, oblique incidence anisotropy, and the earth's magnetic field.

The extent of skew corresponds to the film's departure from ideal. The skew creates a component of the word field along the easy axis. Although skew is defined in terms of the actual position of an element's easy axis relative to its nominal position, it actually varies from point to point within a single element. Skewness of a film is measured with the help of B—H loop tester by applying an ac field with an amplitude larger than anisotropy field along the hard direction. When the field is exactly in the average hard direction, the magnetization in one half of the film makes clockwise rotations while that in the other half of the film rotates anticlockwise, so that the net magnetization component in the easy direction is zero for all field strength. This is measured by a pick up coil with the axis parallel to the easy direction. When the signal is not zero, the film is compared with some reference direction to give the skewness.

Both the skewness and dispersion are effects of film's polycrystalline nature and the failure of all the crystals to line up perfectly with the magnetic field in which the film is deposited. Skew has two principal effects in thin film memories, it increases the amount of digit current required to write, and it reduces the reversible limit of switching material.

5.7.4 Dispersion

Another parameter that affects the operation of film memories is known as dispersion. Although skew is defined in terms of the actual position of an element's easy axis relative to its normal position, it can acutally vary from point to point within a single element. There are two broad classes of dispersion, the anisotropy dispersion that is due to the microscopic structure of the film and the angular dispersion which occurs in thin film samples due to demagnetizing effect. Dispersion relates to microscopic angular deviation in the easy axis direction within film due to variation in internal stresses, grain boundaries, and atomic pair alignment. The effect of dispersion is to increase the digit current and limit the amplitude of word current in NDRO mode of operation.

A Kerr magneto-optical B—H loop tester can be used to measure the angular dispersion in thin film. Mathematical expressions have been derived relating dispersion to the film thickness, its magnetization at saturation and its degree of anisotropy. The measured dispersion angle $\propto$, is the angle from the hard axis at which a large magnetic field must be applied in order to assume that, as the applied field is reduced to 90 per cent of the film's magnetization, it will rotate in the same direction. To denote this specific measure of dispersion a subscript 90, for 90 per cent, is frequently added as α_{90}. For angles less than α_{90}, more than 10 per cent of the film will be rotated in the opposite direction, resulting in a multi-domain state.

The two rotated critical curves shown in Figure 5.18 represent the extreme values for $\alpha + \beta$ in the memory array. To guarantee full switching, the bit field and word field should be

$$H_b \geqslant H_k \sin (\alpha + \beta) + kH_{de}$$

and

$$H_w > H_k + H_{dh}$$

where H_{de} is the easy direction magnetizing field and $H_{dh} = 4\pi Mt/L$ is the demagnetizing field, t is the film thickness, L is the width of the device in hard direction and M is saturation magnetization. The word field must exceed the anisotropy field plus demagnetizing field of the bit when driven into the hard direction. The constant k assumes a value between 0 and 1 depending on the angle of M at the time of writing. The range of permitted values of H_b are the device operating margins which must accommodate variations from the nominal bit drive plus a variety of other effects. The two oppositely shaded rectangles in Figure 5.18 indicate the acceptable operating range for disturb fields as bounded by minimum and maximum H_b and an assumed maximum hard direction field.

5.7.5 Wall Motion and Creep Effect

The packing density of thin film memories is, however, limited by the effect known as creep. This was first observed in 1962 and it occurs only when the applied field has an ac or pulse component in the hard direction and a dc component in the easy direction. This is rather a field activated wall creeping and is different from thermally or ultrasonically activated creeping that occurs in films as well as in bulk materials. The creep effect really consists of small wall jumps at the moments when the field is switched on or off. It is, therefore, believed that wall creep under pulse conditions occurs during the leading and trailing edge of the pulses. The speed with which the walls creep depends on the amplitude of the pulse field in the hard direction, the magnitude of dc field in the easy direction, and the pulse repetition frequency.

Different theories exist on the mechanism of this process, namely, (i) the Bloch line motion theory, (ii) wall structure change theory, and (iii) Lever theory. Of all these theories, the Bloch line motion theory offers a rather satisfactory explanation of various creep behaviours as a function of film thickness. The most important changes with respect to the wall are the variations of the wall energy and width and motion of the Bloch or 90° lines due to wall transition. Films in which no Bloch lines or other lines occur, because they are too thin or of a special structure (double films) or because of a dc field applied in the hard direction, will not exhibit wall creeping. The main idea of the Bloch line motion theory is that when a hard direction field is applied it causes the motion of the Bloch or 90° lines. The wall will still advance over a short distance which is a function of number of lines present and the distance through which the wall moves. For detailed analysis of Bloch lines and wall creep, it is necessary to group the films into four parts according to their thickness. The typical width of Bloch line is only about 100 Å, and as the domain walls themselves are much wider, about 1000 Å, a Bloch line represents a constriction in a wall. When fields are applied in the hard direction, this constriction is displaced along the wall.

It is, therefore, necessary to reduce the creep effect. The memory should be designed with high coercive materials and should remove stray word field which means that the spacing between the film spots should be increased. The vector sum of the applied field and the stray word fields must be confined within the shaded region of the creep threshold curve in Figure 5.18. The two oppositely shaded rectangles indicate the acceptable operating range for disturb fields as bounded by minimum and maximum H_b, and an assumed maximum hard direction disturb field.

References

Agajanian, A.H., Ravi, C.G. (1967): 'Flexible ferrite keepers and their applications in thin film memories, *IEEE Trans. on Magnetic*, V. MAG-3, September, pp. 500-502.

Ahn, K. and Freedman, J.F. (1968): 'Magnetic properties of vacuum deposited coupled films', *IBM J. Res. and Devel.* V. 12, No. 1.

Almasi, G.S. and Genovese, E.R. (1969): 'Signal sensing and magnetic film memory array design', *IEEE Trans. on Magnetics.* V MAG-6, No.4, December.

Almasi, G.S. and Feth, G.C. (1960): 'Thermal noise from long sense lines', *IEEE Trans. on Magnetics*, V. MAG-5, March, pp. 64-70.

Ammon, G.J. and Neitsert, C. (1964): 'An experimental 65 nsec thin film scratch pad memory system', *Proc. EJCC*, pp. 649-660.

Anacker, W., Bland, G.F., Pleshko, P. and Stuckert, P.F. (1966): 'On the design and performance of a small 60 nsec destructive readout magnetic film memory', *IBM J. Res. and Devel.*, V. 10, pp. 41.

Annett, R.C. and McNichol, J.J. (1960): Characterization of keeper for film memories. *IEEE Trans. on Magnetics*, V. MAG-5, No. 3, pp. 304-306.

Bean, W.R. and Siegle, W. (1965): 'Anisotropy control of Ni-Fe films through sequence film depositor', *IEEE Trans on Magnetics.* V. MAG-1., March, pp. 66-67.

Beingoff, M., Carmarate, J. and Sherman, M. (1963): 'Some considerations in the design of plated wire memory systems', *IEEE Batch Fabrication Conf.*

Bertelson, B.I. (1967): 'Multilayer process for magnetic memory devices', *IEEE Trans. on Magnetics.*, pp. 635.

Billing, H. (1962): 'Coincident current magnetic film memory', presented at the Symp. on Fast Memory Technology.

Bittman, E.E. (1964): 'A 16 k word 2 MC Magnetic thin film memory', *Fall Joint Computer Conf.* (California), October 27.

Bittman, E.E. (1963): 'Thin Film Memories—some problems limitations and profits'. *Proc. INTERMAG Conf.* (Washington DC), April 17.

Bittman, E.E. (1961): 'Designing thin magnetic film memories for high speed computers', *Electronics*, V. 34, No. 9, March.

Bland, G.F. (1973): 'Directional coupling and its use for memory noise reduction', *IBM J. Res. and Devel.* V. 7, pp. 252-356.

Blatt, H. (1964): 'Random noise considerations in the design of magnetic film sense amplifiers', M.I.T. Lincon Lab., Laxington, Mass., Rept, 1964-6, August.

Blois, M.S. Jr. (1955): 'Preparation of thin magnetic films and their properties', *J. Appl. Phys.* V. 23, August, pp. 975-980.

Bradley, E.M. (1962): 'Properties of magnetic films for a memory system', *J. Appl. Phys.*, V. 33, March, pp. 1051.

Chang, H. (1967): 'Coupled film memory elements', *J. Appl. Phys*, p. 1203.

Chang, C.F. and Fedde, G.A. (1968): 'Plated wire memory, present and future', *Proc. International Conf. on Magnetics*.

Chow, W.F. and Spandorfer, L.M. (1967): 'Plated wire bit steering for logic and storage', *Spring Joint Comp. Conf.*, AFIPS Proc. V. 28.

Chow, W.F. (1967): 'Plated wire content addressable memories with bit steering technique', *IEEE Trans. on Electronic Computer*, V. EC-16, No. 5, October.

Chu, K. and Singer, J.R. (1959): 'The film magnetization analysis', *Proc. IRF*, V. 47 July, pp. 1237-44.

Cohn, S.B. (1954): Characteristics impedance of shielded strip transmission line', *IRE Trans. on Microwave Theory and Techniques*, V. MTT-2, July, pp. 52-57.

Crowther, T.S. (1964): 'High density magnetic film memory techniques', *Proc, INTERMAG Conf.*, paper 5-7-1 to 5-7-6.

Crowther, T.S. (1962): 'Angular Q-magnetic dispersion of the anisotropy in magnetic films', *Conf. on Thin Films*, (Frenwood springs, Colorado), August.

Danylchuk, I., Gianola, U.F., Perneski, A.J. and Sagal M.W. (1964): 'Plated wire magnetic film memories', *Proc. INTERMAG Conf.*, papers 5-4-1 to 5-4-6.

Deughton, J.M and Pohm, A.V. (1963): 'Dispersion in thin magnetic films', *International Conf. on Nonlinear Magnetics*, April.

Dietrich, W., Proebster, W.E., Dunlop, L.J. and Louis, H.P. (1963): 'The design of a one million bit 100 nsec magnetic film memory', *Proc. INTERMAG Conf.*, pp. 9-2.

Dove, D. (1967): 'Demagnetizing fields in thin magnetic films', *Bell Syst. Tech. J.*, V. 46, pp. 1527-1559, September.

Deve, D. and Long T.R. (1966): 'Magnetization distribution in flat and cylindrical films subject to uniform hard direction field', *IEEE Trans. on Magnetics*, V.MAG-2, p. 194.

Doyle, W.D., Josephs, R.M. and Baltz, A. (1969): 'Electrodeposited cylindrical magnetic films', *IEEE Trans. on Magnetics* V.MAG-5, pp. 241-246.

Eide, J.E. (1965): 'Closed flux thin magnetic film memory prepared by electroplating', *J. Appl. Phys.*, V. 36., March, pp. 1365.

England, W.A., (1970): 'Applications of plated wire to the military and space environments', *IEEE Trans. on Magnetics* V.MAG. 6, No. 3, September.

English, T.D. and McNichol. J.J. (1965): 'Integrated transmission lines for magnetic thin film memories', *IEEE Trans. on Magnetics* V. MAG-1, No. 4, December.

Fedde, G.A. (1967): 'Plated wire memories—Univac's bet to replace toroidal ferrite cores', *Electronics*, May 15, pp. 101.

Feldtkeller, E. (1963): 'Ripple hysteresis in thin magnetic films', *J. Appl. Phy*, V. 34. September, p. 2646.

Felte, H., and Harloff, H.J. (1966): 'Flux keepers in magnetic thin film memories', *IEEE Trans. on Magnetic*, V. MAG-2, No. 3.

Felte, H., and Harloff, H.J. et al. (1970): 'Dielectric effects of ferrite flux keepers in thin film memories', *IEEE Trans. on Magnetics*, V. MAG-6, No. 1, March.

Fowler, C.A., Fryer, E.M. and Stevens, J.R. (1956): 'Magnetic domains in evaporated thin films of Ni-Fe.', *Phy. Rev.* V. 104, November, pp. 645-649.

Freeman, J.F. (1969): 'Soft magnetic thin film memory materials', *IEEE Trans. on Magnetics*, V. MAG-5, pp. 752-764.

Freitag, W.O., Mathias, J.S. and Diguilic G. (1964): 'The electrodeposition of Ni-Fe phosphorus thin films for computer memory use', *Electrochemical Society Journal*, January, pp. 135.

Furuoya, T., Oakada, T., Tobite, N. et al. (1968): 'Plated wire memory with flexible keeper, *IEEE Trans. on Magnetics*, V. MAG-4., September, pp.375-378.

Gianola, U.F. (1958): 'Nondestructive memory employing a domain oriented steel wire,' *J. Appl. Phys.*, V.29, May, pp. 849-853.

Gilbert, T.L. (1955): *Phys. Rev.*, V.100, p. 1243.

Goto, E. (1959): 'The parametron—a digital computing element which utilises parametric oscillation', *Proc. IRE*, V.47, pp. 1304.

Goto, E., et al. (1965): 'Magnetisation and switching characteristics of composite thin film', *Proc. INTERMAG Conf.*

Hayt, W.H., Jr. (1955): 'Potential solution of a homogeneous stripe line of ferrite width', *IRE Trans. on Microwave Theory and Techniques*, V. MTT-3, pp. 16-18.

Higoshi, P. (1966): 'A thin film Rod memory for the NCR 315 RMC Computer', *IEEE Trans. on Electric Computer*, EC. 15, No. 4.

Jutzi, W. (1964): 'Nondestructive readout in thin magnetic film memories', *Proc. IEEE*, V. 52, pp. 875.

Kaufman, B.A., and Hammond, J.S. (1963): 'A high speed direct coupled magnetic sense amplifier employing tunnel diode discriminators', *IEEE Trans. on Electronic Computers*, V.EC.12, pp 282-295.

Kaufman, B.A. Ellinger, P.B. and Kuno, H.S. (1966): 'A rotationally switched rod memory with a 100 nsec cycle time, *Fall Joint Comp. Conf. AFIPS Proc.*, V.29.

Kaufman, B. and Ulzurrun, E. (1963): 'A new technique for using thin magnetic films as a phase script memory element', *AFIPS Conf. Proc.* V.24, pp. 67-75.

Kinniment, D.J. and Aspinall, D. (1967): 'Small capacity thin cylindrical magnetic film storage system', *Conf. on Comp. Technology*, July, pp. 44-49.

Kohn, G. and Jutzi, W. et al. (1965): 'Design principles of nondestructive read thin magnetic film memories with read cycle time of 15 nsec', *Proc. INTERMAG Conf.*, 8-3-1.

Kohn, G., Jutzi, W. et al. (1967): 'A very high speed nondestructive read magnetic film memory', *IBM J. Res. and Develop.*, V.11, No. 2.

Lampert, R.E, Gorres, J.M. and Hanson, M.M. (1968): 'The magnetic properties of Co-Ni-Fe films' *IEEE Trans. on Magnetics*, V. MAG-4, pp. 525-528.

Leilich, H.O. (1967): 'The chain—a new magnetic film memory device ', *J. Appl. Phys.*, V. 41, pp. 13-62.

Luborsky, B.F., Skoda, R.E. and Barbar, W.D. (1971): 'Origins of nondestructive read-out in plated wires', *J. Appl. Phys.*, V. 42, pp. 1428-1430.

Luborsky, F.E. and McCary, R.O. (1971): 'Magnetic film materials', *Proc. IEEE*, V. 59, No. 10.

Luborsky, F.E. and Drummond, B.J. (1974): 'Selected characteristics of plated wires from various sources', *IEEE Trans. on Magnetics*, V. MAG-10, No. 1.

Maeda, H. and Matsushita, A. (1964): 'Woven thin film memories', *Proc. INTREMAG Conf.*, papers 8.1.1 to 8.1.6.

Maeda, H., Matsushita, A. and Takashima, M. (1966): 'Woven wire memory for NDRO system', *IEEE Trans. Electronic Computers*, EC. 15, No. 4.

Mathias, J.S. and Fadde G.A. (1969): 'Plated wire technology—a critical review,' *IEEE Trans. on Magnetics*, V. MAG. 5, December, p. 728.

Matick, R., et al. (1966): 'A high speed read only store using thick magnetic films', *IBM J. Res. and Develop.*, V., 10, No. 6.

Mathias, J.S. and Fedde, G.A. (1969): 'Plated wire technology—a critical review', *IEEE Trans. on Magnetics*, V. MAG-5, pp. 728-751.

Matcovich, T.J. and Flannery, W.E. (1967): 'A magnetic thin film integrated circuit memory system', *IEEE Trans. Magnetics*, V. MAG-3, No. 1.

McCallister, J.P. and Chong, C.F. (1966): 'A 500 nsec computer memory utilising plated wire elements', *Conf. Proc. AFIPS.*, V. 29, p. 305.

McQuillan, J.P.R. (1962): 'The design problems of a megabit storage matrix for use in a high speed computer', *IER Trans. Elect. Comput.*, V. EC-11, pp. 390-404.

Meier, D.A. (1960): 'Magnetic Rod memory' *Proc. Electronic Components Conf.*, May, pp. 122-128.

Meier, D.A. and Kolk, A.J. (1962): 'A magnetic Rod, a cylindrical thin film memory element', in *Large Capacity Memory Techniques for Computing Systems*, MC. Yovitz (Ed)., Mcmillan, New York, 195-212.

Middelhoek, S. and Wild, D. (1967): 'Review of wall creeping in thin magnetic films' *IBM J. Res. and Develop.*, V. 11, No. 1.

Nishino, H. (1965): 'High speed thin film woven memory', *IFIP Congress*.

Oakland, L.J. and Rosing, T.D. (1959): Coincident current nondestructive readout from thin magnetic films. *J. Appl. Phys.*, V. 30, pp. 54S-58S.

Olmen, R.W. and Rubens, S.M. (1962): 'Angular dispersion and its relationship with other magnetic parameters in permalloy films', *J. Appl. Phys.*, V. 33S, No. 3.

Overn, W.M. (1968): 'Status of the planar film memories', *IEEE Trans. on Magnetics*, V. MAG-4, September, pp. 308.

Pearl, J. (1968): 'Field distribution of plated wire memory elements and its effect on memory characteristics', *International Conf. on Magnetics*.

Petschauer, R.J. and Turnquist, R.D. (1961): 'A nondestructive readout film memory', *Proc. Western Joint Computer Conf.*, May, pp. 411-425.

Phillips, R.J.D , Richards, H.D. and Stapleton, D.C. (1968): 'The influence of surface topography on switching time of plated wire memory elements', *IEEE Trans. Magnetics*, V. MAG-4, September, pp. 345-356.

Pohm, A.V. (1966): 'Magnetic film scratch pad memories', *IEEE Trans. Elect. Comp.*, V. E.C. 15, No. 4.

Pohm, A.V. et al. (1965): 'An efficient small thin film memory', *Proc. INTERMAG Conf.*

Pohm, A.V. et al. (1959): 'High frequency magnetic film parameters for computing logic', *Proc. NFC.*, V. 15, October, pp. 202.

Pohm, A.V. and Mitchell, E.N. (1960) : 'Magnetic film memories—A survey', *IRE Trans. Electronic Computers*, V. EC-9, pp. 308.

Proebster, W.E. (1962) : 'The design of a high speed thin film memory', Digest of technical papers, Intern. Solid State Circuit Conf., pp. 38.

Pugh, E.W. et al. (1967) : 'Device and array design for a 120 nsec magnetic film memory', *IBM J. Res. and Develop*, V. 11, No. 2.

Rado, G. and Suhl, H. (Eds) : Magnetism—III, Academic Press, New York, 1963, pp. 525-525.

Raffel, J.I., Anderson, A.H. et al. (1968) : ,A progress report on large capacity magnetic thin film memory developments', *Spnig Joint Conf.*, AFIPS Proc., V. 32, pp. 259.

Raffel, J.I.(1959) : 'Operating characteristics of a thin film memory', *J. Appl. Phys.*, V. 30, pp. 60S-60S.

Rajchman, J.A. (1963) : 'Magnetic memories—capabilities and limitations', Computer Design, September, pp. 34.

Ravi, C.G. and Koerber, G.G. (1966) : 'Effect of a keeper on thin film magnetic bits,' *IBM J. Res. and Develop*, V.10, No. 2, pp. 130.

Rowland, C.A. and Berge, W.O. (1963): ' A 300 nsec scratch pad memory'. *AFIPS Conf. Proc.*, V. 24, pp. 59-65.

Smith, D.O. (1958) : 'Magnetization reversal in thin films', *J. Appl. Phys.*, V. 29, pp. 264-273.

Waaben, S. (1967) : 'High speed plated wire memory system,' *IEEE Trans. Electronic Computers*, V. EC-16, No. 3, pp. 335.

Waaben, S. (1969) : 'High speed, interlaced write and read only operation of a plated write memory system', *IEEE Trans. Electronic Computers*, V.C-17, pp. 1062-1065.

Weniger, K. (1967) : 'Memory system comparisions', Electronic Engineering, V. 26, No. 5, pp. 118.

Wilts, C.H. and Humphrey, F.B. (1968) : 'Magnetic anisotropy in flat ferromagnetic films : A review', *J. Appl. Phys.*, V. 39, pp. 1191.

Yao, F.C. (1966) : 'Propagation of sense signals in large scale magnetic thin film memories,' *IEEE Trans. Electronic Computers*, V. EC-15, No. 4.

6. SEMICONDUCTOR MEMORY SYSTEMS

Rapid advances in semiconductor technology since the invention of the transistor only twentyfive years ago, brought about a technical revolution in the electronics industry. Silicon planar technology led to a significant improvement in the transistor as an electronic device and a logical development of this technique is the presentday integrated circuits.

Integrated circuits were developed initially for space research and military projects where their size and low power consumptions were obvious advantages. Other less obvious qualities soon became apparent, such as reliability, low cost and high speed. Large scale integration (LSI) is one more step in the progress of electronic components and equipment practice. The impetus is basically the interaction of supply and demand, where reduced cost is alternately the cause and the effect. By-products of this progress are improved quality, performance and miniaturization which at times is an end in itself, reduced cost being a subsequent result.

The development of the third generation computer using integrated circuits started from the point of view of complexity, price, and reliability. LSI introduced a second level of integration, application of which brought about the so called fourth generation computers. In integrated circuits we integrate the components to circuits; and in LSI we integrate the circuit to systems. This involves:

(i) Fabrication of circuit cells.
(ii) Testing and verification of good cells.
(iii) Formation of interconnections.

6.1 METAL OXIDE SEMICONDUCTOR (MOS) TRANSISTOR CHARACTERISTICS

Strangely enough some of the ideas, concepts and components used in the design of first generation computers are reappearing in the third and fourth generation computers. Employment of flip-flops as storage units makes it possible to combine a small memory with drive, sense, and decode circuitry on the same chip. Also, the MOS technology is capable not only of superior packing densities and lower power dissipation but also provides very high speed.

To understand the operation of these integrated circuits and to appreciate the design constraints, it is necessary to examine the characteristics of a single MOS transistor. Construction of a p-channel MOS transistor is shown in Figure 6.1. Two highly doped p-type areas are diffused into an n-type silicon substrate. The resistivity of silicon substrate varies from 1 to 10 ohm-cm and the gap between the two diffused areas is of the order of 0.5 mil. These two regions act as source and drain. Then a thin insulating material, usually some type of SiO, of thickness 800 to 2000 Å is deposited over the surface of the silicon between the source and drain—forming the gate dielectric material. Metal is deposited over the surface of the slice, forming contacts, interconnecting leads and the gate electrode.

Usually all n-channel devices are initially 'on' (at zero gate bias) and all p-channel devices are initially 'off', because of the conditions created by the interfacing at the surface of the silicon and oxide. Since it is desirable to use an initially 'off' device for switching digital circuits, all commercial MOS integrated circuits are at present single polarity p-channel units. The source is used as reference electrode and the drain is the output of the devices. The three leads—source, gate, and drain—are roughly analogous to the bipolar's emitter, base and collector, respectively.

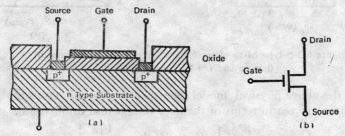

Figure 6.1 Typical MOS transistor in enhancement mode:
(a) Structure; and (b) MOS symbol.

With drain and source grounded, the gate controls the charge in the channel—the region in the substrate surface between the source and the drain. With zero voltage applied to the gate and with drain negative with respect to source, no channel current flows between source and drain (like reversed bias pn junction). As the gate potential is taken negative with respect to source and on charging the metal oxide semiconductor capacitor, conduction starts due to surface inversion of the n type substrate. Figure 6.2(a) shows the V-I characteristic curve for a family of gate voltages. The voltage at which inversion occurs (turn on voltage V_T) is known as the gate threshold voltage. It depends primarily on the magnitude of the surface state charge at the silicon dioxide/silicon interface, Q_{SS}, and the bulk charge in the substrate material, Q_B.

For a constant gate voltage, an increase in the drain voltage alters the situation in the channel region. As the drain voltage increases because of voltage drop across the channel, the voltage across the gate oxide near the drain diffused region is reduced. When this voltage drop ($V_D = V_G - V_T$) reaches a value to just reduce the field such that inversion layer is no longer formed, the channel pinches off and the drain current tends to saturate at a constant value (independent of drain voltage). In this condition the device is said to be in saturation. The inversion layer is thickest at the source and decreases to zero at the point of pinchoff. The voltage across gate oxide just at the point of saturation is called the *pinchoff* or *threshold* voltage. Further increase in drain voltage, drives the MOS hards into saturation. Too much of an increase in drain voltage can cause drain depletion region to punch through all the way to the source, resulting in unrestricted current flow if it is not limited by the external circuit.

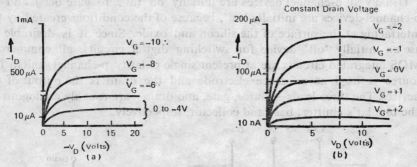

Figure 6.2 p-type MOS characteristic curves: (a) Enhancement mode device; and (b) Depletion mode device.

Using the above physical model one can derive an expression for the source drain current in terms of the gate voltage and drain voltage as

$$I_D = \mu_{eff} \frac{W}{L} C_0 \left[(V_G - V_T)V_D - \frac{V_D^2}{2} \right]$$

where W and L are respectively the channel width (perpendicular to current flow) and effective channel length (in the direction of current flow), μ_{eff} is the effective mobility of majority carriers in the channel, C_0 is the gate capacitance per unit area, and V_D is the drain to source voltage.

The output current variation for a given increment of gate voltage increases as the gate voltage is increased above threshold voltage. It can be shown that output current is proportional to square of the input voltage. That is why MOS is often referred to as square law device. The transfer characteristic of a MOS device for a constant drain voltage is shown in Figure 6.3.

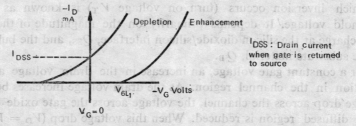

Figure 6.3 Transfer curves showing drain current versus gate voltage.

Most MOS logic circuits fall into one of the two categories—static or dynamic. Figure 6.4 shows the simple inverter stage which forms the basis for MOS linear amplifiers, and which when examined as a switch, can yield design information about MOS logic circuits of only two small MOS structures.

In static MOS circuits transistors are used as conventional dc amplifiers, with other MOS devices used as pull-up resistors. Static MOS circuits are often analogous to bipolar circuits. Dynamic MOS circuits make use of very low leakage current which is associated with gate circuits and junctions of well made MOS devices. These leakage currents are small enough to permit the circuit parasitic capacitances to exhibit time constants from milliseconds to seconds, which may be used to provide temporary storage.

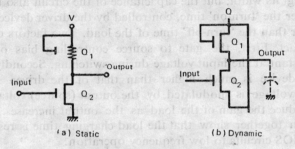

(a) Static   (b) Dynamic

Figure 6.4 MOS inverter circuits.

In static MOS inverter (Figure 6.4a), when the input signal is a '0' (at ground) Q_2 is turned 'off', and the output is a '1'. When the input becomes negative, Q_2 turns 'on' and the output becomes '0'. The one level of the output is approximately the same as the supply voltage, because the load draws essentially no current and there is no voltage drop across the resistanc eof Q_1. The zero level is generally not at ground because Q_1 and Q_2 become a voltage divider when both are turned 'on'. More precisely, the '0' level is

$$V\left[\frac{1}{R_1/R_2 + 1}\right]$$

where R_1 and R_2 are the resistance of Q_1 and Q_2 respectively. R_2 is usually much smaller than R_1, because the '0' level must be kept below threshold that turns on the next stage; the '0' level is, therefore, approximately

$$V(R_1/R_2)$$

The output of logic stage always sees a node capacitance—the sum of the next stage's gate capacitance, the capacitance of the line connecting the two stages, and a few other parasitic odds and ends. This node capacitance charges slowly through Q_1 when the circuit is switching from 0 to 1, and discharges quickly through Q_2 when the switching occurs from 1 to 0.

In a dynamic circuit (Figure 6.4b), when ϕ is negative (p-channel devices) the output is charged via Q_1 to a negative potential. The only loads permitted are capacitive (except for junction leakage). Therefore, when ϕ returns to ground potential, the output will remain negative unless Q_2 conducts—which occurs only if the input is a '1'. After a short delay following application of a pulse on the line ϕ, the output will, therefore, represent the logical inverse of the input. Since the circuit operation does not depend upon the ratio of the device resistances, both devices can be of minimum geometry. Thus some of the tradeoffs between the static and dynamic circuits become obvious; the dynamic circuit is less expensive and faster than the static equivalent, but requires more elaborate drive signals.

So far as speed is concerned the MOS circuit is slower than the bipolar circuit, as the later possesses much higher transconductance or gain per unit area than does the former. The gain of the MOS circuits can be increased by increasing its width, but the capacitance of the circuit also increases. In MOS inverter the 'turn-on' time, controlled by the driver device, is normally much shorter than the 'turn-off' time of the load. Two factors contribute to the above fact. First, the gate to source controlling bias of the driver remains constant at the input voltage during switching. Secondly, resistance of the load device is much higher than that of the driver. As a result the control voltage is modulated by the output (source) voltage in such a way as to reduce the gain of the load as the output increases. These two factors taken together show that the load charging time is responsible for restricting MOS circuits to low frequency operation.

6.2 SEMICONDUCTOR MEMORY INTEGRATED CIRCUIT TECHNOLOGIES

Integrated circuit (IC) family is divided into three broad divisions, namely,

(i) Thin film circuits.
(ii) Semiconductor/Monolithic circuits.
(iii) Hybrid circuits.

The first two classifications are generic, utilizing entirely different design and fabrication principles; while the third type represents a combination of two generic systems. In thin film, passive parts are deposited in the form of thin patterned films of conductive and nonconductive materials on a passive substrate, in semiconductor, all circuit components are fabricated on a semiconductor substrate by diffusion and epitaxial processes, and in hybrid, passive components are fabricated by thin film techniques and active components by semiconductor techniques.

Semiconductor circuits have the advantage in that the active components become the integral parts of circuit itself. Techniques for building semiconductor memory ICs are in a continuous state of change. The tree like representation of the major semiconductor integrated circuit technologies, as shown here, includes the most important factors involved and the more common options available.

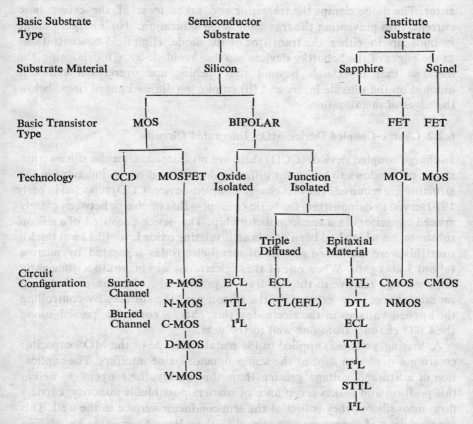

Of the various types of processes the following techniques are widely accepted by the manufacturer for the development of the semiconductor ICs. Although these are not only very exhaustive, the recently reported VMOS (or V-groove MOS) technique, in which the transistor is formed on the side of a groove anisotropically etched in the silicon, shows high performance but it does not appear to be a viable near future LSI technology.

6.2.1 Schottky Process Integrated Circuit

In a typical Schottky process IC, the Schottky diode is formed by the junction of the aluminium metallization and the n type silicon below, and this results in a lower forward voltage drop than that exhibited by discrete, diffused pn junction Schottky diodes. The electrons flowing out of the semiconductor to metal, are in equilibrium with the electrons present in the metal, as a result no (stored) charge is accumulated, and the device has higher speed capabilities than ordinary devices.

This absence of stored charge can be used with advantage if the Schottky diode is placed in parallel with the base to emitter junction of an npn transistor. The diode clamps the transistor and takes most of the excess base current, thus preventing the transistor from saturation. No charge storage is built up in either the transistor or the diode. High field concentrations at the edges of the Schottky devices can be avoided by (i) depositing the metal so that it extends beyond the opening and overlaps a sufficient amount on the dioxide layer, and (ii) employing diffused guard rings below the edges of metallization.

6.2.2 Charge-Coupled Device MOS Integrated Circuits

In charge coupled devices (CCD) there are no transistor on the silicon substrate, no windows to be cut for diffusing dopent, and no pn junctions in the structure are required. The first charge-coupled-device (CCD) reported in early 1970 served to demonstrate the basic concept—that of charge between closely spaced capacitors in a semiconductor chip. The device consisted of a silicon substrate, on which had been grown an insulating oxide layer (0.12 μm thick); over this were fabricated a series of metal electrodes separated by narrow (about 3 μm) gaps. When one of these electrodes was biased to a sufficiently large voltage relative to the substrate, a potential 'well' capable of storing mobile charge was created in the silicon near the surface. By controlling the applied voltages in the electrodes, this charge could be passed along the CCD channel from one well to the next.

A biasing voltage is applied to the metal electrode of the MOS capacitor creating a depletion zone at the semiconductor-oxide interface. The application of a 'storage' voltage greater than this bias voltage opens a well at this position and makes acceptance of carriers possible. If minority carriers flow into silicon, they collect at the semiconductor surface in the well. This accumulation of charge may be moved to the adjacent capacitor by placing a larger 'transfer' voltage on the metal electrode. The larger voltage deepens the well and transfers to new electrode.

At present 64K bit CCD memories are fabricated with minimum geometries of 4-6 μm on chips with sizes of 26-27 mm^2 using a double level polysilicon gate process, very similar to that used for 16K bit MOS dynamic RAMs. This simple stored charge cell, when used in memory, has the advantage that loading is minimum but the drawbacks are—readout process is destructive, stored charge redistributes between the cell and the bit line capacitances, and writing speed is limited by the information storage capacitor which must be made large enough to yield a reasonable sense charge.

6.2.3 Complementary-Symmetry MOS Integrated Circuits

Complementary-symmetry MOS technology has long been regarded as the ideal solution to many of the difficulties encountered in single polarity MOS complex ICs. In conventional bipolar and p-channel MOS ICs, most of the power dissipation is the quiscent power contributed by the load resistance, while in complementary structures, the transistor's load resistor is replaced by a transistor of opposite polarity. As a result they dissipate negligible power and are stable in the presence of noise and heavy loads. These characteristics make the complementary symmetry MOS flip-flops excellent elements for arrays that can be used as memories with capacities up to several hundred bits per chip.

When both p and n devices are fabricated together they have different characteristics, the n-channel devices are in depletion mode, while the p-channel devices are in enhancement mode. Manufacturers use the substrate for the p-channel and diffuse a p-type well for the n-channel. First, the oxide layer is opened and then p-well diffused into the n substrate. A new oxide is grown, and two new holes are opened for p-diffusion, these regions become the source and the drain of the p-channel transistor.

Good operating speeds are expected from the devices built with complementary MOS because the output node capacitance is always charged and discharged through the 'on' transistor. The drawbacks are : (i) since both polarity devices exist side by side, some form of isolation must be used, resulting in significant increase in area per function, (ii) the number of devices required to implement a given function is greater than in the single polarity use.

6.2.4 Silicon-On-Sapphire MOS Integrated Circuits

The use of sapphire rather than silicon as the underlying structure of an integrated circuit offers an advantage of extremely high insulation resistance between components of ICs. This is the most modern technology, particularly suited to diode arrays used as read only memories (ROM). The simple structure and processing make the arrays easy to build; the low capacitance of the silicon-on-sapphire (SOS) diode's junction makes the arrays fast, and the silicon film's large sheet resistance permits resistor to be included in the array without taking too much room. Furthermore, the arrays are highly radiation resistant.

Fabrication techniques under study for the SOS ICs vary considerably. The fabrication of SOS integrated circuits begins with the growth of a single crystal layer of silicon on a polished substrate of sapphire (aluminium oxide). Since silicon and aluminium oxide are different substances, the thin film must be grown heteroepitaxially. After the silicon film is grown on the sapphire, it is selectively doped, using the conventional oxidation, photolithographic, and diffusion processes, to form semiconductor junctions. The two diffusions, one with n-dopent and one with p-dopent, need not be precisely controlled because the dopents are driven at high concentration through selective exposed areas of silicon all the way to the silicon-sapphire interface. After these junctions have been formed, the unwanted parts of the silicon films are etched away to produce electrically isolated islands of silicon supported by the insulating sapphire. A layer of oxide, grown over the remaining islands, seals them thus reducing the probability of short circuits at the crossovers. The final steps in the procedure are open contact holes in the oxide, deposit an aluminium film and etch the metallization pattern.

Complementary MOS SOS circuits can be built employing the same number of diffusion steps needed to fabricate p-channel MOS ICs. This is possible because the dopents for both n-channel and p-channel devices can be applied simultaneously. A typical complementary MOS SOS fabrication process requires one more oxide deposition and one more etching step than the conventional MOS process used for silicon MOS ICs.

6.2.5 Integrated Injection Logic (I²L), Circuits

Integrated injection logic (I²L) is the new and brightest star in the bipolar LSI sky. Integrated injection logic (I²L) or merged transistor logic (MTL) structures show a high packing density and are excellent power delay products. The minimum propagation delay time of conventional I²L, however, is rather long compared with those of high speed TTL gates. The name injection logic (I²L) is given to the process because the operation of the proposed logic cell based on the direct injection of proposed minority carriers in the inverse transistors. There have been several approaches to high speed I²L, for instance, by means of optimized impurity profiles, oxide isolation and Schottky technology.

The key reason that I²L looks so promising is the fact that it appears to have overcome the traditional drawbacks of bipolar approaches to LSI, namely, the low packing density and high power dissipation per gate. I²L features packing densities better than MOS technologies (>200 gates/mm²) and power dissipation that can compete with that of CMOS, at the same time bipolar speeds.

The processing steps for an MTL or I²L structure vary depending on their performances. In the so-called standard technique, on the top of a p-type substrate with an n⁺ buried layer, an n-type epitaxial layer is grown. In this layer p-type base and n⁺ layers are diffused in the conventional way. The memory cell thus consists of two lateral pnp load transistors and two npn transistors which are inversely operated. Thus the high packing density is mainly a result of the elimination of all space consuming resistors and a sort of superintegration whereby pnp and npn transistors are formed such that the collector area for the pnp transistor also functions as the base area of the npn and the base area of the pnp is integral with the emitter area of the npn transistor. I²L is essentially a current mode logic, and relative amplitude of signal and reference are mainly defined by dimension of active base injector interface. It lends itself, per excellence, with the use of current mirrors, to threshold gate implementation.

One of the most interesting technical aspects of integrated injection logic is the possibility of realizing complex digital circuits and analog functions on the same (bipolar) chip. This allows the design of logic circuits with powerful driver stages which should lead to cost effective 'one chip' solutions. The excellent speed performance, even at lower power level, results from the low stray capacitances, the lack of storage time problems, and the very low voltage swings at the signal modes.

The main question about I²L centers around its newness and the lack of understanding its potentiality over other technologies to a significant extent. It appears at this stage that I²L can cover the entire spectrum of the application with the exception of the very high performance end (ECL), the essential zero standby power area (CMOS) and the extremely low-cost low-performance application of calculators (p-MOS).

6.3 SEMICONDUCTOR READ/WRITE MEMORIES

Semiconductor read-write memories are built of pure MOS and bipolar assemblies or in hybrid arrays containing both types of circuits, and are available in a wide range of capacities and speed. Large-scale integration through MOS technology promises to enhance the performance and cut the cost of these random access memories.

The circuits on these chips can be either static or dynamic. In static circuits, the MOS transistors are used as conventional dc amplifiers, with other MOS devices being used as pull up resistors. Dynamic MOS circuits take advantage of the very low leakage associated with the gate circuits and junctions of well made MOS devices. The dynamic type requires refreshing from time to time, but its elements can be densely packed and it, therefore, lends itself to memories of large capacity. Both kinds of circuits can include decoding transistors on the same chips; the address decoding can be partial or complete, but the more complete decoding often involves a speed penalty. With or without the decoding, both circuits can be made compatible at input and output with diode-transistor, and transistor-transistor logic circuits.

Before going further into the consideration of semiconductor memories, it will be helpful to examine some of the properties of these memory devices.

6.3.1 Bipolar Memory Cell

Most bipolar memory devices use relatively standard flip-flops as the storage cells. Two types of memory cell exist—one uses epitaxial layer for resistors and is multiple emitter memory cell while the other uses Schottky barrier diodes to improve the speed response.

The typical bipolar memory cell is shown in Figure 6.5. It is nothing more than a familiar cross coupled flip-flop with multiple emitter transistors. The inner pair of emitters is connected in parallel to the word driver and the outer pair of bit line emitters is used to differentially sense and store information into the cell. Multiple emitter transistors are easy to fabricate in monolithic technology and the circuit shown in Figure 6.5 uses only two resistors. Resistors are used as little as possible in integrated circuits, because they require a large area compared with transistors. The smaller the area, the more circuits per wafer and the lower is the cost per circuit. The cell operates in quiscent, read and write modes.

In the quiscent state the transistor Q_1 is 'on'. The word emitter is held at a low voltage level relative to the B_0 line voltage so that virtually all the current flowing in Q_1 flows to the word line and none flows in the B_0 line. Thus no signal is seen in the digit differential pair line. The current flowing in Q_1 creates a voltage drop across R_1, causing the collector of Q_1 to be at low potential. This low potential is also seen by the base of Q_2, thereby holding Q_2 'off'. The collector of Q_2 and base of Q_1 are then relatively at a high potential since the only voltage drop across R_2 is caused by the comparatively small current flowing into the base of Q_1 and the negligible leakage current. This keeps Q_1 in an 'on' condition.

In order to read the information contained in a cell, the word line potential is made higher than that of the emitters connected to digit lines. This causes the current that was flowing in the word line to switch into either digit or $\overline{\text{digit}}$ line, depending upon whether Q_1 or Q_2 is on. This current causes an increase in potential on either the digit or the $\overline{\text{digit}}$ line, and the change is sensed by the differential sense amplifier to indicate whether the selected cell is in a '0' or a '1' state. After reading is completed, the word line is again lowered to its original potential and the cell reverts to its quiscent state. Note that the state of the cell has not been changed during this operation and therefore a nondestructive readout (NDRO) has occurred.

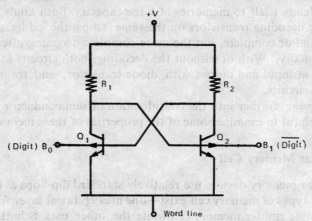

Figure 6.5 Bipolar storage cell.

Writing of information into the cell is done in a manner similar to reading information with the exception that the digit and $\overline{\text{digit}}$ lines are actively energized to cause the cell to enter the desired state. As in reading, the word line is raised in potential forcing current into one of the digit lines. When the potential of digit line is raised, the current flowing in it is decreased, thereby raising the collector potential of Q_1. The increased potential causes base current to flow in Q_2, turning Q_2 'on', and the collector potential of Q_2 drops, reducing base current in Q_1. This feedback effect continues until Q_1 is 'off' and Q_2 line is fully 'on'. For opposite information storage, the digit line is pulsed positive.

In typical memory module, arrays of these cells are arranged on a chip with all cells in a column sharing a digit drive and digit sense circuits; cells in a row are selected by a column word line. Chips often have decoder circuits to drive a single word line from a binary (or other code) address, as well as write and read gates to combine the digit drive and sense circuits to a small number of input and output pins. More emitters may be used in the cell transistors to increase the level of selection at the expense of array complexity.

6.3.2 Static Memory Cell

From the early development of semiconductor memory circuitry, it was realized that metal oxide semiconductor (MOS) devices offer simplicity of processing and economy of layout. MOS is made with only one diffusion and perhaps two-thirds the number of masks as bipolar devices. Although there are occasional exceptions, MOS cells take up only one half to one-fourth the area of bipolar and thus offer a processing cost advantage over the bipolar cells by four to one.

Figure 6.6 shows the basic cell. The two static inverters are wired together to make a flip-flop. The two transistors Q_3 and Q_4 are merely load 'resistors', while transistors Q_5 and Q_6 are used as two-way transmission gates. Transistors Q_1 and Q_2 are the cross coupled elements of the flip-flop and have relatively low impedances. The interior nodes of the flip-flop are connected to the digit lines through two gating devices, which can be switched on by the word line.

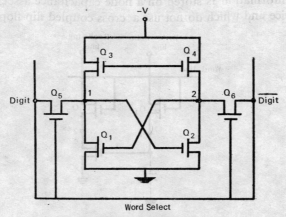

Figure 6.6 Static MOS cell.

In the quiscent state of operation, word line is at ground and the transmission gates are 'off'. Information is retained in one of the two stable states of the flip-flop circuit. The cell dissipates power due to the current flowing through the load device in one side of the flip-flop.

To read the cell, assuming that node 1 is high and node 2 is low, the word line is pulsed turning the gate devices Q_5 and Q_6. Both digit lines are kept at a supply potential. Current flows between the digit line and ground through Q_2 and Q_4. The state of the cell is determined by detecting on which digit line the sense current occurs. There is essentially no cell delay in reading. The sense current will flow in the gating devices in direct response to the word line voltage pulse. The drain of the gating device is connected to the digit line supply and its source is connected to ground through the 'on' flip-flop, which is of comparatively low impedance. To the first order, the sense current does not charge or discharge capacitance and it can flow to the sense circuitry without delay.

Writing is performed by forcing the digit lines to the value desired in the cell, thereby over-riding the contents of the cell. The word line is pulsed, and if the digit line is grounded, then the cell is already in the state to which it was to be written, and no change occurs. If the digit line is grounded, node 1 is pulled down towards the ground through the gating device Q_5. As the level of node 1 drops below the threshold voltage of Q_2, the device turns 'off' and node 2 is pulled up through Q_6 and Q_4. The writing process thus consists of two transients—discharging the initially high node through a gating device operating in common source mode and charging the initially low node through the other gating device in source follower operation. The transients overlap to some extent, but it is the charging transient which largely determines cell writing delay in practice.

6.3.3 Dynamic Memory Cell

The dynamic storage cell for use in a random access memory is shown in Figure 6.7. Information is stored on a node capacitance associated with the gate of a device and which do not use a cross coupled flip-flop circuit. With

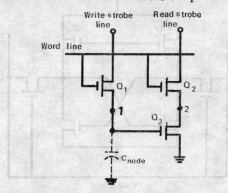

Figure 6.7 Dynamic memory cell.

no dc paths in the circuit, all the transistors can have the same impedance. This impedance can be relatively high, and the area occupied by each transistor is small. The node is either pulled up or down by the logic transistors depending upon input conditions. The node has a capacitance which holds the voltage down. Leakage current exists, however, and the logic inputs must be applied in sufficient time, otherwise the 'precharge' will leak away in a millisecond or so. This time dependency is the reason for the name 'dynamic' as opposed to static logic, which is stable with time.

Data are stored in this cell as a charge on the capacitor C_{node}, which is actually only the parasitic capacitance on the line to which it is shown connected in the diagram. The cell is written by turning on the gating device Q_1 with the word line which establishes the condition of the write strobe line on node 1. In reading the cell the word line is turned 'on'. Devices Q_2 and Q_3 form an AND gate. Q_3 will be 'on' or 'off', depending upon the charge condition of node 1 and the presence or absence of current in the read strobe line can be detected to determine the state of the cell. A lower word line voltage is used in read to prevent inadvertent writing of the cell. This is aided by the fact that the word line must be atleast two 'threshold drops' above ground to turn on Q_2 if Q_3 is already on.

The write transient of the dynamic storage cell can be inherently faster than that of the cross coupled cells due to the absence of gain ratio requirement. This three-device cell also has the advantage that only a single transient is required for writing, rather than the discharge transient followed by an overlapping. Read may be slightly slower in dynamic cells because some sense current may be lost in charging node 2, or because a false sense current spike may charge node 2 even if Q_3 is 'off'.

These dynamic circuits are examples of two phased clocked circuits, but other versions require more or fewer phases. Where, for example, four-phase clocking is employed, the phase pulses often relate to different stages and overlap in various ways to improve the circuit operation. These multiple phases, however, place an additional burden on the system designer who has to provide time phase pulses over a wide area.

6.3.4 Complementary Memory Cell

In complementary logic circuits both p and n channels are used. Such circuits have some unique characteristics and advantages over the other semiconductor memory devices. The area required to perform many logic functions in an integrated complementary MOS (CMOS) array is much smaller than that required by the bipolar technology. CMOS processing requires fewer steps than are used in the manufacture of bipolar ICs. Also, CMOS ICs are operated from a single power source and considerable flexibility is offered to system designer for speed-power optimization.

Before going into the basic storage operation, the characteristics of CMOS inverters are briefly discussed. Consider the case of simple complementary circuit as shown in Figure 6.8. In this circuit, when the input is equal to supply voltage the n-channel device is turned 'on', the p-channel device is 'off', and the output is at ground potential. Conversely, when the input voltage is at ground, the n-channel device is 'off', the p-channel device is 'on', and output is at supply potential. The circuit acts as an inverter, but has the very desirable characteristics that in either quiscent condition, one of the two devices in the circuit is 'off'. No dc current other than the leakage current flows, and the standby power dissipation is essentially eliminated.

The transfer characteristic of the device is shown in Figure 6.8(b). The channel width is held to a minimum in order to maximize transconductance, speed and packing density of the array. When the input goes from a low to a high value the output is pulled down through the n-channel device in common source mode of operation. The upward output node transient occurs through the p-channel device, also in common source operation. Thus the source follower transient is eliminated. This not only gives a faster mode of operation for the transients, but also eliminates the voltage loss between gate and source which occurs with enhancement mode devices in source follower operation.

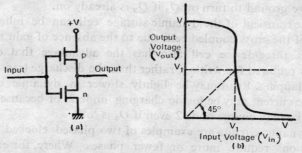

Figure 6.8(a) Complementary MOS inverter; and (b) CMOS inverter transfer characteristic.

Addition of two inverters lead to the complementary flip-flop circuit as shown in Figure 6.9. These circuits dissipate negligible power and are stable in the presence of noise and heavy loads. These characteristics make the

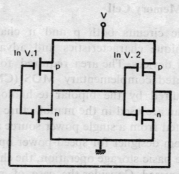

Figure 6.9 CMOS flip-flop.

flip-flops excellent elements for arrays that can be used as memories with capacities up to several hundred bits per chip.

The operation of the circuit is qualitatively similar to static MOS flip-flops. In writing, the complementary load device can be used to help the pull up transient; however, initiating the writing cycle is more difficult because the initial pull down transient of the high node must be accomplished against the common source load device that is turned on hard. If the load device is made low again, writing becomes easier to initiate, but the speed advantage gained in the upward transient is sacrificed.

When the two inverters are connected as in Figure 6.9, the characteristics of two types of devices are effectively multiplied together, and the transfer characteristics of the two-in-series becomes extremely nonlinear. The cross connection provides large noise margins, and well-defined output levels of ground and supply voltage. Since each leg of the flip-flop always contains one conducting and one nonconducting transistor, there is always a relatively low impedance path from the output terminal to either the power supply or ground, depending upon the state of the inverter. The low impedance minimizes the capacitive noise pick up. The switching response of these CMOS logic circuits is determined solely by the capacitance loading at the input and output and the amount of current available to charge this capacitance. The design of these cells is relatively complex and requires large layout areas.

6.4 SEMICONDUCTOR LOGIC CIRCUITS

Workers in the field of switching theory have occasionally turned their attention to the certain issues of LSI, such as attributes of simple wiring patterns, wire layer minimization, and universal logic blocks. The problem of standard logic chips, however, is that universality may not particularly be efficient from a selection area or I/O pin terminal viewpoint at a level much above the simple NOR gate. Functional groupings, such as, decoders, and address register cells are useful and can be readily built, but are far from being universal. A number of studies on universal logic modules have been carried out of which an early paper by Earle is particularly worth mentioning.

The logic gates suitable for LSI should satisfy the following three important requirements: (i) processing should be simple and under good control in order to obtain an acceptable yield of reliable ICs containing about thousand gates, (ii) the basic gate must be as simple and compact as possible, (iii) the power delay time product must be such that operation at a reasonable speed does not cause excessive dissipation on the chip. These circuits have only two states—'off' and 'on' (conducting or nonconducting). It has an input network of active elements that determines the condition under which the circuit provides an output. The present semiconductor MOS memories are actually long shift registers or array of flip-flops, which in turn, are combination of simple logic blocks. A discussion of high speed memories, therefore, begins with logic.

The present trend in digital system design is directed towards the use of reduced power and high performance logic circuits. This trend has helped to achieve increased speed and efficiency in the logic taking advantage of the high packing density capability of integrated circuit. Most modern logic families are based on the inverting gate concept. Such an all purpose element is capable of performing the three basic Boolean functions, AND, OR and INVERT. Various circuit approaches are available to the designer of semiconductor memory system such as RTL, transistor-transistor logic (TTL), Schottky-diode clamped transistor-transistor logic, hybrid MOS-bipolar logic, emitter coupled logic (ECL), etc. Certainly any one family of ICs can neither satisfy the demands of all logic designers, nor meet completely all the specifications of a given digital system. TTL circuits, for example, have short propagation delay but high power dissipation; diode-transistor logic (DTL) circuits, on the other hand, are slower in switching speed but at the same time involve reduced power consumption. Many different logic types available today permit selection of one that comes close to satisfying most of the requirements. In this section we shall consider only the two most popular form of logic suitable for fabrication in integrated circuit form, namely, the ECL and TTL. However, any logic gate design should take account of the following considerations: (i) device geometrics, power dissipation, and propagation delay, (ii) noise margin, (iii) TTL compatibility, and (iv) sensitivity of power supply variation.

6.4.1 Transistor-Transistor Logic (T^{2}L)

Transistor-transistor logic, referred to as T^{2}L or TTL, is similar in many respects to diode transistor logic. Like other logic circuits such as RTL, RCTL or DTL, the coupling element in this integrated logic structure is a transistor. Figure 6.10 shows both discrete and integrated form of TTL circuits. In discrete form the collector terminals and base terminals of all input transistors are connected in parallel. In integrated form this feature offers a significant advantage in that the corresponding collector and base regions of the input transistors need not be isolated from each other. In fact all input transistors can be reduced to one transistor as shown in Figure 6.10(b). The technology used for fabrication of TTL circuits employs epitaxial material with buried collector regions in it. Electrical isolation between devices is achieved with p-diffused region.

The operation of TTL circuits is very simple. Instead of input diodes in a DTL, multiple emitter transistor is used here. The offset diodes have been eliminated, their function being performed by the collector base diode of T_1. With no inputs at the emitter, the input transistors T_A, T_B, T_C are used merely as diodes. The current will flow through these diodes to the base of the transistor T_2 which will turn on. If the emitter of one of the input transistors say, T_A, is connected to ground, the base current will flow through R_1, forcing the transistor T_A to its saturation value. The collector voltage has now reached to almost ground potential making the transistor T_2 cut off. Thus the function of the gate is NAND, and

$$F = \overline{ABC}$$

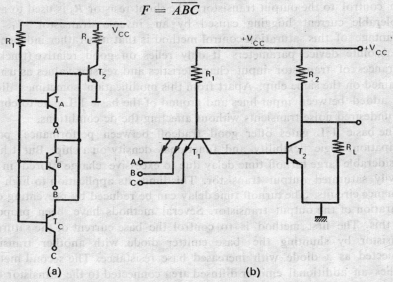

(a)   (b)

Figure 6.10 (a) Discrete form of T²L gate; and (b) Integrated form of T²L gate.

There are some disadvantages in this simple circuit. Since the driving gate must supply the input current to an 'on' TTL gate, a current hogging problem can also exist. Transistor T_2 turns on as soon as one of the inputs drops below 0.7 V approximately. Since the inputs are fed from the output transistor of a similar circuit with its associated saturation voltage, only a small voltage difference exists, resulting in high noise sensitivity. The noise margin can be improved by adding one or more diodes between the collector of T_1 and base of T_2 thus increasing the required turn on voltage. But the addition of extra diodes will cause the turn off time of TTL circuits to increase.

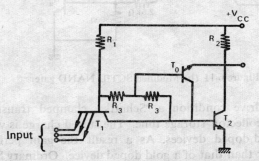

Figure 6.11 (a) Modified T²L gate with feedback transistor.

Without sacrificing the speed advantage, design modifications have been made to the T²L gate in order to achieve greater noise immunity than of Figure 6.10. This is shown in Figure 6.11(a) in which an additional feedback transistor T_0 is used with the conventional T²L circuit to provide a saturation control to the output transistor. The shunt resistor R_3 is used to avoid intolerable current hogging caused by an inverse transistor T_1. The advantage of this saturation control method is that it is rather independent of absolute device parameters. It only relies on good relative (tracking) tolerances of transistor input characteristics and resistor values as usually obtained on the same chip. Apart from this modification sometimes diodes are added between input lines and ground of the basic T²L gate to control the undesired noise transients without affecting the dc conditions.

The basic T²L gates offer good tradeoff between performance, power dissipation, logic flexibility and functional density on a chip. But it has a considerable large turnoff time delay due to excessive charge stored in the heavily saturated output transistor. This limits its application to high performance circuits. The turnoff time delay can be reduced by preventing deep saturation of the output transistor. Several methods have been proposed for this. The first method is to control the base current of the saturated transistor by shunting the base emitter diode with another transistor connected as a diode with increased base resistance. The second method applies an additional emitter diffused area connected to the transistor base as saturation control device. These two methods, though successful in controlling the saturation effect to some extent, are not very effective. The most useful approach is to use a Schottky-barrier diode for clamping voltage of the base collector diode at a relatively low forward voltage.

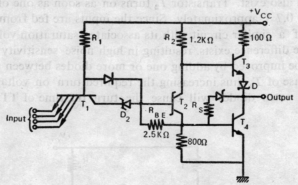

Figure 6.11 (b) Modified SCT²L NAND gate.

Under normal drive condition a Schottky clamped transistor (SCT) exhibits no base collector storage time. The stored charge is very small as compared with gold doped devices. As a result the gain performance of SCT is much better than that of a gold doped device. Ordinary SCT, though possesses good current gain and fast switching times, has a high V_{CEsat} value.

This can be optimized by adding a resistor R_S in series with Schottky-barrier diode (SBD). A modified SCT in a T^{2}L circuit based on 7420 NAND gate is shown in Figure 6.11(b). The resistor R_{BE} across the base emitter of SCT considerably reduces the h_{fe} at low current level and forces a minimum amount of current through R_{BE} before T_2 (and consequently T_4) turns on. The resistor R_S in series with the Schottky diode clamping transistor T_4 brings that transistor into slight saturation. The combination of junction diode D_1 and Schottky diode D_2 between base collector of input transistor enhances the noise margin by clamping the base of T_1 at a higher voltage.

This modified SCT^{2}L circuit has a lower margin of noise (occurring due to different physical properties of a SCT) than a gold doped transistor. Typical propagation delay of SCT^{2}L circuit is of the order of 3.5 nsec at a power dissipation of 20 mw giving a speed power product of $T_{av} \cdot P_D = 70$ pJ. Since these modified SCT^{2}L circuits incorporate additional elements, they require approximately two per cent area more than a single doped NAND gate if bonding pads are included.

The feasibility of utilizing low voltage logic in digital systems permits the exploitation of simplified bipolar technologies. The collector diffusion isolation (CDI) structure enjoys a slight advantage over T^{2}L structure in that it requires a fewer process steps. Because of the relatively shallow diffusion required to penetrate the epitaxial layer and the elimination of the conventional isolation mask and its associated tolerances, a significant area reduction is easily achieved using the CDI process. The highly doped collector region of the CDI transistor leads to unique characteristics. It has relatively high inverse current gain which results from a high collector injection efficiency. This combined with a very low collector series resistance results in very low collector emitter saturation voltages and offsets, and makes the device attractive for use in bilateral switching application.

The TTL circuit configuration is shown in Figure 6.12 which is designed to take advantage of high packing density. This requires low power and results in small signal swing and small dc noise margin. The CDI processing characteristic results in only three masked diffusion steps required in the fabrication of the CDI device structure, while five are required to fabricate a typical standard buried collector (SBC) structure. The CDI bipolar device is competitive in performance with more conventional bipolar device struc-

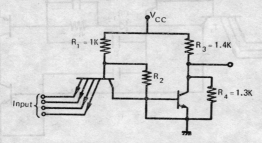

Figure 6.12 TTL gate in CDI configuration.

tures. It also offers economic advantages in that CDI is simpler to process and provides higher component packing densities. The relative merits of CDI technology compared with SBC technology depend on the thickness of the epitaxial layer used for the latter. Regarding the maximum switching speed, CDI presents a problem. The most specific areas with respect to speed degradation are the collector substrate capacitance of the input array, capacitance associated with resistors, and the base collector capacitance of the output transistor, the latter appearing as Miller capacitance, thus limiting rise time. The electrical characteristics generally obtained with CDI transistors are given in Table 6.1

6.4.2 Complementary Transistor-Transistor Logic (CT²L)

The potential for complementary logic has been known for some time in the field of bipolar transistors and more recently in the field of MOS transistors. For high speed low power logic circuits, the combination of pnp and npn transistor offers many advantages. This concept was first proposed by Baker which provides excellent drive capabilities and fast switching speeds. The objective of micropower circuit design is to minimize power supply voltages. The principal reasons are: (i) for a given power level, the signal impedance decreases as the square of the voltage reduction, and (ii) certain devices including bipolar transistors, cannot be operated below a particular current level. So power reductions can only be achieved by lower supply voltages.

The most desirable approach to micropower design in switching circuit is to eliminate standby power through complementary switching so that all the current from the supply is utilized to drive the load impedance and parasitic capacitances in the circuit. This micropower operation is enhanced through the use of complementary transistor circuits. The fabrication process generally adopted uses an epitaxial slice of silicon with a buried

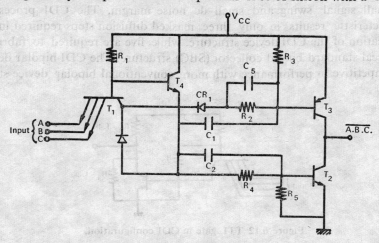

Figure 6.13 CT²L NAND gate.

layer of n$^+$ type dopant. The buried layer is used as a diffusion spot that allows for the formation of the pnp collector and the pn junction isolation with the same diffusion. Independent diffusions are used for each type transistors. The process includes three diffusions for the purpose and two for the npn transistor.

A complementary transistor NAND gate is shown in Figure 6.13 in which the multiemitter transistor T_1 performs the AND operation and the NOT function is performed by the complementary output transitors T_2 and T_3. For the case in which any input is at a '0' level, base current flows through R_1 from V_{cc} supplying base current to T_1 which, in turn, supplies base current to T_3 through R_2. For the case of all inputs at a logic '1' level, all gating emitters are reverse biased and the base current is supplied to T_2 through T_4 and R_4. In both cases, however, the current is supplied through an active device providing symmetrical drive conditions to T_3 and T_2. This is responsible for fast switching at low power levels. The speed up capacitors C_1 and C_2 are used in parallel with the base resistors. The maximum frequency response of this type of gate is limited by T^{2}L type input rather than the complementary inverter section. The circuit speed is dictated by the amount of parasitic capacitance associated with the input transistor.

The operation of complementary transistor-transistor logic circuits in micropower region can be enhanced by simply adding one extra diffusion to the standard monolithic bipolar transistor process. The monolithic micropower logic gate using bipolar transistors can be operated from a very low power supply. Several complementary gate configurations are shown in Figure 6.14(a) with their transfer characteristics in Figure 6.14(b). Speed up capacitors are avoided in the design to minimize the area required per gate. Figure 6.14 (i) is the simplest of the three complementary transistor-transistor logic (CT^{2}L) NAND gate. The base drives of the output complementary pair are derived through the base emitter and base collector diodes of the input transistor, respectively. Since the V_{cc} of the circuit is only slightly higher than two diode drops, the pnp transistor is cut off when all the inputs are high.

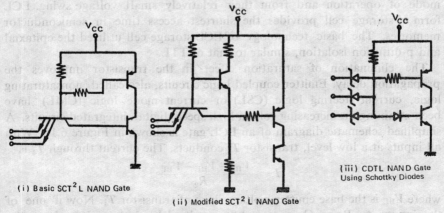

(i) Basic SCT^{2}L NAND Gate

(ii) Modified SCT^{2}L NAND Gate

(iii) CDTL NAND Gate Using Schottky Diodes

Figure 6.14 (a) Different configuration of complementary gate structures.

The clamping of input transistor is necessary to minimize the input leakage current arising from high inverse current gains. The gates shown in Figure 6.14 (ii) and (iii) are designed to have higher low input dc noise margin. The noise margin of the low voltages is approximately given by

$$V_N \simeq V_{DS} - V_{CES}$$

where V_{SD} is the Schottky diode voltage which is typically 300 mV and V_{CES} is the saturation voltage of the previous stage and is approximately 100 mV, so that $V_N \simeq 200$ mV, for the Schottky clamped CT^2L gate. The basic Schottky clamped CT^2L gate has smaller noise margin, the best power speed product and the smallest number of components. Thus adding one extra diffusion, the design flexibility in monolithic integrated circuit can be greatly enhanced.

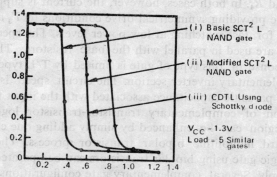

Figure 6.14 (b) Transfer characteristics.

6.4.3 Emitter Coupled Logic (ECL)

Basic logic design with noninverting gate concept cannot provide higher speed in digital circuits because of the saturation effect in the transistor. The high speed performance may be achieved with emitter coupled logic (ECL) or current mode logic (CML) design because of their nonsaturating mode of operation and from their relatively small voltage swing. ECL form of storage cell provides the shortest access time in semiconductor memories. The basic technology of ECL storage cell utilized the epitaxial and p-diffusion isolation, similar to that of TTL.

The elimination of saturation effect in the transistor improves the propagation delay. Emitter coupled logic circuits, also called nonsaturating logic, current steering logic (CSL) or current mode logic (CML) have been attaining an increasing role in high speed digital integrated circuits. A simplified schematic diagram of an ECL gate is shown in Figure 6.15. With all inputs at a low level, transistor T_4 conducts. The current through T_4 is

$$I = \frac{V_{BB} - V_{BE} - V_{EE}}{R_2}$$

where V_{BE} is the base emitter voltage drop of transistor T_4. Now if one of the inputs A, B or C is moved to a voltage level above V_{BB}, the entire current switch from T_4 to the corresponding input transistors T_1, T_2, or T_3. Now the point X moves from $+V_{CC}$ to a level

$$V_D = V_{CC} - R_1 \frac{V_{in} - V_{BE} - V_{EE}}{R_2}$$

It follows that the outputs are

$$V_x = \overline{A + B + C}$$
$$V_y = A + B + C$$

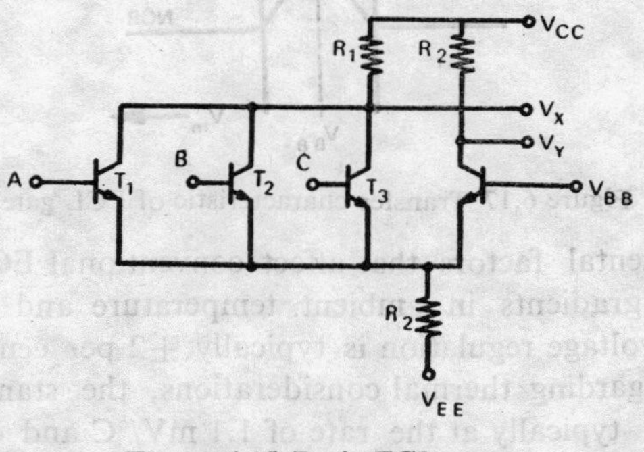

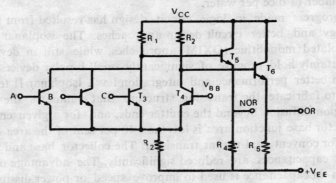

Figure 6.15 Basic ECL gate.

This simple circuit has some disadvantages, namely, it requires more than one supply voltage and these supply voltages should be quite large in order to maintain a constant current with temperature and supply voltage variation which means a higher power dissipation and lastly for maintaining the transistor out of saturation, the dc voltage level at the output must be higher than that of the inputs.

In order to make input-output compatible, emitter followers can be connected to one or both outputs as shown in Figure 6.16. The output emitter followers provide higher drive capability through impedance transformation and allow increased logic swing. This reduces output voltage by the V_{BE} of transistor T_5 and T_6 and improves the driving capabilities of the outputs. The transfer characteristic of this type of gate is given in Figure 6.17, which shows that the output continues to decrease with increased base drive on

Figure 6.16 Modified ECL gate.

an input transistor until that transistor saturates. The OR output under the same condition is one base emitter drop below ground.

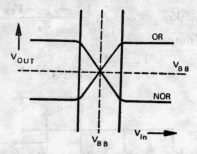

Figure 6.17 Transfer characteristic of ECL gate.

The environmental factors that affect conventional ECL are variations and intrasystem gradients in ambient temperature and in power supply voltage. Supply voltage regulation is typically ± 2 per cent in conventional ECL systems. Regarding thermal considerations, the standard ECL input threshold moves typically at the rate of 1.1 mV/°C and output level track at the rate of 1.5 mV/°C and 0.6 mV/°C for output voltage threshold high and low respectively. Obviously, the temperature difference between interfacing devices should be kept low in order so ensure the noise immunity.

Development work to improve the performance of conventional ECL gate is going on. One approach is to use a fully compensated ECL system in which modifications in the design of current switch and the reference network are made. The system incorporates a temperature compensation feature, so that larger temperature differentials between interfacing circuits can be tolerated. Noise immunity stays virtually invariant with changes in supply voltage and ambient temperature. Nominal ac parameter and power dissipation are identical to conventional ECL. The speed power product for a 25 mV gate is typically 50 pJ. Due to the increased complexity of the reference network and the temperature compensation network required on every output, chip area increases. This increase in die size will reduce the gross number of dice per wafer.

The progress made in logic circuit design has resulted from improved technology and better circuit design approaches. The isoplanar II, and oxide isolated monolithic (OXIM) approaches, while still in development stage, certainly hold promise of significantly small bipolar devices, and resulting in better performance and integration level. Isoplanar II technology is used to fabricate the transistor structure that eliminates the need for base region diffusion beyond the emitter ends, and for a given emitter size the collector base junction area is less than 40 per cent of the area otherwise needed for conventional planar transistor. The collector base and collector isolation capacitances are reduced significantly. The advantage offered by reduction in capacitance is used to improve speed or power dissipation of integrated circuits.

Another technology which offers a much improved performance over the existing standard buried collector (SBC) or collector diffusion isolation (CDI) is known as oxide isolated monolithic (OXIM) technology. The technique of selective oxidation is used to fabricate a 'walled emitter' structure which allows a subtsantial reduction in transistor size for a given active area over standard fabrication technique. This size reduction results in a substantial reduction of parasitic capacitances. The OXIM transistors exhibit relatively small parasitic capacitances and the transistors have small forward and inverse base transit time. This technology when applied to logic gate fabrication, the minimum power delay characteristics of CML gate is about 1 pJ, that of the LSI T²L gate is about 2 pJ and that of the SSI T²L is about 5 pJ. Also in the OXIM technology when applied in fabrication of TTL gate, the power delay product of TTL gate is improved by a factor of 5 over the standard CDI technology. The typical TTL gate fabricated by using OXIM technology can be operated at a power level of 1 mw and a speed of about 5 to 6 nsec. The logic levels are typically 0.2 V maximum for '0' and 1.0 V minimum for '1' with a fan out of eight. Similar data are available for ECL gate operating at −2 V with a logic swing of 0 to 0.2 V.

6.4.4 Emitter Function Logic (EFL)

The emitter function logic (EFL) designed for large-scale integration is based on the noninverting gate philosophy and has several advantages over the standard ECL circuits. The gate is similar to ECL gate but it eliminates a few steps of standard ECL gate. In this structure, the components associated with the complementary output, the emitter follower, its pull up and pull down resistors are eliminated. Also, the parallel input devices forming OR function are replaced and a multiple emitter on the output emitter follower is inserted to perform wired OR functions. The logic design is simplified since minimized Boolean equations are implemented directly without transformations.

A simple EFL gate is shown in Figure 6.18(a). Most of the logic functions are implemented by multiple emitter transistors. Multiple emitters of

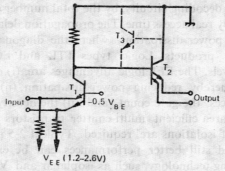

Figure 6.18 (a) Basic EFL gate.

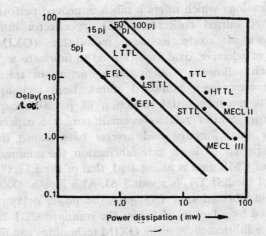

Figure 6.18(b) Power delay comparison for Exclusive ORs (in log scale).

transistor T_1 acts as input stage and this peforms the AND function while a common collector current amplifier T_2 performs the output wired OR function. The clamping diode T_3 is added to prevent the saturation of input device. There is only one internal node, and parasitic capacitances associated with this node, together with the pull up resistor, determine the speed of the circuit. The logic capability of the noninverting OR gate and the AND function can be increased by simply adding emitters to the input transistor.

A comparison of typical EFL performances with other popular logic families is shown in Figure 6.18(b). Many possibilities exist to improve memory logic circuits. Switching time alone is not a satisfactory measure, because larger supply voltages leading to much larger power dissipation will often increase the switching time of logic gates. Also the measurement of power per bit is not very useful, because a low power dissipation might be obtained at the cost of large switching delays. Thus in comparing logic gates, the practice of indicating the speed-power product has been adopted. This is calculated for one logic gate or one memory cell, but in comparing memories it is more useful to divide the total power per chip, including the decoding circuits, by the total number of bits on the chip, and multiply this by real access time. The propagation delay in Figure 6.18(b) is plotted against power dissipation where the diagonal lines show constant power delay products. Logic types TTL and ECL are shown in different power levels. The EFL logic advantages are: (i) operation with low supply voltage, thereby reducing power dissipation, (ii) noninverting gate logic design reduces the gate count, and (iii) the density of integration is increased because area efficient multi-emitter transistors are used and only a small number of isolations are required. Typical 2-5 pJ power delay has been achieved and still better performances can be expected with more advanced processing technology, such as isoplanar and V-groove.

TABLE 6.1
Typical TTL Gate Characteristics
(2 μm epitaxial layer, 5 μm lines and spaces)

Transistor	CDI	SBC
BV_{CEO} (10 μA)	5.4-5.9 V	6-10 V
$V_{CE(sat)}$ (10 mA)	60-120 mV	160-200 mV
h_{fe} (5 mA)	20-90	20-90
f_t (peak)	0.7 GHz (10 mA)	0.7 GHz
f_t (100 mA)	0.5 GHz	0.3 GHz
Gate	1.2 μm epitaxial layer, 2-3 μm lines and spaces	
Delay	20 ns	5 ns
Power (2 V supply)	0.4 mW	1 mW
Power delay product	8 pJ	5 pJ

6.5 MEMORY ORGANIZATION AND SYSTEM OPERATION

During the several generations of computers, CPU speeds have increased by a factor of a few hundreds; such high speeds have resulted in demand for much larger memory capacities. Moreover the memory system designer not only wants large capacity; he also wants high speed operation, speed comparable to those of the CPU. Large-scale integration (LSI) memories show considerable promise. They include low cost, high speed, high capacity, high reliability, and low standby power.

Serious work on random access semiconductor memories began in early 'sixties; first publication appeared in 1965. In contrast with LSI logic, scratch pad and main memory configurations are almost ideally suited for exploitation of the advantages of large chips. The high degree of two dimensional memory cell replication and wiring regularity results in comparatively simple chip design and, with the availability of selection logic directly on the chip, provides a powerful partitioning flexibility. Trade-off possibilities exist between chip storage capacity, speed, input-output pad requirements, and power dissipation which are simply unavailable in discrete logic technology.

The demand for high speed, large capacity and low standby power cannot be met by either MOS or bipolar technology alone. MOS technology offers small memory size, low standby power, and low cost. High speed operation does not seem possible with all MOS designs due to low speed of MOS decoding, driving and sensing circuits. Bipolar technology enables high speed operation, but the standby power of commonly used bipolar flip-flop cells is high. Combination of MOS memory cells and bipolar interface circuitry results in higher speed, but causes severe interconnection problems as MOS and bipolar circuitry cannot be fabricated economically on the same chip.

Upon the introduction of 1k bit MOS dynamic random access memories (RAMs) in 1970, the semiconductor industry was able to challenge the core as the computer main frame memory element. The memory cost is minimized through the use of small chip size with high memory density (3 device/cell silicon gate technology) and by developing an easy interface memory chip which reduces the overhead circuits associated with the building of memory systems by eliminating the special driver circuits and critical multiphase timing generation. The memory system is based on MOS technology for the storage array and on bipolar technology for the interface electronics. The random access storage matrix and the address decoders used to select a particular location of the memory cell can be processed simultaneously on a common substrate. Most active memory cells currently in use employ flip-flops to store binary information; logic gating is incorporated in the cells to ensure that information is written into, or readout of the selected memory location. To decrease cycle time, the state of the cell is sensed in a nondestructive readout mode.

6.5.1 Memory Cell and Memory Array

Performance considerations and limitations can be illustrated by several examples of general design. The key to the attainment of low power dissipation in general lies in the design and method of operation of the storage cell. The guiding factor of MOS RAM design is economy. Significant economic progress to increase MOS storage element packing density has been made during the last six years.

The solid memory products can be used in a wide variety of configurations. The basic storage cell may be static, dynamic or multiple emitter bistable circuits. The multiple emitter configuration requires small area and ease of wiring when using a single metallization layer. On the other hand, dynamic circuit requires extremely low power for data retention. In static circuit there is no need for refreshing while in dynamic configuration it is necessary to provide several timing pulses for periodic refreshing of data and for restoration of the memory selection after read and write operation.

A quite successful way of reducing the cell area is to eliminate circuit elements of the storage cell. The cost is minimized through the use of small chip size with high memory density (3 device/cell, silicon gate technology). There are other possible configurations of the 3 device cell. The smallest configuration is shown in Figure 6.19 as it has minimum interconnecting lines. Another configuration which eliminates the two transistors from three transistors configuration, is the single transistor memory cell which has been tried by several semiconductor memory manufacturers. Although single transistor configuration has the advantages of fewer elements, fewer lines and fewer contact holes, it has the disadvantages that readout of the cell is destructive, the cell output voltage is highly damped so that a highly sensitive refresh amplifier is needed.

The three transistor memory cell is shown in Figure 6.19. The information is stored in the form of a charge on the capacitor C_S which is the combination of MOS gate capacitance of transistor Q_2 and the capacitance of the drain diffusion region of transistor Q_1. This three transistor dynamic memory cell requires five interconnect lines, two select lines—one for reading (read select) and the other for writing (write select)—a read output line, a data input line, and one ground line. The read and write select lines in the memory cell in Figure 6.19 are combined into a common select line, reducing the number of interconnections and thereby the overall memory cell area. Combination of read and write select line requires the use of a three level signal to drive the select lines. The first level is off, the second or intermediate level is for reading and the third level is for writing into the cell. The Q_2 transistor samples the state of the storage node, whereas the Q_3 transistor samples the state of the Q_2 transistor when the 'select' line is at the intermediate level. The Q_1 transistor is employed to refresh the stored information or to write into the cell.

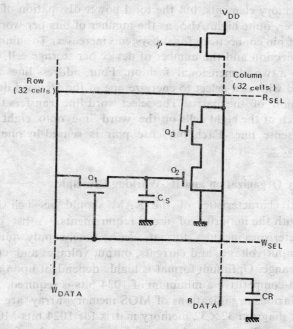

Figure 6.19 Three transistor dynamic memory cell.

In the dynamic cell of Figure 6.19, information is stored on the capacitance C_S of gate Q_2. Data on the W_{DATA} line is written into the cell by enabling Q_1 with W_{SEL}. To read from the cell, the R_{DATA} line with capacitance C_R is discharged to V_{DD} (enabled by signal ϕ). When the signal R_{SEL} enables Q_3, the R_{DATA} line will be charged to V_{SS} through the inverter Q_2 if and only if the capacitor C_S contains a low. Therefore, the R_{DATA} line then contains the logical complement of the cell data. The readout operation from the cell is nondestructive but due to leakage associated with the junction of Q_1, the charge stored in C_S may be lost. To keep the data stored in the cell it is necessary to regenerate the data periodically. This regeneration is done by reading the contents of the cell out onto the read data line, inverting and amplifying the signal and applying it to the W_{DATA} line, and then rewriting back into the cell by activating the W_{SEL} line. A circuit which performs the inversion and amplification function is called a *refresh amplifier*. Separate refresh amplifier is provided for each column of cells in the array. To refresh the entire memory, each row of cells must be individually refreshed.

Low cost, small size, highly reliable LSI memory subsystem can be built by combining monolithic semiconductor memory technology with multi-chip beam lead packaging techniques. LSI subsystems can be organized as linear select system and are built as 256 word × 4 bit, 128 word × 8 bit or 16M word × 4N bit system. In fact, memory arrays with any bit capacity and any bit per word organization can be achieved by combining a number of 64 bit memory elements, but the total power dissipation of such a system is, however, quite high. Also, as the number of bits per word increases, the number of pin connections for subsystems increases. To minimize the on-chip interconnection and the number of device per storage cell, the array is organized in a two dimensional fashion. Four address lines are decoded and combined with row select to energize one of the 16 word drivers in the word dimension of the matrix. The select word line transfers the informations from each of the eight cells on the word line onto eight differential pairs of bit/sense line. Each bit/sense pair is sensed by one of the digit pre-amplifiers.

6.5.2 Memory Organization and Its Working Principle

The electrical characteristics of the RAM should be such that they are compatible with the majority of users' requirements. A list of pertinent RAM characteristics includes format, access time, supply voltages, power dissipation, input voltages and currents, output voltages and currents and temperature range. Optimum format is highly dependent upon application, but to be cost-competitive a minimum of 1024 bits is required.

Although various organizations of MOS memory array are possible, a typical block diagram 32 × 32 memory matrix for 1024 bits MOS RAM is shown in Figure 6.20. As regard to configuration, consider, for example, a chip with 1024 word × 1 bit capacity. If an 8 bit word is required, eight chips may be arranged in row; capacity is 8 × 1024 = 8192 bits. For a larger volume, these chips may be arranged in additional rows, eight per row. By this means that memory is readily organized in any desired capacity and word length. A 1024 bit dynamic silicon-gate MOS random access memory chip is generally used by most of the memory designers as it offers some advantages over the static MOS or bipolar memory. In fact, when speed is not important and a relatively large memory is required, the 1024 bit dynamic MOS RAM is the obvious choice. The silicon-gate process has many inherent advantages over the conventional metal-gate MOS

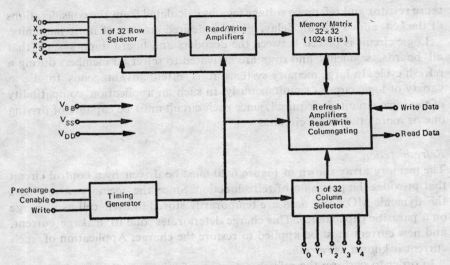

Figure 6.20 Memory chip block diagram.

process. It offers more circuit interconnection flexibility, smaller and faster devices resulting from: (i) the self aligned gate, and (ii) elimination of metal-to-metal separations between the gate and the source or drain.

The memory is organized as 32 row and 32 column array with five address bits selecting the row, and five address bits selecting the column. Two of the 32 decoders provide X and Y decode of the 32×32 storage matrix. The address lines X_0 through X_4 are decoded to select one row of cells. When accessed, the contents of this row are transferred to a row of 32 refresh amplifiers. During read or write, the data is regenerated and written back into the selected row of cells. Address bits Y_0 through Y_5 are decoded to select one refresh amplifier for communication with data input-output terminals. Standard 1024 word by 1 bit dynamic RAM chip is now available. The memory is fully decoded and its differential outputs can be OR-tied. The chip select input allows the selection of individual components in large memory arrays. Stored information is nondestructively read and the differential output voltage is of the same polarity as the differential input voltage during write operation. Since the memory is dynamic, it must be refreshed periodically. The data output is sensed as a current. During the cell cenable if the storage cell is in the read or refresh mode, the current will flow from data output to sense amplifier. If '1' is read from the cell, a high current is available. The current is usually converted to a logical level by a sensitive differential amplifier which measures the voltage drop across the resistor of a few hundred ohms. The choice of sense resistor is influenced by two considerations. Larger values of resistor produce larger output voltages, but increase the time constant of data output lines and therefore, increase the access time of the memory. Lower value, on the other hand, results in high speed but reduces the noise immunity of the system. The optimum value of sense resistor and reference voltage may be calculated from the considerations of the last added circuit delay, given a desired amount of noise immunity.

Logic circuit is placed between the decoders and board inputs such that all boards, segments and rows are activated to select all members during a refresh cycle. In large memory systems it is often advantageous to use a variety of logic circuits simultaneously. In such an application, compatibility of the logic circuits is required, since each circuit must be capable of driving one or more other logic circuits.

Refresh Action

The memory array shown in Figure 6.20 must be driven by a control circuit that provides the provision of refresh action. Since the memory array uses the dynamic MOS cell, data are temporarily stored in each cell as a charge on a parasitic capacitance. This charge deteriorates due to leakage current, and new current must be applied to restore the charge. Application of such current is known as *refresh*.

In order to perform the refresh action, a refresh controller may be attached to the memory unit. The rate at which the refresh action should occur, depends on the specific value of charge and the amount of leakage current, which is a function of temperature. A typical refresh rate at 70°C is every 2 msec. The simplest arrangement for refreshing is to use a refresh buffer for each of the 32 columns and whenever this buffer receives a write or read pulse, all 32 cells in its column are refreshed. Thus 32 write or read cycles are needed to refresh the entire array, and also this arrangement requires a logic subsystem to keep track of columns which have been read or written into.

There are other modes of refreshing, namely, automatic refresh during a write cycle, periodic refresh with every read cycle (called read/refresh or invisible refresh), and single pulse refresh either periodically every 2 msec, or segment by segment as demanded. In a read only cycle there is no change in read/write line. The read pulse lies with chip enable pulse, and its width depends on the amount of time one wishes to look at the output of a particular module. In a write cycle the system writes into a particular cell and automatically refreshes all other cells in the array. Cycle time for a write cycle is longer than for a read only cycle since the write cycle needs a longer delay to get the addresses set up, and its minimum pulse width is greater. In the invisible refresh mode of operation, the memory array is refreshed during each cycle by an 80 nsec, pulse on the read/write line. Since read/write pulse lies outside chip enable pulse, it refreshes the cells in the array without writing any data. Segment-by-segment refresh on demand is useful in memory system where the arrays are grouped in segment. In each segment, there is a one shot which begins timing from the last write operation.

Invisible refresh is most appropriate in the systems where cycle times are around 400 nsec or greater. For fast systems single pulse technique would be more appropriate, whereby the memory can be refreshed by a single pulse—either with a periodic pulse every 2 msec or with segment-by-segment refresh on demand using one shot.

Timing Structure

As the basic memory cell is a dynamic one and data is stored as charge on a parasitic capacitance C_s of transistor Q_2, several timed signals must be provided for periodic refreshing of data. Some of these signals have critical time relationships. These signals can be generated by delay lines, shift registers or by monostable multivibrators. A total of three control pulses are generated—precharge, cenable, and write. A typical memory timing diagram is shown in Figure 6.21.

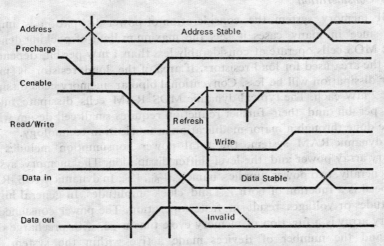

Figure 6.21 Timing diagram of a read/write cycle.

Initially all controls are at high state, at a voltage approximately equal to V_{SS} (off). To begin a cycle, precharge is first brought low to V_{DD} (on). This operation activates the row and column decoders and also charges all read and write data lines negatively. Since the charging circuitry is somewhat slower than decoder circuitry, addresses need not be stable until somewhat precharge is applied.

After precharge and addresses have been active long enough for the data lines to discharge and the decoders to stabilize, the cenable clock is turned on. At this time the particular read select line is activated and the read data line charging circuits are disabled. These data lines begin to discharge selectively, with the signals on them approaching values corresponding to the complements of the data stored in the selected row of cells. As the read data lines are selectively charged, the precharge signal is turned off, removing the precharge signal from write data lines and closing the path which enables write select line to restore the contents of the memory cells.

There is an overlap between precharge and cenable. The signal level on the data line in the cell is a function of the overlap time. Too much or insufficient overlap will cause improper operation and ultimately the data will be lost. This problem which is caused due to unavoidable capacitive coupling between data and select lines and the cell storage capacitor should be kept into consideration in the memory design process.

Similar timing is necessary in writing into the the storage element. Write cenable energizes write select which, in turn, energizes the write drivers when information is stored. When write line is activated, the read data lines are discharged. This disconnects the refresh amplifiers from the write data lines, enabling a path from the data input line to the selected cell. The signal on the data input line will then overwrite the contents of the cell.

Power Consideration

In LSI memory system, the consideration of power dissipation is important, since in many cases it sets the maximum limit of packing density. Static MOS cells operate at considerably less than 1 mW per bit, depending upon the area used for load resistors. If area of the load resistor is more, power dissipation will be less. Conventional bipolar memory cells dissipate about 2 mW each. The typical dynamic MOS RAM cells dissipate microwatts per bit and their further reduction requires small cell design which can be done through a major modification in fabrication technology.

In dynamic RAM system, the total power consumption includes the memory array power and the level shifter dissipation. The memory system uses generally, two power supplies, namely, V_{BB}, V_{SS}. In dynamic MOS, RAM cell speed is a function of both V_{SS} and clock amplitudes. In general higher amplitudes or voltages result in faster operation. The power consumed by memory array is a function of memory cycle time used, with precharge duty cycle and the number of devices made active within the system. For memory cycles which differ significantly in timing, the average current per device executing a cycle may be estimated from the duty cycles associated with precharge, overlap, cenable and transition period.

The next bigger power consumable unit in MOS RAM system is the level shifter circuits. Typical $4K \times 16$ bit memory requires sixteen data level shifters, ten address level shifters and from 6 to 10 clock level shifters depending upon the clock decoding scheme used. Also for the level shifter circuits that are driving large capacitive loads the power associated with charging and discharging the capacitance should be taken into consideration. However, some reduction in power consumption may be achieved by gating the data level shifters such that they deliver low outputs only during cenable period of write cycles.

When the RAM is not being addressed, it is placed in a standby mode in order to save power. This mode is used to make the memory appear nonvolatile to the user. The data is not accessible during this mode. A special precharge is needed to bring the memory out of standby. This precharge sets up the address decoding and permits the RAM to receive the address signals required for a read/write.

6.6 DESIGN CONSIDERATIONS OF SEMICONDUCTOR RAMs

The rapid development of integrated circuit technology has already made semiconductor memory an economic alternative to magnetic memory, both for large capacity memories in conventionally organized systems and for small memories in intimate combination with logic and peripheral circuitry. With magnetic core, film, or plated wire memory, low cost is achieved by having very large magnetic arrays driven by a relatively small number of electronic circuits. Present generations of LSI memories are also built around this consideration and a very large system, such as CDC 7600, clearly show this type of architecture. As discussed earlier, semiconductor memory comprises the memory array, address registers, address decoders and output encoders including the necessary drive circuitries. With LSI array the address decoding takes a little time; but once addressed, a non-destructive read occurs and the stored word so addressed remains available. The addressed word can therefore be used for either or both reading and writing as if it were a register in the machine system. This is not true in magnetic memories where a destructive read occurs and the data must be stored immediately in some other register for regeneration and for other use. LSI memory designs can be made such that a bit mask is inherent within the memory to allow selective reading and writing of bits into and out of a memory word. Such a bit mask can be loaded directly from a stored word and is proposed as an integral part of the LSI memory.

6.6.1 Choice of Basic Memory Cell Technology

The priorities in selecting a technology and designing a storage cell should incorporate different considerations. The storage cell area must be as small as possible to offer minimum cost, power dissipation must be well below 1 μw/bit to permit free air cooling of a large storage system. In fact, low power dissipation and high speed performance have traditionally been incompatible. For the last few years memory designers are suggesting the use of p-channel silicon gate MOS RAMs. But only a few commercial computer systems employ these RAMs in their main memory applications. The main reasons are: (i) p-channel dynamic MOS RAMs require complicated timing and control circuitry to incorporate them in computer systems with existing CPUs which in turn entails a great deal of logic system redesign since virtually all of these CPUs have been designed to be used with magnetic cores, and (ii) p-channel dynamic MOS RAMs are volatile and so data within them must be restored (refreshed) periodically. During each refresh interval, the memory is unavailable for accessing.

The advantages of MOS transistor as a basic element in LSI arrays are quite obvious. The most important of these are processing simplicity, high packing density, and low power dissipation, all of which enable fabrication of complex arrays with high yields and low cost. The cell area is primarily or entirely determined by the area required for metal or polysilicon interconnecting lines and the spaces between them and the area associated with contacts between layers of metal, polysilicon, and silicon. A fundamental measure of memory cell density is the number of metal lines required for cell interconnection in an array together with the number of contacts from metal or polysilicon to silicon required for each storage cell.

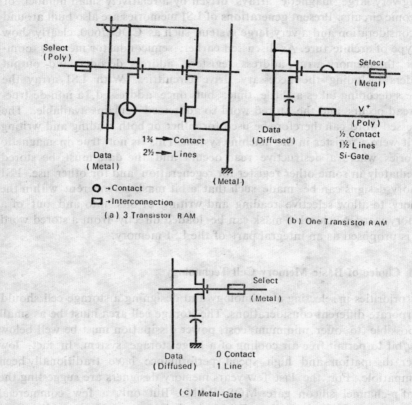

Figure 6.22 Different contacts and interconnections of a RAM cell.

Typical RAM bipolar, MOS, and complementary MOS (CMOS) transistor static read/write memory cells require $1\frac{1}{2}$ to 4 array interconnect lines and $3\frac{1}{2}$ to 10 contacts per storage cell. Several three tran- sistor dynamic MOS RAM cells are in use, and these require $1\frac{1}{2}$ to 3 line and $1\frac{3}{4}$ to $2\frac{1}{2}$ contacts per cell and are thus denser than static cells. Figure 6.22 shows the different interconnections and contact of RAM cell. The speed of operation of MOS design is limited due to low speed of MOS decoding, driving and sensing circuits. On the other hand, the superiority of bipolar technology for high speed performance applications is unquestionable, but its potential for storage chips with high bit density and low power dissipation has been doubted. Finally, the combination of MOS memory cells and bipolar interface circuitry, although results in higher speed, causes severe interconnection problems.

The general technique to reduce the standby power of memory cells is to use dynamic operations. Dynamic circuits conditionally transfer stored charge from one capacitive node to another. They conserve power by drawing current only when the nodes are being charged or discharged. A successful way of reducing the cell area is to eliminate circuit elements of the three-transistor MOS storage cell. This can be done by eliminating the amplifying transistor and the read selection transistor from three transistor cell and sharing these among many cells. This leads to single transistor memory cell that has the advantages of fewer lines, fewer contact holes and fewer elements in the electrical circuits. The overall layout of single transistor cell is almost reduced to approximately one half of that of three-transistor cell. Different single transistor memory cells and refresh circuits have been realized in silicon gate technology. Storage densities of typical 2.6 mil^2/bit operated with a read/write cycle time of 350 nsec has been developed. Advocates of three-transistor-structure feel that the higher signal levels and proven circuitry make for less critical manufacture and higher yields. The single transistor cell, on the other hand, has the obvious advantage of circuit simplicity and reduced area should aid in achieving higher bit storage capacity in future generation designs.

Shift register, bucket-brigade, and charge coupled (CCD) serial-access memories can also provide the system-level access time required for the file storage. Bucket-brigade and CCD serial-access memory arrays require 2-3 metal or polysilicon lines and no contacts per bit, thus providing the same storage density as single transistor RAM cells. The single transistor RAM, the bucket-brigade, and the CCD memories offer the possibility of more than two level storage because a continuous range of values of charge may be stored and accessed.

A still further reduction in cell size and faster operation of the memory can be made by using surface charge storage cells. The surface charge transfer structures offer not only the topological simplicity, but also permit the reduction in number of contact holes between metal layers and the silicon. A surface charge random access memory differs from the other dynamic RAMs in (i) length of bit line, (ii) area and aspect ratio of storage cells and (iii) operating voltages of the memory. These differences are reflected on the overall system design.

Several nonvolatile semiconductor storage devices are based on storage of charge on a conductor or at a charge trapping interface, either of which is totally surrounded by high quality insulator(s) such as silicon dioxide, silicon nitride, and/or aluminium oxide. The surface charge storage cell is a modification of surface transistor. The source of the surface charge transistor forms the storage region and the transfer of charge into and out of the storage region is controlled by the transfer gate. These devices are based on nonequilibrium storage of charge and as such they require refresh action.

The speed with which charge can be transferred out of the storage region is proportional to the total amount of the charge stored. This quantity is proportional to both the potential applied to storage electrode and the cell area. Thus, speed can be tradeoff against either the power dissipation or the bit density. However, the operating voltage, which must exceed the MOS threshold and below the oxide breakdown value, can be varied over a wide range. Thus there is a tradeoff between bit density and ultimate speed.

Regarding the clock rate of MOS memories, it is usually correct to consider a speed power product, that is, at a given value of voltage capacitances charge and discharge at a rate proportional to current, and since the power dissipation under these conditions is proportional to the current, power and speed are directly related. The same is true for surface charge devices. Here at a constant value of charge, speed is proportional to applied voltage and since capacitance is inversely proportional to the voltage at constant charge, the power per bit (CV^2) is proportional to speed.

Wide range of characteristics of semiconductor memories in the various forms of realization are now availabe in the market. Cycle time, storage capacity, power consumption, physical size and cost are parameters of first order importance for these memory technologies. The significant advantage of semiconductor memory relative to magnetic memory is the better electrical compatibility between semiconductor storage elements and integrated logic circuitry. The energy difference between readout and write signals in a semiconductor memory array is typically three to five orders of magnitude.

6.6.2 Array Design

It has been explained in the previous sections that the realization of reliable, high speed, economic semiconductor memory depends critically on several interrelated problems of interconnection and packaging. In the design of large memory systems, some standardization of circuit design is inevitable to keep the amount of design time and effort required reasonable. The most effective layout design methodology for memory array has not been developed so far because the number of variables influencing the preliminary layout design problem increases when the *customerized* approach to MOS array design is attempted. The basic array design process consists of the following major design stages: (i) system design, (ii) preliminary array design, (iii) detail array design, (iv) test design, and (v) mask design.

After the system design is tentatively complete, the preliminary array design stage permits the device designer to survey candidate layout designs with regard to assessing design optimization, performance objectives and packaging constraints. This stage is initiated by extensively simulating the allocated Boolean equation set, expressed in mechanization form in the array level environment. Once the device engineer is confident that the behaviour of the MOS array model is correct, he starts to explore its preliminary layout characteristics and identify any inherent peculiarities. First, the device designer derives the quasi-optimal order for the Boolean equation set that minimizes the metallization length. Secondly, he derives the minimum number of metallization groups (channel) and their quasi-optimal order that minimizes the total pseudo-p-diffusion length. The device designer can now assess the realization of mechanizing the allocated Boolean equation set with a view to attain the layout design optimization objectives and satisfy the packaging design constraints. If this assessment is positive, then the device designer is technically prepared to commence the detail array design stage.

The array layout design scheme is shown in Figure 6.23 which is centred about the U shaped area allocated to mechanization of the Boolean equation set. Bounding this central U shaped area is an area allocated to the clocking functions servicing these Boolean equations. Nested within this U shaped area is an area allocated to driver mechanization that generates the MOS array output assigned to pads in this vicinity. Similarly, the MOS array inputs are allocated to the lower pads together with the adjacent vicinity allocated for their respective receiver mechanizations. The boundaries defining these various functional areas depend on the mechanization complexity of the logic diagram, the clocking scheme and the input/output requirements. The central area can also assume I or S shape without invalidating the concepts underlying the layout scheme.

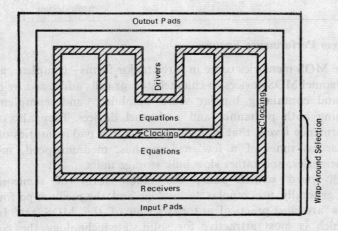

Figure 6.23 Area allocations for customerized MOS arrays.

Having established the layout design scheme, it is necessary to characterize the layout analytically so as to efficiently orient the device designer to the organizational aspects and technical layout peculiarities accompanying the Boolean equation mechanization process. It is rather difficult to analytically formulate layout design optimization criteria for customerized MOS array, as the criteria are strongly influenced by application problems associated with noise, speed, testing and packaging plus the economic influence of yield, which depends on the manufacturing capability supporting MOS technology.

The complex design optimization problems are solved by using computer oriented techniques in which the main problem is divided into smaller manageable problems. This decomposition reflects the hierarchy of technical importance associated with each of the smaller problems. The hierarchy presented in Table 6.2 is appropriate for customerized MOS array and improves the layout design methodology by providing definite milestones during the preliminary array design stage.

TABLE 6.2

Layout Design Optimization for Customerized MOS Array

Hierarchical level	Analytical optimization criterion	Device optimization objective
1	Minimize metallization requirements per equation	Maximize packing density, minimize noise
2	Minimize total metallization length	Maximize yield and speed, minimize noise, simplify mask design
3	Minimize number of metallization groups	Maximize packing density, minimize noise
4	Minimize total p-diffusion length	Maximize yield and speed, minimize noise, simplify mask design

6.6.3 System Performance Factors

Read/write MOS memories come in three major forms—complete assemblies of p-channel MOS devices, p-channel storage cells addressed by bipolar decoders and containing bipolar sense amplifier, and complementary systems using both p-channel and n-channel devices. They also come in three performance levels, that is, high speed scratch pad memories of a few bits with access times of a few nanoseconds, medium-speed, medium-capacity memories, and rather slow bulk storage units.

The high speed scratch pads, the oldest form of semiconductor memories, generally use bipolar technology and the medium-performance p-memories are most practical at today's state of the MOS art. In bulk storage which is most attractive for solid state technology, the common approach is an array of MOS flip-flops driven by bipolar decoders and sensed with bipolar sense amplifiers. Sometimes four-phase or polyphase clocking techniques are used to increase the internal speeds without boosting power consumption or enlarging transistor size. In some circuits, all the four clock phases are externally generated, while in others, only one phase is external, the rest being generated within the circuit. The latter arrangement works best with low voltage MOS circuits.

Four phase clocking can be used with many circuit configurations and with a variety of time relationship between the phases. The input logic signals appear during the first phase and turn the gates of an isolated MOS switching network on or off. Due to the residual charge on the gate, these switches retain their states when the logic signals are disconnected. In the second phase another switch is turned on and it stays on until the third phase arrives when it discharges through the logic network established in the first phase. Finally, in the last phase, the logic network is disconnected again and the switch that was turned on during the second phase produces its new state as the circuit output.

The transistor in a four-phase circuit can be small and thus have a very high resistance. Since they charge open circuited capacitors, the voltage drop across them is relatively unimportant. Likewise the capacitors are very small and charge quickly so that circuit speed is high. Finally, the circuit dissipates very little power because the energy loss when charge passes from one capacitor to another is proportional to the capacitor and the square of the voltage difference, but is independent of the resistance. The only power dissipation stems from leakage in the capacitors and diodes, an almost negligible factor.

The storage capacity of a memory module may be expanded by increasing the number of words and/or the number of bits per word that share a single set of select, drive and detect circuits. But there is an optimum word length L_0 for a memory module of specified total storage capacity of N bits. Power dissipation, array delays, or cost may be minimized by proper choice of word length. If X be the parameter to be minimized, optimum word length may be determined as

$$X = F_w(W) + F_l(L); \quad N = W \times L$$
$$\frac{dX}{dL} = 0$$

where F_w is the component associated with word dimension and F_l is the component associated with word length. However, to a first approximation power dissipation, cost, and array delays are linear functions of word and bit dimensions of the array. If the constants of proportionality for a chosen parameter are X_w and X_l for the word and bit dimensions, respectively, then the optimum word length is

$$L_0 = \sqrt{N\frac{X_w}{X_l}}$$

In dynamic MOS memories, where a capacitor charge rather than the state of a bistable circuit defines a stored unit of information, any capacitor leakage requires data refreshing. The frequency of periodic refreshing depends on transistor leakage which increases sharply with temperature. At 70°C, refreshing is typically required every 2 msec; at lower temperature, that interval may be increased to hundreds of milliseconds. Loading of the MOS device is mainly capacitive. To avoid deterioration of the array performance over that of an individual cell by introducing long time, the array is usually driven and sensed by low impedance bipolar transistor circuits. The memory cell presents a capacitive load to word, bit and sense lines, and to an approximation these lines can be treated as a lumped resistance and capacitance as shown in Figure 6.24. If R_L and C_L are the resistance and capacitance, respectively, of the loaded lines per cell, the time constants of the drive line will be

$$\tau = \frac{N^2 R_L C_L}{2}$$

and the corresponding drive current will be the capacitive charging current, i.e.,

$$I_{\text{Drive}} = NC_L \frac{dv}{dt}$$

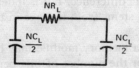

Figure 6.24 Lumped equivalent of
drive and sense lines.

The above equation is an approximate one since it assumes a low value of series resistance. For large value of series resistance of the line, the drive current will be limited and will give greater delay in the array. The transition time which is a design parameter, may be chosen on the basis of allowable delay in the array, and the voltage swing is fixed by device tolerance considerations. Hence there is a tradeoff between drive current and speed for a given number of cells in a line.

Similarly, the sense line is driven from a high impedance approximating a current source, and is sensed at a low impedance approximating short circuit. The sense line time constant is also given by the above equation so that there is once again a tradeoff between speed and number of devices on the line. The maximum possible number of cells on a line will depend on whether one or two layers of metallization are used in the array fabrication. One layer of metallization necessitates diffuse crossunders where lines intersect. Diffused crossunders can be avoided with two layers of metallization. The capacitance per unit area of diffused and metallized lines is roughly the same.

Because of the low standby power in the cell, the overall memory system power will be determined by the drive and sense circuitry, except in the case of an unusually large array. For a memory of N bits, the power dissipation per bit will be minimized if:

$$W = \sqrt{N \frac{2P_B + P_S}{P_W}}$$

and

$$B = \frac{M}{W}$$

where N is the total number of bits;
  W is the total number of words;
  B is the number of bits per word;
  P_B, P_S and P_W are the dissipation of bit driver, sense amplifier and word driver respectively.

In the performance of semiconductor RAMs, it has been found that array delays increase linearly with extension of the length of lines, decoder delays increase less than linearly with the number of words and word select, digit driver and digit decoder delays are almost independent of array size. The total propagation delay time is determined by the amount of current supplied to memory cells and logic gates. At low current levels the propagation delay is determined by junction and parasitic capacitances. This delay time τ will be proportional to the time t needed to charge or discharge the capacitances. As $Q = CV$ and $t = Q/I$, τ will be proportional to CV/I. The dissipation D will be $D = VI$, in which V is the voltage over a forward biased junction. From this it follows that the power delay time product $D\tau$ is proportional to CV^2 which is constant. At medium current levels the main influence on the propagation delay time comes from the active charge in the memory transistors and at high current levels there are two phenomena that cause a worst propagation delay—first, the series resistance of the base prevents fast charging or discharging of active charges, and secondly, these active charges increase more than linearly with increasing currents.

The design of a large capacity semiconductor memory begins with the determination of the maximum module capacity that can be used within the limits imposed by system requirements and assembly considerations. If system requirements allow flexibility in word length, this parameter should be adjusted to minimize array delays, cost or power dissipation.

6.6.4 Yield Analysis and Reliability

Packaging and interconnection techniques have a major bearing on the reliability, cost, and physical size of large capacity semiconductor RAM. The manufacture of large array of ICs, containing several thousand devices on a single silicon slice, is limited by the device yield. To attain the improved performance of LSI memories it is necessary that a number of integrated circuit process refinements and additional process controls should be employed. Digital circuits based on bipolar transistors are particularly sensitive to metallization related to increases in resistance. Multilevel metallized arrays require control of the contour of the edges of the delineated metal and dielectric. In MOS memory circuits close control of surface properties and stability must be maintained and more effective input protection against static charges is also desirable. As main memories p-channel MOS circuits are attractive for their ease of fabrication, low power dissipation, relatively high yield and high density. They can be processed in 25 steps, compared to about 150 for bipolar circuits and 50 for complementary MOS circuits, which use both p and n channel devices. All large area memory circuits require improved processing that yields lower densities of localized material defects.

In the manufacture of integrated circuits a rectangular or square array of circuit chips is processed from an essentially round slice. Bulk silicon is the substrate material used for basic MOS processes, although other materials, such as sapphire, are used for improved speed performance and radiation hardening properties. A number of effects occur during processing that make the outer periphery of the slice unusable. These are: (i) rounding of slice at the edge, which causes pattern distortion, (ii) beading of the photoresist at the edge also resulting in physically distorting the pattern, and (iii) non-uniform diffusion effects caused by variations in temperature at the outer edge. All these phenomena have an adverse effect on chips located near the slice edge. These effects can be accounted for by defining an effective slice radius that is smaller than the actual radius.

Smaller geometry of an integrated circuit pattern tends to increase its susceptibility to registration and resolution problems, alignment effects, bridging by conductive particles, corrosion effects and photolithographic problems. However, the purpose of using smaller geometry is to increase function density to permit given circuits to be fabricated on chips of smaller size. The reason is that the probability per chip of encountering a localized material defect depends on the amount of active device area of the chip. Broadly speaking, defects in ICs are due to: (i) defects existing in the silicon crystalline structure, (ii) defects formed during the fabrication process, and (iii) defects created during final assembly and packaging. The statistical nature of defects of ICs may be classified as random or nonrandom. Nonrandom defects are more prevalent near the edge of the slice. Many defects occur at random on the slice. The defects due to pinholes are random in nature. For a given number of defects on the slice, the yield of chips from the slice will depend on the manner in which the defects are distributed. The highest yield will occur when none of the defects falls within any chip and the lowest when the defects are distributed uniformly among the chips. When the defect distribution is governed by Boltzmann statistics, the yield is given by:

$$\text{Yield} = \left(1 - \frac{A_a}{S}\right)^{SD}$$

where A_a is the active area of chip, S the area of slice, and D the number of defects per unit area. In the limiting case when $A_a/S \ll 1$, we have

$$\text{Yield} = \exp\left(-A_aD\right)$$

In the case of random defects, yield is the same regardless of placement of chips on the slice. So the number of good chips obtainable from the slice will be maximum when the number of chips on the slice is maximum. However, this is not true in the case of nonrandom defects. In this case, yield depends on placement of chips on the slice.

In MOS devices which contain thin oxide in certain regions, one of the most common failure modes is short circuit or leakage path through localized region in the thin oxide. Also, MOS devices are fabricated on higher resistivity material and operate at higher voltages than bipolar devices. Thus they are more sensitive to surface related failure mechanisms that involve continuity of metallization or high current density in metals and contacts. Surface related failure mechanisms are caused by changes that occur in the electrical properties of $Si\text{-}SiO_2$ interface as a result of motion of mobile charge in/or on the SiO_2, trapping of charge in the SiO_2 or existence of fast states at $Si\text{-}SiO_2$ interface. Instability in the fundamental parameters of that interface can cause channelling either under or beyond metal. This can also change the voltage at which punch through occurs and increase diode reverse current. Also localized defects in the silicon and thermally grown SiO_2 are factors in IC reliability and are major factors affecting the yield when they occur in active device areas. Thus yield falls off severely as circuit area increases and the probability of occurrence of localized defects that can cause reliability problem increases with increasing chip area. However, the yield and reliability of very large chips decrease less rapidly than the exponential decrease that is predicted for purely random distinguishable defects.

Higher reliability that can be attained in the LSI systems is due to the fact that they use fewer wire bonds and external interconnections and due to a reduction in the number of packages and circuit components such as drivers. Available data on failure rates of integrated circuits under various levels of stress indicate that failure of wire bonds is one of the principal limitations of integrated circuit reliability. Other failure mechanisms are ion migration, microstacks in metallization at oxide steps and electromigration. The degree to which reliability improvement can be made by the use of LSI depends to a large extent, on the degree of success in partitioning the system to obtain high gate-to-pin ratios. The resulting improvement in gate-to-pin ratio is directly proportional to the increase in circuit complexity. In fact, one of the main advantages of LSI system is that the increase in the array complexity also reduces the number of packages required and, therefore, reduces the probability of failures in a system due to package failure.

In order to exploit the advantages of MOS/LSI fully, one should construct the system with groups of highly regular circuits with as few I/O lines as possible. Partitioning, the task of allocating logic functions between individual MOS/LSI devices, is the main problem in MOS/LSI computer design. Using conventionally packaged MOS/LSI devices, only a limited number of interconnecting pins are available (usually in the order of 40 to 60). Using beam lead technology, it is possible to increase the number of leads although in most cases the limit is set by the chip area devoted to output drivers. Two types of partitioning schemes, namely, vertical or bit slicing and functional partitioning, are employed. In a vertical partitioning scheme, logic is divided so that functions associated with a certain bit (or bits) in the computer are contained in one chip, while with functional partitioning, complete functional building blocks, such as accumulators, adders, etc. form the basis for a chip. The optimum partitioning scheme is one where the logic is grouped in such a way that as much interconnecting as possible is done on the device itself, thus minimizing the interconnection requirements between devices while at the same time minimizing the number of device types.

6.7 SEMICONDUCTOR READ ONLY MEMORY

While in the past memory designers have perpetually tried to increase speed and performance of their computers, the era of LSI has opened up many new horizons in this field. The LSI circuit leads to extremely low cost for digital circuit elements. This is particularly true when the chip is in the form of iterative arrays, such as random access memory or read-only memories. These arrays have a large number of functions per connection, which is the main driving force behind LSI.

The semiconductor read-only memories (ROMs), that are well suited to LSI manufacturing process have received a great deal of attention in recent years due to their versatility and diversity of applications in which they can be used. As the name implies they are intended to store nonchanging information. If one removes the write capability from a RAM, a ROM results. Most of these memories have read cycle characteristics similar to RAMs read/write counterparts, but the data are 'written' at the time of fabrication. Although some ROMs can be written in or altered, the write time is relatively long. These memories, apart from the name ROM, are sometimes called fixed program memory, or read-only store (ROS), or permanent memory or dead memory. Either bipolar or MOS technology may be used in the manufacture of ROMs. In general, bipolar devices are faster and feature higher drive capability, while MOS circuits consume less space and power. Thus MOS ROMs are preferred where speed is not critical, as in character generator. Basically read-only memory is an $N \times M$ matrix of intersections between a set of input and output data lines. The coupling elements commonly used are diodes, bipolar and metal oxide semiconductor transistors. The presence or absence of a coupling element at each of the intersections of the matrix determines the type of memory. Practically any active or passive electrical component can serve as coupling element. Each of these types of ROM is subject to a number of tradeoffs with respect to cost, flexibility, speed, fabrication, external circuits, reliability and commercial availability. However, general observations can be made regarding the various design criteria which are discussed in this section. The applications of semiconductor ROMs are together with other type of ROMs are discussed in Chapter 8 of this book.

6.7.1 ROM Elements

Read-only memories, developed since 1951, have been widely used in data processing equipment to store data that seldom or never have to be changed. One of the earliest uses of ROM was in ENIAC computer which used them to store multiplication tables and tables of other functions. Resistor matrices were used in ENIAC but they are now out of favour. Apart from resistors, capacitive and inductive matrix arrangements can be made but the bidirectional properties of these linear elements give rise to many indirect or 'sneak' path through the matrix. The most effective solution to read-only memory is to use semiconductor technology. Reasons for increased usuage of semiconductor ROMs or alterable ROMs is obvious as they require little power and are characterized by small volume, low cost and nonvolatility. Typical ROM may be addressed in a fixed time interval, regardless of location, so that it is actually a type of RAM.

Figure 6.25 shows a simplified arrangement of ROM elements. The associated circuitries are much less complex than read/write memories and are ideally suited to MOS or bipolar manufacturing processes. Data storage, as shown in Figure 6.25(a) is indicated by the presence or absence of a diode at the intersection point of the X and Y lines. Any crosspoint may be identified as a '0' or '1' by making the X line positive, the Y line negative. A diode presented at the crosspoint will conduct while the diode in the corresponding sense line will be blocked, thus providing the readout. Both discrete or monolithic diode arrays are used in the ROM structure. These diode arrays are simple, reliable, and flexible. The external circuits used with diode arrays are rather standard and are not very complicated.

Like diode arrays, monolithic bipolar transistor arrays or MOS arrays can be used in ROM construction. Monolithic bipolar transistor arrays, as shown in Figure 6.25(b), though very reliable, are fast and rugged, and require a very expensive production equipment. In this array, connection is made from an input line to the base of a transistor whenever a '1' is to be stored; transistors corresponding to stored '0' are left disconnected. Similarly, for MOS arrays (Figure 6.25c), the gate of MOS transistor is connected to an input line for a '1' and left disconnected for a '0'. The predominant type MOS device is the p-channel enhancement mode (p-MOS) unit, in which holes are the vehicle of current flow. The arrays include one or two levels of decoding, and store thousand bits, each accessible in about a microsecond.

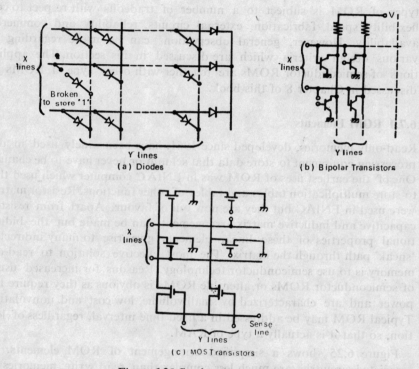

Figure 6.25 Semiconductor ROM.

In programming MOS arrays, the manufacturer must use a customerized masking operation (the mask being computer generated) to produce the required pattern of stored data. ROM manufacturers usually provide convenient forms on which users may clearly state their required contents. The data on these forms can directly be translated to a computer pro- gramme for automatic programming equipment.

There is also a variety of specialized ROMs for use in recurring applica- tions. For applications requiring both nonvolatility and field alterability, one technique used a semiconductor material (amorphous or polycrystalline), that is electrically alterable between two stable phases. Another device is based on a metal—nitride oxide silicon—technology in which a layer of silicon nitride is introduced by a high voltage pulse. The advantage of this type of devices is that they may be cleared, then reprogrammed by a process similar to writing data into a RAM without removal of circuit board.

6.7.2 Classifications and Implementation of ROM

The extensive use of microprogramming technique in digital control and data processing field creates a need for versatile read-only memories. Many kinds of ROMs have been proposed and some of them have been put to practical uses. As they are used in various fields, ROMs must generally be programmed to suit individual applications. This programming may be carried out as a routine part of the manufacturing process. A special mask is required, the cost of which is justified only for large production requirements. However, ROMs are divided into the broad categories: (i) mask programmed, and (ii) field programmed.

Whether the device is mask or field programmed, the data, usually in the form of truth table, are entered into the array. In case of mask programmed devices, the truth tables, tapes, computer punched cards, etc. are submitted to IC manufacturer, who uses them to prepare at least one of the photomask's used for processing the wafers of ROM devices. He also uses these data to prepare the test program for testing wafer. The presence or absence of the connection in mask programmed ROM is established during metallization process. Using computer aided mask making techniques, design costs and turn around time can be minimized, but the overall circuit costs become large. In addition, it is not always possible to completely specify the memory configuration in the early design phases of the system in which the memory is to be used. It is in these instances where mask programming can have some rather undesirable economic implications. Because of the limitations of mask programmable ROMs, memory designers have paid their attention in electrically programmable semiconductor ROMs in which the information pattern is permanently recorded by application of an electrical signal. The electrically programmable ROMs can be divided in two categories: (i) ROMs in which a permanent change in the memory interconnection pattern is affected by an electrical pulse, and (ii) reprogrammable ROMs in which a reversible change in active memory device characteristics is induced electrically. The programmable ROM is preferred where a system design is tentative or where memory variability is an important requirement.

The field programmable ROMs allow the users to enter data into devices in the field. This type of memories may be electrically programmable or electrically reprogrammable. Electrically programmable ROMs were proposed initially in the form of fusible type. Programming is accomplished by fusible links. Connection represented by these links may be opened changing corresponding 1's to 0's by direct currents for selectively fusing appropriate segments of the circuit. This allows stocking a basic ROM for programming directly by the user.

Programmable ROM construction may begin with a basic bipolar design including cross-coupling transistors in all locations. MOS programming devices are not very suitable since the resistance and current levels required for the fusing process are incompatible with MOS impedance levels. But the disadvantage of the fusible type system is that they cannot be reprogrammed, which makes the write-in operation test impossible before shipment. Although programmable ROMs are individually more expensive, they do not require a special mask and are, therefore, particularly convenient for small to moderate quantity applications.

The other type, known as electrically reprogrammable ROMs, is widely used and this eliminates the disadvantages of the fusible type ROMs. Reprogrammable feature of ROM devices permits later correction of errors made in the write-in operation while makes the device reusable. These are basically charge storage devices which rely on charge storage in a dielectric that forms part of an insulated gate field effect transistor structure. Charge storage effects have been observed in a number of gate structures, namely, a floating gate buried within the gate insulator, a metal-silicon-nitride thin silicon dioxide silicon (MNOS), a metal aluminium-thin silicon dioxide-silicon (MAS) and a floating gate avalanche injection MOS (FAMOS). Also the ovonic amorphous semiconductor memory device has been demonstrated in which the amorphous layers change its conductivity by means of the voltage application across the layer above a certain critical value.

The wide use of ROMs in the field of computer memory system require certain basic properties such as, electrical reprogrammability, high speed, on-chip address decoding and long term non-volatility. The semiconductor ROM memories with customerized masks need a long turn around time and are expensive. Metal nitride oxide silicon (MNOS) memories have been studied but they require complicated manufacturing process and their nonvolatility is insufficient to read-only memory use. The MNOS memory transistor works as an MOS transistor with alterable threshold voltage. The threshold voltage can be altered back and forth between two levels by applying large gate voltages of either polarity. On the other hand, the utilization of MAS transistor in ROM configurations has shown improved performances. The memory function is based on electron injection from either a semiconductor or a metal electrode into aluminium, which corresponds to positive or negative bias. The injected electrons can be excited by radiation, such as X-rays and electron beam. The MAS-ROM devices, apart from the above requirements, have several other advantages, namely, the readout is nondestructive, the memory is erasable and reusable, the written data are nonvolatile, and their half decay time is pretty large.

6.7.3 ROM Organization

Most of the advancements of semiconductor memory are based on improvements in process, mask and alignment technologies. The most rapid progress, however, continues to come from ingenious applications. The users demand for high speed and low cost read only memories for microprogram and other control applications. These call for developments of various types of ROMs with the features of long term nonvolatility, electrical reprogramability, high speed, on chip address decoding, etc.

The design considerations of a high speed integrated circuit ROM should include minimum power dissipation, minimum propagation delay, minimum circuit area and maximum reliability. The circuit configuration can be optimized to achieve fast switching action and good capacitive driving capability without incurring excessive power consumption. Power gating techniques can be utilized especially in the address decoders to effect power reduction without speed degradation. Minimization of active and passive device area leads to reduced capacitance and higher speed. Reduced circuit area can be achieved by straightforward shrinkage of component area and also by considerations of logical organization and circuit design.

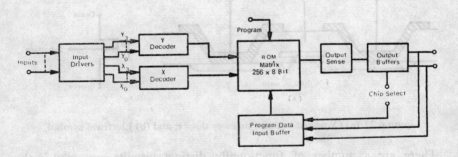

Figure 6.26 Block diagram of ROM organization.

The block diagram of the logical organization of a 256×8 bits ROM is shown in Figure 6.26. It is fully TTL compatible and can be operated in both the static or dynamic mode. The state-of-art programmable ROM is a 512×8 bits device having a maximum access time of 70 nsec and DTL/TTL compatibility on its inputs and outputs. Of course many ROMs include a variety of options. For example, a mask programmable memory may be organized as either 512 words $\times 4$ bits or 256×8 depending on the mode control input logic level. A chip cenable input is usually included to allow paralleling of chips for expanded capacity.

The basic memory cell is a floating gate avalanche-injection MOS charge storage device in which no electrical contact is made to the silicon gate. Memory arrays using the basic structure of Figure 6.27 can be fabricated. The starting material is silicon and the floating poly-silicon gate is isolated from the silicon substrate by a SiO_2 layer of approximately 1000 Å thickness and from the top surface by 1.0μ of vapour deposited oxide. A high voltage between source and drain removes positive carriers from the floating gate, and the isolated negative carriers on the gate create a conducting channel. Operation of the FAMOS structure depends on charge transport to the floating gate by avalanche injection of electrons from either the source or drain pn junction. The memory cell is cleared by exposure to ultraviolet radiation which discharges the gate. The informations can be stored in FAMOS device as a '1' corresponding to no charge on the floating gate or as a '0' corresponding to a charge on the floating gate when the device is on. Information can be decoded and sensed in either the static or dynamic mode. The static mode of operation eliminates the need for clocks at the expense of increased power dissipation and reduced speed, while the dynamic mode offers advantage in both performance categories.

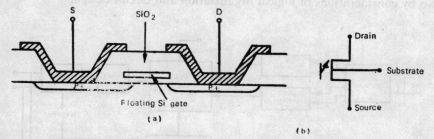

Figure 6.27 (a) Cross-section of a memory device; and (b) Electrical symbol.

There are a number of functionally distinct circuits contained in the FAMOS-ROM organization, as shown in Figure 6.26, and all these circuit blocks are common to both the 'PROGRAM' and 'READ' modes with the exception of the PROGRAM data input buffers. The input/output buffers provide for full TTL compatibility and addressing is accomplished by the X and Y decoders. A selected memory cell with a charged FAMOS device will be reflected by a low '0' TTL level at the output, while a memory bit that is not charged will result in a high '1' TTL level. A memory bit is selected by a coincidence of signals on the X and Y select lines. Information in the selected memory cell is sampled by the output sense circuit. Programming of the memory is similar to the operation in the read mode and can be performed from punched paper tape or other data input devices through the programming terminal. The typical timing diagram for the program mode is shown in Figure 6.28. Initially all the bits in the memory are in '1' state and the information is introduced by selectively programming '0' in the proper bit location through charging FAMOS devices

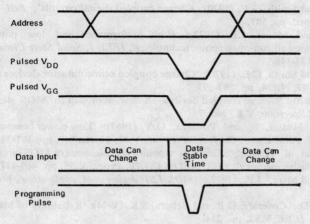

Figure 6.28 Timing diagram.

from the PROGRAM terminal. In the PROGRAM mode the eight output terminals are used as data inputs to determine the information pattern in the eight bits of each words, while word address selection is performed by the X and Y decoders through the input drivers. Inhibition is accomplished by applying a negative voltage to the data input terminal. This voltage level is transferred to the inhibit transistor (chip select is enabled), which turns on and overrides the Y select signal. To allow programming of a selected bit, the data input terminal is kept at ground potential.

References

Abbott, R.A., Regitz, W.M. and Karp, J.A. (1973): 'A 4K MOS dynamic random access memory', *IEEE J. Solid State Circuit*, V.SC-8, October, No. 10.

Ahrons, J.W. and Gardner, R.D. (1970): 'Interaction of technology and performance in COS-MOS integrated circuits', *IEEE J. Solid State Circuits*, V.SC-5, pp. 24-29.

Amelio, G.E., et al. (1970): 'Experimental verification of the charge coupled device concept', *Bell Syst. Tech. J.*, V.49, pp. 593-600.

——(1971): 'Charge coupled imaging devices—design considerations, *IEEE Trans. on Electronic Device*, V.ED-18, pp. 986-992.

Altman, L. (1974): Charge coupled devices move in on memories and analog signal processing,' *Electronics*, V.47, pp. 91-101.

Bakar, W.D. (1973): 'Oxide isolation brings high density to production bipolar memories', *Electronics*, V.46, March, pp. 65-70.

Barrett, J.C., Bergh, A., Horank, T. and Price, J.E. (1970): 'Design consideration for a high speed bipolar read only memory', *IEEE J. Solid State Circuits*, V.SE-5, No. 5.

Bentchkowsky, Frohman, D. (1969): 'An integrated metal-nitride oxide silicon (MNOS) memory', *Proc. IEEE*. V.57, June, pp. 1190-1192.

Berger, H.H. and Wiedmann, J.A. (1972): 'Merged transistor logic,' presented at the 1972 ISSCC, February 16-17.

Boyle, W.S. and Smith, G.E. (1970): 'Charge coupled digital circuits', *Bell Syst. Tech. J.*, V.49, April, pp. 587.

Boleky, E.J. and Mayer, J.E. (1972): 'High performance and low power CMOS memories using silicon-on-sapphire technology', *IEEE J. Solid State Circuits*, V.SC-7, April, pp. 135-146.

Boyle, W.S. and Smith, C.E. (1970): 'Charge coupled semiconductor devices', *Bell Syst. Tech. J.*, V.47, No. 4, pp. 587-593.

Boyle, W.S. (1970): 'Charge coupled devices—A new approach to MOS devices structure', *IEEE Spectrum*, V.8., No. 7.

Brewer, D.E., Nissim, S. and Podraza, G.V. (1967): 'Low power computer memory system', *Fall Joint Comp. Conf. AFIPS Proc.* V.31, November, pp. 381-393.

Burns, J.R., et al. (1969): 'Silicon-on sapphire complementary MOS circuits for high speed associative memory', *FJCC AFIPS CONF. Proc.*, V.35, pp. 469-477.

Carr W.N., and Mize, J.P. (1972): '*MOS/LSI design and application*', McGraw-Hill, New York.

Colbourne, E.D., Coverley, G.P. and Behara, S.K. (1974): 'Reliability of MOS/LSI circuits', *Proc. IEEE*, V.62, pp. 244.

Cricchi, J.R., Brewer, J.E., Williams, D.W., Blaha, F. and Fitzpatrick, M.D. (1974): 'Nonvolatile block oriented RAM', in *ISSCC Dig. Tech. Papers*, V.XVII, pp. 204-205.

Critchlow, D.L., Dennard, R.H. and Schuster, S.E. (1967): 'Design of large scale integrated logic using MOS devices', Presented at the Microelectronic Symp. St. Louis, M.O.

Davis, S. (1974): 'Selection and application of semiconductor memories', *Computer Design*, V.13. No.1.

Dhaka, V.A., Muschinske, J.E. and Ownes, W.K. (1973): 'Subnanosecond ECL gate circuit using isoplanar II', in *ISSCC Dig. Abstract FAM*, 13.6.

Dhaka, V.A. (1968): 'Design and fabrication of subnanosecond current switch and transistors', *IBM J. Res. Devel.*, V.12, November, pp. 472-482.

Dussins, R.R. and Zieve, R.M. (1972): 'Read-only Memory in computers—where are they headed', *Electr. Des. News.*, 1 August, pp. 24-31.

Earle, J. (1964): 'The impact of microelectronics on digital computers', *Electronic Design*, V.37, pp. 86.

Embinder, J. (1971): '*Semiconductor Memories*', Wiley Interscience, New York, Engler, W.E. Tiemann, J.J. and Deertsch, R.D. (1972): 'A surface charge random access memory system', *IEEE J. Solid State Circuits*, V.SC-7, October, pp. 330-335.

Engler, W.E. et al. (1972): 'A surface charge random access memory system', *IEEE J. Solid State Circuits*, V.SC-7, pp. 330-335.

Evans, W.J., Tretola, A.R. et al. (1973): 'Oxide isolated monolithic technology and applications', *IEEE J. Solid State Circuits* V.SC-8, October, No. 5.

Fehr, G.K. (1970): 'Microcircuit packaging assembly-state of the art', Solid State Technol., August, pp. 41.

Frohman-Bentchkowsky, D. (1971): 'A fully decoded 2048 bit electrically programmable MOS-RAM', ISSCC Digest, pp. 80.

Gray, P.A., Pedarsen, R.A., Soloway, B.H., and Reed R.A. (1970): 'Design of high performance TTL integrated circuit employing CDI component structures', *IEEE J. Solid State Circuits*, V.SC-5, October, pp. 227-235.

Garrett, L.S. (1970): 'Integrated circuit digital logic family II TTL devices', *IEEE Spectrum*, V.7. November, pp. 43-50.

Hart, C.M. and Slob, A. (1972): 'Integrated injection logic—A new approach to LSI', presented at the 1972 ISSCC, Feb. 16-17.

Hewlett, F.W. (1975): 'Schottky I²L', *J. Solid State Circuits*, V. SC-10, pp. 343-348, October.

Hodges, D.A. (1975): 'A review and projection of semiconductor components for digital storage', *Proc. IEEE*, V.63, No. 8, August.

Hodges, D.A. (1968): 'Large capacity semiconductor memory', *Proc. IEEE*, V.56, July, pp. 1148-1162.

Hoffman, W.K. and Kalter, H.L. (1973): 'An 8k bit random access memory chip using one device FET Cell'. *IEEE, J. Solid State Circuits*, V.SC-8, October, pp. 298-305.

Igarashi, R., Kurosawa, T. and Yaita, T. (1966): 'A 150 nsec associative memory using integrated MOS Transistor', *ISSCC Digest of Technical Papers*, pp. 104, February.

Keonjian, E. (Ed.) (1963): *Microelectronics*. McGraw-Hill, New York.

Keyes, R.W. (1969): 'Physical problems and limits in computer logic', *IEEE Spectrum*, V.6, May, pp. 36-45.

Kute, B.A. (1971): 'Design considerations of semiconductor random access memory systems', *IEEE Computer* V. 4(2), March/April, pp. 11-17.

Kvamme, F. (1970): 'Standard read only memories simplifies complex logic', *Electronic Design*, V.43, January, pp. 88-95.

Larsen, R.P. (1971): 'Computer aided preliminary layout design of customized MOS array', *IEEE Trans. on electronic computers*, V.C-20, No. 5, May.

Lewin, M.H. (1965): 'A survey of read only memories', *Proc. Fall Joint Computer Conf.*, pp. 775-788.

Luecke, G., Mize, J.P. and Carr, W.N (1973): in *Semiconductor Memory Design and Application*, R.E. Sawyer, (Ed.) McGraw-Hill, New York.

Lund, E., Allen, C.A., Anderson S.R. and Tu, G.K. (1970): 'Design of a megabit semiconductor memory system', *Fall Joint Comp. Conf. AFIPS Proc.*, pp. 53-62.

Lynes, D.J. and Hodges, D.A. (1970): 'Memory using direct coupled bipolar transistor cell', *IEEE J. Solid State Circuits* V.SC-5, pp. 186-191.

Marley, R.R. (1971): 'Design considerations of temperature compensated emitter coupled logic', Presented at IEEE Intern. Conv., March.

Martin, W. and Croxen, B.F. (1972): 'The inverting cell concept for MOS dynamic RAMs', *IEEE ISSCC Dig. Tech. Paper*, February, pp. 12-13.

Matick, R. (1963): 'Operating characteristic of a thick film ROM model', *IBM Res. Rep. RC 903*, March 1.

Matick, R., et al. (1966): 'A high speed read only store using thick magnetic films', *IBM J. Res. and Dev.*, V.10, No.4, pp. 328.

Melay, G.E. and Earle, J. (1963): *The Logic Design of Transistor Digital Computers*. Prentice Hall, Englewood Cliffs, N.J.

Miller, L.F. (1970): 'A critique of chip joining techniques', *Solid State Technol*, April, pp. 50-62.

Moore, G.E. (1970): 'What level of LSI is best for you', *Electronics*, V.43, February, pp. 126-130.

Muller, H.H., Owens, W.K., et al. (1973): 'Fully compensated ECL—eliminating the drawbacks of conventional ECL', *IEEE J. Solid State Circuits*, V.SC-8, No.5, October.

Murphy, B.T., Glinski, V.J., Gray, P.A., and Pederson, R.A. (1969): 'Collector diffusion isolated integrated circuits', *Proc. IEEE*, V.57, September, pp. 1523-1527.

Nichols, John L. (1967): 'A logical next step for read-only memories', *Electronics*, June 12, p. 711.

O'Donnel, C.F. (1968): 'Engineering for systems using LSI', *Fall Joint Camp. Conf.*, *AFIPS Conf. Proc.*, V. 33, pt. 1.

Pasqualini, R. (1976): 'Design considerations for a pararllel bit organized MOS memory', *IEEE Trans. on Electronic Computers*, V. EC-16, pp. 551-57.

Peltzer, D. and Herdon, W. (1971): 'Isolation method shrinks cells for fast, dense memories', *Electronics*, March 1, pp. 52-55.

Perkins, H.A. and Schmidt, J.D. (1965): 'An integrated semiconductor memory system', *Proc. AFIPS Fall Joint Computer Conf*, pp. 1053-1064.

Pleshko, P. and Terman L.M. (1966): 'An investigation of the potential of MOS Transistor memories', *IEEE Trans. on Electronic Computers*, V. EC-15, No. 4.

Procebsting, R. and Green, R. (1973): 'A TTL Compatible 4096 bit N channel RAM', *ISSCC Dig. Tech. Pap.*, pp. 28-29.

Reley, W.B. (1971): *'Electronic Computer Memory Technology*, McGraw-Hill, New York.

Regitz, W.M. and Karp, J. (1970): 'Three transistor cell 1024 bit 500 ns MOS RAM', *IEEE J. Solid State Circuits*, V. SC-5, pp. 181-186.

Rosenbaum, S.D. and Caves, J.T. (1974): 'CCD Memory arrays with fast access by on chip decoding', in *ISSCC Dig. Tech. Paper*, Vol. XVII, pp. 210-211.

Rothstein, L. (1971): 'Speed/power chart for digital ICs', *Electronic Engineering*, V. 24, June.

Schlacter, M.M., Keen, R.S. and Schrable, G.L. (1971): 'Some reliability considerations pertaining to LSI technology', *IEEE J. Solid State Circuits*, V. SC-6, No. 5.

Schmidt, J. (1965): 'Integrated MOS transistor random access memory', *Solid State Design*. V. 6, January, pp. 21.

Seeds, R.B., et al. (1964): 'Integrated complementary transistor nanosecond logic', *Proc. IEEE*, V. 52, December, pp. 1584-1590.

Seeds, R.B., (1967): 'Yield and cost analysis of bipolar LSI', Presented at the Int. Electron. Devices Meeting, Washington D.C., 1 October.

Sheets, J. (1970): 'Three state switching brings wired OR to TTL', *Electronics*, V. 43, September, pp. 78-84.

Siegfried, K. Wiedmann (1972): 'A novel saturation control in TTL Circuits, *IEEE J. Solid State Circuits*, V. SC-7, No. 3, June, pp. 243-250.

Skokan, Z.E. (1973): 'Emitter function logic—logic family for LSI', *IEEE J. Solid State Circuits*, V. SC-8, No. 5, October.

Slob, A. (1968): 'First logic circuits with low energy consumption', *Philips Tech. Rev.*, December, pp. 363-367.

Stein, K.U. and Friedrich, H. (1973): 'A mil² single transistor memory cell in an silicon gate technology', *IEEE J. Solid State Circuits*, V. SC-8, October, pp. 49-55.

Stein, K.U., Sihling, A. and Doering, E. (1972): 'Storage array and sense/refresh circuit for single transistor memory cells', *IEEE J. Solid State Circuits*, V. SC-7, October, p. 336.

Stehlin, R.A., Niemann, G.W. (1972): 'Complementary transistor—transistor logic (CT²L) — An approach to high speed micropower logic', *IEEE J. Solid State Circuits*, V. SC-7, No. 2, April.

Sut, S.C., Meindl, J.D. (1972): 'A new complementary bipolar transistor structure', *IEEE J. Solid State Circuits*, V. SC-7, No. 5.

Tada, K., Laraya, J.L.R. (1967): 'Reduction of storage time of a transistor using Schottkybarrier diode', *Proc. IEEE* (letter), V. 55, November, pp. 2064-2065.

Talbert, C.D. (1972): 'Simplify random access memory selection', *Electronic Design*, V. 18, August 16, pp. 70-74.

Tarui, Y., Teshima, H., Hayashi, Y. and Sekigawa, T. (1969): 'Transistor Schottky barrier diode integrated logic circuit', *IEEE J. Solid State Circuits* V. SC-4, February 12, pp. 3-12.

Tarui, Y., Hayashi, Y. (1972): 'Electrically programmable nonvolatile Semiconductor memory', *IEEE J. Solid State Circuits*, V. SC-7, October, pp. 369-375.

Tarui, Y., et al. (1969): 'A 40 ns 144 bit n-channel MOS-LSI memory', *IEEE J. Solid State Circuits*, V. SC-4, No. 5, pp. 217-279.

Taub, D.M. (1963): 'A short review of read only memories', *Proc. IEEE.*, V. 110, pp. 157-161.

Terman, L.M. (1971): 'MOSFET memory circuits', *Proc. IEEE*, V. 59, July, pp. 1044-1058.

Tsang, F. (1974): 'A 1024 bit bipolar RAM', in *ISSCC Dig. Tech. Papers*. V. XVII, pp. 200-201, 249.

Vadass, L.L., Grove, A.S., Rowe, T.A. and Moore, G.E. (1969): 'Silicon gate techology' *IEEE Spectrum*, V. 6, October, pp. 28-35.

Vadass, L.L., Chua, H.T., and Grove, A.S. (1971): 'Semiconductor Random-Access Memories', *IEEE Spectrum*, V. **8**, No. 8, pp. 40-48.

Walther, T.R. and Mccoy, M.R. (1972): 'A three transistor MOS memory cell with internal refresh', *ISSCC 72. Dig. Tech. Paper*, pp. 14-15.

Weinberger, A. (1967): 'Large scale integration of MOS complex logic—a layout method', *IEEE J. Solid State Circuits*, V. SC-2, December, pp. 182-190.

Wiedmann, S.W. (1973): 'Injected-coupled memory; A high density static bipolar memory', *IEEE J. Solid State Circuits*, V. SC-8, October, pp. 283-288.

7. SOME ADVANCED MEMORY TECHNOLOGIES

Technology is advancing so rapidly that it is extremely difficult to keep pace with developments in one's own field. It is, therefore, reasonable to expect that developments outside some speciality may go unnoticed or unappreciated. A persistent theme of development of memory technology has been the quest for larger and faster systems. The stunning success of silicon semiconductor technology for information processing has not completely stifled the search for alternative technological bases for memory and logic. Thus there has been interest in research related to logic based on magnetic bubbles, optical devices, and superconducting devices in the past decade. The physics of these devices and their performance characteristics will be discussed in this section.

Widespread use of magnetic bubble devices for low-cost low-power memories may be forthcoming in the not too distant future. Improvements in fine line lithography have spurred the development of smaller bubble technologies in the hope of realizing higher data rates, higher bit densities, greater yields, greater margins and accompanying reduction in cost. The results of the preliminary experiments which attempt to establish the proper design criteria for small bubbles have now become available on such electron beam and X-ray lithographically defined circuit. Great progress has been made in the development of magnetic bubble devices in the period from 1967 and at present, prototype of memory modules employing 4-5 μm diameter bubbles are in operation. Although both semiconductors and bubbles belong to integrated circuit technology, bubble devices are intrinsically and significantly simpler in structure and fabrication than MOSFET devices, though they are rather slow. However, the question of whether bubble memories will eventually be used for large capacity ($>10^9$ bits) computer—memory storage is still open, and depends on future technological progress.

Another area in which considerable advancement has recently occurred is optical memory technology. Optical data storage presents many unique advantages, notably the high storage density and low access time, not attainable by conventional recording techniques. With a coherent laser beam and diffraction limited optics, the expected packing density could exceed 100 million bit per cm^2 of medium area. Moreover, the system allows parallel processing, and inertialess addressing. These attractive capabilities of optical system can be further enhanced by applying holographic techniques. At present there are two basic approaches to storage, namely, bit by bit recording and holographic storage. No alterable optical memory, either bit oriented or holographic, has yet been brought to a commercial product stage uptil now to the knowledge of the present authors.

In many cases experimental optical memory systems have been constructed to demonstrate the concepts and acquire tradeoff knowledge. In the area of fundamental research, many new optical materials for memory as well as for generation, modulation, deflection, and detection of coherent optical beam have been prepared, physical phenomena analyzed and characterized. In the device research area, impressive progress has been made in the components required for optical beam addressing, and in quantifying the material memory characteristics. From these extensive investigations some important results have been obtained. Although some progress has been made undoubtedly regarding the optical memory technology, a careful assessment of the present status reveals that the technology, though proved technically feasible, is not yet economically competitive with existing mass memory technologies. Much work remains to be done to bring down the cost, especially in the area of lasers and optical components.

Superconductive memory devices also deserve consideration. Advances in cryogenic array fabrication have made it feasible to consider thin film superconductive devices as being potentially competitive in the computer field, particularly for parallel data processors. Cryoelectric devices are recognized as the only imminent means of economically achieving and evaluating very large capacity data handling systems. Enthusiasm for these devices stems from this consideration continued with relative simplicity of their fabrication. In fact in a superconductive unit, the memory element can work very fast with minimum noise because they have very low power consumption and an extremely nonlinear transition occurs between the superconducting and normal states.

Early attempts to develop superconductive computer elements were based on the cryotron, in which the magnetic field produced by current in one conductor was used to destroy superconductivity in another conductor. The transitions between the superconducting and normal state is, however, a first order transition, involving latent heat and nucleation events, and difficulties connected with the first order nature of the transition plagued efforts to develop large computing systems based on cryotrons. A more promising approach to superconductive computing elements was provided by Josephson's discovery of the effects associated with tunnelling between superconductors that are known by his name. These gates provide very fast switching of the order of picoseconds and have power dissipation of few microwatts only. The physics of these devices and all other memory techniques are discussed in the following section.

7.1 MAGNETIC BUBBLE MEMORIES

In recent years, a number of new techniques have been developed and explored for memory applications. Notable among them are, large scale integration using semiconductors, magneto-optic memory and the magnetic 'bubble' domain devices. Magnetic bubble memories have the potential capabilities of having a high bit density and large capacity per chip and also are less expensive. Being a solid state technology, they eliminate the mechanical motion associated with the presentday disk and tape systems. Long term nonvolatility of the stored information is provided much more easily than with most semiconductor devices. In addition, logic and display functions are possible. The ability to store, transmit and process information in the same medium eliminates or reduces the problems of electrical interconnections, signal conversion, and the associated power dissipation.

The bubble domain technolony has now reached the point where it is destined to play a leading role in the future development of computer hardware. The generation, propagation and sensing of magnetic 'bubble' domains are really different aspects of the same phenomenon—the interaction of bubble domain with its magnetic environment. A unified theory of this interaction remains a challenge to workers in this field. The future of magnetic bubbles for binary storage applications is now well established. The materials which support bubble domains have been studied extensively over the last few years and a thorough understanding of their properties has been gained. In binary storage applications, individual bubble domains are manipulated in the garnet medium by either current loops or permalloy propagation tracks.

7.1.1 Physical Principles of Bubble Memory Devices and Their Material Considerations

A uniaxial magnetic film with its easy axis normal to the film exhibits serpentine domains in the demagnetizing state. When a suitable dc bias magnetic field is applied along the easy axis, these serpentine domains having their magnetization opposite to the applied field will shrink and become cylindrical domains, as shown in Figure 7.1. Further increase of the bias field reduces the bubble size and finally they disappear. The size of these bubbles ranges between 1 and 100 μm and depends on the properties of material used. Actually such cylindrical domains or 'bubbles' represent cluster of magnetic spins stable under the combined influence of the applied field, domain wall energy and the magnetostatic energy.

Cylindrical magnetic domains called bubbles can exist in certain thin platelet crystals of anisotropic material having an easy axis of magnetization normal to this platelet. The research and development in this at the initial stage was primarily devoted to the search of suitable magnetic materials. In order that the bubble technology may provide an economic alternative to conventional computer memories, it must satisfy the following stringent requirements, namely:

(i) the packing density of one million per square inch restricts the maximum bubble diameters to about 7.5 microns. This requires a film thickness of same magnitude and constant within 1 per cent.

(ii) Film material must have a low magnetization value, since the anisotropy field that is necessary for turning the magnetization from easy direction to the plane of the film, should be at least 1.5 times the magnetization.

(iii) A minimum mobility of 200 cm/sec/oersted is required, which means that a low coercive material is necessary so that the walls can move freely in response to in plane magnetic fields.

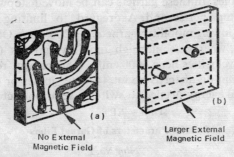

(a)
No External
Magnetic Field

(b)
Larger External
Magnetic Field

Figure 7.1 (a) Stripdomains as observed in orthoferrite and garnet platelets; (b) Strip collapse into bubbles as the critical field is reached.

A renewed interest in the domain structure occurred after Bobeck published his paper on the properties and device applications of magnetic domains in orthoferrites in 1967. Extensive research has been made for the last few years to find materials that give rise to small bubbles that can move at high velocity. The minimum objectives have been to attain a packing density of a million bubbles per square inch and a mobility allowing a data processing rate of a million bits per second. For a constant in-plane gradient of the bias field H, simple theory predicts a bubble velocity V given by

$$V = 0.5 \ \mu_{\mathrm{w}} \ [\Delta H - 8H_c/\pi] \qquad (1.1)$$

where μ_{w} is the *straight wall* mobility, H is the change in bias field over a bubble diameter and H_c is the wall motion coercivity. For orthoferrite materials of chemical formula $RFeO_3$, where R is any rare earth ion, Equation (1.1) remains valid for all practical drive field H, and velocities as high as 10^5 cm/s have been achieved corresponding to a data rate of 3M bits/s.

However, domains in orthoferrites are too large for practical purposes (~ 50 to $100 \ \mu m$). Very small bubbles ($\sim 1 \ \mu m$) should be available in hexaferrite. However, experiments with somewhat larger bubbles ($\sim 10 \ \mu m$) in these materials indicate that a limiting velocity of about 200-250 cm/s is reached for large drive fields. Such velocities correspond to limiting data rates between 10 and 100 Kbits/s which is too slow for practical devices.

Another class of materials, which show some better results is the magnetic garnet crystals of general formula $A_3Fe_5O_{12}$, where A can be yttrium, or an of the rare earths, or at least in part lanthanum or bismuth. It was an un-expected discovery since the garnets are cubic crystals and laws of magnetism do not permit such crystals to be uniaxial. During the process of crystal growing small strains are introduced which are responsible for this uniaxial property. By using the process known as liquid phase epitaxy single crystal the magnetic garnet film is grown on the [111] plane of gadolinium gallium by liquid phase epitaxy. The material properties of garnet film is given in Table 7.1. The most common substrate is gadolinium gallium garnet ($Gd_3Ga_5O_{12}$). In the most satisfactory garnet sample the bubble dia-meter is about 3 μm, which allows the packing of a million bubbles per square inch. Bubbles in these garnets can be moved stepwise at the rate of at least a million steps per second. As regard to limiting velocity, it has been found that lower mobility garnets ($\sim$200 cm/s Oe) do not exhibit velocity saturation, whereas some high mobility garnets ($\sim$2000 cm/s Oe) do exhibit this, at velocities near 4000 cm/s. The energy required to move a garnet bubble 4 μm diameter is about 44×10^{14} joules or only a very small fraction of the total energy needed to switch a semiconductor active element.

TABLE 7.1

Material Parameters of Garnet Films

Composition	Film No. 1 $Y_{2.75}Sm_{0.25}Ga_{1.1}Fe_{3.4}O_{12}$	Film No. 2 $Y_{2.75}Sm_{0.25}Ga_{1.1}Fe_{3.4}O_{12}$
Saturation magnetization ($4\pi M$)	206 Gauss	210 Gauss
$H_{collapse}$ (Free bubble)	124 Oe	122 Oe
Demagnetizing strip width	5.6 μm	5.6 μm
Film thickness	6.5 μm	6.5 μm
Initial mobility	320 cm/sec/Oe	—
Meterial length	0.58 μm	0.75 μm

7.1.2 Generation of Magnetic Bubbles

The generation of bubbles can be accomplished by two distinct means, namely, nucleation and stretch cut. The latter type of generator usually keeps a seed bubble which is stretched into a strip either by pulsed current carrying conductors or by a permalloy element and then split into two with the same or different conductors or permalloy elements. This type of gene-rator consists of a permalloy disk, a conductor loop and a propagating channel. A seed bubble is circulated around the disk under the influence of an in-plane rotating field. As it crosses a conductor loop, a suitable current pulse is applied which splits the seed into two and transfers one of them to the nearly propagating channel. The conductor stretch type generator is similar to the above with the only difference that it has a three terminal conductor pattern as shown in Figure 7.2 (b). Within the proper phase angle the conductor path 3-2 is pulsed to stretch the seed bubble across the gap to the propagating channel, followed by a pulse in the conductor path 1-3 to split it into two.

Two types of permalloy stretch generators are commonly used. In the first type, which is also known as Chevron generator, a doughnut shaped permalloy feature is used to circulate the seed bubble. The performance of this type of generator depends on the amplitude and the width of the current pulse. A relative position in time between the current pulse and the rotating field direction (referred to as phase angle) is also important. The other type, known as T-bar pattern generator, possesses the finest dimensions and further require the highest accuracy since they have direct influence on chip operation margins.

The permalloy and conductor patterns are designed mainly by trial and error, with the objective of obtaining the widest possible magnetic field margins and temperature range of operation, the highest possible data rate, and the lowest possible current and power for the memory control functions. The optimum designs vary with the properties of the magnetic bubble material used.

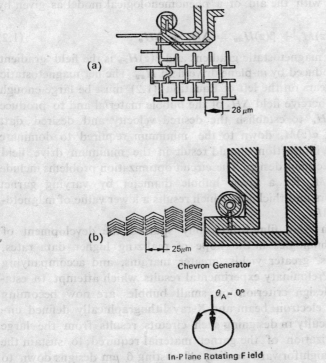

Figure 7.2 Magnetic bubble generators: (a) Permalloy stretch type;
(b) Conductor stretch type.

The operating bias range of the permalloy stretch pattern depends upon the thickness and the saturation magnetization $(4\pi M)$ of the garnet films. The potential well, which a bubble experiences under the permalloy elements, is determined by the vertical component of the permalloy field averaged along the domain wall and does not depend upon $4\pi M$. The most important factor affecting the stability range of the propagating bubbles is the magnetic pole distribution of the permalloy elements. These distributions can be theoretically calculated or experimentally simulated including the bubble field and the two dimensional shapes of the permalloy elements. It is rather complicated, however, to apply the results to the analysis of the stability range of bubbles under the permalloy elements. Potential well depth measurement techniques and the analysis of maximum limiting frequency give some practical approaches to analyze the bubble propagation.

A number of device models have been proposed which are capable of predicting what happens to the drive field when the bubble size is scaled down by increasing the saturation magnetization of the garnet materials. In designing the submicron circuits, care must be taken to insure that the permalloy is thick enough so that it is not saturated by the applied fields. The spacing dependence of the minimum drive field and the field gradient can be understood with the aid of a phenomenological model as given by Equation (1.2).

$$\alpha(z)M_s + \beta(z)H_{xy} = \Delta H_c + \Delta H_v \qquad (1.2)$$

where $\alpha(z)M_s$ is the magnetostatic gradient and $\beta(z)H_{xy}$ is the field gradient on the bubble produced by in-plane drive field H_{xy}. The net magnetostatic gradient which appears on the left of Equation (1.2) must be large enough to overcome the coercive field ΔH_c of the bubble material and to produce enough gradient ΔH_v to establish the desired velocity and desired data rate. Reduction of $\alpha(z)M_s$ down to the minimum required to dominate the bubble—bubble interaction, should result in the minimum drive field and in an optimum circuit design. The circuit optimization problems include the reduction of M_s for a given bubble diameter by varying garnet material's parameters and thickness, which results a lower value of magnetostatic gradient $\alpha(z)M_s$.

Improvements in thin film lithography spurred the development of smaller bubble technologies in the hope of realizing higher data rates, higher bit densities, greater yields, greater margins, and accompanying reduction in cost. Preliminary experimental results which attempt to establish the proper design criterion on small bubbles are now becoming available on such electron beam and X-ray lithographically defined circuits. A major difficulty in designing such circuits results from the large saturation magnetization of the garnet material required to sustain the small bubbles. Straightforward scaling of existing 6 μm designs down to submicron sizes results in impractical rotating field requirements, particularly at high data rates.

7.1.3 Propagation of Magnetic Bubbles

While search for the right material was on, technologists had already started fabricating devices for the creation, annihilation, transfer, interaction and detection of bubbles. So far we have seen that a magnetic bubble is a round cylindrical domain of upward magnetization surrounded by a sea of downward magnetization or vice versa. Such domain exists in thin sheet of certain magnetic materials when a uniform bias field of proper magnitude is applied perpendicular to the sheet. They repel one another like parallel dipoles, and are kept about diameter apart (centre to centre) in practical devices to prevent excessive bubble to bubble interaction. Logic devices, on the other hand, make use of this interaction and thus use a closer spacing.

Bubble technology involves the creation and manipulation of these cylindrical domains. Information is transmitted by propagation of these bubbles. Two general techniques have been used to provide control structures and to propagate or guide paths on the magnetic material for bubbles. They can travel along the paths guided by current loop called 'conductor access' device. The other so-called 'field access' method uses the induced magnetic field in specially shaped magnetic structures (normally of patterned permalloy whose polarity is induced and controlled by an external rotating magnetic field). Typical field access propagation structures are the T-bar, the Y-bar, the contiguous disk, and the Chevron type.

One of the earliest devices constructed using the bubbles was the shift register. The bubble propagation device was simply a series of three interleaved conductor loops which when energized sequentially, would attract and guide a bubble along a desired path. The sizes of the bubble and the conductors are chosen in such a way that the bubble is in contact with the field gradient of the next loop. The reverse motion of the bubbles are prevented by using three-phase system and the bubbles are shifted by the sequential application of currents through the loops. A data rate of 475 KHz has been experimented with a current of 100 mA for domains with a diameter of 100 μm. The required current will be reduced linearly with bubble diameter. The conductor loop technique has the advantages that only an external dc magnetic field is required while the disadvantage is that one flaw in a conductor of a memory circuit makes the, whole device worthless.

The second method of propagation, based on field access technique is known as angelfish propagation. It utilizes the fact that the diameter of the bubbles can be modulated by modulating the biasing field. Motion is achieved by manoeuvring these pulsating bubbles in and out of asymmetrical energy traps. These energy traps are created by wedge shaped thin films of high permeability permalloy placed in contact with the magnetic film. The advantage of this approach is that it eliminates the need for electrical connections to the bubble chip in order to achieve propagation. The required driving force is also small compared with other approaches. While the disadvantages of this approach are that the operating margins are rather tight and that the oscillating component of the bias field must have very good spatial uniformity, implying large inductance coils. This would make high frequency operation difficult. For these reasons, this device is used in special purpose display and printing processes rather than in memory applications.

The third and most widely used type of propagation which removes the drawbacks of angelfish type of propagation, is known as T-bar propagation. This approach uses an external in-plane field rather than an external perpendicular field to control bubble propagation. In this process the size of individual bubble remains same but they are moved from point to point by a rotating magnetic field acting in conjuction with a pattern of thin film permalloy T's and vertical bars. A pattern of magnetically soft material, such as permalloy, is used to convert a rotating in-plane field to a translating pattern of attracting magnetic poles. The permalloy pattern is composed of bars whose length to width ratio is chosen so that the bar will become magnetized only by a parallel magnetic field. The bubble acts like magnetic dipoles that follow the moving pattern. Figure 7.3(a) shows the bubble generation and propagation under the action of rotating magnetic field. Writing is accomplished by superimposing a single conductor that can either aid or inhibit the 'snapping off' of a new domain.

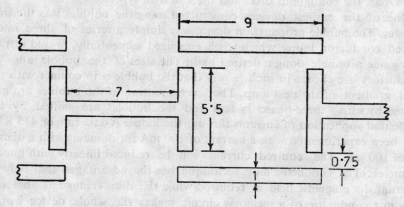

Figure 7.3 (a) Structures of a T-bar permalloy pattern.

The various access methods discussed above can also be used to generate new bubbles. In the conductor-access method a new bubble can be produced by equipping one of the loops with a hairpin conductor that can be separately energised, while in the field access scheme that employs a rotating magnetic field, one can install a bubble generator at the head of any row of T's and bars as shown in Figure 7.3(b). Under the influence of rotating field a new bubble will be produced for every complete revolution of the field, and will be propagated from one place to another, under the control of applied field.

The variation of bubble diameter with applied in-plane field is shown in Figure 7.4. For a given element, the well depth increases with increasing

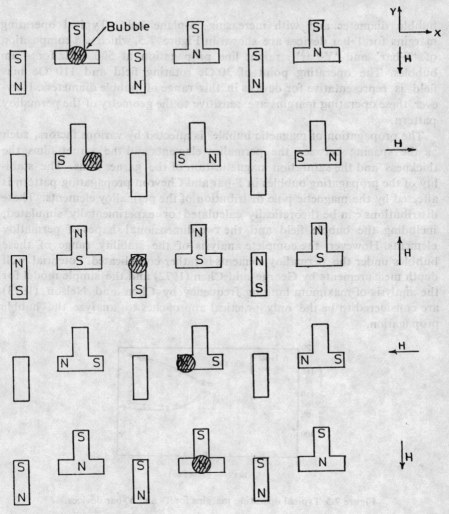

Figure 7.3(b) Bubble generation in a T-bar circuit.

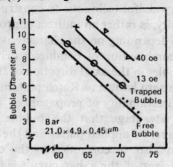

Figure 7.4 Variation of bubble diameter with applied fields.

bubble diameter and with increasing in-plane field. Typical operating margins for T-bar devices are shown in Figure 7.5, which is a composition of 'T-bar' and 'Y-bar' straight line propagation at 500 KHz for 4 μm bubbles. The operating point of 30 Oe rotating field and 110 Oe bias field is representative for devices in this range of bubble diameters. However, these operating margins are sensitive to the geometry of the permalloy pattern.

The propagation of magnetic bubbles is affected by various factors, such as the spacing between the permalloy elements and the garnet films, the thickness and the saturation magnetization of the garnet films. The stability of the propagating bubbles in T-bar and Chevron propagating pattern is affected by the magnetic pole distribution of the permalloy elements. These distributions can be theoretically calculated or experimentally simulated, including the bubble field and the two dimensional shapes of permalloy elements. However, the complete analysis of the stability range of these bubbles under the permalloy elements is rather complicated. Potential well depth measurements by George and Chen (1972) and the simple model for the analysis of maximum limiting frequency by Chen and Nelson (1973) are considered to be the only practical approaches to analyze the bubble propagation.

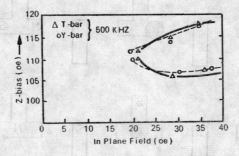

Figure 7.5 Typical operating margins for T- and Y-bar devices.

Other approaches have also been tried for bubble propagation. The T-bar pattern which is a very skilful technique to construct memory circuits with high information density, is rather an indirect approach, and the bubble propagation speed varies depending on the characteristics of the soft magnetic thin film patterns. A combination of conductor drive and the angelfish type circuit propagates bubbles in the axial direction of the conductor. Sometimes a modified angelfish pattern known as Ratch pattern gives the stable location of the bubble and a directionality of propagation. Ratch bubble propagation circuit has the advantage that the bubble can be propagated in proportion to the number of applied pulses and the distance through which the bubble moves can also be controlled by the current pulse amplitude. Another interesting variant of the T-bar circuit is the 'Chevron' pattern as discussed earlier in which attempts have been made to increase the operating margins by propagating the bubbles in elongated form rather than in round form. The elongation occurs transverse to the direction of propagation making such devices particularly useful in sensing applications.

7.1.4 Magnetic Bubble Logic Circuits

The technology of discrete magnetic domains has introduced a variety of possibilities for new modes of realizing logic and memory devices that might be used for construction of digital information processing systems. The proposed logic circuits have shown the feasibility of realizing basic logic operations using magnetic bubbles as carriers of information, and the technology of magnetic bubble memories already shows promise of yielding practical systems. The method of bubble logic circuits is based on the construction of cells and the driving conductors that perform simple logic operations. In conductor access devices, logic can be performed by bubble transfer operations, while in field access devices, logic is performed by providing alternative paths which are selected by interaction between bubbles. Examples include the conjugate logic gates, resident bubble cellular logic and the Chevron 3-3 logic circuits. Logic can also be performed by counting bubbles, such as, in symmetric switching function implementation.

A simple bubble logic gate using current loop as driving element is shown in Figure 7.6. Consider two bubble positions A and B which store the values X and Y respectively. When the current loop at B is energized to perform the bubble transfer operation, the following situations may arise:

(i) If there are no bubbles at A, nothing happens.
(ii) A bubble at A will be attracted to B, if there are no bubbles at B.
(iiii) If both A and B are occupied by bubbles, then there is mutual

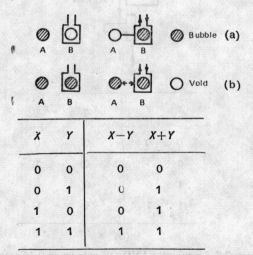

X	Y	$X-Y$	$X+Y$
0	0	0	0
0	1	0	1
1	0	0	1
1	1	1	1

Figure 7.6 A conjugate AND/OR gate using bubble transfer operation.

repulsion and this repulsive force will cancel the force exerted by loop current.

All possible situations in such transfer operation are shown in the truth table in Figure 7.6. After transfer operation the state of A represents AND while that of B represents OR operation. More detailed study on transfer operation has been made by Graham (1970) at the Bell Laboratory.

In field access devices, the bubbles follow the paths guided by a permalloy overlay structure. To perform the logic, the permalloy pattern is designed to provide easy and hard paths for the bubbles. Repulsion between bubbles is utilized to influence the choice of a path by a bubble.

The conjugate logic gates use the T-bar pattern to provide two kinds of bubble paths, the easy and the hard path. One bubble always travels along the easy path and in case of repulsion between the two bubbles, one will travel along the hard path. Consider the AND/OR gate as shown in Figure 7.7. When a single bubble enters the gate from either X or Y, it travels

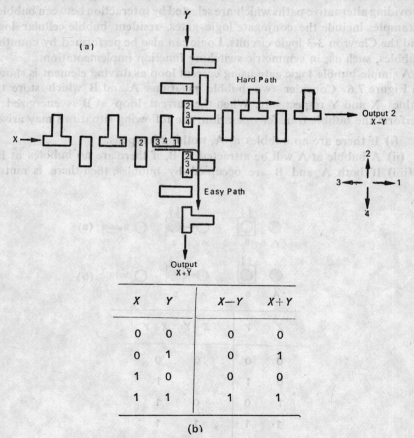

X	Y	X−Y	X+Y
0	0	0	0
0	1	0	1
1	0	0	0
1	1	1	1

(b)

Figure 7.7 A conjugate AND/OR gate using field access devices.

along the easy path. When two bubbles simultaneously enter the gate at X and Y, they repel each other. The X bubble, as there is no other path, will travel along the easy path and the Y bubble will travel along the alternative hard path. Therefore, output 1 gives an 'OR' function $(X + Y)$, while the output 2 gives an 'AND' function $(X \cdot Y)$.

In this logic the number of bubbles entering the gate is exactly equal to the number of bubbles leaving the gate, so that total number of bubbles remains constant. Nonconservative logic gates can also be implemented in which extra bubbles may be generated or annihilated within the gate. Since these conjugate logic operations are based on bubble repulsion force they are not suitable for logic gates having more than two inputs.

The third type of logic circuit known as Resident-bubble cellular logic, possesses advantages over the conjugate logic, and is based on the construction of cells that perform simple logic operations and that can be combined to realize more complex functions. There are four types of cells: the transmission cell, the two dimensional cross-over cell, the NAND cell, and the flip-flop cell. An important property of these cells is that no bubbles ever enter or leave any cell, all inter-cell communications being done by bubble interactions near the cell boundaries. The cross-over cell contains two resident bubbles, while each of the other three cells contains one resident bubble. The function of a cell is determined by its internal structure. The input is considered to be 1 if there is a resident bubble in the adjacent cell travelling along the input terminal, otherwise 0. The output is 1 if the resident bubble of the cell travels along the output terminal, otherwise 0.

The resident bubble cellular NAND gate is shown in Figure 7.8. The NAND cell contains a single internal bubble, circulating clockwise, which takes the hard path to bypass the output position, if and only if, both the inputs are received. The internal paths are divided into four parts. A zig-zag line in the figure denotes a hard path. If none of the inputs is 1, the resident bubble travels along the paths 1 and 4, and the output is 1. If only input Y is 1, the resident bubble still travels along the paths 1 and 4, since it follows a path remote from the adjacent bubble at Y. If only input X is 1, the resident bubble is repelled by the adjacent bubble at X and travels along path 2 and then path 4, the output is still 1. If both inputs are 1's the resident bubble is repelled by the adjacent bubble at X to travel along path 2, and again repelled by another adjacent bubble at Y to travel along the path 3, and thus bypassing the output path 4, yielding 0. The various situations as described are summarized in truth table in Fig. 7.9, indicating that the device performs NAND operation.

This kind of logic requires neither bubble generator nor annihilator. Different functions can be realized in basic cells. Once the basic cells have been designed, the logic designers can proceed to combine them to realize the desired functions in a manner quite similar to classical design techniques. However, such cell design results in extensive area and long delay for each

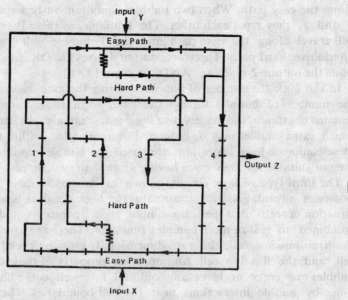

Figure 7.8 Resident bubble cellular NAND gate.

X	Y	Paths of the Resident Bubble	Z
0	0	1, 4	1
0	1	1, 4	1
1	0	2, 4	1
1	1	2, 3	0

Figure 7.9. Truth table.

cell. The initial loading and synchronization of resident bubbles on all cells also present practical difficulties.

Another class of logic circuit, known as Chevron 3-3 circuit, is an extension of the usual logic connections from 2 inputs to 3 inputs, and 2 outputs to 3 outputs. In this case three permalloy paths are designed to converge at an interaction channel and the variation in spacing or width of Chevron patterns at the channel defining various kinds of interactions. Though this type of logic circuit has extended the number of inputs than others, it cannot however, overcome the basic physical limitation that the bubbles can only interact effectively within 3—4 diameters. Hence it cannot further increase the number of inputs in a logic gate. Also this type of logic reduces the device operating margins significantly below that of conventional T-bar shift register devices.

All these bubble logic devices are limited either by irregularity of circuit connection or by low density. The most important type of logic device, that provides higher density and low connectivity, can be realized by bubbles such as in the symmetric switching function implementation. It offers competitive performance (space and delay) as the conventional logic connectives when implemented by bubbles. Moreover, these devices offer rewrite ability to eliminate the part number problem, and accommodation for large number of inputs to ease interconnection and delay equalization problems.

If a symmetric switching function of n variables has the value of 1 when exactly m variables $(0 \leqslant m \leqslant n)$ are 1's, then it is called elementary, and can be written as $_nS_m$. Also, any symmetric switching function $_nS_m$ of n variables can be expressed in terms of $n + 1$ elementary symmetric switching functions as:

$$S = a_0 \cdot {_nS_0} + a_1 \cdot {_nS_1} + a_2 \cdot {_nS_2} + ... + a_n \cdot {_nS_n}$$

where
$$_nS_n = \Sigma x_1, x_2, ..., \bar{x}_m \bar{x}_{m+1} \bar{x}_{m+2} ... \bar{x}_n$$

for
$$m = 0, 1 ... n$$

Each coefficient a_i is either 0 or 1. These $n + 1$ coefficients completely determine a symmetric switching function and are called personalization coefficients. In order to compute a symmetric switching function by a bubble device, we need to count the number of bubbles at the inputs and to compare it with personalization coefficients. The personalization coefficients are represented as bubble stream which consist of $n+1$ bit positions. The ith bit position from the left of the personalization stream represents the value of a_{i-1} at which a bubble denotes a 1 and a void 0. After counting the input bubbles the number is also represented in a similar way, i.e., a bubble in the ith position from the left denotes that there are i-1 bubbles at the input. A bubble at the first position indicates that there is no input.

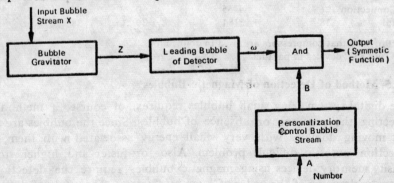

Figure 7.10 Block diagram of bubble implementation of symmetric switching function.

The mechanism of realizing a symmetric switching function using magnetic bubble is shown in Figure 7.10. This is a block diagram and can easily be implemented by the permalloy pattern. The bubble gravitator which consist of empty idlers takes all the input bubbles serially and gravitates them towards one end. The streams of all bubbles are then flushed into the leading bubble detector, which has three idlers. The leading bubble detector translates the total number of input bubbles to the position of one bubble in an otherwise all void data stream (W). The personalization control bubble stream defines the logic function by placing bubbles in a data stream to represent a number (B). The interaction of data streams and B yields the output.

The characteristics of a symmetric switching function device is determined by its personalization stream, and not by the device structure; thus it is amenable to rewriting. The multiple input capability is determined by the number of idlers allowable to the device. The capability of multiple inputs and the capability of performing high level functions greatly reduce the interconnection and hence delay equalization problem in this type of devices. A comparison amongst the various bubble logic devices is shown in Table 7.2. Since the delay and chip area required for each logic device is a measure of its merit, we have shown these parameters for realizing a full adder. The chip area required for each logic implementation depends on the device configuration, the permalloy pattern and the circuit connections. We estimate the area required for each device in units of a storage cell area.

TABLE 7.2
Characteristics of Various Logic Gates

	Conjugate logic gate	Resident bubble cellular logic	Chevron 3-3 circuit	Symmetric switching function device (SSF)		
Delay	2*	504	10	9**	*or*	18
Area						
Gate	12	729	30	28**	or	14
Connection	6	4455	0	0		
Total	18	5184	30	38**	or	14

*Provided that compressors are used in connections.
**Two SSF devices in parallel.

7.1.5 Method of Detection of Magnetic Bubbles

The digital system using small bubbles requires, of course, a method for detecting the presence or absence of bubbles. Since the bubbles are tiny, fast moving domains with very small energy associated with them, their detection poses a difficult problem. Also for faster and higher storage density memory devices using magnetic bubbles require the detection of magnetic domains of the order of 1 μm in diameter. The mode of detection will then become a significant limiting factor in memory design. A number of methods have been tried so far. The detection of these bubbles could be either destructive or nondestructive, that is, the detector could either annihilate the bubble stream or 'sample' the bubbles without destroying them as they travel by.

Nondestructive techniques are based on several physical principles, such as, electromagnetic induction, direct optical sensing, Hall effect and magnetoresistance. A bubble being a dipole, has a typical dipole field pattern. A moving bubble produces a transient magnetic field in a conductor pick-up coil while passing below it. This small voltage in the conductor loop is then amplified in the external control circuit. During the course of calculation a given bubble may return many times to the readout site. Moreover, this type of detection becomes increasingly difficult as the bubble diameter decreases because of the small amount of available flux. Magneto-optical detection is another method which has been tried in the initial phase of development. The orthoferrites and garnets, being transparent to optical radiation, permit the magnetic domains to be observed and photographed under a microscope using polarized light.

Modern bubble sensors used in practice fall into two categories—the semiconductor Hall effect devices and the magnetic film magnetoresistance devices. In each case, the flux from the bubble is used to modulate the power supplied from an external source. The bubble can be stretched in order to increase the available flux, thus providing signal amplification. In Hall effect sensor as shown in Figure 7.11 the vertical component of bubble domain's external field applies a Lorentz force to moving charge carriers within a semiconductor causing a voltage V_s to appear at right angles to both magnetic field and the direction of carrier flow. The signal is given (in MKS unit) by

$$V_s = BI/ent$$

where B is an average vertical component of flux density emanating from the bubble, I is the input current, e is the electronic charge, n is the effective carrier concentration, and t is the sensor thickness. The above equation shows the importance of small carrier concentration and thin samples in achieving large signal voltages. However, this will also increase the noise voltage. The above equation assumes that $B\mu' \ll 1$, where μ' is the effective carrier mobility in semiconductor. For a square and symmetric semiconductor, i.e. $R_x = R_y$, the signal power P_s is related to input power P_{in} as given by:

$$P_s = (B\mu')^2 P_{in}$$

The only way to increase the power output is to increase the carrier mobility. The earliest detectors were made from silicon which has a low mobility μ'. Technologists are now trying for better sensor materials which should have higher carrier mobility but low noise factor. GaAs has carrier mobility five times that of silicon but it has considerably more recombination noise than silicon, and also it cannot stand as large an applied voltage because it breaks into Gunn oscillations. Another material InSb, which has one of the highest room temperature mobilities, has been used for sensor element. 10 μm bubbles have been detected with this type of sensors.

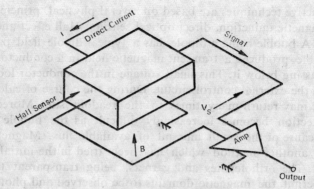

Figure 7.11 Hall effect sensor.

The magnetoresistance sensor method appears to be most compatible with the ultraminiaturized solid state devices. In this method the presence of a bubble lowers the resistance and hence voltage, as measured between the two poles of a bridge circuit; the result is a small output signal. For the magnetoresistance sensor, the uniaxial and shape anisotropies are so chosen that in the absence of a bubble domain, the sensor magnetization lies parallel to sensor current (high resistance state). When a bubble passes by, its in-plane external field component switches the sensor magnetization partly perpendicular to current (low resistance state). If a constant current I is supplied to the sensor, this resistance change appears as a voltage change.

The signal output from the sensor, however, decreases with bubble diameter, going approximately as the inverse cube root of bubble diameter. The permalloy sensor has the advantages of better temperature stability, since its resistance changes about 0.1 per cent per °C. Moreover, it is thinner and requires a less elaborate evaporation procedure. By reducing the thickness of permalloy sensor down to 0.02 μm, it is possible to detect 4 μm bubbles. But if the bubble diameter reduces further then these sensors are not so effective. Reducing the thickness of permalloy sensors further cause a sharp increase of the demagnetizing field, as a result of which the switching threshold increases. The detection of domains of the order of 1 μm in diameter can be done optically by the Faraday effect using a single mode optical waveguide structure and a photomultiplier.

The optical detector is basically a photomultiplier. A polarizer is mounted before the photomultiplier so that the optical discrimination would be obtained between the bubble domain and the reverse domain via the Faraday effect. By adjusting the analyzer one can either null the rotation to the bubble producing a dark bubble on a bright background or null the background produciug a bright bubble. A more practical structure will be a photomultiplier mounted directly to the back of the garnet substrate with a thin polarizing element in between. The only limitation to this approach is the saturation of the detector by the dc background light.

7.2 OPTICAL MEMORIES

Presentday electronic computers employ logic gates that perform the switching operation in approximately 10^{-8} second and are capable of storing 10^4 to 10^7 bits of information which are accessible in 10^{-6} to 10^{-7} second. It now appears that in order to achieve higher speeds in micrologic gates some basically new phenomena need to be explored. To this end extensive effort has been devoted to the exploration of the possibility of optical computer logic element.

At the start it is useful to distinguish three broad categories which have emerged in the field of optical processing of information. The first technique, having the origin in spatial filtering studies, is the coherent optical processing technique and this has reached a certain maturity in the sense of being a readily useful method of processing data. The second category includes all the electro-optical effects and devices which are useful in logic, memory or input/output. The third category is the all optical processing in which signals are carried by light and logic is performed by interaction between light beams. The status of this category may be described as exploratory. The current activity is directed towards uncovering the effects which show promise in optical logic or storage.

The strongest stimulus to develop an optical information processing technique is its potential for enormous data-handling capacity. The key to high storage density is the submicron wavelength of light, since the theoretical limit of closeness of stored bits to each other is set by the wavelength of the recording energy. The practical limit is set by particle size in the recording medium and the photographic emulsions that contain particles of few tens of millimicron in diameter.

The unique properties of optical signals which differentiate them from their counterparts in electronic computers are:

(i) Lack of electrical charge of photons, leading to complete decoupling, and isolation of signals and very large fan-in.

(ii) The wavelength of signals will be much shorter than any of the circuit dimensions. Therefore, one could eliminate, for example, all the reactive effects in the interconnections. One might still have to be contented with mismatched transmission lines, but this is not a major problem since the decay times are very short.

(iii) The two-dimensional wave nature of optical radiation at very short wavelengths which in turn involves: (a) easy way of propagation of many independent signals through simple channels without need for any conductors; (b) potentially, very small components including 'waveguides', perhaps leading to smaller interlogic distances and hence, higher operating speeds; (c) extremely high carrier frequencies; and (d) propagation of two dimensional signals, which may be viewed as parallel propagation of one dimensional signals.

7.2.1 General Approaches to Optical Memories

The introduction of optical techniques to memory applications, originally conceived as a revolutionary development, is now undergoing a more cautious evolutionary process. Designers of optical memories take advantages of all the advanced techniques, such as holography, high resolution photographic emulsion and photochromism. Two basic approaches, namely, holographic recording and bit-by-bit recording are widely used by the present memory designers. With a laser source, a unique advantage can be gained by making full use of the coherent properties of optical beams with the technique of holographic recording.

Of the various techniques, the bit-by-bit system requires a laser source, the beam modulator for intensity control, the beam deflector for addressing. The memory medium will respond to the beam to effect a WRITE function as well as it interacts with the beam to provide the readout function at the detector. In certain media, an additional electric or magnetic field is required in conjunction with the beam for write, or read operation. The other technique utilizes holographic method for data storage. A holographic memory is page oriented and a single page of data, containing 10^3 to 10^5 bits, is written or read out one time. A holographic memory therefore utilizes parallel storage, and the optical system and the component requirements are different from that of bit-by-bit system.

7.2.1.1 HOLOGRAPHIC TECHNIQUE

It has long been recognized that photographic emulsion is capable of storing an enormous amount of information. Since many holograms can be superimposed on the same photographic plate and as the impinging optics are a built in property of holograms, holographic memories are currently under investigation. Holography, sometimes called *lensless photography* or *wavefront reconstruction photography*, is a way of recording the unfocussed light reflected or transmitted by an object or objects. The term 'wavefront reconstruction' refers to a process in which the amplitude and phase of scattered electromagnetic wavefront is recorded (usually photographically) together with a suitable coherent background in such a way that it is possible to produce at a later time a reproduction of the electromagnetic field distribution of the original wavefront. The coherent background is necessary for the separation of the 'reconstructed' wavefront from the rest of the field scattered by the hologram.

Taking advantage of rapid developing techniques of coherent light beam deflection, the holographic memory combines the high information storage potential of the photographic plate with the possibility of rapid random access. There are a lot of reasons for considering holography as a means for data storage. These memories are basically read-only type. Its memory can be changed by replacing the storage medium by a new one. Permanent magnet twistor memories operate on the same principle, the information is stored on cards, which have to be removed physically and remagnetized if the information needs changing.

The basic components of the experimental holographic memory include a laser source, a deflection system, a storage medium and an array of photodetector. With respect to the storage of digital data in a read only holography memory, a page-organized memory storing 10^8 bits with access time of $1\,\mu s$ to a single page of 10^4 bits appears feasible. The stored data are recovered at the speed of light with very little decoding computations. Efforts are under way to find suitable materials for read write memories. When random access times in the microsecond range are sought, inertialess beam deflecting techniques such as electro-optic or acoustic-optic effects will have to be used. Materials having these effects can deflect light beam directed to them through a change in their indices of refraction, induced electrically or acoustically.

Typical holography storage plane is a $3'' \times 3''$ photographic plate containing approximately 10,000 individual holograms arranged in a 100×100 array. Each hologram stores 10,000 bits of information, so that the entire plate stores $10,000 \times 10,000$, that is, 100 million bits. The memory is read by directing the laser beam with the X-Y deflector to the appropriate hologram. As it passes through the hologram, the beam is split into a large number of separate beams in a pattern depending on the information stored. These separate beams then illuminate certain diodes in the readout array of 10,000 photodiodes. It is interesting to note, incidentally, that these holograms not only store information but also act as lenses. Each directs the transmitted beam to the single, stationary array of photodetectors. Proposals for associative memory based on holographic techniques have been reported by many workers. However, details of holographic technique will be discussed subsequently.

7.2.1:2 PHOTOGRAPHIC TECHNIQUE

With the introduction of photography it became possible to record and store the information contained in an optical image. Using optical technique, high resolution photographic emulsions can be efficiently used in high density information storage application. The recording densities greater than 10^9 bits per square inch can easily be achieved with various coating methods. The writing methods, which are similar to holographic approach, use diffraction technique.

The term photographic film refers to an emulsion that is a suspension of silver halide crystal in a protective colloid (usually gelatin). Photographic processes involve an interaction of light with certain of the silver halides. Generally for photographic purposes silver halides are considered to be either silver bromide or silver chloride, or silver iodide. When radiation falls on a photographic silver halide film there is a tendency for a decomposing reaction to occur.

When a high level of light is being imaged on a photographic film, some light passes through the film. Some of this is reflected back into the emulsion from the rear surfaces of the emulsion and its support. Some of the light will be refracted, some diffracted, and some reflected as it passes through the film. This will cause the light to spread out or diffuse beyond the image boundaries, resulting in reduced image sharpness.

A very high resolution emulsion is placed in contact with a reflecting surface such as mercury. Parallel incident light waves will pass through the glass plate and emulsion to mercury from which it will be reflected back on itself. The incident waves would normally expose portion of emulsion. In this case, however, the portion of waves reflected back by the mercury will interfere with the incident waves in the emulsion. Now only the areas of the emulsion where the incident and reflected waves reinforce will be exposed. No exposure will take place where the incident and reflected waves cancel each other. For monochromatic light the location of exposed areas will be related to the wavelength of incident light. In effect these exposed areas form a diffraction grating.

Standing waves within the thickness of the photographic emulsion, which is based on Lippmann process, offer another approach toward increasing information storage density. In this process, a panchromatic photographic emulsion is placed in contact with a metallic mirror, and sufficient coherent light passes normally through the emulsion. This standing wave occurs when a light beam exposing the film to store a 1 reflects off the substrate below the emulsion and interferes with itself. In doing so, a periodic layer structure of reduced silver is set up and this has a spacing related to the light's wavelength. Light is marked out of the areas where 0's are stored, so that these spots remain unexposed.

The reflected light can be detected by photodetector. Of the several methods, one uses a dispersive material, such as grating which spatially separates the wavelengths, allowing each bit to be read in parallel. Another method is to use Bragg effect, which causes the reflected light to shift to shorter wavelengths as the angle of incidence increases. The information storage density can be further increased by exposing the same region of emulsion to several wavelengths. Each colour will set up a separate layer structure, provided the grain size is sufficiently small and the reflected light from the emulsion will contain all the original wavelengths. Conceivably 'n' colour sources spaced appropriately over the band of sensitivity could provide 'n' information bits, one per colour, at each location.

In high resolution photographic emulsion, optimization of the readout characteristics of standing wave memory is controlled by proper choice and matching of both exposure and processing. The spot size is controlled or degraded by: (i) the optical purity of crystals, (ii) the diffraction limit due to aperture of the detector and associated optics, (iii) the effective light source collimated. The signal-to-noise ratio at the output of the deflector is affected by the half wave voltages. Since the half wave voltage is a function of wavelength, it may be necessary to use two optical rotator crystals per stage to obtain high signal-to-noise ratio. Although this technique is very suitable for large capacity storage, its application in computer is quite limited. The chemical amplification process is very slow and access to this kind of storage can be cumbersome.

7.2.1.3 PHOTOCHROMIC TECHNIQUE

Effects involving change of states in a material due to the direct interaction between the photons and the material medium have been found useful for optical memory application. Since, in this case beam energy is not converted to heat, some of the limitations of material sensitivity are avoided. Basically both holographic and high resolution photographic techniques can be classified as permanent stores. A beam-alterable optical memory can be constructed by using holography in combination with photochromism. These memories provide still larger storage density since information can be stored three dimensionally as volume instead of area of the medium available for storage.

Photochromism, a characteristic of many organic dyes and other organic compounds such as, alkali halides (potassium chloride, potassium bromide crystals), calcium fluoride, strontium titanate crystals doped with Fe-Mo and Ni-Mo, and a variety of photochromic plastics and glasses, is a reversible change in a compound's absorption spectrum irradiated with specific wavelength of light. This colour change results in an increase or decrease of absorption of other wavelengths which coincides with the read beam wavelength. In general, short wavelength causes the spectrum to shift towards red; longer wavelength shifts it back towards blue. The induced colour change may be erased by illumination with light of a longer wavelength or by heating. This reversible nature of the process will give only temporary storage.

The use of photochromic material for large capacity memories has the advantages of (i) high resolution since these materials are basically grainless (resolution greater than 3000 lines/mm has been demonstrated), and (ii) high angular wavelength sensitivity enabling a large number of holograms to be recorded in the same volume that can be selectively readout by angular rotation of the medium. The memory system using this process can retain stored information without power consumption and the cost per bit is extremely low. The switching speed of photochromic materials is inherently high. The read function in photochromic memory system is performed through CRT illumination of the photochromic memory matrix, with readout by means of an image dissector tube. The write and erase operation can be performed by laser beams of appropriate spectral content, focussed at the photochromic memory plane. The focussed spot can be scanned across the memory matrix by the 2D acoustic scanner as directed by scan control. However, the disadvantages of photochromic media are (i) relatively low sensitivity for writing, (ii) relatively poor thermal stability (for most photochromic media, stored information is rapidly bleached out at temperatures ranging from 50 to 100°C), and (iii) poor spectral response (most photochromic media are only sensitive to one or two primary colours).

7.2.1.4 MAGNETO-OPTIC TECHNIQUE

The basic element of magneto-optic memory consists of a laser source, polarizer and a collimator, magnetic memory matrix, analyzer and a detector as shown in Figure 7.12. The optical read-write technique, when applied to certain magnetic materials, the combination results in a novel approach for reversible storage. The theoretical and experimental magneto-optic characteristics of ferromagnetic films have been investigated extensively. This special interest in the field of magneto-optics is due primarily to its utilization for information retrieval in magnetic domain studies and possible application for optical beam memory system.

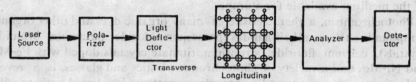

Figure 7.12 Magneto-optic read/write memory system.

The detailed requirements on materials for opto-magnetic recording depends on the particular technique utilized for read, write and erase. However, the fact that the basic physical phenomenon for readout is the magneto-optic effect and for writing-erasing is the thermomagnetic effect, allows us to make a general assessment of the material requirements. Investigations have been made on several magnetic materials and garnet for memory purpose. In evaluating potential materials, the Faraday constant normalized to the absorption is an important guide. The other important factors for thermomagneto-optic memory include coercive force, mechanism of thermal writing, thermal excursion for reading, and efficiency of heating. A compromise of these factors should be made before selecting the proper material for thermomagneto-optic memory application. Light falling on these magnetic materials is efficiently converted into heat through absorption and there are many useful thermomagnetic effects that lead to the desired strong variation of coercivity with temperature. The light beam then acts as gate that allows magnetic switching by a magnetic field only of the illuminated bit. As the thermomagnetic effects are highly nonlinear, only digital recording is considered. Different thermomagnetic effects are used in Curie point, compensation point and thermostrictive recording. In all these methods the switching thereshold is thermal. Therefore, small well defined heat spots are required for successfull operation of memory unit.

Generally manganese-bismuth (Mn-Bi) is used for the magneto-optic memory purpose as it has a very high Faraday rotation. This rotation is about a fraction of a degree per centimetre of the material thickness. Sometimes other ferromagnetic materials are used; such as, Europium Selenide (EuSe) and Europium Oxide (EuO). These materials also have very large Faraday rotations, but their Curie temperatures are very low of the order of $4.2°$ K for EuSe and $60°$ K for EuO, so that they must be operated in a cryogenic environment. Single crystal garnet material (e.g. Gadolinium Iron garnet) is also tried for magneto-optic memories. The total magnetization of this material is attributed to two operating sublattice magnetizations which cancel each other at compensation temperature giving rise to a large coercive force over its normal value.

The writing of information into a magnetic film requires a laser beam focussed onto a small region. This is known as thermomagnetic recording. The use of thermomagnetic effect in a ferromagnetic or ferrimagnetic media was the first approach to be introduced for alterable optical data storage, and has been the most widely studied approach to optical memory. In this case the optical beam energy is used for heating a bit location to a temperature at which magnetization reversal can be affected.

Information retrieval from the film can be made by using magneto-optic Faraday effect. A beam of plane polarized light from a beam deflector passes through the desired region of the film. Because the film is magnetized, it rotates the plane of polarization of the transmitted beam, in one direction for the stored '1', and in another for the stored '0'. If an analyzer has been set to extinguish light from a '0' bit, then a region magnetized the other way will rotate the beam in the opposite direction, so that it is partially transmitted by the analyzer. A photo-detector reads the stored information.

The problem of signal-to-noise ratio arising from magneto-optical signals and shot noise in a photo-detector has been considered by various authors. The analyzer is not necessary if the incident light is polarized at a large angle to the plane of the incidence. In this case the conversion from magneto-optical rotation to amplitude modulation occurs at the reflecting surface. There are other sources of noise, namely (i) surface noise due to imperfections in the magnetic film, and (ii) laser noise. However, these noises can be reduced to some extent by using an aperture stop to eliminate the diffracted depolarized light from the small pinholes, and secondly by using a split-beam dc signal processing in which the signal is additive in the two beams while the noise cancels.

7.2.2 Optoelectronic Memory Devices

Although the batch fabricated semiconductor logic arrays and superconducting circuits such as, cryotrons at liquid temperature bath offer a solution of interconnection problem in high speed logic, they present severe problems in terms of designing for adequate speed, low enough power dissipation, manufacturing yield and complication of organizing logical interconnections on a large array. The alternative approach of realizing arrays of logic circuits which offer faster logic operations, is to use optoelectronic circuits. With the help to solid state light emitting devices, it has become possible to construct a large number of optoelectronic digital logic circuits. Unlike 'all optical' laser devices whose operation is based on the interaction of optical signal with laser materials, optoelectronic circuits require conversions between optical and electrical energies. Much of the interest in optoelectronics stems from its low cost potential which depends on the fact that: (i) individual active and passive circuit elements are not required, and (ii) relatively large and complex arrays may be fabricated using polycrystalline materials and straightforward manufacturing techniques. Moreover, in optoelectronic memories storage elements are completely independent of their detectors. Readout from the memory can be serial, parallel, or by block.

The electroluminescent light source is required to be both fast and efficient. A high speed computer storage element with little present commercial usage is the GaAs tunnel diode using injected luminescence. It possesses both bistability and high switching speed. When it is employed in a circuit as a bistable device, the state of the device is determined either by measuring voltage across the device or the current through it directly; or by applying a stimulus and observing the presence or absence of a switching transient.

The construction of a tristable storage element requires only that a semiconductor tunnel diode be placed with elementary circuit ass hown in Figure 7.13. The values of R_L and V_0 are chosen to permit the circuit to have two stable states. One stable state occurs in the tunnel current region where no observable light is emitted while the other state occurs in a region of detectable light emission. Thus the state of this bistable storage circuit can be determined unambiguously by coupling a suitable photodetector to the circuit. Because of the extremely rapid transient response of both the tunnelling mechanism and the direct recombination mechanism, it is possible to design high speed nondestructive readout (NDRO) storage cells and related circuitry by utilizing this device concept.

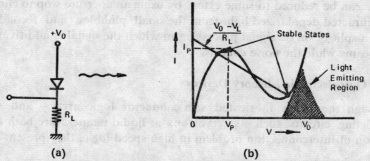

(a)   (b)

Figure 7.13 (a) Bistable storage element; (b) Schematic V-I plot of GaAs tunnel diode.

The availability of visible radiation from electroluminescent arrays provides useful nondestructive readout properties in the memory function. Electroluminescent arrays are sources of broad area diffused light emission. It is, thus, possible to form compact groups of individually controllable light emitting areas, which respond very rapidly to direct electrical excitation. The electroluminescent materials are either crystalline or powder, dispersed in dielectric medium. The resulting light emission is generally termed intrinsic electroluminescence. Both electroluminescent and photoconductive materials have been well developed and lend themselves to fabrication of multicell arrays capable of logic, memory and a number of display functions.

Several types of devices or combinations of devices meet the requirements of an optoelectronic memory. The simple combination unit is the electroluminescent-photoconductor (EL-PC) cell which is connected as a series circuit with optical feedback to establish bistability. Once the EL device begins to emit, its light reduces the PL's resistance, ensuring that the emission continues. In addition, the emitted light indicates the storage cell's state. It is turned 'on' by applying a momentary over-voltage to the series circuit and it is turned 'off' by removing the power. Another version requiring much smaller area is the combination of the silicon integrated flip-flop and a light emitting diode. The silicon IC provides the threshold and storage action. The light emission in this case is solely for external detection and it does not enter into circuit function.

The main problem with regard to EL-PC circuits is their slow response, which is usually attributed to the relatively slow speed of the photoconductor (millisecond to several seconds) in responding to changes in optical excitation. Although some speed advantage can be gained in parallel operation of EL-PC circuit since parallel operation requires PC conductivities which are approximately N times those used in serial circuits (where N is the ratio of parallel fan-out to serial fan-out). The size reduction of an optically coupled EL-PC element will eventually be limited by (i) the minimum PC electrode spacing, given the ratio of allowed electric field to supply voltage, (ii) the amount of light loss through the edge of the EL cell which becomes significant when the EL cell width is less than twice the phosphor thickness. Another consideration in size reduction is the undesired optical coupling between adjacent cells.

The most promising optoelectronic memory element in a single device is the light emitting switch (LES) which contains a layer of semi-insulating material between P and N regions of the P-N diode. The LES structure is well suitable for batch fabricated memory system, since the individual LES element consists of a P region and a N region formed on opposite faces of a high resistivity wafer.

The LES, when properly biased, maintains a steady state with either high or low impedance. In 'on' state, or low impedance state, the LES emits radiation characteristics of the handgap. For gallium arsenide (GaAs) structure, this radiation occurs near 8.800 Å, similar to the GaAs p-n emitter. The LES emits no radiation in high impedance mode, its state can be interrogated by optical output. The data retrieval is optical and hence it is independent of switching electronics. The read part of the memory consists of an image sensor system that can sample each of the storage locations. This can be done serially, in parallel, or in a combination of both. The most important detector system is an array of photodetector elements.

7.2.3 Physical Principle of Magneto-optical Memories

The theory of various *magneto-optic* (M/O) effects that can be utilized to detect the magnetic state of memory is reviewed briefly in this section. The M/O effects result from magnetically induced interactions between electromagnetic waves and the electronic current carriers in matter. At optical frequencies, most ferromagnetic materials appear to be nonmagnetic and are considered to be gyroelectric. The electric field of the light wave is somehow coupled with the uncompensated electron spin moments. This coupling was described by Voigt in 1908 as a tensor dielectric constant. Voigt simply considered M/O effects as equivalent to the well-known Hall effect in materials. In other words, when the optical electric field causes current carriers to move in the presence of a magnetic field the carriers experience a magnetic force normal to their motion and the applied magnetic field, this magnetic force being equivalent to Hall voltage.

When linearly polarized light is either reflected by or transmitted through a magnetized medium it is effected in a way that depends linearly on the direction cosines of the magnetization. In the longitudinal and polar reflection effects and in the Faraday transmission effect, the plane of polarization is rotated; in the transverse reflection effect, the reflectivity changes. Among the three reflection effects, the polar Kerr effect is a few times larger than the longitudinal and transverse ones, but in common with Faraday effect, it requires a magnetization component normal to the surface. This choice is then practical for MnBi due to its very high magneto-crystalline anisotropy and for GdIG due to its very low saturation moment near its compensation point. Between longitudinal and transverse effects, the former is preferred, as the later is a modulation of reflectivity and is thus very susceptible to light source noise.

The high speed, low energy and rotational switching of magnetization vector $\overline{M}$ which is possible with thin films of permalloy is well known, and consequently, considerable work has been done in attempting to use permalloy films for light switches. In a M/O system, the figure of merit f for switch design is given by the ratio of the Faraday rotation F to the absorption coefficient α, i.e., $f = F/\alpha$. The Faraday effect, neglecting absorption, is proportional to thickness of the material and is approximately equal to the polar effect for a very small thickness. Thus, for films of the order of a few hundred angstroms thickness the two effects are equal. This should be taken into account in choosing the optimum material for an M/O memory.

Magneto-optic effects are described through Maxwell's equation by introducing a gyrotropic (skew symmetric) dielectric tensor (ε). To a good approximation, (ε) can be taken as

$$(\varepsilon) \simeq \varepsilon \begin{bmatrix} i & -iq & 0 \\ iq & 1 & 0 \\ 0 & 0 & 1 \end{bmatrix} \tag{2.1}$$

where ε is related to complex index of refraction $n \, (= n' + in'')$ by $\varepsilon = n^2/\mu_0 c^2$ and $q \, (= q' + iq'')$, the complex gyroelectric constant.

The problem of reflection and transmission of light in plane paralleled structures which do not contain gyrotropic media is characterized by two noninteraction polarization modes, namely, modes with the optical electric vector $\bar{E}$ perpendicular ($\perp$) or parallel ($\parallel$) to the incidence plane, respectively. If a gyroelectric medium is present, two different types of interaction can occur: (i) If the magnetization $\bar{M}$ is perpendicular to the light propagating vector $\bar{S}$ (transverse effect), and $E_\parallel$ mode will be amplitude modulated when $\bar{M}$ is reversed in direction while the $E_\perp$ mode will be unaffected. (ii) For any orientation of $\bar{M}$ mode interaction occurs with a transfer of energy from one mode to the other. In the first case the effect is one of impedance modulation, and the resulting light modulation can be optimized by adjusting the impedance mismatch between the incident wave and magnetic material by means of dielectric layers. In the case of mode conversion the effect cannot, in general, be described by means of an impedance which is a constant of the magnetic material. However, in the presence of large isotropic optical absorption, mode conversion is maximized by impedance matching to the isotropic loss.

For light obliquely incident on a boundary, the associated magneto-optic effects are distinguished by the orientation of the magnetization $\bar{M}$ with respect to the plane of incidence defined by incident, reflected, and transmitted light. The Kerr effect is observed in the reflected light, and the Faraday effect in the transmitted light for each orientation of $\bar{M}$, as shown in Figure 7.14.

In order to switch $\bar{M}$ with field of few oersteds, $\bar{M}$ must be in the film plane, since only component $\Delta \bar{M}$ out of the plane must overcome a demagnetizing field $4\pi\Delta M$ ($4\pi M \sim 10^4$ in permalloy). The longitudinal effect ($\bar{M}$ in the film plane, $\bar{S}$ at oblique incidence and coplaner with $\bar{M}$) and the transverse effect ($\bar{M}$ in the film plane and perpendicular to $\bar{S}$) are therefore of interest for possible use as a light switch. The polar effect ($\bar{M}$ perpendicular to the film plane) is not of practical interest.

The problem of maximizing either the M/O signal or modulation is not just a material problem, but also a device compatibility and system problem.

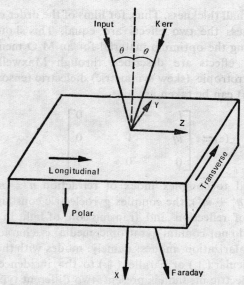

Figure 7.14 Geometo of magnetic-optic effects

Once M/O material is specified, the only variables available for independent variation are the film thickness, angle of incidence, incident index and exit index for a single film structure.

The longitudinal M/O effect is used for reading out random access memories. In longitudinal effect incident light, polarized with $\bar{E}_{\parallel \text{ or } \perp}$ to the plane of incidence, is reflected with a component in the opposite state of polarization. The component of incident and reflected electric fields $\bar{E}_{\parallel}^{i}$ and $\bar{E}_{\parallel}^{r}$ which are parallel to M do not contribute to mode conversion but only dissipate energy by optical absorption. Hence the Kerr coefficient, defined as $k_{\perp, \parallel} = \bar{E}_{\parallel, \perp}^{r} / \bar{E}_{\perp, \parallel}^{i}$ will be maximized if a very thin magnetic film is placed in an optical standing wave at a position such that tangential $\bar{E}_{\parallel} = 0$ (very thin means $D = 2\pi d / \lambda_0 \ll 1/10$, where d is the film thickness and λ_0 the incident wavelength). Once again the condition of $\bar{E}_{\parallel} = 0$ suggests placing the magnetic film on the surface of a highly reflecting metal (a mirror) since then the total tangential $\bar{E} \simeq 0$. A surface with tangential $\bar{E} = 0$ will be called an electric mirror. Calculation then shows that the maximum Kerr coefficient for a very thin film is

$$|k|_{\max} = R \frac{|n|^2 |q|}{I} \qquad (2.2)$$

where R is a constant and I is the electric current. A measure of improvement can be obtained by considering $|k|_{\max}$ for a thick magnetic film or magnetic substrate. For magnetic substrate

$$|k|_{\max} = \frac{\gamma_0 |q|}{2n'} \qquad (2.3)$$

where γ_0 is the direction cosine. The ratio of Kerr coefficients for the two structures, namely, the thin and thick films, is then

$$\frac{\sqrt{3}\,|\,n\,|^2}{4\gamma_0 n''} \qquad (2.4)$$

For $\gamma_0 = 0.87$, this ratio is 2.5 and 1.7 for Fe and permalloy respectively. In order to maximize the value of $|\,k\,|$ it is necessary to match the incident wave to gyrotropic properties of magnetic material.

The reading process uses the longitudinal magnetic Kerr effect as shown in Figure 7.15, in which light wave linearly polarized either ∥ or ⊥ to the plane of incidence, is reflected by the mirror like magnetic film surface. A polarization analyzer is introduced in the path of the reflected beam. Information is inserted into a digit plane by coincidence of half select currents on orthogonal lines. Since illumination is longitudinal to $\overline{M}$, steady illumination will result in an average level of light passing through the analyzer which depends on the information content of the digit plane. This implies that the light on the detector must be scanned. At one extreme only one bit is illuminated at a time and one detector views all bits, and at the other extreme the illumination is complete and only one bit detector is turned on at a time.

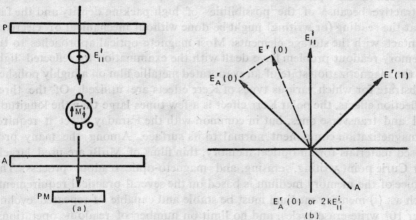

Figure 7.15 Destructive or nondestructive readout signal.

In Figure 7.15 $\overline{M}$ is oriented as in longitudinal effect when the film is in 1 or 0 state, and the analyzer is set to extinction for, say, the 1 state (Figure 7.15 b). When the film is rotationally switched to the 0 state (or the light turned on when in the 0 state), a steady light signal ΔI is generated where

$$\Delta I \simeq 2\,|\,k\,|^2 I_0 \qquad (2.5)$$

The corresponding electron current I_0 at the cathode of the photo-multiplier tube is then

$$I_0 = Q\,\Delta I \qquad (2.6)$$

where Q is the quantum efficiency of the cathode. The electronic noise N at the photo-multiplier cathode is

$$N = (2\Delta f)^{1/2} (I + TQI_0)^{1/2} \qquad (2.7)$$

where Δf is the bandwidth and T is the transmission coefficient of the crossed polarizer-analyzer. For $T \sim 10^{-4}$ or 10^{-6} for polaroid sheet or Nichol prism, respectively, $TQI_0 \ll I$ and the noise becomes

$$N \simeq (2\Delta f I)^{1/2} \qquad (2.8)$$

Hence the signal-to-noise ratio for the cell is

$$\text{Signal/noise} = (I/2 \; \Delta f)^{1/2}$$

$$= 2 \mid k \mid \left(\frac{QI_0}{2\Delta f} \right)^{1/2} \qquad (2.9)$$

which is actually the maximum possible value. Validity of Equation (2.9) depends on the increase in $\mid k \mid$ from 10^{-3} to 2×10^{-2}.

7.2.4 Magneto-optic Read-Write Processes

The idea of an optical readout or of an optical write-in has long been attractive because of the possibilities of high packing density and the fact that the reading (or writing) might be done without mechanical or electrical contact with the storage elements. Most magneto-optical approaches to the memory readout problem have dealt with the examination by reflected light of the magnetization state of an evaporated metallic film on a highly polished substrate for which various types of Kerr effects are utilized. Of the three reflection effects, the polar Kerr effect is a few times large than the longitudinal and transverse ones, but in common with the Faraday effect it requires a magnetization component normal to its surface. Among the many proposed materials for an optical memory, thin films of MnBi are used largely for Curie point writing, erasing, and magneto-optic readout process. The choice of the memory medium is based on the several practical requirements such as: (i) memory medium must be stable and capable of repeated cycling over 10^6 write-erase cycles, and no limit on number of readout operations, (ii) power requirement for basic memory operations must be reasonable, (iii) the packing density should be sufficiently higher than the magnetic disk type memory, and (iv) the medium must be suited for high speed memory operations ($> 10^6$ bits/s) and lastly, the readout signal-to-noise ratio must be suitable. The other medium, namely, the gadolinium iron garnet (GdIG) is also used in memory applications due to its low saturation moment near its compensation point.

The most obvious mechanism of thermal writing is to exceed the Curie point. A small spot on the film is momentarily heated to above the Curie temperature. The magnetization vector of the heated spot after cooling is determined by the combined influence of the demagnetizing field and the applied field. The latter must be smaller than the coercive force of the unheated region. The sources of heating energy can be heated pen, an electron beam or a laser beam. When a laser beam is used, the heated spot size can be made comparable to the laser wavelength, and the rapid heating and cooling results.

There are basically four types of lasers under consideration, namely, gas lasers, solid dielectric lasers, semiconductor lasers and tunable dye lasers. Since the diffraction limited spot size is linearly proportional to the laser wavelength, the use of long wavelength laser will unnecessarily erode the packing density of the memory. Furthermore, long wavelength optical components and detectors are less available than those operating in the visible wavelength. For these reasons, laser of wavelength much longer than 1 μm are considered unsuited for optical memory application. The energy required for heating a bit of volume V is

$$E_T = C_v V \Delta T$$

where C_v is the volume heat capacity and ΔT is the temperature rise required for writing. For most solid materials C_v is in the range of 10^{-2} to 10^{-3} nJ/(μm^3 °C). Besides making the bit dimensions small, it is most desirable to make ΔT small. Most thermally induced recording materials have $\Delta T \sim 100$°C with an effective volume of 1 μm^3. Therefore, the energy required per bit is about 0.1-1.0 nJ. At a 10 M bit/s rate, the laser power required is about 1 mW. Readily available lasers of approximately 10 mW power should be adequate for this to allow for optical losses.

The laser power required to raise a spot on MnBi above the Curie temperature depends upon the spot size, pulse duration, starting temperature, film reflectance, absorption, substrate conductivity, and the crystallographic phases of the film. Power requirements measured in this system are shown in Table 7.3 for room temperature operation of the films having an optical density of two and a reflectance of about 20 per cent. When the film temperature is raised, write power requirement decreases sharply and is almost zero at Curie temperature. The erase field requirement is governed by the demagnetizing field at the boundary between the area above and below the Curie temperature. A typical erase field is about 600 Oe for the normal phase and 300 Oe for the quenched phase.

TABLE 7.3

Laser Writing Requirements

Lens f/stop	Pulse duration	Pulse power (mW)
2	2 μsec	3.0 (0.75)[a]
2	100 nsec	12. 5 (3)[a]
4	2 μsec	11.0 (3)[a]
4	100 nsec	45[b] (11)

[a]Typical quenched phase power requirements are in parentheses.
[b]Estimated.

Another approach of write-erase method is known as compensation temperature technique. In ferrimagnetic materials such as gadolinium iron garnet (GdIG), the two sublattice magnetizations are in opposite directions. At a certain temperature called the *compensation temperature* (T_{comp}), the magnitude of these sublattice magnetizations cancel out each other and the medium attains extremely high coercivity. A few degrees away from this compensation temperature the coercivity drops and the magnetization switching becomes easy. This is the basic mechanism for the compensation point writing technique. By operating the medium at T_{comp}, and applying a magnetic field H_a in coincidence with the laser heating pulse, the heated spot is raised to a temperature at which the applied field is greater than the local coercivity. The magnetization of the heated spot can therefore be switched. Typically in single crystal GdIG, $T_{comp} \simeq 15°C$ which is nearly equal to room temperature, the coercivity is reduced from a few hundred oersted to 50 Oe by a temperature rise of 3°C.

A compensation point memory is shown in Figure 7.16, the information is stored in the magnetization state of small polished section of GdIG mounted on a transparent sheet with a high thermal conductivity. The magnetization in each chip is either parallel or antiparallel to the light path. The chip along with the substrate is placed in a thermostat at its compensation temperature so that the magnetization is stable.

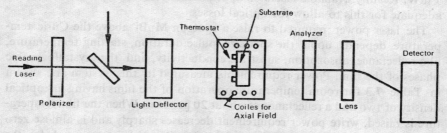

Figure 7.16 Compensation point memory.

Reading of information from the memory is performed by sending a light beam from the reading laser through the light deflection switch. The polarization axis of this beam will be rotated by $\pm \theta$. If the analyzer is set at, say, $90° \pm \theta$, these two alternatives can be readily distinguished from the size of the signal at the detector. Writing of information into the memory is done by directing the light pulse from the heating laser to the appropriate bit and a pulse current is applied to the coils which loop the memory array. The wavelength and power level of this laser have been chosen so that the sample will absorb the radiation and will heat up perhaps a degree above T_{comp}. At this temperature the coercive force is such that the applied field can switch the one heated bit but leave the other undisturbed. Because of the small size of GdIG chip and its good thermal contact with the bath, it cools down rapidly to the bath temperature as soon as the heating laser is no longer directed towards it.

The problem of signal-to-noise ratio arising from the M/O signals and the shot noise in a photodetector tube are of considerable interest to the memory designers. The shot noise is due to average current. Contribution to this current may come from such sources as stray light that bypasses the analyzer. The analyzer is not necessary if the incident light is polarized at a larger angle to the plane of incidence. In this case the conversion from magneto-optical rotation to amplitude modulation occurs at reflecting surface. There are other sources of noise, namely, the surface noise due to imperfections in the magnetic film and the laser noise. The media noise due to pin holes, scratches, dust and graininess of the polycrystallite mirror like metal film is almost impossible to eliminate, because these imperfections lie in the manufacturing and handling processes. It is, therefore, imperative to find means to minimize their effect. However, noise reduction can be done by using spatial filtering technique. By reducing the optical resolution of the viewing system to the minimum required to resolve the information bits, one rejects most of the light scattered by the imperfections. For example, this can be done by an objective lens stop. The improvement in signal-to-noise ratio can be of the order of $(D/d)^2$, where D and d are the dimensionso f the bit and defect respectively.

7.2.5 Physical Principle of Holographic Memory

The aspect of coherent waves which is vital to holography is that two or more intersecting coherent wave trains can form standing wave patterns, that is, if at a particular moment one is able to examine in detail the brightness of light in the intersecting region, a very definite pattern of light and dark areas would be observed. If a photographic plate is placed in the intersecting region and is properly exposed to the standing wave light pattern, the intensity of light pattern can be recorded as the hologram. The term *wavefront reconstruction* refers to a process in which the amplitude and phase of a scattered electromagnetic wavefront is recorded (usually photographically) together with a suitable coherent background in such a way that it is possible to produce at a later time a reproduction of the electromagnetic field distribution of the original wavefront. The coherent background is necessary for the separation of the *reconstructed* wavefront from the rest of the field scattered from the hologram. Although the rigorous electromagnetic theory of scattering, diffraction and polarization is required for an exact treatment of holography, we shall briefly discuss the principles of the process by the method originally introduced by Gabor and later modified by Rogers.

The magnitude and phase of a scattered wavefront can be recorded photographically by superimposing a coherent 'reference beam' or background wave on the field striking the photographic plate. The simplest technique for carrying out this superposition is one illustrated in Figure 7.17, wherein a plane wave illuminates a region containing a scattering object and

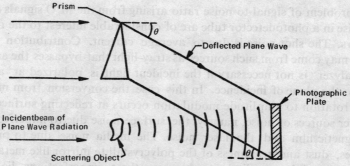

Figure 7.17 Arrangement for recording of holograms.

a plane mirror or simple triangular prism, respectively. The object, of course, diffracts the incident radiation to generate a field with some magnitude $A(x)$ and some phase $\phi(x)$ at the photographic plate, while the prism simply turns the incident plane wave through an angle θ to contribute a field with a uniform magnitude A_0 and a linear phase variation αx, where α is constant relating to angle θ and the wavelength λ according to the relation:

$$\alpha\lambda = 2\pi\theta \tag{2.10}$$

Thus the amplitude striking the plate is

$$A_0 e^{-i\alpha x} + A(x)e^{i\phi(x)} \tag{2.11}$$

Hence the intensity, i.e. the quantity to which the emulsion is sensitive is

$$I(x) = A_0^2 + A(x)^2 - 2A_0A(x)\cos[\alpha x + \phi(x)] \tag{2.12}$$

It will be noted that the phase $\phi(x)$ of the scattered wavefront has not been lost in computing the intensity, as it would be if the reference beam were not present. The emulsion, of course, records some power of intensity, that is, the amplitude transmittance $T(x)$ of the resulting photographic plate, providing one's work in the linear range of the $H-D$ curve, is proportional to

$$T(x) \propto [I(x)]^{-\gamma/2}$$
$$= [A_0^2 + A^2(x) - 2A_0A(x)\cos\{\alpha x + \phi(x)\}]^{-\gamma/2}$$
$$\simeq A_0^{-\gamma-2}[A_0^2 - \tfrac{1}{2}\gamma A(x)^2 + \gamma A_0 A(x)\cos\{\alpha x + \phi(x)\}]$$

This on simplification is given by

$$T(x) = 2A_0^2 - \gamma A(x)^2 + \gamma A_0 A(x)\exp[i\alpha x + i\phi(x)]$$
$$+ \gamma A_0 A(x)\exp[-i\alpha x - i\phi(x)] \tag{2.13}$$

where γ is the slope of the $H-D$ curve. It has been assumed that the intensity of the reference beam greatly exceeds that of the radiation scattered by the object, so that the approximation made in dropping the higher order terms of the binomial expansion is justified. The photograph described by Equation (2.13) is called a hologram after Gabor.

If the object, which is used in the recording process is an opaque plate with a very small hole in it, and is illuminated with a plane wave, then the aperture will act as a simple spherical radiator according to Huygen's principle. Thus the amplitude striking the photographic plate will be of the form

$$A_0 \exp(-i\alpha x) + A \exp\left(i \frac{\pi}{\lambda f} x^2\right) \qquad (2.14)$$

where λ is the wavelength of radiation, and f is defined in Figure 7.18(a). Hence according to formula (2.13) the transmittance of the hologram corresponding to elementary source will be of the form

$$T(x) \propto 2A_0^2 - \gamma A^2 + \gamma A_0 A \exp\left(i \frac{\pi}{\lambda f} x^2 + i\alpha x\right)$$

$$+ \gamma A_0 A \exp\left(-i \frac{\pi}{\lambda f} x^2 - i\alpha x\right) \qquad (2.15)$$

When the hologram, as described by Equation (2.15), is placed in a parallel beam, three distinct components of radiation are generated as shown in Figure 7.18(b). The first component arises from the first two terms of Equation (2.15), which, being constants, uniformly attenuate the incident

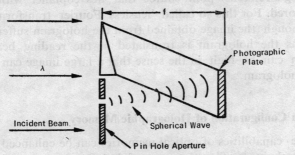

Figure 7.18 (a) Hologram of a pinhole aperture.

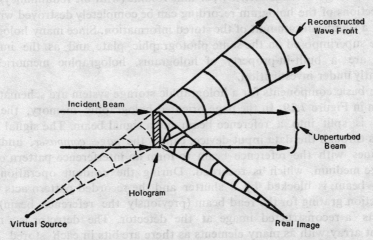

Figure 7.18 (b) Wavefront reconstruction and image formation.

waves producing another parallel beam to the right of the hologram. The third and fourth terms produce two additional components by deflecting the incident waves upward and downward, respectively and by virtue of the linear phase shift in their components. The third term of Equation (2.15) acts not only as an upward deflecting prism, but also as a negative lens on incident radiation, i.e. an incident plane wave will be deflected upward, giving a convex spherical wavefront. This spherical wavefront will, in fact, be identical to one which exposed the hologram. Similarly, the fourth term of Equation (2.15) acts not only as downward deflecting prism, but also a positive lens on incident radiation, and the spherical wavefront will in the normal way come to focus at a distance f from the hologram. Thus, illumination of the hologram with a plane wave not only reconstructs the scattered wavefront, but also obtains as a 'bonus' an image of the object, which in this case is a point source.

The important advantage of holography, particularly in high density storage system, comes from the ability to obtain high magnification of the registration errors. This property is most pronounced when the hologram is recorded using a reference point source that lies coplaner with the object data to be stored. For this so called 'lensless Fourier transform' recording geometry, though the image obtained from the hologram suffers absolutely no motion as the hologram is translated in the reading beam, yet the magnification can be high in the sense that a large image can be obtained from a tiny hologram.

7.2.6 System Configuration of Holographic Memory

The attractive capabilities of optical memories can be enhanced by applying holographic techniques. The advantage of hologram storage device would include a high storage density per unit volume (with bit redundancy) such that sections of the hologram recording can be completely destroyed without losing a significant amount of the stored information. Since many holograms can be superimposed on the same photographic plate and as the imaging optics are a built-in-property of holograms, holographic memories are currently under investigation.

The basic components for a holographic storage system are schematically shown in Figure 7.19. In the page oriented holographic memory, the laser beam is split into a reference beam and a signal beam. The signal beam passes through the data input device, called the *page composer*, and then combines with the reference beam to form an interference pattern on the storage medium, which is recorded. During the readout operation, the signal beam is blocked by a shutter and the recorded pattern acts like a diffraction grating for the read beam (previously the reference beam) and projects a reconstructed image at the detector. The detector is a multi-element array with as many elements as there are bits in each stored page. Therefore, the entire page of the data is immediately available for electronic

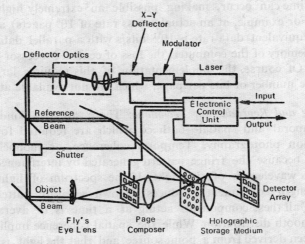

Figure 7.19 Schematic diagram of holographic memory system.

accessing during readout. The optical system is so arranged as to provide coincidence of the reference and signal beams at the storage medium, and the signal beam always fills and pivots about the page composer for all address location. Since each deflected beam location is used to address an entire page, the system speed and capacity can greatly exceed the deflector speed and capacity, whereas in the bit-by-bit system they are the same.

The page composer is used to convert the incoming data to be recorded into a one- or two-dimensional optical object that can be recorded holographically. It is usually considered to be an array of electrically controlled light modulators although the array could also be optically addressed. The page composer is located in the object beam of the two beam holographic systems. During readout, the recording beam is reconstructed and the stream of ones and zeros will be focussed onto the photodetector array.

In experimental holography memory, light from the laser source passes through a pair of deflectors provided for horizontal and vertical scanning. Each deflector is essentially a water-filled transparent container with an ultrasonic transducer. These deflectors operate with the acusto-optic effect using Bragg diffraction. In 1966, Korpel showed that both phase and amplitude distribution of a sound beam is modulated onto a light beam if it travels through some common space with the sound. The mechanism which is active in the transfer of phase and amplitude of information from the sound wave to the light wave is Bragg diffraction of the light off the phase grating which generates sound.

The transducer (read, write, erase, head) for optical recording is the final lens. For a given lens position a large number of bits can be read, recorded or erased, limited by the field of view of the lens. Thus many bits can be accessed simultaneously. In holographic memory, the data are organized in blocks (pages) of 10^4 to 10^5 bits each. Thus parallel transfer of an entire block at a time can occur, making possible an extremely high equivalent data rate. For example, at an actual access rate of 10^6 page(s) and 10^5 bit/page, the equivalent data rate is 10^{11} bits/s with a parallel data transfer to the main memory of the computer, the loss of central processor time will be minimized. Of course, the implementation of this requires large channels equal to the number of bits per page, which are not available at present.

Recording and Reproduction Technique: There are two kinds of coherence— temporal and spatial—both of which are required for wavefront reconstruction photography. Temporal coherence, or monochromaticity, is required because the fringe pattern generated by interference is a function of the wavelength of the light. If the spectrum of light is broad, each wavelength component produces its own separate pattern and the resultant of all these components acting at a time is to average out the fringes to smooth distribution. While the spatial coherence implies that the light has been derived from a point source and that the light is capable of being imaged to small spot or point. If the source lacks spatial coherence then each element of the source produces interference fringes that are displaced from those of other elements. The sum of many such set of fringes averages to some very nearly uniform value.

Recording media reveal their reactions to radiation by changing the complex function which characterizes their transmission. Hence, information may be recorded on the medium by changing the optical absorption, or by changing the optical path length through the material, or both. The recorded interference pattern between a temporally coherent light wave from an object and a reference beam (from the same source) is referred to as hologram, and the density of silver in photography plate can be made linearly proportional to the light intensity in the standing wave. Each hologram, which is about one millimeter in diameter, has a unique address in the array and each can store a block of information which is called a page.

In conventional photography only intensity and wavelength (colour) can be recorded, while in holography the phase of the light reflected or transmitted by an object is recorded in addition to the parameters recorded by conventional photography. For high density optical recording, usually high resolution photographic films or plates are used. Both Kodak and Agfa have prepared these films which provide a linear resolution greater than 2000 line/mm, and a writing sensitivity of about 10^{-4} to 10^{-3} nJ/μm^2. The readout technique from the film is either by intensity modulation from exposed bits or by phase modulation. For high quality hologram dichromated gelatin (DG) films are used. Transparent polymer material is mixed with liquid monomer and catalyst solution to form the film medium. Upon illumination by light (usually in ultraviolet region), cross-links are either formed (negative photoresist) or removed (positive photoresist). Regions where there are no cross-links can be dissolved in the developing process, producing relief phase holograms.

Generally holograms are divided into two categories of 'thin' and 'thick' depending on the ratio of the thickness to the grating spacing. Thin holograms may be reconstructed from any angle and with any wavelength, although the diffraction efficiency will depend on these factors. On the other hand, for a thick hologram the readout process must use the same wavelength and angle as those used during recording. By changing the angle (or the wavelength) during recording, numerous individual holograms can be recorded in the same volume of the material and can then be selectively read.

At places where the signal bearing waves have their greatest amplitude the interference fringes have the greatest contrast whereas at places of low signal wave amplitude the fringe contrast is low. Thus variations in the amplitude of the waves reflected from the object produce corresponding variations in contrast of the recorded fringe pattern.

Again, the spacing of fringes is related to the angle between the signal-bearing wave and the reference wave. At places where the signal-bearing waves make a large angle with the reference waves, the resulting fringe pattern is comparatively fine; at places where the waves meet at a smaller angle the fringe pattern is coarser. Therefore, variation of the phase of the signal-bearing waves produce corresponding variations in the spacing of the fringes on the photographic record. Thus, in brief, we have made two significant observations that both the amplitude and phase of the signal-bearing waves can be preserved respectively as modulation in contrast and spacing of the recorded interference fringes.

In order to record the phase content of light wave, the source must emit temporally coherent light. Hence to make the hologram, it is necessary to use light that has high degree of coherence. It is for this reason that a laser is usually used as the light source for producing a hologram. Electrons at an excited high energy level are made to emit this energy only when they are stimulated. The light emitted from a laser source is essentially monochromatic and therefore temporally coherent.

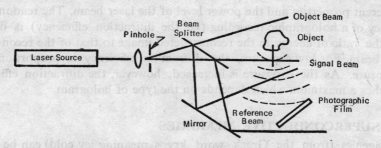

Figure 7.20 Schematic diagram of hologram recording.

The simplest hologram is formed by dividing a parallel (collimated) laser beam into two collimated beams by using a partially reflecting mirror, and causing one half to intersect the other as shown in Figure 7.20. The result-ing standing wave pattern will be simple straight line fringes observed in classical optics. In case of holographic storage array, the process of recording of data mask contains digital information as arrays of pin holes. The data mask represents the contents of a page. Each mask is basically an array of pin holes, blocked for 0's and transparent where 1's are need-ed. This recorded data mask has the property that by the application of an electric signal to the transducer, it generates an ultrasonic wave in water and this wave deflects the laser beam passing through water. The deflector should provide a narrow, collimated beam that can be moved parallel to itself in two dimensions to scan the holograms. When the hologram is addressed by the pair of deflectors, the stored data are projected onto the readout plane. Since the information stored is binary, one should get the presence or absence of light dots in the readout plane. The detectors which transform the light signal to electrical signal are an array solid state photodetectors (phototran-sistors)—one detector for each bit in a page.

The page organized arrangement is essentially for achieving large storage capacities. The reason lies in the inherent limitations of all currently known techniques for high speed light deflection. When random access time in microsecond range is sought, inertialess beam deflection techniques, such as electro-optic or magneto-optic effects, will have to be used. Such deflec-tion can be characterized by speed and capacity. Speed refers to how fast the deflector can move the laser beam from one address to another random-ly selected address, while the capacity is determined by the number of distinct positions that the deflector can produce.

Sometimes nonlinearities and other imperfections in the hologram tend to give rise to ghosts in the reconstructed bit pattern. Periodic structures tend to give ghosts that cause '1's at point where '0's should be. Randomiz-ing the position or phase of the bit pattern reduces these ghosts and increases the dynamic range, or, alternatively, allows a larger number of bits per hologram.

Holographic recording imposes much more stringent requirements both on coherent properties and the power level of the laser beam. The readout effi-ciency of a holographic recording (i.e. the diffraction efficiency) is defined as the ratio of energy in the reconstructed image to that of the reconstruct-ing beam. For low exposure, the diffraction efficiency is proportional to exposure. As the exposure is increased, however, the diffraction efficiency reaches a maximum which depends on the type of hologram.

7.3 SUPERCONDUCTIVE MEMORIES

Cryogenics (from the Greek word kryos, meaning icy cold) can be dated from 1908 when H. Kamerlingh Onnes first liquefied helium. The pheno-menon of superconductivity was discovered three years later by the same Dutch physicist, when he found that there is an abrupt disappearance of resistance in certain elements (such as, mercury) at low temperature. The substances which exhibit this effect are referred to as superconductors. In 1916 Sailsbee observed that the application of magnetic field can cause a superconductive-to-normal transition in a specimen. Sailsbee hypothesized that the superconductive to normal transition caused by a current could be related to the critical magnetic field resulting at some point on the surface of the specimen. Superconductors which follow Sailsbee's hypothesis are called *soft* superconductors; others are called *hard* superconductors. The soft superconductors produce the sharpest transitions and so the computer devices use only soft superconductors. In fact, whether a superconductor is superconducting or resistive depends on the temperature, the magnetic field, and the current. The state of the superconductor may be controlled by either of the above three parameters.

The possibility of using superconducting switch in computer circuits received widespread considerations in the early part of 1960s. Suppercon-ducting devices have been recognized as the only imminent means of econo-mically achieving and evaluating very large capacity data-handling systems with high data processing rates accomplished through use of highly parallel system organization and operation. The basic idea for a superconducting switching element originated with Buck (1956) who invented the cryotron. The essential characteristics of superconducting element that tempted the researchers in using them as memory devices are:

(i) The suppression of superconductivity by a magnetic field, called the *critical field* which is a function of temperature.

(ii) The complete exclusion of external magnetic flux in a supercon-ductor, that is, when external applied magnetic field in a supercon-ductor is less than the critical field, the flux density within the superconductor remains uniformly zero. A sheet of superconducting material can thus provide perfect magnetic shielding.

(iii) The persistence of an induced current in a superconductor. This persistence is an immediate consequence of the disappearance of the detectable resistivity in the material.

These properties of superconductive materials are particularly attractive for computer memories because of the potential low cost per bit stored for memo-ries larger than several million bits. The zero resistance of superconductors permits stored currents to persist indefinitely without any maintenance power. These currents can be used in microminiaturized computer circuits for the permanent storage of information and also in large high field mag-nets. In a typical superconducting or cryoelectric unit, one driver can actuate up to several thousand times as many stage elements as in conven-tional magnetic or semiconductor memories and a single amplifier can sense as many more memory positions. Moreover, cryoelectric principle permits both switching and storing by the same techniques and, therefore, presents a unique possibility. These elements can work very fast with minimum noise. Economic considerations dictate that commercially competitive forms of superconducting memories must have high speed storage with capacities in excess of 10^7 bits and a potential for 10^9 bits capacity. The cost attributable to refrigeration and room temperature electronics becomes relatively independent of storage capacity for very large memories.

For the present discussion we are concerned with the subclass of superconductors that also display diamagnetic behaviour in the superconductive phase. These effects suggest exploitation for both small signal and switching devices. The thin-film-cryotron has received perhaps the greatest attention of a variety of superconducting devices, with the continuous sheet memory a close second for mass memory application. Before proceeding deep into the operations of superconductive memories we shall briefly discuss the physical principles underlying the superconductivity process.

7.3.1 Physics of Superconducting Devices

The microscopic characteristics of superconductor have been the subject of a number of phenomenological treatments. The remarkable properties of superconductors, as well as superfluid flow in liquid helium, are consequences of quantum effects operating on a truly macroscopic scale. The general line of explanation was suggested by Fritz London. The present theories are in accordance with his ideas. The superconducting state has the characteristics of a single quantum state extending throughout the volume. There is a long range order which maintains the value of the momentum constant over large distances in space. As stated by London: "a superconductor is a quantum structure on a macroscopic scale, which is a kind of solidification or condensation of the average momentum distribution", is no doubt a very good description of the present microscopic theory. In fact, London's theory is particularly useful in explaining changes in properties of a superconductor which occur when its dimensions become very small.

The conductivity of metals can be explained by conduction electrons which have an effective mass m, charge e, density n, and an average velocity v. When a metal becomes superconducting, the conduction electrons divide into two parts, namely, superconducting and normal phases. This two-fluid model of superconductivity has been proposed by Gorter and Casmir in 1934. The so-called superelectrons are accelerated in an electric field. The superconducting phase, which has a density of n_s, first appears at critical temperature T_c. The ratio $n_s/n \ll 1$ for temperature close to T_c, and approaches 1 as the temperature approaches to absolute zero.

Considering the force (per unit length) due to an electric field E on an electron in an undisturbed medium, the electrons will be accelerated according to Newton's law

$$F = m \frac{\partial \bar{v}}{\partial t} = e\bar{E} \tag{3.1}$$

The superconducting current density J_s, is given by

$$\bar{J}_s = n_s e \bar{v} \qquad (3.2)$$

Substituting Equation (3.1) into (3.2) we obtain

$$\bar{E} = \frac{m}{e} \frac{\partial \bar{v}}{\partial t} = \frac{m}{n_s e^2} \frac{\partial \bar{J}}{\partial t} \qquad (3.3)$$

The electric field is therefore related to the time derivative of the current density by a constant. Using Maxwell's equation

$$\nabla \times \bar{E} = -\frac{\partial \bar{B}}{\partial t} = \mu_0 \frac{\partial \bar{H}}{\partial t}$$

$\bar{E}$ can be eliminated from Equation (3.3), so that it becomes

$$\frac{m}{n_s e^2 \mu_0} \nabla \times \bar{J}_s = -\dot{\bar{H}} \qquad (3.4)$$

London's theory assumes that any variation of $\bar{B}$ and $\bar{H}$ in a superconductor placed in a uniform magnetic field is caused entirely by induced currents of superconducting electrons and not by any magnetization of the superconductor. Thus

$$\bar{B} = \mu_0 \bar{H}$$

Similarly, J_s can be eliminated from Equation (3.4) by using Maxwell's equation

$$\nabla \times \bar{H} = \bar{J}_s$$

$$\lambda^2 \cdot \nabla \times (\nabla \times \dot{\bar{H}}) = -\dot{\bar{H}} \qquad (3.5)$$

where λ, defined as the *penetration depth*, is

$$\lambda^2 = \frac{m}{n_s e^2 \mu_0}$$

Equation (3.5) can be simplified by using $\nabla \cdot (\nabla \cdot \dot{\bar{H}}) = \nabla(\nabla \cdot \dot{\bar{H}}) - \nabla^2 \dot{\bar{H}}$. Since $\nabla \cdot \dot{\bar{H}} = 0$, Equation (3.5) becomes

$$\dot{\bar{H}} = \lambda^2 \nabla^2 \dot{\bar{H}} \qquad (3.6)$$

Integration of Equation (3.6) gives

$$\bar{H} - \bar{H}_0 = \lambda^2 \nabla^2 (\bar{H} - \bar{H}_0) \qquad (3.7)$$

where $\bar{H}_0$ is the constant of integration and is equal to the initial field in the superconductor. However, from the Meissner effect, we know that the initial field $\bar{H}_0$ must be zero inside a bulk superconductor. Thus, Equation (3.7) becomes

$$\bar{H} = \lambda^2 \nabla^2 \bar{H} \qquad (3.8)$$

The constant of integration of Equation (3.7) is inherently zero. However, Equations (3.7) and (3.8) clearly show that the magnetic field is expelled ($\bar{H}_0 = 0$) and not frozen into superconductor.

The solution of Equation (3.8) for superconductive half space occupying $x \gg 0$ is

$$H = H_0 \exp(-x/\lambda) \tag{3.9}$$

which shows that for $x \gg \lambda$, $H \simeq 0$ in accordance to Meissner effect. H_0 is the applied field at the boundary. The field penetrates with exponential decay into superconducting half space as shown in Figure 7.21. λ is termed the penetration depth in the analogous manner to skin depth. However, unlike skin depth, the penetration depth is independent of frequency.

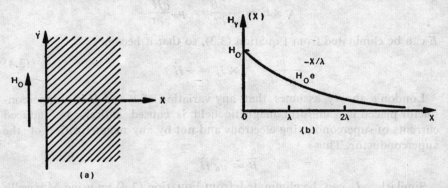

Figure 7.21 (a) A semi-infinite superconducting media with applied field parallel to the surface; (b) Variation of magnetic field inside the superconducting media.

Equation (3.9) shows that the approximation $\bar{B} = \bar{H} = 0$ inside a superconductor can only be used if all dimensions of the superconductor are much greater than λ. If any superconductor is of the order of λ, such as in a thin film, appreciable flux penetration will occur in the presence of magnetic field.

In practice the value of λ as stated in the deduction is slightly smaller than that found by measurement of magnetic moments. The penetration depth is also found to be a function of impurity concentration which also cannot be accounted for by the above stated value of λ. In fact, both the critical field and the penetration depth are functions of temperature. The variation of field with temperature is shown in Figure 7.22. Empirically it was found that the critical field can be closely approximated by the relationship

$$H_c(T) = H_c(0)\left[1 - \left(\frac{T}{T_c}\right)^2\right] \tag{3.10}$$

Using the two fluid model of Gorter-Casimir, the fraction of normal electrons when the material is superconducting is given by

$$\frac{n_n}{n_0} = \left(\frac{T}{T_c}\right)^4 \tag{3.11}$$

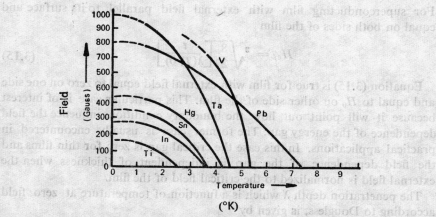

Figure 7.22 Phase portraits of the superconducting boundaries.

Thus the equation for superconducting electrons is

$$\frac{n_s}{n_0} = 1 - \left(\frac{T}{T_c}\right)^4 \tag{3.12}$$

Using the value of λ and Equation (3.12) we obtain

$$\left[\frac{\lambda(T_c)}{\lambda(0)}\right]^2 = \frac{1}{1 - \left(\frac{T}{T_c}\right)^4} \tag{3.13}$$

that is, λ falls from infinity at T_c to $\lambda(0)$ at absolute zero. The quantity $\lambda(0)$ is a constant of the particular material. For tin and lead, λ $(0) \sim 5 \times 10^{-8}$m. This equation agrees reasonably well with the experimental data.

It was shown later that the London Equations (3.8), (3.6) and (3.3) are only exact when the temperature is close to T_c and the field is much weaker than H_c. Nevertheless, Equations (3.8) and (3.6) are sufficiently accurate for most weak-field calculations at any temperature if λ is determined experimentally rather than derived from Equation (3.3). For fields approaching to the critical field H_c, a phenomenological theory has been developed by Ginzberg and Landau (1950).

Critical Field: Ginzberg and Landau theory, is particularly applicable to the calculation of cirtical field of thin films. It is very useful for understanding the behaviour of various factors influencing memory operation and in computing approximate values of the currents required for driving.

Let H_{cf} be the critical field of the film under consideration, t be the film thickness, and H_{cb} be the critical field of the bulk material. According to Dougless, the critical field in the superconducting material for $t/\lambda \ll 1$ will be

$$H_{cf} = \sqrt{24}\left[\frac{\lambda(T,0)}{t}\right] H_{cb} \tag{3.14}$$

For superconducting film with external field parallel to its surface and equal on both sides of the film

$$H_{cf} = \sqrt[3]{\frac{8}{27}} \left[\frac{t}{\lambda(T, 0)} \right] \tag{3.15}$$

Equation (3.15) is true for film with external field equal to zero on one side and equal to H_0 on other side of the film. This particular case is of interest because it will point out how the boundary conditions influence the field dependence of the energy gap. The former case is usually encountered in practical applications. In this case the critical gap is zero for thin films and the field dependence of the gap is independent of thickness when the external field is normalized to the critical field of the film.

The penetration depth λ which is a function of temperature at zero field according to Dougless, is given by

$$\lambda = G(\rho)\lambda_B (0, 0) \left[1 - \left(\frac{T}{T_c} \right)^4 \right]^{-1/2} \tag{3.16}$$

where λ_B is the penetration depth of the bulk material, and $G(\rho)$ is a complicated expression of ρ which is related to Pippard coherence length ξ_0 (which, in turn, is a property of the material) as

$$\rho = 1 + \frac{\xi_0}{t}$$

From Equations (3.14) and (3.15) values may be obtained for the drive currents for film memory and the control currents for switching cryotrons. Strictly speaking, these equations apply only when the thickness of the film and hence ξ_0 is less than λ. Under these conditions, the superconductor will satisfy the local limit ($\xi_0 < \lambda$).

7.3.2 Basic Superconducting Memory Elements

Apart from the general class of superconductors that exhibit zero resistivity at an ambient temperature and magnetic field, there is a subclass of superconductors that also display diamagnetic behaviour in the superconductive phase. These effects suggest exploitation for both small signal and switching devices. The basic idea for a superconducting switching element originated with Buck (1956) who invented cryotron. This consists of a layer of thin niobium wire usually called 'control' wound on to a thicker tantalum 'gate' wire. When the structure is placed in liquid helium, then both the niobium and tantalum wires become superconducting. The magnetic field, due to sufficiently large current in the niobium solenoid wire will restore resistance to that part of the tantalum wire subject to the field. The two materials are chosen because the convenient operating temperature of 4.2°K is only a little below the critical temperature of tantalum, but much lower than that of niobium, so that a control current sufficient to 'open the gate' is still much less than the critical current of the control. The diameter of the gate is further kept large so as to maximize the amount of gate current I_g, which can be controlled by the control current I_c. Calling H_c as the critical field of the tantalum gate at the operating temperature, and D its diameter, we get

$$(I_g)_{max} = H_c \pi D$$

and

$$I_c = \frac{H_c}{n}$$

where n is the number of turns per unit length of control winding. Thus

$$\frac{(I_g)_{max}}{I_c} = n\pi D$$

This is the 'gain' of the cryotron, which must be kept at a value greater than unity in order that the gate current of one cryotron can be used to control the other.

A wide variety of logical circuits can be built up by making use of this reciprocal control of a number of cryotrons. Buck gave a unified and complete treatment of the uses of the cryotron in various logic circuits such as flip-flops, AND, and OR circuits. Figure 7.23 shows an arrangement of

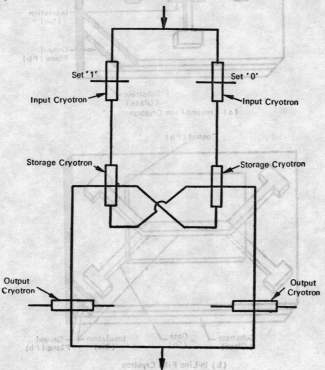

Figure 7.23 Cryotron bistable circuit.

cryotrons for bistable operation. When the input current flows in the left hand branch, it must also flow in the control of the right hand storage cryotron, the gate of which is, therefore, held resistive. Current is then forced to flow in the left hand branch and the condition is stable. The circuit has two stable states with current flowing in one or other of the two branches. To set the circuit to a known state, a control current is passed through one of the input cryotrons, thus forcing the supply current to flow in other branch. The state of the element is sensed by means of output cryotrons, only one of which is resistive.

The film cryotron was later introduced and because of its small dimensions, it increased the operating range in terms of speed. Because of the

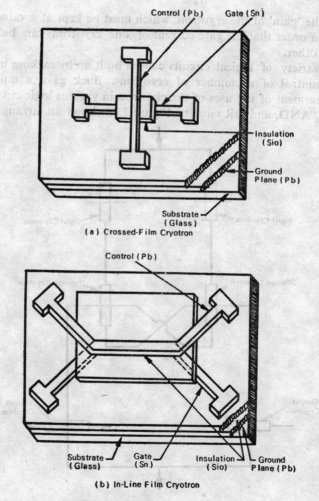

(a) Crossed-Film Cryotron

(b) In-Line Film Cryotron

Figure 7.24 Thin film cryotron

simplicity of the evaporated device, the thin film cryotron can be batch fabricated and is sufficiently attractive to overcome the disadvantage of a low ambient temperature. A thin film cryotron is shown in Figure 7.24, which has two versions—the crossed-film and the in-line cryotrons. The crossed-film cryotron as shown in Figure 7.24(a) consists of a tin gate region sandwiched between and insulated from a diamagnetic lead shield plane beneath and a lead control line above. Lead film also provides electrical connections to the tin gate. Gate resistance can be restored by either a self-current I_g or a control current I_c or a combination of these. The current gain of this structure is a function of the ratio of the widths of the gate and control films and also of the depth to which a magnetic field penetrates a superconductor. The geometry of the thin film cryotron reduces the time constant, and so faster operation is possible than the original wire wound devices. To reduce the time constant still further, the resistance of the gate may be increased by employing an in-line structure as shown in Figure 7.24(b). For other than right angle crossing in thin film cryotron, an assymetry will exist in the gate control current characteristics, since the two fields combine vectorially to determine the net ambient field at the gate. Thus we have two types of cryotrons, one is sensitive only to control current magnitude and the other is polarity sensitive counterpart known as in-line cryotron.

Crossed-film cryotrons display variable current gain by appropriate line width control. The large width to thickness ratio of the shielded films implies the first order dependence of the magnetic field strength on film current

$$H \simeq \frac{1}{W}$$

where W is the film width. In the absence of control current there is a critical gate current I_{cg}, for which the induced field is necessary to restore gate resistance. Conversely, there is a critical control current I_{co}, below which there is

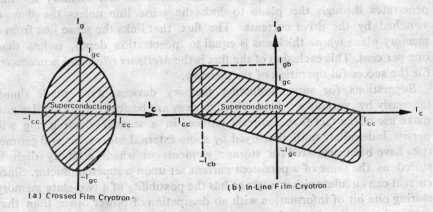

(a) Crossed Film Cryotron

(b) In-Line Film Cryotron

Figure 7.25 Phase diagram for cryotron.

insufficient external field generated to restore gate resistance, in the absence of gate current. The ratio of these currents is the static gain defined as

$$G = \frac{I_{cg}}{I_{cc}}$$

This gain is, in principle, proportional to the ratio of gate and control currents as shown in Figure 7.25. In crossed-film the phase boundary forms an ellipse and the ratio of intercepts, called the large signal gain G, is governed by the ratio of widths of the two strips as stated previously. While in case of in-line cryotron the phase boundary forms a parallelogram. The cryotron is biased to point $-I_{cb}$ for positive current operation. The gain for biased in-line cryotron is, therefore,

$$G = I_{cb}/(I_{cc} - I_{cb})$$

which can be greater than unity.

Under steady state conditions, the power dissipation is zero as long as there is atleast one path which remains superconducting. The speed with which the resistance can be inserted, that is, the speed with which a gate can be made normal, depends on the basic phase transition time and is too small to be a limiting factor. Basically these cryotron circuits consist of parallel superconducting paths between which the current can be switched by the insertion of a resistance into the nondesired branches. The switching time for one current path to another is determined by the ratio L/R, where L is the inductance of the superconducting loop made by the current paths and R the resistance introduced by an opened gate. However, the usefulness of wire wound cryotron is severely limited by the fact that switching time which depends on L/R is comparatively large, even if the gate consists of a tantalum film evaporated onto an insulating cylinder. Although the resistance of the thin film gate is comparable to that of wire gate, but the ground planes confine magnetic flux in a small region and thus results in a lower L/R values lower than the wire-wound cryotrons. In continuous film memory no flux penetrates through the plane to link the sense line unless the phase is switched by the drive currents. The flux that links the sense line from a memory plane whose thickness is equal to penetration depth, is less than one per cent. This exclusion of the flux is the *Meissner effect* and is necessary for the successful operation of the memory.

Suggestions for superconducting memory devices were made simultaneously by various workers. These devices are basically quite similar and make use of the fact that a current induced in a superconducting ring will persist indefinitely until destroyed by some external means. Several geometries have been suggested for storage elements in which a binary digit is stored as the sense of a persistent current set upon a superconductor. Since current can circulate either way one has the possibility of a two-state memory storing one bit of information with no dissipation of power other than that required to maintain the low temperature. Of the various suggestions it is that of Crowe (1957) on which most attention has been concentrated and we will briefly describe it here.

The Crowe cell basically consists of a thin film of superconducting material (with a small hole of a few mm in diameter) which has a narrow cross-bar running across it as shown in Figure 7.26. The cross-bar which traverses the hole is made of tin and acts as the transitional element. All other strips and sheet films are made of lead which always remain super-conducting at the operating fields and temperatures. As long as the entire configuration remains superconducting, the magnetic flux threading the hole must retain its original value which is taken to be zero. The drive currents X and Y perform two functions—(i) they couple a current into the circuit formed by the bridge and the region surrounding the holes, and (ii) their field together with this coupled current causes the bridge to become resistive (normal). This coupled current will decay until an equilibrium point is reached. This equilibrium point is the point at which the current in the bridge is limited to a value at which the bridge is on the brink of being normal with respect to the drive currents. When the X, Y drives are removed, these remain stored as presistent current. The positive drive currents of X and Y results one direction of stored current while the other direction of stored current is obtained by negative drive currents.

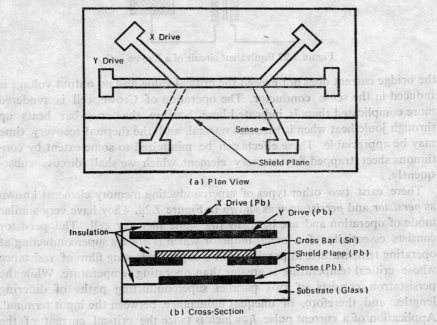

(a) Plan View

(b) Cross-Section

Figure 7.26 Persistent-current storage element.

The equivalent circuit of a Crowe cell is shown is Figure 7.27. When the current I is sent into either of the X, Y drive lines, a current I_s is induced in the cross-bar. When $I_s = I_c$, the cross-bar becomes resistive and heated above its initial temperature very quickly. The cross-bar is then no longer superconducting, and hence I_s decays to zero. During this period a sharp voltage spike is induced in the sense wire. The temperature of the cross-bar cools down to ambient temperature at the rate depending upon the substrate. If I is now switched off, a circulating current I_s will be generated in opposite direction and it will again be quenched as it passess through the critical value.

Readout operation of the cell is destructive. In the superconducting state, the bridge acts as the shield for the sense line as shown in Figure 7.26. When the bridge becomes normal, some energy is coupled into the sense line and a sense pulse is recorded. To write information into the cell, the persistent current must be left in the same sense as it exists at the end of the read pulse. This can be achieved by limiting the effective drive current to half the amplitude required to write 'one' so that the current in the bridge does not exceed the critical value. When a read pulse is applied to a cell storing 'zero',

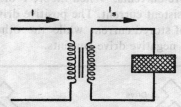

Figure 7.27 Equivalent circuit of a Crowe cell.

the bridge current does not exceed the critical value and no output voltage is induced in the sense conductor. The operation of Crowe cell is rendered more complicated than is indicated here because the cross-bar heats up through joule heat when it becomes normal, and the thermal recovery time may be appreciable. These effects can be minimized to some extent by continuous sheet trapped flux memory element which we shall discuss subsequently.

There exist two other types of superconducting memory elements known as *persistor* and *persistatron* as shown in Figure 7.28. They have very similar mode of operation and are basically the same memory cell. The persistor consists essentially of a metal inductor which is always superconducting at operating temperature, in parallel with a superconducting film of resistance whose critical temperature is greater than operating temperature. While the persistatron consists of two parallel superconducting paths of differing lengths, and therefore, of unequal inductance, between the input terminal. Application of a current pulse I_{in} which is twice the critical current of the film element, causes the current change in resistive element first as they have low inductance compared to other. Since the film becomes resistive above its critical value I_c, any film current above I_c will, however, be diverted to the superconducting inductance. This process takes place with a time constant

L/R, where L is the coil inductance and R the effective resistance of the film. After the switching operation the film current I_f is equal to I_c as shown in Figure 7.28(b).

When the input pulse is terminated, most of the current flows through the film, which again becomes superconducting, and a persistent current, equal to critical current, is left circulating through L and R. A second input pulse of opposite polarity sets up a persistent current which circulates through L and R in the opposite direction.

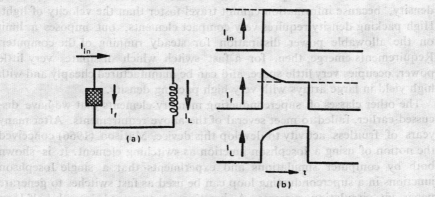

Figure 7.28(a) The persistor; (b) Current waveforms of a
persistor memory cell.

The persistor can therefore be used as a storage element which represents the digits '0' and '1'. The voltage drop, which appears across the film when it becomes resistive, can be utilized to read out the stored information. A relatively large voltage appears across the storage loop whenever the film becomes resistive.

The persistors can be operated in a two dimensional selection array similar to those used in certain magnetic core random access memories. The input current for all presistors in the selection array is uniform, which puts a restriction on the critical current tolerance on the films in such an array.

There are other classes of cryogenic devices based on some other principles and these are principally of academic interest. Some researchers are studying Josephson junction, a sandwich of thin normal layer between two superconductors that behaves somewhat like a tunnel diode. Some people have tried the Ryotron, a variable inductance cryogenic device. The Ryotron is superficially similar to the cryotron but operates on a different principle. The cryotron is a resistance switch and steers current between alternate paths by inserting a small resistance in one path while the other path remains superconducting. The Ryotron is an inductance switch and can route currents between zero resistance paths. The simple cryotron circuit suffers from a fundamental time constant limitation on its speed. The Ryotron circuit avoids this limitation as it operates on the principle of reactive current division.

7.3.3 Josephson Junction Devices

The basic technical reason for searching new devices to use in the computers is the increasing trend towards faster machine of larger capacity, to handle even more complex operations in a reasonable time. Speeds can be limited either by the switching speed of individual elements or by the packing density, because information cannot travel faster than the velocity of light. High packing density requires very compact elements, but imposes a limit on the allowable power dissipation for steady running of the computer. Requirements emerge, then, for a fast switch which dissipates very little power, occupies very little space, and can be manufactured cheaply and with high yield in large arrays with very high packing density.

The other classes of superconducting memory elements that we have discussed earlier, failed to meet several of the above requirements. After many years of fruitless activity to develop this device, Matisoo (1966) conceived the notion of using a Josephson junction as switching element. It is shown both by computer simulations and experiments that a single Josephson junctions in a superconducting loop can be used as fast switches to generate persistent circulating currents. A junction is arranged in each half loop according to known concepts. Only one junction is switched by coincident word and digit fields to generate clockwise or counter-clockwise circulating currents, representing binary information. During switching, the loop circuit is critically damped. The information is read out nondestructively by sensing the magnetic field of the stored and select current with an additional Josephson junction underneath the loop.

Josephson tunnelling junctions have been proposed in 1962 for memory and logic application. A tunnelling effect can be observed between superconductors when the tunnelling barriers become very thin, less than 10 Å or

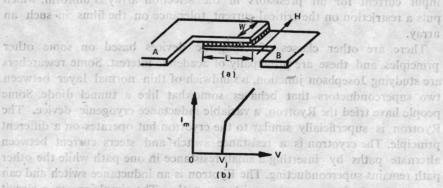

Figure 7.29 (a) Josephson tunnelling structure; (b) Current-voltage characteristic of the structure.

so, provided the magnetic field in the barrier is small (a few gauss or less). This is Josephson tunnelling, which is characterized by the absence of any potential drop across the tunnelling junction for currents less than certain maximum current. The barrier behaves as if, it too, were superconducting and as if both superconductors were now joined to form one continuous superconductor. The most striking characteristic of Josephson effect is the sensitivity of tunnelling supercurrent to small magnetic field.

Typical 'Josephson gate' for computer applications consists of a Josephson tunnel junction over a semiconducting ground plane. Niobium is used for superconducting ground plane and lead alloy films are used for the junction. A Josephson tunnelling element is shown in Figure 7.29(a). Current flows either by superconducting pair or by normal electron tunnelling through an insulator of thickness d between the electrodes A and B. The nature of the current depends on the applied magnetic field H and the voltage V between electrodes A and B. The ideal current voltage characteristic, measured between terminals A and B, is shown in Figure 7.29(b). The voltage is a two valued function of the current at small currents ($I<I_m$); the voltage may be zero or it may be somewhat greater than V_j. The property of this element that makes it useful as a computer device is that maximum zero-voltage current I_m depends on the magnetic field roughly as shown in Figure 7.30. The field H_0 at which I_m vanishes is determined by a remarkable macroscopic quantum effect; H_0 is the field for which the flux through the tunnelling region is equal to one quantum of flux, a quantity defined in terms of fundamental constants by $\phi_0 = h/2q$. The flux is related to the field by

$$\phi = \mu_0 H dL$$

where d is the thickness of the flux containing layer and L the junction length as shown in Figure 7.29(a). The flux is not strictly confined to the insulator, but penetrates a small distance λ into the superconductor and d is 2λ plus the insulator thickness.

If dimension L in Figure 7.29 is large enough, the magnetic field does not penetrate the insulating region uniformly, it is rather localized in region known as vortices. If the applied magnetic field is not homogeneous there

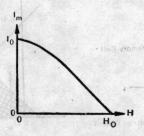

Figure 7.30 Dependence of maximum zero-voltage current
on the magnetic flux through the tunnelling region.

will be energetically preferable positions for a vortex. Variation of the magnetic field by applying currents through additional conductors allows the preferred vortex site, and thus the vortex to be moved. Thus a vortex can be used to represent information, and the information can be moved from places in a fashion somewhat similar to the way that magnetic bubbles are moved. Even in smaller junctions the applied magnetic field does not uniquely determine the vortex structure and the possibilities of different magnetic configurations allow the information to be stored in a single vortex. Currents of few milliamperes are required to change or move the information in these vortex devices, and the energy associated with storage of a bit $\phi_0 I$ is of the order of 3×10^{-18} joule.

The single flux quantum (SFQ) storage element, based on flux shuttle principle can be used in random access memory array. The memory core is simply a Josephson junction. With a large enough L/λ_J ratio to allow stable storage of a flux quantum written, the function can be detected by appropriate means. The advantages of single flux quantum storage cells are simplicity of fabrication and potential for large array densities. Moreover, this memory can be made nonvolatile by shaping the junctions (cells) so that these can hold on SFQ without current or magnetic bias field.

The flux quantization effects occur in Josephson junction when it is driven by a current I_g. The magnetic field associated with the control current I_c induces in the junction an equal current. The combination of I_g and I_c gives rise to junction control characteristic, as shown in Figure 7.31(b). Below the envelope (thick line), the junction is always superconducting if the envelope is approached from below (starting with $I_g = I_c = 0$). Above the envelope the junction is in the voltage state and a voltage equal to the gap voltage exists across the junction. In Figure 7.31(b), the thick line has been extrapolated (dashed line) down to $I_g = 0$. For small dimension and/or low current density junction, the magnetic field produced by the junction current can be neglected. Then the applied field dependence of the Josephson current is a well known Fraunhaffer diffraction pattern. For large current

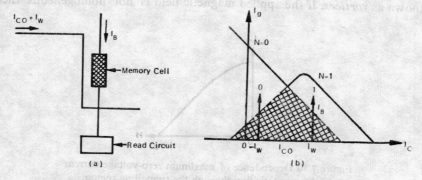

Figure 7.31 (a) Memory operation; (b) Control characteristics.

densities, such that $L/\lambda_j > 1$, the self fields created by the junction current alter the field dependence drastically depending on the L/λ_j ratio. For a very large junction $(L/\lambda_j \gg 1)$ the junction exhibits the Meissner effect, screening the external magnetic field within the Josephson penetration length from the edges by creating circulating currents in the junctions. These are several eigen modes of the long junction and the so-called vortex modes have been analysed by Owen and Scalapind. This adjacent vortex mode has quite large regions of overlap in long (large L/λ_j ratio) junctions.

A cross-section of a Josephson memory is shown is Figure 7.31. It is driven by a bit current I_B and is controlled by a bipolar word current I_W. The shaded region in Figure 7.31(b) represents the overlap region between $N = 0$ and $N = 1$ modes. In $N = 0$ modes the flux in the junction is essentially zero, while in the $N = 1$ mode the junction contains roughly one flux quantum. Writing of 'one' into the cell requires a word current I_W and a bit current I_B so as to cross the $N = 0$ mode boundary, leaving the cell in the $N = 1$ mode. Similarly, in writing 'zero,' a word current of $-I_W$ is sent which leaves the cell in the $N = 0$ mode. The word and bit currents are chosen so that each 'one' individually is unable to make the cell to change state. Both have to be applied in coincidence for writing information into the cell.

Reading of information from the cell requires that both I_W and I_B are to be applied simultaneously. If the cell was in $N = 1$ mode, the operation will leave the state of the cell unchanged and produce no output signal. If, on the other hand, the cell was in $N = 0$ mode, the combination of I_W and and I_B will make the cell to switch to $N = 1$ mode, giving an output signal in the form of a short spike. This signal, which carries the information that a zero was written in the cell travels down the bit line until it reaches the read circuit. Reading of information from the cell is a destructive process so that the cell will have to be reset into its original state after readout. The advantages of these type of memory elements are their obvious simplicity and potential for yielding high packing densities in a memory array, both the advantages stem from the single device cell concept and the fact that readout is done outside the array itself.

7.3.4 Operation of a Superconductive Memory System

It is apparent that a cryoelectronic random access memory, either of discrete-cryotron or of continuous sheet form, has potential applications. The cryoelectronic memory can compete favourably on an economic basis where the storage capacity requirement exceeds 10^7 bits at a one microsecond cycle time. At capacities in excess of 10^8 bits, cryoelectronic memories appear to be the only feasible medium retaining few microsecond cycle time capability at reasonable system cost. These requirements may be translated into necessary capabilities for device fabrication in the light of practical assembly and packaging considerations.

A photomask-photoresist technique is generally adopted for fabrication and this circumvents the several physical limitations encountered in the mask stencil techniques. This approach is conceptually similar to that extensively used in semiconductor fabrication. The basic photomask-photoresist operation consists of transferring the pattern defined in a high contrast photographic transparency (the photomask) to a photosensitive coating (the photoresist) over the material to be patterned. Either the exposed or the unexposed region of this photoresist is then selectively removed (developed) by appropriate reagents. The remaining coating resists the attack of a selective etchant for the material to be patterned. After etching, the photoresist is selectively removed (stripped) from the patterned material with another reagent.

The photomask-photoresist fabrication method has not only provided a means of achieving high resolution circuitry in a practical minimum of material layers but also has permitted a vital breakthrough in low temperature insulation practices. In order to photoetch lead selectively in the presence of prior layers of lead or tin, an etch resistant coating must be applied to the structure as well as to the areas to be retained in the current layer. The method used is to insulate each preceding layer everywhere except at points where electrical contact is to be made from above; it is important to select an insulating material that is also unaffected by subsequent process steps. The highly effective solution is the use of a 'photoresist' itself as the insulator. Photoresistive materials are photosensitive polymers that are self-patternable by virtue of intended photographic exposure and development properties. They also possess excellent surface-wetting and adhesion characteristics and do not thermally stress-relieve under repeated temperature cycling.

The optical system used to transfer the photomask pattern to the photoresist coating may take either of two forms depending on the minimum line width to be resolved. Contact printing is the simplest method and is accomplished by bringing the photomask and resist coated substrate into near contact. Uniform illumination can be achieved by a broad light source. At very smaller dimensions, the small photomask substrate separation can lead to undesirable diffraction effects in the developed photoresist. Projection printing must then be used, with an accompanying requirement for very high quality lenses and filtered sources to avoid aberration effects. Clearly, this photomask-photoresist approach will permit definition of line widths, and therefore, device density and count per substrate, well in excess of those required for commercially interesting applications.

Of the various types of superconductive memory cells that have been proposed, the cryogenic continuous sheet memory cell appears to be most attractive from the point of view of bit density and fabrication requirements. The simple cell geometry consists of two perpendicular drive lines placed above a thin memory storage plane of a soft superconductor, such as, tin. When current pulses are applied to the drive lines, the superconductivity of the memory sheet requires that magnetic flux should not penetrate through the sheet. To satisfy this requirement, currents equal and opposite to the drive currents are induced in the superconducting memory plane which cancel the normal field component of the drive currents. The characteristics of the sheet are selected such that the current density at the intersection of the drive lines is sufficient to quench superconductivity in the local bit area but not along a single drive line.

The value of the drive currents can be estimated from Equation (3.15) since the field is applied to one side only. The drive current is approximately given by

$$I_c = \frac{WH_{ef}}{4\pi} \tag{3.17}$$

Combination of the above equation with Equation (3.15) yield

$$I_{\text{critical}} = \frac{K(T)\,tW}{\lambda(T,\,0)} \tag{3.18}$$

where K is a function of temperature, t film thickness in angstroms, W is the line width in mils and λ is the penetration depth which is a function of temperature and $G(\rho)$. Equation (3.18) for various film thickness for four different line widths is plotted in Figure 7.32(a). The critical current for driving the film depends inversely on the penetration depth. Several factors other than the thickness of the film and the temperature affect λ. One of these is the mean free path. Short mean free path makes λ larger and thus reduces I_c. This is undesirable since the trouble from half select signals completely offsets any advantages obtained from lowering the drive currents by putting impurities into the film.

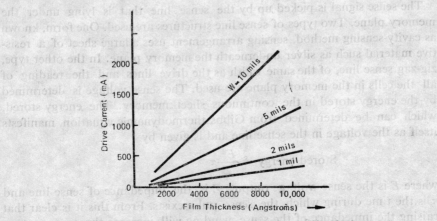

Figure 7.32 (a) Memory drive current as a function of film thickness.

Crossed-film cryotrons are used in the selection trees of film memory. These are simply control films of lead passing over and insulated from a gate film of tin. The magnetic field generated by a current passing through the control film causes the tin film to become resistive and thus the gate film can be switched from the zero resistance condition to the resistive condition. The value of the control current can be determined in the same manner as that of the self-switching current, except that Equation (3.14) is applicable for critical field since the field from the control is applied to both sides of the cryotrons. This is shown in Figure 7.32(b). For faster operation of selection trees, sometimes in-line cryotrons are used, but this places some complications in masking and fabrication processes.

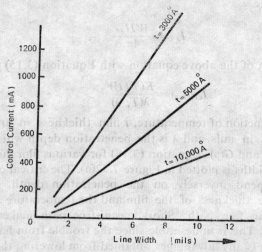

Figure 7.32(b) Control current as a function of line width

The sense signal is picked up by the sense line that is lying under the memory plane. Two types of sense line structures are used. One form, known as cavity-sensing method, sensing arrangement uses a large sheet of a resistive material such as silver underneath the memory plane. In the other type, zig-zag sense line, of the same width as the drive lines and the reading of all the cells in the memory plane are used. The sense voltage is determined by the energy stored in the continuous sheet memory. The energy stored, which can be determined from Gibbs thermodynamic equation, manifests itself as the voltage in the sense line and is given by

$$\text{Stored energy} = \frac{E^2}{Z}\tau$$

where E is the sense voltage output, Z is the impedance of sense line and τ is the time during which the sense pulse exists. From this it is clear that raising the impedance of the sense winding will increase the sense output voltage. For large capacity planes, zig-zag sense line is generally used, although they have a relatively large time delay. Cavity sensing method can also be incorporated provided certain modifications are made to raise their impedance.

7.3.5   Refrigeration

Lastly, we shall add a few words regarding the problem of refrigeration. The reason for cooling an electronic device to very low temperatures is either to perform a function more cheaply than is otherwise possible or to perform a function that is not otherwise possible. It is the first reason that prompts the development of large superconductive computer memories. Cryogenic electronics will be only as useful as the cost and the reliability of the refrigeration permits. The base cost of liquid helium refrigeration will principally determine the lower economic bound on information handling capacity of such system.

Liquids are better refrigerants than either solids or gases because of their combination of fluidity and a condensed state makes them convenient to store and to transfer from vessel to vessel. At very low temperatures, the only liquid substances are those which are gases at room temperature. Heat flows into the bath from the surrounding medium, the temperature of the bath is kept constant since the liquid is always at its boiling temperature. The boiling temperature can be varied by changing the pressure of the gas above the liquid surface.

A closed cycle helium refrigerator is used in superconducting memory system. The two refrigerators must be designed to run for longer periods without significant chance of failure. Typical closed cycle cooling power required at 3.5°K for significant superconducting data processing system will be in excess of a few watts. The heat load stems principally from thermal leakage through the refrigerator walls and along the data link conductors.

References

Magnetic Bubble

Almasi, G.S., Keefe, G.E. and Terlep, K.D. (1972): 'High speed sensing of small bubble domains', *Conf. on Magnetism and magnetic material, AFIP Conf. Proc.*, No. 10, pp. 207-211.

Almasi, George, S. (1973): 'Bubble domain propagation and sensing', *Proc. IEEE.*, V.16, No. 4.

Beausolail, W.F., Brown, D.T. and Phelps, B.E. (1972): 'Magnetic bubble memory organisation', *IBM J. Res. Dev.*, V. 16, No. 6.

Bobeck, A.H., Fischer, R.F. and Perneski, A.J. (1969): 'A new approach to memory and logic cylindrical domain devices', *AFIPS Conf. Proc.*, V. 35, pp. 544-553.

Bobeck, A.H., Fischer, R.F., et al. (1969): 'Application of orthoferrites to domain wall devices', *IEEE Trans. on Magnetics*, V. MAG-5, September, pp. 544-553.

Bobeck, A.H., Danylchuck, J., Rossol, F. and Strauss, W. (1973): 'Evaluation of bubble circuits processed by a single mask level', *IEEE Trans. on Magnetics*, V. MAG-9, No. 3.

Bonyhard, P.I. (1970): 'Application of bubble devices in digital systems,' *IEEE Trans. on Magnetics*, V. 6, No. 4.

Bonyhard, P.I. and Nelson, T.J. (1973): 'Dynamic data—real location in bubble memories', *Bell. Syst. Tech. J.*, V. 52, No. 3, pp. 307.

Bonyhard, P.I., Geusic, J.E., Bobeck, A.H., Chen, Y., Michaelis, P.S. and Smith, J.L. (1973): 'Magnetic bubble memory chip design', *IEEE Trans. on Magnetics*, V. MAG-9, pp. 433-436.

Borrelli, N.F. (1973): 'Magnetic bubble detection using waveguide fiber optics', *J. Appl. Phys.*, V. 44, No. 4.

Bosch, L.J., Downing, R.A., Keefe, G. E., Rosier, L.L. and Terlep, K.D. (1973): '1024 bit bubble memory chip', *IEEE Trans. on Magnetics*, V. MAG-9, pp. 481-484.

Chang, H., Fox, J., Lu, D. and Rosier, L.L. (1972): 'A self-contained magnetic bublbe domain memory chip', *IEEE Trans. on Magnetics*, V. MAG-8, No. 2.

Chen, Y.S. and Nelson, T.J. (1972): 'The effects of spacing between garnet film and permalloy overlay circuit in magnetic bubble devices', *IEEE Trans. on Magnetics*, V. MAG-8, December.

Chen, Y.S. and Nelson T.J. (1973): 'Maximum speed of propagation of magnetic bubbles by permalloy overlay circuits', *J Appl. Phys.*, V. 44, July, pp. 3306-3309.

George, P.K. and Chen, T.T. (1972): 'Magnetostatic potential well and drive fields, in field access bubble domain drive circuits', *Appl. Phys. Lett.*, V. 21, September, pp. 263-264.

Godstein, R.M., Shoji, M. and Copeland, J.A. (1973): 'Bubble forces in cyhudrical magnetic domain system', *J Appl. Phys.*, V. 14, November, pp. 5090-5095.

Graham, R.L. (1970): 'A mathematical study of a model of magnetic domain interactions', *Bell Syst. Tech. J.*, V. 49, No. 8.

Hewitt, B.S., Pierce, R.D., Blank, S.L. and Knight, S. (1973): 'Techniques for controlling the properties of magnetic garnet film', *IEEE Trans. on Magnetics*, V. MAG-9, pp. 366-372.

Ishihora, H., Seki, N. and Watanabe, T. (1974): 'The single conductor and ratch bubble propagating circuit', *IEEE Trans. on Magnetics*, V. MAG-10, No. 3.

Jones, M.E., and Enoch, R.D. (1974): 'An experimental investigation of potential wells and drive fields in bubble domain circuits', *IEEE Trans. on Magnetics*, V. MAG-10, No. 3.

Michaelis, P.C. and Danylchuck, I. (1971): 'Magnetic bubble repertory dialer memory', *IEEE Trans. on Magnetics* (Corresp), V. MAG-7, September, pp. 737-740.

Minnick, R.C., Bailey, P.T., Standfort, R.M. and Semon, W.L. (1972): 'Magnetic bubble logic', *WESCON Proc.*, 8/4.

Orihara, S. and Hirano, A. (1974): 'A study of the bubble stability range in T bar and chevron circuits', *IEEE Trans. on Magnetics*, V. MAG-10, No. 3.

Perneski, A.J. (1969): 'Propagation of cylindrical magnetic domains in orthoferrite', *IEEE Trans. on Magnetics*, V. MAG-5, No. 3.

Rossol, F.C. (1971): 'Stroboscopic observation of cylindrical domain propagation in a 'T-bar structure', *IEEE Trans. on Magnetics*, V. MAG-7, March, pp. 142.

Shirakura, T. and Yoshihiro, S. (1973): 'A conductor permalloy loop bubble domain memory chip', *IEEE Trans. on Magnetic*, V. MAG-9, No. 3.

Thiele, A.A. (1970): 'Theory of static stability of cylindrical domains in uniaxia platelets', *J. Appl. Phys.*, V. 41, March. pp. 1139-1145.

——(1971): 'Device implications of the theory of cylindrical magnetic domains', *Bell Syst. Tech. J.*, V. 50, March, pp. 725-773.

Varnerin, L.J. (1972): 'A perspective of magnetic materials for bubble mass memories', *IEEE Trans. on Magnetics*, V. MAG-8, pp. 329-333.

Optical Memories

Anderson, L.K. (1968): 'Holographic optical memory for bulk data storage', *Bell. Lab. Record*, November, pp. 319.

Anderson, L.K. (1970): 'High capacity holographic optical memories', *Microwaves*, V. 9, March, pp. 62-66.

Anderson, L.K., Brojdo, S., Lamacehia, J.T. and Lin, L.H. (1967): 'A high capacity semipermanent optical memory', Conf. on Laser Engineering and Applications, Washington D.C.

Bray, T.E. (1959): 'An Electro-optical shift register', *IEEE Trans. on Electronic Computers*, V. EC-8, No. 2, June.

Chang, J.T., Dillon, J.F. and Gianola, U.F. (1965): 'Magneto-optical variable memory based upon the properties of a transparent ferrimagnetic garnet and its compensation temperature', *J. Appl. Phys.*, V. 36, pp. 1110-1111.

Chen, D. (1974): 'Magnetic materials for optical recording', *Applied Optics*, V. 13, April, pp. 767.

Chen, D., Hook, J.D. (1975): 'An overview of optical data storage technology', *Proc. IEEE.*, V. 63, No. 8, August.

Clapp, L.C. (1962): 'High speed optical computers', *Proc. Western Joint Comp. Conf.*, May 9-11, pp. 475-489.

Collier, R.J., Lin, L., Burkhasdt, C. (1971): *Optical Holography*. Academic Press, New York.

Collier, R.J. (1967): 'An up-to-date look at holography', *Bell Lab. Record*, V. 45, No. 4, pp. 102.

Cookee-Yarbrough, E.H., Gibbons, P.E. and Iredale, P. (1964): 'Proposed optoelectronic method of achieving very fast digital', *Proc. IEEE* (London), V. 111, No. 10, p. 1641.

Carran, R.K. and Shankoff, T.A. (1970): 'The mechanism of hologram for action in dichromated gelatin', *Appl. Opt.*, V. 9, July, pp. 1651-1657.

DeBouard, D. (1968): 'Feasibility study of a large capacity magnetic film optical memory', *IEEE Journal on Quantum Electronics*, May, pp. 378.

Dorin, G.H. and Weissbein, L. (1963): 'Photochromism discovery', January.

Fan, G.Y. and Greiner, J.H. (1968): 'Low temperature beam addressable memory' *J. Appl. Phys.*, V. 38, February, pp. 18.

Fleisher, H., Pengelly, P., Reynolds, J. Schools, R. and Sineys, G. (1965): 'An optically accessed memory using the Lippman process for information storage optical and electro-optical information processing', MIT Press, p. 1.

Feriser, M.J. (1968) 'A survey of magneto-optic effects', *IEEE Trans. on Magnetics*, V. MAG-4, pp. 152-161.

Gabor, D. (1949): 'Microscopy by reconstruced wavefront', *Proc. Roy. Soc* (London), V. 197, pp. 454.

Goldberg, N. (1967): 'A high density magneto-optic memory', *IEEE Trans. on Magnetics* V. MAG-3, December, pp. 605.

Goodman, J.W. (1971): 'An introduction to the principles and applications of holography', *Proc. IEEE*, V. 59, No. 9.

Hunt, R.P., (1969): 'Magneto-optics, lasers and memory systems', *IEEE Trans. on Magnetics*, V. MAG-5, pp. 700.

Hunt, R.P., Magyary, A.K. and Dickey, B.C. (1970): 'Optical scanning for a magneto-optic memory', *J. Appl. Phys.*, V. 41, pp. 1399.

Leith, E.N. and Upatneiks, J. (1965): 'Photography by laser', *Sci. Am.*, V. 212, June, pp. 29-35.

Lin, C.H. and Beauchamp, H.L. (1970): 'Write-read-erase in situ optical memory using thermoplastic hologram', *Appl. Opt.*, V. 9, September, pp. 2088-2092.

Lissberger, P.H. (1964): 'Modification of the longitudinal kerr megneto-optic effect by dielectric layers', *J. Opt. Soc. Am.*, V. 45, pp. 804.

Loebner, E.E. (1955): 'Optoelectronic devices and network', *Proc. IRE.*, V. 43 pp. 1897-1906.

MacDonald, R.E. and Beek, J.W. (1968): 'Magneto-optical recording', 14th Annual Conf. on Magnetics and Magnetic Materials, Nov. pp. 18-21.

MacDonald, R.E. and Beck, J.W. (1969): 'Magneto-optical recording', *J. Appl. Phys.* V. 40, pp. 1429.

Mayer, L. (1958): 'Curie point writing on magnetic films', *J. Appl. Phys.* V. 29, June, p. 1003.

Mee, C.D. and Fan, G.J. (1967): 'A proposed beam addressable memory', *IEEE Trans. on Magnetics*, V. MAG-3, pp. 72-76.

Mezrich, R.S. (1970): 'Magnetic holography', *Appl. Opt.* V.19, October, pp. 2275-2279.

Miata, J.J. (1960): 'Optical readout of digital magnetic recording', *Proc. Nonlinear Magnetics and Magnetic Amplifier Conf.*, pp. 22-35.

Naiman, M. (1965): 'Content-addressed memory using magneto-resistive readout of magnetic thin film', *Proc. INTERMAG Conf.*, pp. 11, 2-1-11, 2-5.

Neblette, C.B. (1962): *Photography, its materials and processing*. Van Nostrand, New Jersey, pp. 338.

Pennington, K.S. (1965): 'How to make laser holograms', *Microwaves*, V. 4, October, pp. 35-40.

Rajchman, J.A. (1970): 'Promise of optical memories', *J. Appl. Phys.* V. 41, March, pp. 1376-1383.

Rajchman, J.A. (1970): 'An optical read-write mass memory', *Appl. Opt.*, V. 41, October, pp. 2269-2271.

Raffel, J.I. and Crowther, T.S. (1964): 'A proposal for an associative memory using magnetic film', *IEEE Trans. on Electronic Computers* (short notes), V. EC-13, pp. 611.

Reich, A. and Dorion, G.M. (1965): 'Photoc romic high speed large capacity semi-random access memory', Optical and Electro-optical Information Processing, MIT Press, Cambridge, pp. 567.

Riesz, R.P. (1962): 'High speed semiconductor photodiodes', *Rev. Sci. Instr.* V. 33, September, pp. 994.

Rogers, G. (1950): 'Gabor diffraction microscopy: the hologram as a generalized zone plate', *Nature*, V.166, pp. 237.

——(1950-51): 'Artificial hologram and astigmatism', *Proc. Roy. Soc.* (Edinburgh). V. 63 pp. 193.

Shulmen, A.R. (1970): *Optical Data Processing*, John Wiley, New York.

Smith, D.O. (1967): 'Magnetic films in computer memories', *IEEE Trans. on Magnetics*, V. MAG-3, September, pp. 434-452.

Smith, D.O. and Harte, K.J. (1966): 'Content addressed memory using Magneto or Electro optical interrogation', *IEEE Trans. Electronic Computers* (correspondence), V. EC-15. No. 1.

Stroke, G.W. and Labeyrie, A.E. (1966): 'White light reconstruction of holographic image using Lippmann-Bragg diffraction effect', *Phys. Letters*, V. 20, pp. 367-369.

Treves, D., Hunt, R.P. and Dickey, B. (1969): 'A wide band magneto-optic memory system', *IEEE Trans. on Magnetics* V. MAG-5, p. 440.

Treves, D. (1967): 'Magneto-optic detection of high density recording', *J. Appl. Phys.* V. 38, pp. 1192-1196.

Treves, D., Wolf, J.W. and Ballard, N. (1969): 'Temperature sensitive magnetic film for magneto-optic memory', *J. Appl. Phys.*, V. 40, pp. 976.

Tufte, O.N. and Chen, D. (1973): 'Optical techniques for data storage', *IEEE Spectrum*, February.

Urbach, J.C. and Meir, R.W. (1969): 'Properties and limitation of hologram recording materials', *Appl. Opt.* V. 8, pp. 2269.

Van Santen, J.G. (1961): 'The technology and applications of opto-electronic circuit'. *Intern. Solid State Circuits Conf. Digest*, February, pp. 14-15.

Superconductive Memories

Anacker, W. (1969): 'Potential of superconductive Josephson tunnelling technology for ultra-high performance memories and processors', *IEEE Trans. on Magnetics*, V. MAG-5, pp. 968.

Barnard, J.D., Blumberg, R.H. and Casewell, H.L. (1964): 'Operation of the cryogenic continuous film memory cell', *Proc. IEEE*, V. 52, No.10, October.

Basavaih, S. and Broom, R.F. (1975): 'Characteristics of in-line Josephson tunnelling gates', *IEEE Trans. on Magnetics*, V. MAG-11, No.2, March.

Bremer, J.W. (1965): 'Cryoelectric technology' *Proc. 1965 Nat'l Symp. on the Impact of Batch Fabrication on Future Computers*, pp. 27-29.

Bremer. J.W. (1962): *Superconductive Devices*, McGraw-Hill, New York.

Broom, R.R., Jutzi W., et al. (1975): 'A 1.4 mil^2 memory cell with Josephson junction', *IEEE Trans. on Magnetics*, V. MAG-11. No. 2. March.

Burns, L.L. (1964): 'Cryoelectronic memories'. *Proc. IEEE*, V. 52, October, pp. 1164.

Burns, L.L., Christiansen, D.A. and Gange, R.A. (1963): 'A large capacity cryoelectronic memory with cavity sensing', *Proc. 1963 Fall Joint Computer Conf.* pp. 91-99.

Chan, H.W., Lum, W.Y. and Van Duzer, T. (1975): 'High speed switching and logic circuits using Josephson devices', *IEEE Trans. on Magnetics*, V. MAG-11, No. 2. March.

Crane, B.A. and Githens, J.A. (1965): 'Bulk processing in distributed logic memory', *IEEE Trans. on Electronic Computers*, V.EC-14, April, pp. 186.

Crowe, J.W. (1957): 'Trapped flux superconducting memory', *IBM. J. Res. and Dev.*, V. 1, No. 4, October.

Fulton, T.A. (1975): Some aspects of the dynamics of Josephson junction circuits and devices', *IEEE Trans. on Magnetics*, V. MAG-11, No. 2, March.

Greiner, J.H., Basavaih, S. and Ames, I. (1974): 'Fabrication of experimental Josephson tunnelling circuits', *J. Vac. Sci. Tech.*, V. 11, Jan./Feb. pp. 81.

Lynton, E.A. (1962): *Superconductivity*. John Wiley, New York.

Matisoo, J. (1967): 'The tunnelling cryotron—A superconductive logic element based on electron tunnelling', *Proc. IEEE*, V. 55, pp. 172.

——(1967): 'Critical currents and current distribution in Joshephson junctions', *Phys. Rev.* V. 164, pp. 538.

Newhouse, V.L. (1964): *Applied Superconductivity*, John Wiley, New York.

Newhouse, V.L. and Edwards, H.H. (1967): 'Cryotron storage cells for random access memories,' *Radio Electronic Engr.*, V. 33, pp. 161-170.

Pritchard, J.P. Jr. (1966): 'Superconducting thin film technology and applications,' *IEEE Spectrum*, V. 3, pp. 46-54.

Pritchard, J.P., Jr. Pierce, J.T. and Slay, B.G., Jr. (1964): 'Photomask-photoresist techniques for cryotron fabrication', *Proc. IEEE*, V. 52, October, pp.1207-1215.

Shapiro, S. (1963): 'Josephson currents in superconducting tunelling; the effects of microwaves and other observations', *Phys. Rev. Lett.*, V. 11, pp. 80-82.

Young, D.R. (1961): 'Recent developments in high speed superconducting devices', *Brit. J. Appl. Phys.*, V. 12, August, pp. 359-362.

Zappe, H.H. (1974): 'A subnanosecond Josephson tunnelling memory cell with nondestructive readout', *Solid State Physics*, June 10.

8. SPECIAL PURPOSE MEMORIES

8.1 READ ONLY MEMORY (ROM)

Read only memories are not new, although their use in the past has been rather limited. The most common form of ROM is the diode matrix, which has been used since the early days of diode production. Gradually many technologies have been evolved for achieving read only memories. The rapid development of semiconductor ROMs has produced a succession of faster, larger and more flexible devices, which are used in code translation, character generation, microprocessor program storage (microprogrammed control), and look-up tables. Apart from the semiconductor ROM, other types of ROMs include capacitor matrix, inductance matrix, permanent magnet twistor matrix, ferrite core matrix, magnetic film matrix, and so on. Most of these systems are not fast enough to operate with the presently available high speed circuits. The technical limits of capacity of these memories are set by the physical size and electrical delay in the conductors while the main limitation to the use of ROMs is set by the cost.

Both ROMs and RAMs are random access devices. ROMs are well suited to LSI technologies. As the name implies, they are intended to store non-changing information. Although some ROMs can be written in or altered, the write time is relatively long. The primary differences in various ROMs lie in the cell design. They can be logically divided into two types-permanent and semipermanent. A permanent read only memory is fixed by construction so that any necessary change in data require reconstructing at least a part of the storage device. In a semipermanent read only memory, data can be changed by replacing only the changeable data element. The semiconductor ROMs can be constructed by either MOS technology or bipolar technology. The bipolar devices are faster and feature higher drive capability, whereas MOS circuits consume less power and space. The prime advantages of present day ROMs are low cost, low power requirements, fast access and nonvolatility.

This section is divided into three subsections. In the first part the various technologies used to produce read only memories and programmable read only memories are discussed. The second part describes the device from an operational and programming point of view and the last part covers some of the important applications of read only memories. A large number of ROM applications fall into either random access category, or sequential address category. The first category may also be thought of as code translation, while the sequential addressing applications requires a series of codes to be generated in sequence. However, we shall discuss these points in this chapter, the type of ROM that is best in any particular job depends on the specifications and requirements of the job.

8.1.1 Techniques for Implementing ROM Arrays

Semiconductor memories are divided into three broad categories, as shown in Figure 8.1. with two exceptions, each of these generic categories can be implemented with either of the two major technologies MOS and bipolar. These exceptions are the CCDs (charge coupled devices) and EPROM (erasable programmable read only memories), which are uniquely implemented with MOS technology. The various technologies used to produce semiconductor read only memories have been discussed earlier in Chapter 6. In this section a brief discussion of the salient properties of ROM matrices using different techniques have been presented.

A read only memory is an array of selectively open and closed unidirectional contacts. These memories, sometimes called fixed program memories are, however, limited in their applications by the consideration of cost, both for initial cost of a memory, and for the cost of replacing the element. The combination of low cost, high speed, system design flexibility and data non-volatility has made the read only memories an important part of many digital systems in production today.

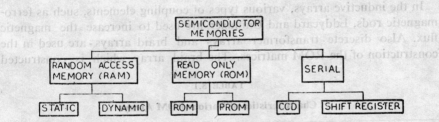

Figure 8.1 Family diagram of semiconductor memory.

The read only memory (ROM), developed in 1951 was initially used in telephone systems in large cities. Gradually many technologies have been employed or suggested for achieving read only memories, each with certain merits and demerits. The various types of ROMs include capacitor matrix, mutual inductance matrix, transformer (Diamond ring) matrix, ferrite core matrix, permanent magnet-twistor matrix and so on. Most of these systems are not fast enough to operate with the presently available high speed integrated circuits. The technical limits of capacity of these memories are set by the physical size and electrical delay in the conductors while the main limitation to the use of ROMs is set by cost.

A large number of resistive, capacitive and inductive coupling elements were proposed in the past twenty years. The principle of most ROM organizations is that at the crosspoint of the drive wires a coupling element is mounted when a '1' is desired, and no coupling element is present in the case of a '0'. The simple resistive coupling element used by the manufacturer provides several benefits. It reduces the complexity of ROM construction, reduces the parasitic signals and it does not require differential sensing of a transient voltage or current pulse. Capacitive and inductive couplings have the advantage that no physical connections need be made at the intersection in the matrix. This simplifies fabrication and makes possible the insertion of data automatically by punching holes in the metal cards. Both capacitive and inductive arrays provide nonerasable type of storage while square loop ferrite core array, permanently magnet twistor and magnetic film arrays offer erasable type of storage.

The capacitor matrix for information storage has been reported by Gatenmakher in 1956. The capacitor matrix is fabricated using the well known printed circuit techniques. The resulting array is a 'sandwich' of two conductor patterns separated by an insulating layer of mylar. The printed card capacitor read-only memory has been used in IBM 360 system. The capacitor arrays are in general more reliable and rugged and can store 10^7 bits at 10 μsec to 10^4 bits at less than 1 μsec. Also the power requirements are extremely low. The fabrication techniques for this type of memories are suited to batch processes that should yield relatively inexpensive stores.

In the inductive arrays, various types of coupling elements, such as ferromagnetic rods, Eddycard and Unifluxer are used to increase the magnetic flux. Also discrete transformer arrays and braid arrays are used in the construction of the ROM matrices. The braid array which is constructed

TABLE 8.1

Characteristics of Various ROM Arrays

ROM arrays	Changeability	Mechanical alignment	Cycle time (μsec)	Output signal (mV)	Access	Bits per storage element	Addressing
Capacitive	Yes	Critical	200	10	Random	1	Linear select
Inductive	Yes	Critical	1	30	Random	1	Linear select
Permanent Magnet Twistor	Yes	Critical	5	4	Random	1	Linear select
Rope	No	Not applicable	6-10	100	Random	Variable	Null decoder

with a loom were developed primarily for spaceborne use, where cost is not as important as speed, density and performance. Moreover, the random access capability of braid memory is definitely valuable for interpreter routines. The advantages of transformer read only store are that, these are simple and inexpensive to build and gives good output signals without requiring much higher word currents. In fact, where speed is not a criterion and the greatest ease in changing the stored information is essential, the transformer read-only store has much to recommend it.

Sometimes, permanent magnet twistor and rope memories are used as ROM arrays. The first category belongs to the class of semipermanent store which is characterized by large capacity, low cost, high reliability and can efficiently be used for program or constant storage where the information content is seldom changed. The twistor is composed of ferromagnetic material and electrical conductors. The twistor derives its name from the fact that it makes use of the effect of torsion on a rod of magnetic material. The rod may be a solid magnetic wire with torsion applied, or a conducting nonmagnetic wire on to which a strain insensitive square loop magnetic tape in the form of thin foil is helically wrapped. While the rope array is a true permanent storage device in the sense that the information contact of the memory is fixed by construction. Any changes in the information content require that the device be rebuilt or exchanged. Usually two types of storage elements can be used in rope memory; bobbin cores and ferrites. Also the rope may be organized in two different ways, namely, 'one-core-output' and 'one-core-per-word'. These memories have been used in a number of computing systems. The rope is essentially a coding switch, and may thus be used to perform logic and table lookup function in a very efficient manner. The main drawback in manufacturing the rope memory is in wiring. However, the application of rope memories in typical supervisory work, information retrieval and association, or in performing logic functions is based on such factors as cost, immunity to environmental noise, speeds, selection techniques and circuit requirements. The different ROM arrays discussed here can be summarized in Table 8.1.

8.1.2 Programmable Read Only Memories (PROM)

The read only memory, like the random access memory, has gone through evolutionary changes in a short period of time. In a just few years, programmable devices have evolved from expensive curiosities used in research to accept common design elements. Innovations in bipolar and MOS technology have resulted in programmable and erasable programmable ROMs, called PROMs and EPROMs respectively. These two types of devices have greatly increased the usefulness and acceptability of read only memories in system applications.

The primary difference in read only memories is in the forming of the open or closed contact; that is, in the design of the cell. In mask programmable read only memories (ROMs) the contact is made by selectively including or excluding a small conducting jumper during the final phase of manufacture. In bipolar programmable read only memories (PROMs) the contact is made with a fusible material such that the contact can later be opened, allowing the data pattern to be configured by the user after the device have been manufactured.

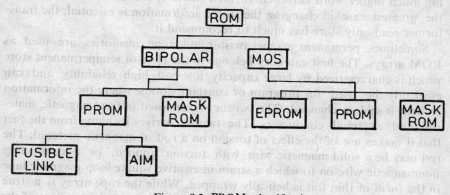

Figure 8.2 PROMs classification.

As discussed in Chapter 6, there are two basic ROM/PROM technologies —bipolar and MOS. Their primary difference is in access time; bipolar access times are approximately 50-90 nsec, and MOS access times are about an order of magnitude higher. Once again these technologies can be sub-divided into mask ROMs and PROMs as shown in Figure 8.2. PROMs are used not only in conventional electronic such as computers and instruments, but also are used increasingly in consumer goods such as cars and ovens. Use of programmable devices is based on the ability to alter a generalized integrated circuit (which can be mass produced) to make it specific to the desired applications. In this section the different technologies have been discussed for the manufacture of programmable ROM devices.

8.1.2.1 ELECTRICALLY PROGRAMMABLE ROMs

Electrically programmable read only memories allow the data pattern to be defined after final packaging rather than when the device is manufactured. Two types of electrically programmable read only memories, commonly called PROMs are available in the market. Basically these PROMs are either Fusible Link (FL) type device or Avalanche Induced Migration (AIM).

Fusible Link devices are completely nonvolatile and once they are programmed, they can not be erased. Continued improvements in fuse technology have resulted in four kinds of fuse material in use today; nichrome, platinum silicide, polycrystalline silicon and titanium tungsten. All four FL technologies are basically similar and are constructed using a cell structure like that shown in Figure 8.3. The fuse material is deposited as a very thin film link to the column lines of the PROM. The memory cell is actually constructed of a transistor switch and the fuse material is as shown in Figure 8.3. The fuses are 'blown' during programming by saturating a bipolar transistor (emitter follower) through selecton of row and column by decoding circuitry. With the cell's transistor base high and the column line near ground, a large current is switched through the transistor and hence through the fuse in the emitter leg. The emitter contact is open circuited by the high current, resulting in the programming of the bit location.

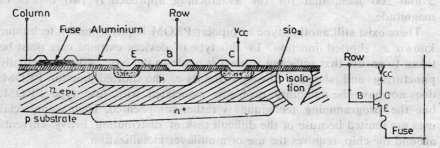

Figure 8.3. Basic cell structure and typical fuse cell.

Of the various fuse materials used in PROM manufacturing techniques, silicon fuses have been preferred by the memory manufacturer, because as the silicon is a standard integrated circuit material, no new contact problems or problems with dissimilar materials are encountered. The thickness of the silicon fuse used in PROMs is nominally 3000 Angstroms, 15 times the thickness of the nichrome fuse. Resistivity of the silicon fuse is controlled by doping, as in standard integrated circuits. Also the 'growback' problem which is associated with nichrome fuse technology does not exist with silicon fuse. As regard the life of the PROM, it has been found that silicon fuses stand maximum number of tests.

The other type of bipolar PROM implementation is the avalanched induced migration (AIM) or shorted junction. The shorted junction cell along with its structure is shown in Figure 8.4. An npn double-diffused

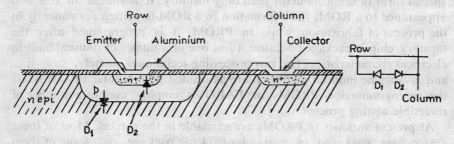

Figure 8.4 Basic cell structure and typical Avalanched induced migration cell.

transistor structure is used, but only the emitter and collector contacts are metallized. As shown in Figure 8.4 the base is left open, thus forming a pair of back to back diodes, D_1 and D_2.

This is based on irreversible process and occurs on the migration of aluminium through silicon to diffused junction. In this cell, D_2 is reverse biased and the heavy flow of electrons in the reverse direction causes aluminium atoms from the emitter contact to migrate through the emitter to the base, causing an emitter-to-base short the avalanching technique requires higher voltage and current than the fuse technique, but the resulting metal migration is a fast process. The fusing time for the nichrome varied between 5 and 200 μsec; that for the avalanching approach is two orders of magnitude.

There exist still another type of bipolar PROM implementation technique known as shorted junction. In this type of devices extreme care must be taken to ensure that sufficient contact is made to the base without actually puncturing and shorting through the base. The shorted junction PROM, does not have the reliability problems associated with fuse type PROM, but the programming technique is rather complicated. Their commercial uses are limited because of the difficult task of distributing heavy currents around the chip, requires the use of multilayer metallization.

8.1.2.2 MASK PROGRAMMABLE ROMs

Fabrication process of integrated circuit devices includes several steps such as, photo masking, etching and diffusing in order to create a pattern of junctions and interconnections across the surface of the wafer with a layer of aluminium, and then to selectively etch away protions of the aluminium, leaving desired interconnecting pattern. In the manufacture of mass programmed ROMs, the row to column contacts are selectively made by the inclusion or exclusion of aluminium connections in the final aluminium etch proces.

8.1.3 Architecture of PROMs

PROMs basically are engineering development aid. The PROM is a special form of semiconductor read only memory. It is similar in size and appearance to a ROM, the information in a ROM is written permanently in the process of fabrication while in PROM, it is programmed after the memory chip is packaged because it has one of a numer of unusual built-in electrical characteristics. The two processing techniques namely, fuse link and avalanche induced migration are associated with bipolar PROM while the reprogrammalbe PROMs or EAROMs employ one of a number of reversible writing process.

At present varieties of PROMs are available in the market. Most of these devices are packaged in a standard 24 pin package, and some of them have a transparent lead to allow erasure. The PROM input is in the form of a binary coded address, five lines for a 32-word device, six lines for 64-words, and so on. when the PROM is addressed, the address is decoded on the chip and the stored word appears at the output. The number of bits in the word depends on the PROM organization.

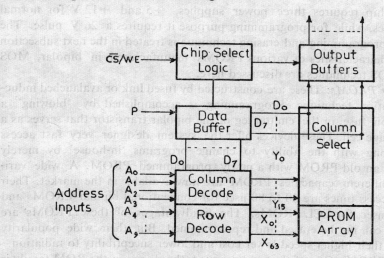

Figure 8.5 Block diagram of PROM (*Courtsey*: Intel Corporation).

The architecture of a PROM is shown in Figure 8.5. These are available in types in which a programmed bit results in a 'high' (logic '1') or in a 'low' (logic '0') level. Some logicians like to think of a PROM as a fixed AND array (the addressing logic), whose outputs feed a programmable OR array (the data). PROM data generally is organized as $N \times M$, where N is the number of addressable words and M is the number of bits per word. Thus 1024×8 PROM has 1024 words, each 8 bit wide and total memory capacity is 8192 bits. Several features such as, integral latches and registers and a 'power down' capability have been included in PROMs to give the designers additional flexibility. The CS/WE connection, serves three functions; at low input voltage (0V), the device is selected for normal read operation; at high input voltage (3 V), the device is deselected and the outputs are placed in the high impedance state, and at an intermediate voltage (~11.5 V) the device is write enabled and ready to receive the program pulses.

The conventional ROM is programmed by altering one of the masks in the fabrication process. PROMs, however, are made with a uniform mask for all chips, thus, bits are initially set to a logic state. The PROM architecture described above corresponds to Intel 2708 device which is a static 8192 bit (1024×8) EPROM. The heart of the 2708 is the single transistor stacked gate cell, consists of a bottom floating gate and a top select gate as shown in Figure 6.27. As there is no electrical connections to the floating gate, erasure is done by non electrical means. Programming, or introducing '0's is accomplished by applying TTL level addresses and TTL level data, $a + 12$ V write enable signal, then sequencing through all addresses consecutively for several times and applying a 26V program pulse at each address.

This chip requires three power supplies, ± 5 and $+12$ V for normal read cycles, while for programming purpose it requires a 26 V pulse. The detailed programming and erasing technique is treated in the next subsection and the characteristics of various PROMs manufactured in bipolar, MOS and MNOS techniques are discussed here.

Bipolar PROMs: These are constructed by fused link or avalanched induced migration technique. Programming is accomplished by 'blowing' a polysilicon fuse in the emitter leg of the bipolar transistor that serves as a data storage cell. These devices offer the system designer very fast access times along with the ability to change programs 'in-house' by merely replacing an old PROM with a newly programmed PROM. A wide varities of different capacities PROM are now available in the market. Their typical access times are 40 to 80 nsec for conventional bipolar PROMs and 15 to 20 nsec, for ECL PROMs. The disadvantages of these PROMs are that they can not be erased and reprogrammed. But their wide popularity is due to their higher speed lower cost and lower suceptibility to radiation.

MOS PROMs: One of the most unique technologies in the ROM family is the erasable PROM (EPROM) which offer system designers maximum flexibility in changing program instructions and so forth in the development of their systems. MOS PROMs were introduced in 1971 and have undergone evolution similar to dynamic RAMs, only at a somewhat slower rate. MOS EPROMs are slower than bipolar PROMs, but they have advantages of reprogrammability and large array sizes. The large arrays correspond to lower package count on production boards and, hence, greater inherent reliability. Like bipolar devices, EPROMs are also available in large varities of bit densities having access times in the range 350 nsec. The unique advantage of MOS EPROMs is that they can be programmed in batches. Bipolar PROMs, which are programmed singly by high current techniques, EPROMs are voltage programmed devices which can be programmed in 'gang' by parallel programming techniques. These EPROMs are now used in various fields—the most important one is their incorporation as an integral part of a microcomputer chip.

MOS PROMs are espacially susceptible to static discharge which can ruin sensitive oxide layers within the device. Hence one should have to take proper care in handling these devices.

MNOS PROMs: In some applications, particularly in evaluating a new system, it is desirable to make changes in the memory content while avoiding the complexity and volatility of read/write memory systems—such as in developing microprocessor system. In this type of applications the programmable ROM (EAPROM) enter the picture.

Another approach to a reversible PROM electrically alters the program using metal-nitride oxide semiconductor (MNOS) technology. These are known as electrically erasable or alterable PROMs (EAPROM) and are in early stages of their development. Compared with floating gate avalanche— injection MOS erasable ROMs, memories using MNOS generally specify faster write and erase time but slower read times. But these are in the early stages of their development. They hold much promise for future designs as their cost, speed and data retention characteristics. Common EAPROM configurations are 32×16, 256×4, 1024×4 and 2048×4. Read access time range from 90 nsec to 10 msec, write times from 1 to 50 msec/word and erase times from 10 to 100 msec/word.

Another type of PROM which belongs to reprogrammed class is known as MAOS PROM. It uses the gate dielectric for charge storage. The dielectric material may be alumina or silicon nitride. This type of memory sometimes called read-mostly memory (RMM) is programmed by the application of a positive or negative gate voltage pulse above a critical polarization level. The application of this type of memory is, however, limited at present day.

8.1.4 Programming Techniques

The PROMs are made with a uniform mask for all chips, thus all bits are initially set in the logic say '1' state. To program a PROM, bit conditions are selectively altered by applying suitable electrical pulses. PROMs are programmed by applying voltages and currents to the device in excess of those encountered in normal operation. This causes a physical change in the programming element. Since the programming element varies among manufacturers, circuit design and programming procedures differ from device to device. Before going into the programming techniques the erasing will be discussed.

Erasing procedure: The standard technique of erasing EPROMs is to illuminate the window with a ultra violet lamp which has a wavelength of 2537 Å. The UV source is placed at a distance of 2-3 cm from the programming element and the radiation is allowed to fall on the element for 10-45 minutes, depending on the type of device and UV source. The total UV energy falling on the window of the programming element is expressed as watt-seconds per sq. cm. Falling of the UV radiation raises the conductivity of silicon dioxide and allows the floating gate charge to leak away. The erasing process is not selective, and results in resetting all cells in the device. It is necessary to check the UV source periodically because the UV source ages with time, its intensity diminishes which means that EPROM left to erase for 'the usual' time may not be completely erased if the UV source is old. Incomplete erasure can cause increased access time or unstable bits. In case of electrically alterable PROM (MNOS PROM) erasing can be performed by applying a reverse gate field which allows the discharge of the interface and thus erases the programmed side. Unlike UV erasable cells an MNOS cell can be erased individually without altering the rest of the array.

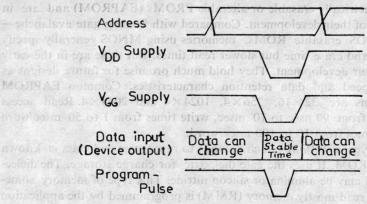

Figure 8.6 Programming waveforms.

Programming procedure: After erasure, all the bits in the memory are in '1' state. Information is introduced by selectively programming '0' into the desired bit locations. The electrical programming of the memory is conceptually the same operation in read mode with exception of the programming voltage pulse. The timing diagram for the program mode is shown in Figure 8.6. The width of the program pulse is from 0.1 to 1.0 msec. There should be N successive loops through all the addresses in the memory. The number of loops (N) required for complete programming is a function of the program pulse width (T_p) according to $N \times T_p > 100$ msec.

Referring to the diagram of Figure 8.5 for Intel 2708 PROM, the word address selection is done by the same decoding circuitry as is used in the read mode. Data to be programmed are presented 8 bits in parallel, to the data output lines of 2708. The chip select $\overline{CS}$/WE input (pin 20) is raised to +12 V for programming. The other logic levels for address and data lines and supply voltages are the same as for the read mode. After the address and date set up, one program pulse (26 V) is applied to the program input (pin 18). Proper care should be taken regarding the end of a program sequence. The $\overline{CS}$/WE falling edge transition must occur before the first address transition when changing from a program to a read cycle.

8.1.5 Applications of ROM

The applications of read-only memories are widespread. They can be programmed to perform a sequence of logic events on a mix of combinational and sequential events. The delay which occurs in large combinational nets are avoided here. The memory is manufactured according to the truth table supplied by users. Read only memories employing one-to-one functional concept can perform as code converters, as logrithmic and trigonometric function generators, and as storage for computer microprograms. Micro-programming also constitutes a growing and particularly important application. The control function in a microcomputer is largely microprogrammed, with the microprogram stored in a separate ROM. ROMs are also used to store fixed user programs. The other important application of ROM is in data terminals with CRT displays. The ROM translates the data transmission code to appropriate CRT beam reflections for character generation.

Semiconductor MOS read-only memories are now an integral part of complex logic functions in control and arithmetic applications because they are electrically and physically compatible with logic ICs and have self-contained decoding and sense circuitry. In old days ROMs were generally treated as subsystem because they require special control and sense circuitries. The system development usually follows six steps, describing the system, designing the architecture, generating the truth tables, generating the logic equations and diagrams, building the hardware, and checking out the system. In these sequences, the input for programming a ROM would be a truth table. Data are loaded in the array by etching away part of the gate oxide of MOSFETs corresponding to 1 bit, so that when they are selected, they begin to conduct and thereby produce a 1 output. In fact the application of ROMs to code converter is really a combinational logic function. Viewed functionally, the memory's input is an address and its output is a word corresponding to the address. In this section some of the important applications of ROM are presented.

In the conventional logic design the standard sum, particularly the least redundant sum, is the starting point for the logic designer. Its result—the minimum sum, is a sum of products, each product is implemented by an AND gate, and their sum by an OR gate. An exactly parallel procedure resulting in a product of sums is also used. The logic implementation by the ROM actually depends on the nature of the coupling element used, that is, for diode or resistor ROM matrix the added operation is a AND while for bipolar transistor with multiple emitters matrix, the logic implemented by each column is positive AND. When inverter is cascaded into each ROM bit line, the overall logic function performed by ROM is positive NAND. With n-channel enhancement type MOS device in coupling element, a negative NAND function is directly obtained.

However, in implementing logic, the minterm is directly programmed into the ROM. This is done directly from the truth table for each of the several functions at once, by passing the minimization process.

8.1.5.1 CODE CONVERSION AND LOGIC IMPLEMENTATION

One of the most obvious and useful applications for read-only memories is in code conversion which is nothing but basically a combinatorial logic function. Combinatorial circuits have no internal storage elements. As a result, the output signals are functions only of the inputs supplied at the time the output is measured (neglecting propagation delays). A ROM may be used to generate combinatorial functions when the number of input signals is not excessive. The ROM system consists of n input lines and m output lines. The input lines consider only the binary systems and are capable of having any of 2^n input combinations. When any such combination appears on the inputs, the output line becomes activated with some particular combination of signals. The logical function of a ROM is thus that of an n input m output decoder. In memory terminology, we would say that it is an $(m \times 2^n)$ bit read-only memory.

The ROM matrix converting all possible combinations of an n bit input code into an m bit output code requires that $n \geqslant m$. From logical point of view we can express the ROM in a Boolean canonical form, which can be implemented by electronic logic elements. For changeability we would have to have $n \times 2^n$ literals and $2^n - 1$ connectives, to be expressed by some implementations with 2^n storage elements at each bit position. It is obvious that a logic approach is not economical since, as a first step towards reduction, we could use a selection tree and drive all m bit locations in a word from a common source.

TABLE 8.2
Code Conversion Truth Table

Inputs				Outputs							
X_3	X_2	X_1	X_0	Y_7	Y_6	Y_5	Y_4	Y_3	Y_2	Y_1	Y_0
0	0	0	0	0	0	0	0	0	0	0	0
0	0	0	1	0	0	0	1	0	0	0	1
0	0	1	0	0	0	1	1	0	0	1	1
0	0	1	1	0	0	1	0	0	0	1	0
0	1	0	0	0	1	1	1	0	1	1	0
0	1	0	1	0	1	1	0	0	1	1	1
0	1	1	0	0	1	0	0	0	1	0	1
0	1	1	1	0	1	0	1	0	1	0	0
1	0	0	0	1	1	1	1	1	1	0	0
1	0	0	1	1	1	1	0	1	1	0	1
1	0	1	0	1	1	0	0	1	1	1	1
1	0	1	1	1	1	0	1	1	1	1	0
1	1	0	0	1	0	0	0	1	0	1	0
1	1	0	1	1	0	0	1	1	0	1	1
1	1	1	0	1	0	1	1	1	0	0	1
1	1	1	1	1	0	1	0	1	0	0	0
Gray or BCD				Gray to BCD				BCD to Gray			

Read only memories lend themselves readily to converting from one binary code to another (such as from binary to Gray). This conversion is particularly useful in electro-mechanical systems controlled by a computer. The problem of code conversion can be solved quickly and easily by writing the two codes in the truth table format. In general, a truth table lists various combinations of a set of input variables, with one or more output functions for each combination; as such, it governs the locations of 1 and 0 bits stored in read-only memories. In these cases, both inputs and outputs are treated on a word basis and the truth table describing the process is simply a listing of two codes.

As an example, consider the case of a Gray to BCD and BCD to Gray code conversion. The truth table shown in Table 8.1 is written by specifying a four input, eight output device programmed according to Table. 8.2. Here the inputs to the ROM are either Gray code or BCD, with the first four outputs (Y_7 through Y_4) gated to the BCD system when the inputs represent Gray code, and second four outputs (Y_3 through Y_0) gated to the Gray system when the inputs are BCD.

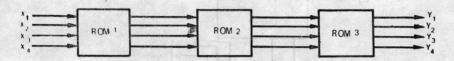

Figure 8.7 Multilevel logic implementation by ROMs.

The conversion from binary to Gray code is only one of the many code conversions possible. ROM/PROMs can be used to encode data for secured data transmission systems. These types of codes can be as simple or as complex as desired. A terminal attached to a central computer can 'talk' to the computer over a secured line if both the terminal and computer have the proper encoding/decoding ROM/PROMs.

For implementing random logic we can use ROMs in cascade connections as shown in Figure 8.7. It permits the input data X_1, X_2,..., etc., to ripple through the cascade of ROMs to provide the desired output functions. Considerable delay time is inherent in the ripple through approach, and we must be careful to avoid the possibility of 'glitches' appearing at the output during the transient. In fact, any static logic circuit with n inputs and m outputs can be replaced by ROM with n inputs and m outputs. This is a powerful feature of ROM and itself permits a host of applications.

8.1.5.2 SEQUENCE GENERATOR

Read-only memories can be programmed to perform a sequence of logic events or a mix of combinational and sequential events. They find wide acceptance in the generation of binary sequences used in controllers, microprogrammers, and data communication systems. In many applications ROM can provide a sixteen word sequence of up to eight bits by either of the two methods—sequential addressing with the use of a binary address counter, or the use of feedback from the ROM output.

Typical sequence generator employing a 16 word, 8 bit ROM unit is shown in Figure 8.8. The address counter which is a simple binary counter, causes each of the 16 words to be addressed in sequence. This technique of generating sequences can be expanded to provide longer, multiple-of-eight word lengths and longer sequences since larger read-only memories are usually required for sequence generation. The code used for each 8 bit word will, of course, depend on the number of different operations to be performed. For example, a 4 input, 8 output device can be designed as a bidirectional one-of-eight sequence generator which provides successive 1's on eight output lines as the count advances. In this system, one of the four inputs is used to control the direction of the sequence while the other three are used to detect the count. The operation of the system is shown in Table 8.3.

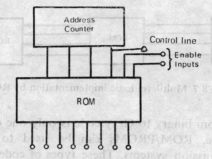

Figure 8.8. Sequence generator.

TABLE 8.3
Truth Table for One-of-Eight Decoder

Input				Output							
Control	Count			Y_0	Y_1	Y_2	Y_3	Y_4	Y_5	Y_6	Y_7
0	0	0	0	1	0	0	0	0	0	0	0
0	0	0	1	0	1	0	0	0	0	0	0
0	0	1	0	0	0	1	0	0	0	0	0
0	0	1	1	0	0	0	1	0	0	0	0
0	1	0	0	0	0	0	0	1	0	0	0
0	1	0	1	0	0	0	0	0	1	0	0
0	1	1	0	0	0	0	0	0	0	1	0
0	1	1	1	0	0	0	0	0	0	0	1
1	0	0	0	0	0	0	0	0	0	0	1
1	0	0	1	0	0	0	0	0	0	1	0
1	0	1	0	0	0	0	0	0	1	0	0
1	0	1	1	0	0	0	0	1	0	0	0
1	1	0	0	0	0	0	1	0	0	0	0
1	1	0	1	0	0	1	0	0	0	0	0
1	1	1	0	0	1	0	0	0	0	0	0
1	1	1	1	1	0	0	0	0	0	0	0

The number of different patterns can be increased by using more of the inputs as control signals. The collection of read-only memories simulates a counter and can be counted either up or down by proper feedback from output to input. Shift registers and other sequential functions could be implemented in this fashion. In typical control application, the output of an ROM is used to gate different logic arrays to perform a variety of functions in data processing systems. They are also very useful in communication applications where the output signals can be used for multiplexing and demultiplexing large number of data channels. A demultiplexer or data distributor using an ROM is shown in Figure 8.9. This routes the input data to one-of-n outputs as directed by the control lines. In this case a single data bus is distributed to one-of-eight data channel according to the binary information received on the three control lines.

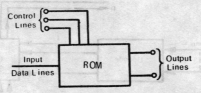

Figure 8.9 A demultiplexer using ROM.

8.1.5.3 Character Generation

Another known important application of ROM is in character generation for alphanumeric display system. This can generally be classified as code conversion in which the inputs to the ROM represent the character to be displayed in some type of binary code, and the outputs, are programmed to actuate the specific visual display mechanism. The digital character generators generally consist of the ROM in which a given input code produces a digital output code for the desired character. Both the input code and the program can vary depending on the particular system in which the ROM is used. There are many character formats which may be coded into the ROM. The characters may be generated by using a dot matrix or an XY-stroke or vector generation scheme. The vector display technique can greatly increase the resolution of the displayed character. Instead of dot, here the image is formed by a series of vectors. A 5×7 dot matrix provides the minimum resolution for display of English alphabets.

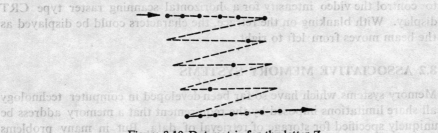

Figure 8.10 Dot matrix for the letter Z.

A typical alphanumeric computer terminal utilizes a cathode ray tube (CRT) as the basic display mechanism, and the ROM is used to convert binary alphanumeric data to its visual equivalent on the basis of the CRT. A fairly common input code is the 6 bit American Standard Code for Information Interchange (ASCII), and the smallest practical matrix size is 5×7. Consider the 5×7 dot matrix to code the letter Z as shown in Figure 8.10. Each dot position represents a light emitting diode and these dot positions would have been coded as binary 1 in the ROM. Similarly, the dark field display points correspond to bits in the ROM coded to binary 0's. The display format shown in Figure 8.11 uses a dot matrix character and a raster with blanked retrace.

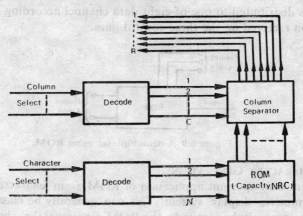

Figure 8.11 A 5×7 dot matrix for character generator.

The dot matrix format is useful for display on billboards, matrix printers, etc., in addition to CRT display terminal. In raster type scan the output from the ROM consists of 7 simultaneous bits which can be used to load control bits into a moving billboard display. A typical logical organization for a MOS ROM with a 5×7 dot matrix output and a 6 bit ASCII input code requires 64×5×7 bit storage capacity. In general, a ROM with C character R rows and N columns per character, will require CRN total storage bits. A common select circuit is used to select one of the five column outputs. The direct output from the character generator with column select is used to control the video intensity for a horizontal scanning raster type CRT display. With blanking on the retrace, the characters could be displayed as the beam moves from left to right.

8.2 ASSOCIATIVE MEMORY SYSTEMS

Memory systems which have so far been developed in computer technology all share limitations imposed by the requirement that a memory address be uniquely specified for storage of retrieval of data. But in many problems these addresses are to be derived from the content of the data points themselves such as in the operations of sorting interpolating and catalog lookup and in more sophisticated applications of information retrieval and pattern recognition. Largely because of the astronomical proportions of the computing task assumed by some real and reasonable problems in these and other areas there has been an increasing interest in the type of memory in which information is stored and retrieved on the basis of content. First work dealing with the concept of associative memory was published by Slade and McMohan in the year 1956. However, numerous implementation problems inherent in the then computing technology limited the applications of associative memory techniques to small and highly specialized systems. Recent advances have made the design of larger and more flexible associative processing systems possible.

8.2.1 Some Definitions

Before proceeding further with this technique, it is appropriate to define the class of systems we are dealing with in this section. An *associative memory* may be defined as a storage device that stores data in a number of cells which can be accessed or loaded on the basis of their contents. An *associative processor* may be defined as an associative memory in which data transformations can be performed on the contents of a number of cells selected according to the contents. Advancing a little further one can define an *associative computer* as a computing system that uses an associative component for storage and/or processing, respectively. It should be understood that most associative memories can be programmed to perform logic and arithmetic operations and can therefore simulate associative processor. Another point to be noted is that while discussing associative memory techniques we exclude array computers and associative devices which are used for performing executive control functions. Associative memory devices have been identified by a variety of names by different authors depending on the salient properties of the devices such as content addressable memory (CAM) (Estrin and Fuller), content addressed memory (Lewin), data addressed memory (Newhouse and Fruin), catalog memory (Slade and McMahon), multiple instantaneous response file (Noe), parallel search memory (Flakoff), distributed logic memory (Lee), and logic-in-memory computer (Stoner). We shall be using the terms associative memory (AM) or content addressable memory (CAM) and associative processor for brevity and consistency to include all the above properties, and an associative device to refer to an associative memory or processor.

8.2.2 Architectural Concepts

There are two fundamentally different concepts of an associative device, depending on the different architectural variations have evolved till now.

The first can be regarded as deterministic in the same manner as a conventional computer memory system where a normal storage address is generated from an examination of the data to be stored. In this version, an item for entry is characterized by as many descriptors as possible and the entry is stored at the intersection of these descriptors. The list of descriptors, if regarded as separate from the data word itself, has been given the name associative criterion by Kiseda and others (1961).

The second conception of an associative memory is concerned almost exclusively with an ability to interpolate between stored data points. This does not imply that exact recall of stored data points are not desired, although this capability is generally compromised. According to this idea, the memory should have the ability to interpolate or extrapolate in a field of statistically related memory entries. At this point we may mention that the biological systems evince both types of memory processes and so they are commonly classified as associative memories. The most important design feature of the biological system is what is termed as *distributed memory*. In general, in a computer memory a particular item is stored in a sharply defined location. But the entries in a biological system are distributed through relatively extended volumes of the neural network, so that even partial extirpation cannot erase a strongly recorded memory trace. The concept of distributed memory has received a great deal of attention in the past few years primarily because of the pioneering work of Rosenblatt (1958) on perceptrons and the researches by Widrow and Adaline. Different algorithms have been suggested for associative addressing in a distributed memory field depending on the architectural requirements of the systems.

8.2.3 Design Concepts

Depending on the application, associative devices can be used in a number of ways in a computer system: (i) as a special purpose peripheral device; (ii) as part of a storage hierarchy; (iii) as a subsystem integrated into a computer system; and (iv) as an autonomous system within a multiprocessor. An associative memory can also be used for performing some executive control functions within a computer system.

Without considering their applications, we can classify the associative devices into six categories: (i) fully parallel word organized; (ii) fully parallel distributed logic; (iii) bit serial; (iv) word serial; (v) byte serial; and (vi) block oriented. These basic methods of organization have been modified and extended to multiaccess capability, hybrid associative memory and read-only associative memory.

Large number of research publications dealing with cryogenic associative memories belong to the category of fully parallel word organized associative devices, because comparison logic must be associated with each bit of memory in such a device. Until recently only exact match operations were proposed to be implemented in fully parallel associative devices. But recent developments in integrated circuit technology have made possible the design of associative processes in which a variety of comparison and arithmetic operations are performed in parallel on each word.

The concept of a distributed logic memory was proposed by Lee. The organization is desirable in dealing with variable length data items. The distributed logic memory is composed of a control unit and a large number of identical memory cells each of which stores one character of information. The cells evaluate the input condition given by the input and the command buses independently and in parallel and depending on the outcome, they will perform or ignore the specific operations. Typical operations are:

(i) Changing of states.
(ii) Transmitting state information to a neighbour.
(iii) Accepting data from the input bus or putting data on the output bus.

Using these commands the distributed logic memory can perform pattern matching operations and is therefore well suited for information retrieval applications.

Shooman (1960) introduced the concept of parallel processing with vertical data which essentially consist of processing one bit of a large number of words in parallel and constitutes the essence of bit-serial systems. This approach represents a compromise between fully parallel and word-serial processing and represents a practically realizable proposal.

When an associative device is viewed as a black box with certain functional capabilities, it is noted that parallel operation on all the words is not essential. As a matter of fact, if the words are operated at a high speed in a serial manner, reasonable speed of operation may be obtained with moderate cost. This is more or less the design philosophy for word-serial associative devices.

For application such as information storage and retrieval, where a large storage capacity is required neither bit-serial nor word-serial systems offer an acceptable solution. As a result several attempts have been made to provide associative capabilities for mass storage. Slotinick proposed a logic-per-track device that consists of a head-per-track disk memory with some logic associated with each track. This system exploits the very high potential data rates of head-per-track disk and is suitable for applications requiring large quantity of random access memory. A system based on combination of Slotinick and Lee's ideas has been proposed by Parhami. It seems that the block-oriented associative processing constitutes the most promising architecture for information storage and retrieval problems.

8.2.4 Hardware Design

In this section the basic functions of associative devices, hardware elements to implement them and their physical characteristics will be discussed. Several good reviews of various implementations techniques have appeared in the literature such as A.G. Hanlon (1966) and B. Parhami (1973).

Regarding basic operations to be performed by an associative device, they largely depend on applications. The simplest search operations are exact match (equality) and its complement (inequality). This operation marks all cells whose contents match (or do not match) the unmasked portion of a key words. Another search operation is similarity or approximate match. A similarity search operation marks all the cells whose contents approximately mismatch in most positions, a specified integer K. Other search operations that are applicable to numerical arguments are as follows (Hanlon, 1966):

Less than	Greater than
Less than or equal to	Greater than or equal to
Maximum value	Minimum value
Between limits	Not between limits
Next higher	Next lower

The other operations that need specific consideration are read, write and arithmetic operations. The read operation is performed as in conventional memories or by enabling a cell directly by a multiple response resolver. The write operation, may be a simple write for modifying a given field of an arbitrary number of cells or multiwrite, which is a very powerful operation used for modifying a given field of an arbitrary number of cells. Arithmetic operations are usually performed as sequences of other basic operations.

Regarding hardware elements for associative devices, Slade and McMahon first presented the idea of using cryogenic or superconductive circuits. But the attention of researchers diverted to other technologies because of the inherent fabrication problems, high refrigeration and maintenance cost of cryogenic devices.

The highly advanced magnetic memory technology resulted in an interest in magnetic associative devices from the beginning. Both discrete and continuous magnetic memory elements have been proposed for the purpose. Considerable work has been done for realizing magnetic associative devices using ferrite cores, transfluxors, biax cores, and multiaperture logic elements. The description of an experimental associative memory using ferrite cores is included in this chapter to introduce the technique of associative devices. Recently, magnetic thin film, and in particular plated wire memories have been popular for realizing bit serial associative devices. Rudolph et al. (1970) reported a plated wire associative memory device that requires 100 to 300 ns/bit for search operations.

The advent of large scale integration (LSI) has resulted in a large number of substantive proposals for solid state associative memories. Wald (1970) reported that MOS associative memories may be constructed with a cycle time of 300 ns for read, write and equality search operations. The advantages of solid state associative devices worth mentioning are: (i) high signal-to-noise ratio allows long associative memory words; (ii) the equivalence of input and output energy levels minimizes cross-talk problems; (iii) the input energy requirement can be made very small; (iv) output signals are compatible with external logic; and (v) components with loose tolerances can be used.

Associative memory and content addressable memory that we have discussed so for are essentially single function memories, that is, they search only for those words that exactly match the compared ones. Addition of a few more features produce even more useful associative memory design. Such additional devices are the response resolver, response store, and the mask register as shown in Figure 8.12. The response store, the sense amplifiers and match/mismatch register are common to all words in the memory. The response resolver contains some additional circuitry that scan the states of the flip-flops in the match/mismatch register at the end of a search operation to produce the desired results. These might include a count of the number of matches or mismatches instead of a mere indication of them. The mask register permits a search to be performed only on selected bits in the comparand, not the whole comparand. With the mask register the programmer defines which fields or portions of the comparand he wishes to use in the search, or a search could locate all words whose number value is greater than the comparand or less than it.

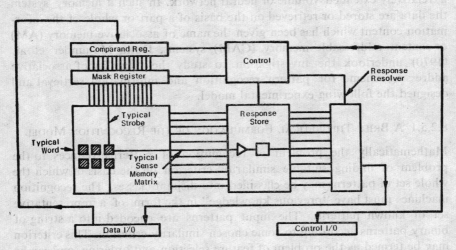

Figure 8.12 Basic associative memory contains an array of storage elements, a comparand register, a response store and a mask register.

In the following subsections we shall describe some experimental hardware realizations of (a) associative memory devices using ferrite cores for application in pattern recognition and information retrieval problems,

(b) integrated circuit content addressable memory devices, (c) a crossed-film cryotron (CFC) catalog memory, and (d) principles of associative memory system using holography.

8.2.5 An Experimental Associative Memory for Pattern Recognition and Information Retrieval Problems

There has been a considerable growth of interest in problems of pattern recognition and machine learning in general and speech recognition in particular. This has created an increasing need for search of suitable methods and techniques. Several different approaches have been proposed. Uptil now it seems that one of the most promising techniques for the solution of problems in pattern recognition and machine learning is the statistical theory of decision and estimation. In all such methods the use of a digital computing system is inevitable, because of the largeness of data and the inherent complications of the recognition procedures. Different systems and models have so far been suggested by several authors such as Forgie and Forgie (1959), Halle and Stevenson (1962). A significant development in this line of research in recent times is that both from the computation point of view and from the learning point of view attention has been diverted towards biological systems. Unlike the conventional digital computer memory where the data are stored in sharply defined locations, entries in the memory organization in biological system is distributed through a relatively extended volume of neural network. In such a memory system the data are stored or retrieved on the basis of a part or whole of the information content which has been given the name of associative memory (AM) or content addressable memory (CAM) systems. Dutta Majumder et al. (1970) undertook the investigation to study the suitability of associative addressing scheme for pattern recognition and information rertieval and designed the following experimental model.

8.2.5.1 A Brief Theoretical Formulation of the Recognition Model

Mathematically the problem of recognition of patterns reduces to the problem of finding suitable similarity criterion on the basis of which the whole set of patterns may be classified into disjoint classes. The recognition machines must have "previous knowledge" in the form of a representative set of known patterns. The input patterns are encoded into a string of binary patterns according to some chosen similarity criterion. This criterion may be termed as the problem of feature selection and ordering, and can be achieved by several methods such as minimization of the distance between matrix of the input pattern from the representative set, or likelihood ratio test, probability ratio test, etc.

Let us suppose that each input pattern has n different characteristics, the value of the ith characteristic can be expressed as K_i binary digits. If we consider an N-dimensional space, where,

$$N = \sum_{i}^{n} K_i \qquad (2.1)$$

then each measurement of the input pattern will correspond to a corner of the N-dimensional hypercube.

In the pattern recognition problems the measurement space M is considered as an N-dimensional space of binary valued functions f_1, $f_2 \dots f_n$ each of the functions being the time domain analysis of different recognition parameters. It can be shown (Sebystyn, 1956) that this input space may best be divided into θ regions, such as R_1, $R_2, \dots R_\theta$, where θ is the total number of distinct patterns, defined by the inequality

$$R_r: P_r \phi_r \geqslant P_s \phi_s, \text{ where } s \neq r \qquad (2.2)$$

and

$$r, s = (1, 2 \dots, \theta)$$

where P_r and ϕ_r are respectively the apriori probability and the probability density function of rth group. The decision boundary between regions in M associated with rth and sth group is

$$P_r \phi_r - P_s \phi_s = 0 \qquad (2.3)$$

This equation can be rewritten as

$$\log \frac{P_r}{\phi_s} - \log \frac{P_s}{\phi_r} = 0 \qquad (2.4)$$

which represents a hypersurface in the N-dimensional space M. In case of say speech pattern recognition the probability density functions for acoustical parameters may be taken as multivariate normals with equal variances (King and Tunis, 1900).

Let

$$\phi_r = [(2\pi)^{N/2} \mid \lambda_r \mid^{1/2}]^{-1} e^{-y^2} (f - \mu_r)^t \lambda_r^{-1} (f - \mu_r) \qquad (2.5)$$

where μ_r is the mean vector and λ_r is the dispersion matrix. From this the density function equation yields:

$$\log \frac{P_r}{P_s} - \frac{1}{2} \log \frac{\mid \lambda_r \mid}{\mid \lambda_s \mid} - \frac{1}{2} [(f - \mu_r)^t \lambda_r^{-1} (f - \mu_r) - (f - \mu_s)^t \lambda_s^{-1} (f - \mu_s)]$$

$$\qquad (2.6)$$

which represents a hyperquadratic equation.

If

$$\lambda_r = \lambda_s = \lambda$$

Equation (2.6) reduces to

$$f_t \lambda^{-1} (\mu_r - \mu_s) - \frac{1}{2} (\mu_r + \mu_s) \lambda^{-1} (\mu_r - \mu_s) + \log \frac{P_r}{P_s} = 0 \qquad (2.7)$$

Expression (2.7) represents the equation of an hyperplane. So the boundaries separating the regions defined by likelihood ratios are hyperplanes.

The optimum linear transformation used to minimize the distance between the points of the same group while keeping the total volume of space constant, is given by

$$A = CW \tag{2.8}$$

$$C(U - v_1 I) = 0 \tag{2.9}$$

where A is the transformation matrix, the rows of C are eighenvectors of the covariance matrix U of the set of vectors and W is a diagonal transformation representing the feature weighting coefficients and is given by

$$W_{nn} = \left[\prod_{p=1}^{N} \sigma_p \right]^{1/N} \frac{1}{\sigma_n} \tag{2.10}$$

where σ_n is the sample variance of the coefficients in the nth coordinate direction.

8.2.5.2 APPLICATION OF ASSOCIATIVE ADDRESS MACHINE IN PATTERN RECOGNITION PROBLEMS

Let us suppose that $x_1, x_2, ..., x_n$ are the associative criteria for a given field of data and let the ith orientation have discrete permissible values that can be expressed by K_i binary digits. Then the data word may be represented by

$$\{\phi; x_1, x_2, ...x_n\} \tag{2.11}$$

Let K_i be the number of binary digits required to express all permissible values of the ith criterion. Then we can conceive of an N-dimensional space where $N = \sum_{i=1}^{n} K_i$, where the data field would be finite point set consisting of the corners of an N-dimensional hypercube. It has been shown in Subsection 8.2.5.1 that for a multidimensional measurement space for such a distribution it is possible to define hyperplanes as separate different patterns according to some chosen criterion of closeness, so that different patterns of the same class represent points distributed in distinctly defined finite volume. It has been shown by Simmons (1964) that in such a space it is possible to define a matrix such that the closeness of two points can always be ascertained. For the purpose of allocation address to an input pattern a randomly selected set of linearly independent points, called association vectors, may be used as reference vectors. It is possible to extend this space to a multidimensional space and preserve the completeness of the matrix. This allows a tremendous increase in the volume efficiency of the data storage space. It is also possible to position a hyperplane of $(r-1)$ dimensions at arbitrary distances from the reference points. The normal distance of input vectors from such a plane may be used as the associative address for storing or retrieving the data. The concept can easily be extended to divide the whole transformed space, as explained in the previous section, into regions separated by suitable hyperplanes. It is clear that the equations of the hyperplanes generated by the constant likelihood ratios or their transforms can also be transformed into vectorial equation of the hyperplanes of the form

$$\alpha_i L = \rho - d_i \qquad (2.12)$$

where α_i is the position vector of the ith reference point, L the r-tuple whose elements are the directon cosines of the hyperplane, d_i the distance of the ith reference point from the plane and ρ is the distance of the plane from the origin.

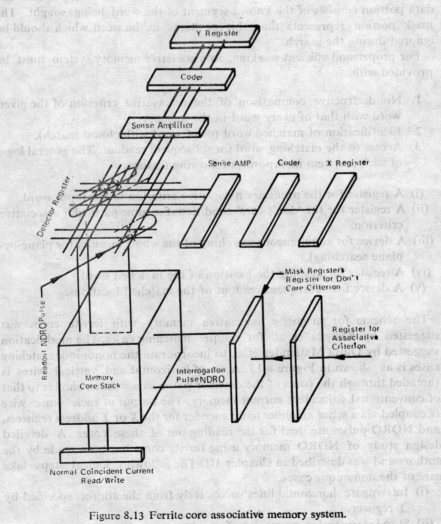

Figure 8.13 Ferrite core associative memory system.

8.2.6 Design Principles of a Magnetic Core Associative Memory Device

In an associative memory the address is generated from an examination of the whole or a part of the input data. The descriptors of a data word for the purpose of its identification has been termed by Kiseda et al. as the *associative criterion*. Thus a single word in memory may have a multiplicity of associative criteria, and several words also may have a common associative criterion. A unique associative criterion results in the location and/or retrieval of a single stored word and a non-unique case can result in the location and/or retrieval of more than one word in storage. The associative criterion consists of two parts—the data portion and the mask portion. The data portion consists of the known segment of the word being sought. The mask portion represents those bit positions in the word which should be ignored during the search.

For proper and efficient working, an associative memory system must be provided with:

1. Nondestructive comparison of the associative criterion of the given word with that of every word in the memory.
2. Identification of matched word (or of word with closest match).
3. Access to the matching word for subsequent readout. The general logic of such a system incorporates following features:

(i) A register for the necessary associative criterion of the input word.
(ii) A register for the 'don't care' conditions for some particular associative criterion.
(iii) A device for simultaneous searching of the whole memory (or plane-by-plane searching).
(iv) A register for keeping the location of the matched word.
(v) A device for subsequent readout of the matched locations.

The scheme for magnetic associative memory with ferrite cores was suggested by Kisseda et al. for unique matching cases. The modification suggested by Dutta Majumder et al. to incorporate the nonunique matching cases is as shown in Figure 8.13. A set of horizontal and vertical wires is threaded through the cores of the detector plane in a manner similar to that of conventional coincident current memory. The output of each sense wire is coupled via a sense amplifier to an encoder for the X or Y address registers, and NDRO pulses are used for the reading out of these cores. A detailed design study of NDRO memory using ferrite cores has been made by the authors and was described in Chapter III. The following logical steps take care of the nonunique cases.

(i) Interrogate horizontal lines successively from the address specified by X register.
(ii) Stop interrogation on receipt of an output signal.

(iii) Start interrogation of the vertical lines from the address specified by the Y register.

(iv) Stop interrogation on receipt of an output signal.

(v) Perform necessary readout and other operations of the main memory, and go back to step (iii).

(vi) If the last vertical wire has been reached, go back to step (i).

(vii) Stop at the end of interrogation of the last location. Obviously, this searching of the detector plane would take considerable time adversely affecting the efficiency of the system. But the use of very fast NDRO pulses would somehow compensate it. For example, with a memory core of 1.5 μsec switching time a memory cycle in a conventional computer would be more than 4 μsec. Whereas experiments performed by the authors on the other hand, showed that NDRO pulses with 200 nanosecond intervals and 80 nanosecond width is quite reliable for the purpose of readout. Thus atleast 20 times faster searching is feasible. Moreover, in the case of nonunique matches the locations once searched need not be again interrogated. Thus in an operational system approximately 80 to 100 times increase in speed may be achieved.

Of course it would be best to have a system in which all the cores in the detector plane could be interrogated simultaneously where some priority network could pick out different matched locations one after another.

8.2.7 The Model for Pattern Recognition Incorporating Associative Addressing Scheme

The modified model as shown in Figure 8.14 is an extension of the earlier model incorporating the ideas explained in the previous sections. The analyzer coder unit B transforms input speech signal into the binary valued time functions f_i of different acoustical parameters which are temporarily stored in C. At D this undergoes preliminary classification. A previously selected and ordered set of acoustical parameters which are broad enough to ensure a sensible input pattern to be matched, is used for interrogation of the associative memory. These parameters would be referred to as *key criterion*.

The key criterion is put into the interrogation register and the rest of the criteria are put into the mask register of Figure 8.13. The interrogation of memory can now produce one of the following three conditions:

(a) No match;

(b) Unique match; and

(c) Nonunique match.

In the second case the address of the matched location straightaway provides a primary selection of the pattern class. In the third case the

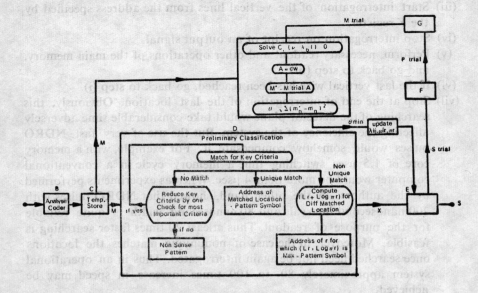

Figure 8.14 Pattern recognition model incorporating associative addressing memory system.

different matching locations are sequentially selected for computation of likelihood ratio for which all the parameters are taken into consideration. These computations provide for preliminary classifications. In the first case, when there is no match, the key criteria are put one by one from least significant ones into the mask register and interrogation of the memory is continued till the match is obtained. If there is no match even when the most important criterion is interrogated the pattern is labelled as non-sense. On the basis of this primary classification the symbol X for the pattern classes is generated. A trial transformation $X \to S$ is made on X at E. The S trial is passed on to F where the transformation $S \to P$ is made using rules simulating speech synthesis from phonetic symbols and its output P trial simulates speech signal patterns. This action is closely analogous to that of B.

The M trial generated from this is fed into a comparator unit. This comparator first transforms M trial $\to M'$ given by relations (2.8) and (2.9). The Euclidian distance matrix between M and M' are computed, and the symbol for which the distance is minimum is taken to be the correct symbol.

8.2.8 Solid State Content Addressable Memory (CAM) Devices

It is clear from the foregoing analysis and discussions that the mode of operation of a content addressable memory (CAM) differs from that of a location addressable RAM operation in the following ways:

(i) For storing and retrieving information the address of the memory location is not necessary.

(ii) During the retrieval process, information is simultaneously sensed from all specified memory locations and processed to determine if it is associated with the desired information.

(iii) All associated information in the specified section can be retrieved, i.e., it is a multivalue output process.

(iv) In a CAM, read is also called a match or search operation. During the search operation, information is sensed from every memory word and is compared with the search key. The search operation also requires the CAM cells to perform the compare logic operation within the cell.

(v) A nondestructive readout (NDRO) cell is necessary for a practical CAM system. While search "1" or search "0" is carried out in the key, the search "Don't Care" condition is carried out in the remaining portion of the word.

To successfully operate the CAM system with integrated circuits, methods or algorithms must be found for locating empty positions to store new information, retrieving data other than the highest priority word in a list of matching words, restoring the memory to quiescent state after each operation, etc. Also it has got to be established that a CAM is a more efficient hardware substitute for a RAM plus a searching algorithm.

Bell Laboratory proposed and experimentally realized an IC-CAM system which claimed solutions to some of the above mentioned problems.

Figure 8.15 shows an integrated circuit CAM cell while Figure 8.16 shows symbolically how these cells are to be interconnected in a memory organization. Transistors T_1 and T_2 constitute the basic inverter stage and T_1, T_2, T_3, and T_4, form a flip-flop circuit having two stable states with the potentials of nodes 1 and 2 either at V_s or at ground. A binary "1" is stored when node 1 is at V_s and node 2 at ground and a "0" is stored for vice versa.

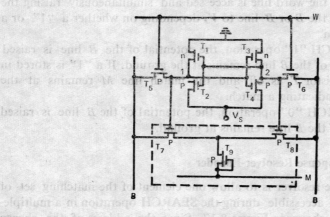

Figure 8.15 Proposed CIGFET CAM cell.

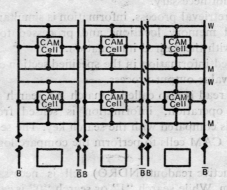

Figure 8.16 Memory organization of proposed CAM.

During the quiescent state the word line W is kept at V_s. The two access transistors T_5 and T_6 are p-channel devices so that when they are in the off state the memory cell is isolated from the bit lines B and $\bar{B}$. Both bit lines are kept at ground potential during standby and read cycles. Transistors T_7, and M is the match line. The gate terminals of the transistors T_7 and T_8 are T_8 and T_9 constitute the match logic circuit connected to those of transistors T_2 and T_4 respectively. T_7 will be on if "0" is stored in the cell and T_8 will be on if "1" is stored in the cell. Transistor T_9 is connected in a diode coupled logic circuit so that the current flows through either T_7-T_9 or T_8-T_9 to the match line. The match line M normally remains at ground potential unless there is a mismatch between the information being searched and that stored in the cell.

During a READ instruction the information is retrieved when the cell is accessed by lowering the potential of the word line to ground. During a WRITE operation the word line is accessed and simultaneously raising the potential of either the B or $\bar{B}$ line to V_s depending on whether a "1" or a "0" is to be written.

During a SEARCH "1" operation, the potential of the B line is raised to V_s while that of the $\bar{B}$ line remains at the ground. If a "1" is stored in the cell, then transistor T_7 is off and the match line M remains at the ground potential indicating a match.

During a SEARCH "0" operation, the potential of the $\bar{B}$ line is raised to V_s while that of the B line remains at ground.

8.2.9 Multiple Response Resolver-Encoder

The function of the resolver is to allow one element of the matching set of words to become accessible during the SEARCH operation in a multiple-match situation as shown in Figure 8.17. Since the address of the chosen element may contain the desired information, the resolver-encoder should not only resolve the multiple matches, but should also provide the address of the chosen element. Figure 8.18 shows the integrated CIGFET resolver encoder proposed by Bell Laboratory. The four inputs of the circuits labelled 00, 01, 10, 11 are normally at V_s potential. Ground potential when applied to any of the inputs will cause the circuit to indicate a match. These terminals are so labelled that when a match signal appears at any one of the four 11, 10, 01, 00 will appear at the input terminals 1 and 2 and match 0 will appear at the terminal 3. Figure 8.19 shows a proposed bipolar transistor for resolver encoder.

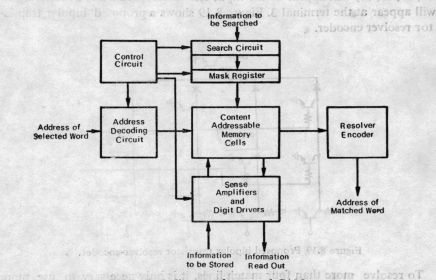

Figure 8.17 Block diagram of a general CAM system.

To resolve more than four match links, it is only necessary to use more identical circuits. Figure 8.20 shows the manner in which these circuits would be connected together for a 16-match line case. The hierarchy of priority of the circuit for the 16-input case is the same as that for the original 4-input case.

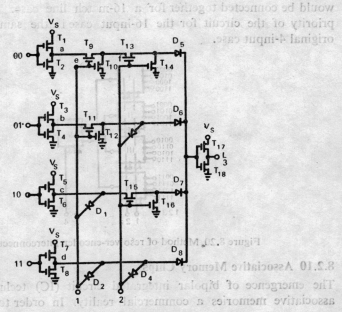

Figure 8.18 Proposed CIGFET resolver-encoder.

inputs, the output at terminals 1 and 2 is the address label of that input terminal. The ground potential being zero the output at terminal 3 indicates whether there is a match signal at any of the four inputs.

If two or more match signals appear at the inputs, then the address of the higher priority input signal (priority from highest to the lowest is 11, 10, 01, 00) will appear at the input terminals 1 and 2 and a match signal will appear at the terminal 3. Figure 8.19 shows a proposed bipolar transistor resolver encoder.

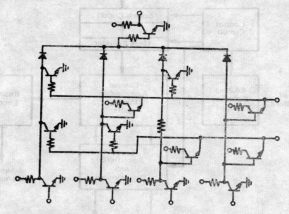

Figure 8.19 Proposed bipolar transistor resolver-encoder.

To resolve more than four match lines, it is only necessary to use more identical circuits. Figure 8.20 shows the manner in which these circuits would be connected together for a 16-match line case. The hierarchy of priority of the circuit for the 16-input case is the same as that for the original 4-input case.

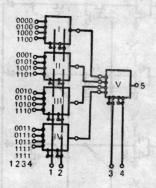

Figure 8.20 Method of resolver-encoder interconnection.

8.2.10 Associative Memory Chips

The emergence of bipolar integrated circuit (IC) technology has made associative memories a commercial reality. In order to attain maximum speed it is necessary to combine the comparison logic circuitry and the data storage elements of the memory on the same structure. Attempt to design MOS associative memory was not satisfactory due to their speeds. With MOS associative memory chips it takes about 300 to 500 nanoseconds to produce a match signal. On the other hand, bipolar associative memory can do the job ten times faster, but have been limited to relatively few bits per chip as they require more space and power.

But of late the improvements in bipolar IC technology have made it possible to commercially produce AM building blocks of adequate size. Fairchild has produced corporation bipolar AM 4102 of 16 bit array organized as four bits by four words on a chip of 80 mils by 95 mils dimension. The 16 cells with its storage elements and comparator circuits occupy most of the space on the chip. The remaining part of the chip contains address selection match detection and input processing circuits. A 16 bit AM processor can be designed with 4 such 4102 chips. An associative memory such as this, is ideally suited for systems where information is stored and retrieved with a keyword.

8.2.11 The Crossed Film Cryotron(CFC) Associative (Catalog) Memory

An elaborate presentation of theory and implementation of cryogenic memory devices and systems has been provided in section 7.3 of Chapter 7. Here we shall present a brief description of realization of associative memory system using cryotron memory cells. Although words can be written in an associative memory just as in a random access memory, the presence or absence of a particular word within a superconducting associative memory can be sensed by a single interrogation process. It is also necessary to indicate the precise location of the desired word.

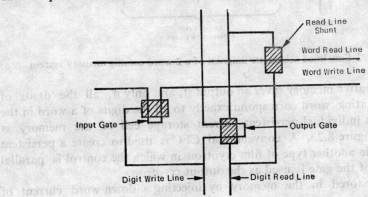

Figure 8.21 CFC random access memory storage cell.

Associative memories are suitable for listing items, since an item can be extracted from anywhere in the memory as long as its "tag" is specified. Slade et al. (1960) proposed a CFC associative memory and called it a catalog memory. Figure 8.21 shows a CFC random access memory storage cell and Figure 8.22 shows a simplified schematic diagram of a 2-word catalog memory system. The basic storage loop is composed of the 'digit write' and the 'word write' lines. By simultaneously pulsing these two lines and terminating the word current pulse before the digit pulse, a circulating current can be stored in the loop. Since this circulating current makes the output gate resistive, it can readily be detected if a voltage pulse occurs on the 'digit read' line when the 'digit read' and 'word read' lines are simultaneously pulsed. The 'word read' line pulse deactivates the shunt in the 'digit read' line. This shunt prevents the circulating currents of words other than the one sensed from creating output voltage signals. The circulating current can be destroyed by pulsing the 'word write' line. Since the 'word read' and 'word write' lines are common to all the storage cells of any one word, all the bits of a word can be stored or read simultaneously.

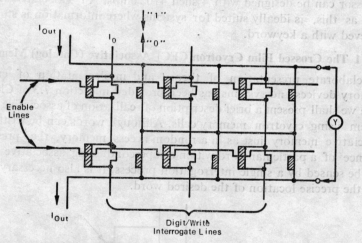

Figure 8.22 Simplified schematic diagram of a 2-word catalog memory system.

The associative memory gives an output if, and only if, all the digits of the interrogating word correspond exactly to all the digits of a word in the memory. An individual persistent current storage cell of the memory is shown in Figure 8.23. A conventional CFC is used to create a persistent current, while another type of film cryotron in which the control is parallel and on top of the gate is used as the output cryotron.

A "1" is stored in the memory by injecting a down word current of magnitude I_0 into a digit write/interrogate line while simultaneously pulsing the enable line of the desired storage word. The cells are constructed with equal inductance in the two write current paths through each cell. This results in a "1" being represented as a clockwise stored current of $I_0/2$. A "0" is a counterclockwise current also of magnitude $I_0/2$ and is obtained by reversing the direction of I_0 on the digit lines.

An experimental memory of this type is reported to have been built and operated. To interrogate the memory for a desired word, the digit currents representing the word are simultaneously injected to all the write/interrogate lines, without the enable line current. Since the interrogating currents of magnitude I_0 divide equally between the two branches, they either add or oppose the circulating currents in the control of the output cryotron. If the currents add in an output control, output gate becomes resistive; if the currents oppose, the gate will be superconducting. If all the interrogating currents match all the circulating currents in one word location of the memory, all the output gates in that location will become resistive and an output voltage will appear at the memory output terminals. Unless there is an exact comparison, there will always be at least one superconducting path through the memory and there will be no voltage output.

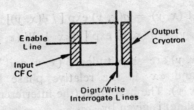

Figure 8.23 Persistent current storage cell.

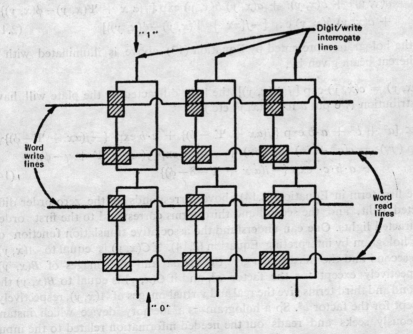

Figure 8.24 An alternative design of catalog memory (Newhouse and Fruin).

The other two interesting variations of superconducting associative memory are ones that were designed by Newhouse and Fruin (Figure 8.24), (1962) and the other by Seeber (1960).

8.2.12 An Associative Memory System Using Holographic Technique

Theoretical and experimental aspects of holographic memory technique are presented in connection with optical memory technology in Chapter 7. Here the principles of a holographic associative memory will be briefly described as suggested by Mitshuhito Sakaguchi et al. (1970).

One of the fundamental properties of holography is the inherent associative translation process which is quite suited for the interrogation operation in AM system. Consider two coherent light beams simultaneously incident on a photographic plate at the point (x, y) given by,

$$A(x, y) = a(x, y) \exp[j\phi(x, y)]$$
$$B(x, y) = b(x, y) \exp[j\{\alpha x + \Psi(x, y)\}]$$

where $a(x, y)$ and $b(x, y)$ are amplitudes, $\phi(x, y)$ and $\Psi(x, y)$ are phases of the incident beams and αx is the relative phase between the coherent beams $A(x, y)$ and $B(x, y)$. The hologram (the interference pattern recorded on the photographic plate) is given by

$$I = [A(x, y) + B(x, y)]^2$$
$$= a(x, y)^2 + b(x, y)^2 + a(x, y)\, b(x, y) \exp[j\{\alpha x + \Psi(x, y) - \phi(x, y)\}]$$
$$+ a(x, y)\, b(x, y) \exp[-j\{\alpha x + \Psi(x, y) - \phi(x, y)\}] \tag{2.13}$$

If the hologram represented by Equation (13) above is illuminated with a coherent beam given by,

$C(x, y) = c(x, y) \exp[j\gamma(x, y)]$, the light diffracted by the plate will have distribution (we put a for $a(x, y)$ etc.)

$$D \propto [a^2 + b^2 + a \cdot b \exp\{j(\alpha x + \Psi - \phi)\} + a \cdot b \exp\{-j(\alpha x + \Psi - \phi)\}\gamma c$$
$$\exp(j\gamma). = c(a^2 + b^2) \exp(j\gamma) + a \cdot b \cdot c \cdot \exp\{j(\alpha x + \Psi + \gamma - \phi)\}$$
$$+ a \cdot b \cdot c \cdot \exp\{-i(\alpha x + \Psi - \delta - \phi)\} \tag{14}$$

The first term in Equation (2.14) above corresponds to the zero order diffracted light, and the second and third terms correspond to the first order diffracted lights. One can understand the associative translation function of the hologram by interpreting Equation (2.14). If $C(x, y)$ is equal to $A(x, y)$, the second and the third terms give the virtual and real images of $B(x, y)$, respectively except for the factor a^2, and if $C(x, y)$ is equal to $B(x, y)$ the second and third terms give the real and virtual images of $A(x, y)$, respectively, except for the factor b^2. So a hologram is a memory device which instantaneously seeks and reads out the needed information related to the input information, that is, the interrogation signal. However, diffracted images can be reconstructed even when $C(x, y)$ does not completely coincide with $A(x, y)$ or $B(x, y)$. Therefore, the interrogation operation based on the logical Exclusive OR has to be introduced even in the holographic associative memory.

8.2.12.1 WORKING PRINCIPLE OF A HOLOGRAPHIC ASSOCIATIVE MEMORY

A schematic diagram illustrating the formation of holographic associative memory plane is shown in Figure 8.25. The hologram memory plane in this case is a photographic plate recording the two dimensional interference patterns between two sets of coherent light beams modulated by interrogated signals and information signals respectively.

The light beams $A(x, y)$ and $B(x, y)$ contain the information $A = (A_1, A_2, A_3...A_n)$ and $B = (B_1, B_2, B_3 \cdots B_m)$, respectively. Here A_i and B_i denote the ith bit of A and B respectively. For convenience of optical logical operations, let the beam A (x, y) consists of a set of $2n$ parallel beams a_1, $\bar{a}_1$, a_2, $\bar{a}_2$, a_3, $\bar{a}_3 \ldots a_n$, $\bar{a}_n$, and the beam $B(x, y)$ a set of $2m$ diverged beams b_1, $\bar{b}_1$, b_2, $\bar{b}_2$, b_3, $\bar{b}_3,...b_m$, $\bar{b}_m$. The ith bit of A, A_i, is represented by a pair of true beam a_i and a complement beam $\bar{a}_i$ Similarly, a pair b_i, $\bar{b}_i$ corresponds to B_i. The coherent beams come out of true or complement sources according to the states "1" or "C" of the corresponding bits. For example, if (A_1, A_2, A_3, A_4) is $(1, 0, 1, 0,)$ and $(B_1, B_2, B_3, B_4,)$ is $(0, 0, 1, 1,)$ then $A(x, y)$ is a set of coherent beams coming out of the positions a_1, $\bar{a}_2$, a_3, $\bar{a}_4$, and B (x, y) coming out of positions $\bar{b}_1$ $\bar{b}_2$, b_3, b_4. In the hologram formed by $A(x, y)$ and $B(x, y)$, the information A is recorded as a spot sequence a_1, $\bar{a}_1$...in a word space, while the information B is contained in very spot of $A(x, y)$. Thus recorded information is expressed logically by $a_1 \sum(b_i + \bar{b}_i)$, $\bar{a}_1 \sum(b_i + \bar{b}_i),....$ The recording of different information is made in quite a similar way, except that the position of the photographic plate is shifted each time.

Figure 8.25 shows a configuration for the interrogation and the readout. The interrogation is made by means of the mismatch detection. A coherent interrogation beam $C(x,y)$ modulated by complement of an interrogation signal $(C' = C'_1, C'_2,...C'_n)$ illuminates the hologram memory plane. $C(x, y)$ also consists of combinations of true and complement beams, that is $C(x, y) = c_1, \bar{c}_1, c_2, \bar{c}_2,...c_n, \bar{c}_n$, where c_i (or $\bar{c}_i$) is a coherent beam simultaneously illuminating the corresponding bit part a_i (or $\bar{a}_i$) of all words subjected to the interrogation. Some of the C_i's may be the DON'T CARE bits which do not participate in the interrogation. No light beams come out of the DON'T CARE bit positions.

Throughout this section, we use the term "Modulation" in the meaning of the spatial modulation. Since $C(x, y)$ is modulated by the complement of the interrogation signal, no images of the information signals are reconstructed from the word spaces of the interrogated signals which completely match

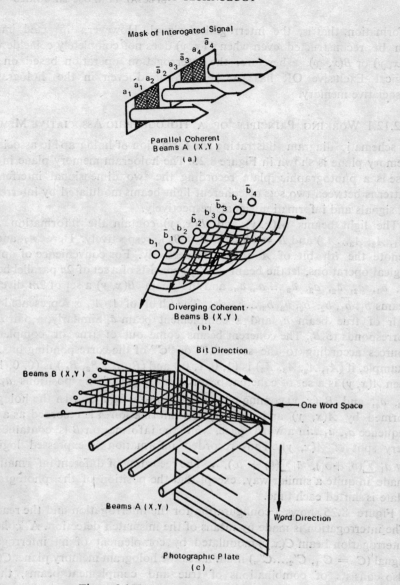

Figure 8.25 Arrangement for interrogation.

the interrogation signal, or in other words completely mismatch the complement of the interrogation signal. In the previous example $A = (1, 0, 1, 0)$ and $B = (0, 0, 1, 1)$ the interference pattern is recorded in the $a_1, \bar{a}_2, a_3, \bar{a}_4$ parts, and each of them contains the whole B information. If the interrogation signal (C'_1, C'_2, C'_3, C'_4) is $(1, X, X, 0)$, where X denotes the DON'T CARE bit, the corresponding interrogation beam $C(x, y)$ consists of two parallel beams coming out of the $\bar{c}_1$ and c_4 positions. Since both $\bar{c}_1$ and c_4 do not coincide with the interference pattern, no image of the B information is reconstructed in the present case. Thus we have found that the interrogation signal $C' = (1, X, X, 0)$ matches the interrogated signal $A = (1, 0, 1, 0)$ related to the information signal $B = (0, 0, 1, 1)$. If the interrogation signal is $C' = (1, X, 0, X)$, the interrogation beams come out of the bit positions $\bar{c}_1$ and c_3. In this case, the image of B information $(0, 0, 1, 1)$ is reconstructed because the interrogation beam c_3 is illuminated on the bit part a_3 where the interference pattern was recorded. Thus we know $C' = (1, X, 0, X)$ does not match A. While the interrogation beam is simultaneously illuminating all of the words, the reconstructed images of the information signals are detected by means of a photodetector array arranged for each word. As mentioned before, the words giving the reconstructed images mismatch the interrogation signal, and those giving no images match the interrogation signal. As a result of the interrogation operation, the following three states are possible: mismatch, single match, and multiple match. In the last case, the multiple match must be changed into the single match by means of an ordered retrieval technique before the readout of the needed information. After the location of the matched word is found by the interrogation operation, the needed B information can be read out by illuminating the matched word of the memory plane by a coherent beam. In the previous example, $(C'_1, C'_2, C'_3, C'_4) = (1, X, X, 0)$ is found to match $A = (1, 0, 1, 0)$. By illuminating the word containing $A = (1, 0, 1, 0)$ by a coherent beam, the recorded information $B = (0, 0, 1, 1)$ is reconstructed on a photodetector array arranged for each bit.

When a practical holographic associative ROM is constructed on the basis of the principle explained above, a light deflector and an array of light modulators would the be important components. In the interrogation operation the coherent beams modulated by the complement of the interrogation signal must be distributed simultaneously to illuminate all the words. This can be done in the following way. The input coherent beam is divided into $2n$ parallel coherent beams corresponding to $c_1, \bar{c}_1, \ldots c_n, \bar{c}_n$, by means of a combination of beam splitters. The $2n$ parallel beams are, then, modulated in accordance with the coherent interrogation signal by means of an array of $2n$ electro-optical light modulators. After having been passed through the light modulator array, the parallel beams are distributed along the word direction by means of a light deflector. The light deflector composed of the polarization switches using electro-optic crystals. The input coherent beam is completely deflected by driving the polarization switch at the half-wave voltage, the input coherent beam will be divided into two directions with equal intensities by driving the polarization switch at half of the half-wave voltage. The readout can be simply done with the same apparatus by setting the light modulator array at the state of all "1" and deflecting the $2n$ coherent beams into the matched word space. The reconstructed images of the needed information are detected by the photodetector array. An array of strip-shaped photodetectors is suited for the purpose since it has simpler construction compared to the matrix type one. An integrated type photodetector array would be used for high speed operation, provided the reconstructed images are reduced by an imaging lens of small focal length. The basic experiment as described by Shakaguchi et al. (1970), on the light deflector composed of $LiTaO_3$ polarization switches and calcite deflectors promises a cycle time up to 1 μsec for both the interrogation and the readout, provided the photodetector arrays have sufficiently fast response times. The ultimate bit density of such holographic associative memory is limited by the aperature of the small hologram expressing a single bit.

8.3 PRACTICAL ASSOCIATIVE MEMORIES

The largest associative memory (apart from those that were built as part of classified projects) that has been used so far as is known, is the 2048-word ferrite core unit developed in 1968 by the Goodyear Aerospace Corpn, for the US Airforce, Rome Air Development Centre (RADC). There are 15 kinds of searches on its 50-bit words and it can perform 31 operations related to the memory's interface with RADC's CDC 1604 B Computer. In associative memories; as in most other memories, the speed, cost and maximum word length are affected by the kind of memory element used. But in associative memories, the cost is greatly increased by the electronic circuits connected to each word. This is the main reason why these memories are not mass produced. Though associative memories have been built with cryotrons and planar metallic films, magnetic ferrite elements both simple toroids and multi-aperture devices have proven most successful in large systems. Plated wire memories have also been reported to be very successful in this context.

It can be said that the cost per bit for associative memories is at least 50 times greater than that for conventional memories. The main reason for higher cost is that the associative memories require logic circuits at each word. Also, an associative memory's response store and resolver make the memory a kind of small computer that can execute a variety of complex instructions. This capability is intrinsically more expensive than mere storage. A few practical associative memories (other than RADC 2048 words × 50 bits one) are: (i) Stanford Research Institute built one in 1963 using split cores 1100 words × 281 bits with exact match associative searches for RADC, US Airforce; (ii) Scope Inc. built one associative memory using transfluxors, 1024 words × 24 bits with exact match associative searches for US Department of Defence in 1963; (iii) Goodyear Aerospace supplied one to US Navy in 1964 with multi-aperture storage device (MALE), 256 words × 30 bits, (iv) Philco Ford supplied in 1965 to US Airforce with multi-aperature storage device (Biax), 1024 words × 48 bits with exact match associative searches, and (v) Texas Instruments supplied to US Airforce Avionics laboratory in 1970 with LSI-MOS device, 128 words × 50 bits with exact match associative searches.

The price differential that exists today between associative memory and conventional memory, is not so great if the total operating system cost is considered. Associative systems require simpler software and save time when searching through a file for data of a particular type. The plated wire technology has already brought the cost down substantially, and semiconductor technology promises to bring it down even further generating new interest in associative memory systems and development of new applications.

References

Read Only Memories

Amdahl, G.M., Blaauw, G.A. and Brooks., F.P., Jr. (1964): 'Architecture of IBM System/360', *IBM. Journal* V.8, No. 2, p. 87.

Barret, W.A., Humphrey, F.B., Ruff, J.A. and Stadler, H.L. (1961): 'A card changeable permanent magnet twistor memory of large capacity', *IEEE Trans. on Electronic Computer*, V.EC-10, pp. 451-461.

Bobeck, A.H. (1967): 'A new storage element suitable for large sized memory arrays the twistor', *Bell. Syst. Tech. J.*, V.36, pp. 1319-1340.

Carr, W.N. and Mize, J.P. (1972): '*MOS/LSI Design and Application*', McGraw-Hill, New York, Chap. 6.

DeBuske, J., Janik, J. Jr. and Simons, B.H. (1959): 'A card changeable nondestructive readout twistor store', *Proc. Western Joint Comp. Conf.* (San Fransisco., Calif.), March.

Dinnely, J.M. (1964): 'Card Changeable Memories', *Computer Design*, V.3, No.6, pp. 20.

Dussine, R. (1971): 'Evaluation of ROM in Computers', *Honywell Computer Journal*, V.5 No. 2, pp. 79-88.

Endo, I. and Yamato, J.(1962): 'The Metal Card Memory, A New Semipermanent Store', *Large Capacity Memory Techniques for Computing Systems*, Yovits (Ed.) Macmillan, New York.

Foglia, H.R., McDermid, W.L. and Peterson, H.E. (1961): 'Card capacitor—A semipermanent read only memory', *IBM Journal*, V.5, No.1, p. 67.

Gutenmakher, L.I. (1956): 'Statistical and information machines of new type', *Vestink Akademia Nawk*, V.26, pp. 12.

Haskell, J.W. (1962): 'Printed cards for the board capacitor memory', *IBM Journal*, V.6, No.4. pp. 462.

———(1966): 'Design of a printed card capacitor read-only store', *IBM J. Res. and Dev.* V.10, No.2, March.

Hemel, A. (1972): 'Square root extraction with read only memories'. *Computer. Design*, April, pp. 100-104.

Hoffman, G. (1970): 'MOS character generator', *Taxas Instrument Application Report*, *Bulletin* CA-145, January.

Hoover, C.W. Staehler, R.E. and Ketchledge, R.W. (1958): 'Fundamental concepts in the design of the flying spot store' *Bell. Syst. Tech. J.*, V.37, September. pp. 1161-1194.

Kilburn, T. and Grimsdale, R.L. (1960): 'A digital computer store with a very short read time', *Proc. IEEE*, V.107B, pp. 567-572.

Krylow, et al. (1963): 'Semipermanent memory—latest use for twistor', *Electronics*, V.36, pp. 80.

Kvamme, F. (1970): 'Standard read-only memories simplify complex logic design', *Electronics* V.43, No.1, January, pp. 88-95.

Kuttner, P. (1963): 'The rope memory, a permanent storage device', *AFIPS Conf. Proc.* V.24, October, pp. 45-58.

Lewin, M.H. (1965): 'A survey of read-only memories', *Proc. FJCC.*, pp. 775-88.

Linford, J. (1971): 'ROMs as Logic', *Electronic Engineering*, July, pp. 52-3.

Looney, D.H. (1959): 'A twistor matrix memory for semipermanent information', *Proc. Western Joint Comp. Conf.*, March, pp. 36-41.

Macpherson, D.H. and York, R.K. (1961): 'Semipermanent storage by capacitive coupling', *IRE Trans. on Electronic Computers*, V.EC-10, No.5, pp. 446.

Matick, R. (1963): 'Thick read-only memory device', *J. Appl. Phys*, V.34, April, pp. 1173.

————(1966): 'Fast nondestructive read slow write memory device using thick magnetic films', *IEEE Trans. on Electronic Computers*, V.EC-15, No.4.

Morgenson, E.O., Jr. (1962): 'Wired core matrix memories', *Instruments and Control Systems*, V.35, pp. 72.

Nichols, John L. (1967): 'A logical next step for read-only memories', *Electronics*, June 12, pp. 111.

Pick. G.C. (1964): 'A semipermanent memory utilizing correlation addressing', *AFIPS Conf. Proc.* V.26, October, pp. 107.

Pick, G.C., Gray, S.B. aud Brick, D.B. (1964): 'The solenoid array—new computer element', *IEEE Trans. on Electronic Computers*, V.EC-13, February, pp. 27-35.

Renand, A.M., and Neumann, W.J. (1960): 'Unifluxor—A permanent memory element', *Proc. WJCC*, p. 128.

Taub, D.M. (1963): 'Analysis of sneak paths and sense line distortion in an improved capacitor read-only memory', *Proc. IEEE*, V.51, No.11, pp. 1554.

————(1963): 'A short review of read-only memories', *Proc. IEEE* V.110, January, pp. 157.

Taub, D.M. and Kington, B.W. (1964): 'The design of transformer read-only stores', *IBM Journal*, V.8, No.4, pp. 443.

Wamsloy, J. (1962): 'Inductive coupled read-only memory', IRE Wescon Convention (Los Angeles), August.

Watanbe, S. and Takahashi, S. (1962): 'Capacitance type fixed memory', in *Large Capacity Memory Techniques for Camputer Systems*, M.C. Yovits (Ed.), Macmillan, New York.

Wier, J.M. (1955): 'A high speed permanent storage device', *IRE Trans. on Electronic Comp.* V.EC-4, pp. 16-20.

Yamato, J. and Suzuki, Y. (1961): Forming semipermanent memories with metal and storage', *Electronics*, V.34, November, pp. 1361-141.

Associative Memory

Ahrons, R.W. (1963): 'Superconductive associative memories', *RCA Review*, V. 24, pp. 325-354.

Anderson, L.K. (1968): 'Holographic optical memory for bulk data storage', *Bell Lab. Rec.*, V. 46, November, pp. 318-325.

Apicella, A. and Frank, J. (1965): 'A high speed NDRO one-core-per bit associative element', *Proc. International Conf. on Magnetics*, April, pp. 14, 5-1.

Bartlett, J. John Modge and Joh Springer (1970): 'Associative Memory Chips: fast, versatile and here', in *Electronic Computer Memory Technology*, Wallace B Riley (Ed.) McGraw-Hill, New York, pp. 217-221.

Cainiello, R.R. (1961): 'Outline of the theory of thought process and thinking machines', *J. Theor. Biology*, V. 1, April, pp. 204-235.

Derickson, R.B. (1968): 'A proposed associative push down memory concept', *Computer Design*, V. 7 pp. 60-66.

Dutta Majumder, D. and Datta, A.K. (1970): 'Some studies on suitability of Associative Memory in Pattern Recognition Systems', Estratto dall' opera Antomazione E Strumentazions Milalono. Federazione delle Associazione Scientific e Techniche, Italy.

Eddey, E.E. (1967): 'The use of associative processors in radar tracking and correlation', *Proc. Nat. Aerospace Electronics Conf.* pp. 39-42..

Estrín, G. and Fuller, R. (1963): 'Algorithms for Content-Addressable Memery', *IEEE Pacific Computer Conference Proc.*, pp. 118-128, March.

Flakoff, A.D. (1962): 'Algorithms for parallel serarch memories', *J. Ass. Comput. Mach.*, V. 9, October, pp. 488-511.

Forgie, S.W. and Forgie, C.D. (1959): *J. Acous. Soc. of America*, V. 31, November.

Halle, M. and Stevenson, K. (1962): *IRE Trans. Inf. Theory*, V-IT 8, No. 2.

Hanlon, A.G. (1966): 'Content-addressable and associative memory systems: a survey', *IEEE Trans. on Electronic Computers*, V. EC-15, pp. 509-521.

King, J.H. and Tunis, C.J. (1966): *IBM J. Res. & Dev.*, V. 10 No. 1

Kiseda, J.R., Peterson, H.E. Seelbach, W.C. and Teig, M. (1961): 'A magnetic associative memory,' *IBM J. Res. & Dev.*, V. 5, pp. 106.

Kogelnik, H. (1965): Imaging of optical modes-resonators with internal lens', *Bell Syst. Tech. J.*, V. 44, March, pp. 455-94.

Lee, C.Y. (1968): 'Content—addressable and distributed logic memories,' in Applied Automata Theory, J.T. Tou (Ed.,) New York, Academic Press.

Lewin, M.H. (1962): 'Retrieval of ordered lists from a content-addressed memory', *RCA Rev.*, V. 23, January, pp. 215-229.

McCulloch, W.S. and Pits, W.H. (1943): 'A logical calculus of the ideas imminent in nervous activity', *Bull. Math. Biophysics*, V. 5, December, pp. 115-133.

McDermid. W.L. and Peterson, H.E. (1961): 'A magnetic associative memory'. *IBM J. Res., Develop.*, V. 5, January, pp. 59-63.

Mundy, J.L, Burgess, F.J.. et al. (1972): 'Low cost associative memory', *IEEE Solid State Circuits*, V. SC-7, pp. 364.

Natarajan, N.K. and Thomas, PAV. (1969): 'A multi-access associative memory.' *IEEE Trans. on Computer*, V. C-18, pp. 424-428.

Newhouse, V.L. and Fruin, R.E. (1962): 'A cryogenic data addressed memory', Spring Joint Computer Conference, *AFIPS Conf. Proc.*, Washington DC, pp. 89-99.

Noe, J.D. (1961): MIRF (multiple instantaneous response file)', *Current Res. Devel.* Document, V.5, November.

Parhami, B. (1973): 'Associative Memories and Processors: An Overview and Selected Bibliograhy', *Proc. IEEE*, V. 61, No. 6, January.

Post, P.B. (1969): 'A life like model of association relevance', *Proc. Int. Joint. Comp. Conf. Artificial Intelligence*, May.

Pritchard, J.P. and Wald, L.D. (1964): 'Design of a fully associative cryogenic data processor', presented at the *INTERMAG Conf.*, April.

Rosenblatt, F. (1958): 'The Perceptron—a probabilistic model for information storage and organization in the brain', *Rev.* V. 65, pp. 386-407.

Rudolph, J.A., Fulmer, L.C. and Willard C. Meilander. (1970): 'With associative memory speed limit is no barrier', *Electronic Computers Memory Technology*, Wallace B. Riloy (Ed.) McGraw Hill, pp. 217-221.

Raffel, J.I. and Crowther, T.S. (1964): 'A proposal for an associative memory using magnetic films', *IEEE Trans. on Electronic Computers*, V. EC-13, No. 5.

Sakaguchi, M., Nishida, N. and Nemoto, T. (1970): 'A new associative memory system utilizing holography', *IEEE Trans. on Computers*, V. C-19, No. 12, December.

Seeber, R.R., Jr. (1960): 'Associated self-sorting memory', *Proc. Eastern Joint Computers Conference*, pp. 179-187.

Seeber, R.R. and Lindquist, A.B. (1962): 'Associative memory ordered retrieval', *IBM J. Res. and Dev.*, V.6, January, pp. 126-136.

Shooman, W. (1960): 'Parallel computing with vertical computing data', *Proc. Eastern Joint Computer Conf.*, pp. 111-15.

Simmons, G.J. (1964): 'Application of an associatively addressed Distributive memory', *AFIPS Conf. Proc.* Washington D.C., pp. 494-513.

Slade, A. E. and McMahon, H.O. (1956): 'A Cryotron catalog memory system', *Proc. Eastern Joint Computer Conf.*, pp. 115-120.

Slade, A.E. and Smallman, C.R. (1960): 'Thin film cryotron catalog memory', *Solid State Electronic*, V. 11, pp. 357-62.

Stone, H.S. (1971): 'Associative Processing for General Purpose computers through the use of modified memories', *AFIPS Conf. Proc.*, pp. 949-55.

Stone H.S. (1970): 'A logic in memory computer', *IEEE Trans. on Computers*, V. C-19, pp. 73-78.

Stroke, G.W. (1965): 'Lenseless fourter-transform method for optical holography', *Appl. Phys. Letters*, May, pp. 201-03.

Widrow, B. (1962): 'Generalization and information storage in network of adaline 'neurons' in self-organizing systems', MC Yovits et al. (Ed). Washington DC, Spartan, pp. 435-461.

9. LIMITATIONS OF EXISTING MEMORY TECHNOLOGIES AND PROSPECTS FOR BIOCHEMICAL MEMORIES

Conceptually, any element or phenomena that exhibits two or more stable states or a delay property, can be utilized for storage. Only a few of these possibilities have, however, proven satisfactory or have given competitive performance in the past or often promise for the future. Today no standard technology exists for large capacity memories; there are several promising approaches such as, magnetic core, magnetic film, magnetic bubble, semi-conductor, optical memories, etc. It seems reasonable that a given technology cannot be improved indefinitely, some ultimate limit must exist which will be approached perhaps exponentially, but a point will be reached where the investment in making improvements exceeds the return. This point of diminishing return may now be appearing more nearly true. In any rapidly advancing technological area one must be concerned with the bounds imposed on the technology by natural laws.

In any attempt to forecast the demand for memory, it is first necessary to segment the wide range of technology and performance found in modern day computer memory into relatively homogeneous categories which can then be analyzed. Ferromagnetic or ferrimagnetic materials possessing binary states of stable magnetization direction have been the backbone of data storage since the beginning of the computer technology. Subsequently, numerous technologies have appeared to offer alternatives for large storage systems. Reliability, size, and speed of response are the fundamental properties with which we shall be mostly concerned. However, these are not independent of each other. For any physical mechanism employed in a device, the smaller the device the faster will be its response. But fast response in any single element is of little avail unless communication time between elements is also shortened. Lastly, the discussion of the ultimate capability of computer memory elements must start with the consideration of reliability. The various parameters that affect the reliability consideration include logical and physical redundancy crosstalk and resulting difficulties of single particle memory elements, and memory element's life time. The discussions on these factors are briefly included in this chapter though we have analysed them in all the previous chapters whenever necessary. In Section 9.1 current technologies are reviewed, in Section 9.2 memory reliability and stability of individual storage elements are discussed, and in Section 9.3 an approach towards the biochemical memories is presented briefly.

9.1 VARIOUS MEMORY TECHNOLOGIES

If one makes an overview of divergent nature of basic memory technologies in the last few years, one finds that, at one end of the spectrum of memory technology currently used in digital computers and other data handling equipment, semiconductor random access memories are gradually replacing ferrite core memories, while at the other end of the spectrum, devices exploiting remanent magnetization, as ferrite cores do, are virtually uncontested. These magnetic devices, including their different varieties provide inexpensive storage at long recovery times by virtue of their mechanical nature. The choice of a particular memory technology depends upon the considerations of speed, size, and reliability parameter. However, all these different technologies can be grouped into three general categories of: (i) continuous media, (ii) semiconductor media, and (iii) discrete components.

9.1.1 Continuous Media Storage

Although the main memory in a computer is being replaced by semiconductor devices, magnetic recording techniques continue to dominate in the area where large storage capacity and nonvolatility are required. Magnetic recording and optical recording systems which fall in continuous media storage system are generally used in mass storage technology. Magnetic disk devices are presently capable of storing approximately 6.4×10^9 bits in a system consisting of eight spindles, each having 20 recording surfaces. Information is stored at a density of approximately 2×10^5 bits/cm^2, providing an active recording area of approximately 10^4 sq. inch. The extension of capacity of these systems to 10^{12} bits/cm^2 requires either an increase in recording area or an increase in bit packing density. In presentday technology, the recording density is not limited by the resolution of the medium but rather by practical engineering considerations, such as, readout signal-to-noise ratio and difficulty in rapid and accurate positioning of the inductive transducer with respect to the medium. The requirement of mechanical motion not only limits the speed but also reduces the reliability.

The optical memories which provide significant advantage over the magnetic disks and tapes, offer large bit packing density since the bit size can approach the wavelength of light. The limitation on the bit density is imposed by the diffraction limit of light, which, for visible wavelengths is approximately 0.5 μm. Besides the wavelength, an important parameter to consider is the response time of the detector. In holographic data storage systems suggested by Graf and Lang, the physical size of the detector array limits the storage capacity just as much as does the physical size of the storage medium itself. They arrived at a result that the capacity is limited by a factor of the from N,

$$N \leqslant \left[\frac{DH}{4\lambda (D + H)} \right]^2$$

where D is the lateral dimension of the detector array and N is the lateral dimension of the hologram plate and λ is the wavelength. This limitation arises because of the diffraction limit and because of the need for oblique incidence of the reconstructed rays on the detector plane. However, the construction of an optical memory requires many components which are too costly. The commercial success of optical memory depends on the reduction of effective cost of those components so that this technology may be extended to both small and large capacity stores.

Returning to the magnetic recording system, it is clear that the basic limitation lies in the particular system approach and not in the use of magnetic materials. One major problem with current mechanically accessed magnetic recording disks is the long access time, particularly with movable head slider. This shortcoming can be removed to some extent by using one head/track system. The requirement of high speed mechanical transportation of magnetic transducer head at extreme proximity of the bit location is a major source of limitations. In fact, an examination of the magnetic recording technique reveals the limitations in the following areas:

(i) *Access time.* For addressing a large recording medium surface area, the mechanical motion of the transducer head imposes a limitation on the access time. Presently available disk technology indicates an access time of about 10^{-2} sec is required for a medium of total area of about 10^{-4} sq. in. Improvement in this area is rather more difficult and also very costly.

(ii) *Packing density.* The readout signal from the memory depends upon the magnetic flux switched from the bit location which is proportional to the dimension of the bit. Therefore increasing the packing density causes reduction in the signal-to-noise ratio. The present status for a disk pack memory is 4000 bits per track and 200 tracks per inch, resulting in 8×10^5 bits/in². Improvement above 10^7 bits/in² may be expected in the future.

(iii) *Reliability.* It has been found that while the mechanical motion has brought simplicity and low cost file storage technology in the past, it is now becoming one of the major problems. For effective coupling of the magnetic flux to the recording transducer, the later is placed at extreme proximity of the memory medium. As bit density increases, the spacing or flying height between transducer and medium must be reduced accordingly. This spacing is typically 2.5 μm. for disk pack memory, and the relative speed is approximately 2500 in/sec. The combination of tight tolerance and high speed mechanical motion resulted in reduced reliability and data security due to failures, such as, head crashes. These difficulties of magnetic recording can be circumvented by using beam addressed type of magnetic memories. Such optically addressed scheme often writes information by using laser beam to heat a small localized domain of a magnetic surface, thereby selectively changing its magnetic properties so that the small region can be switched by an applied magnetic field.

Attempts to circumvent the shortcomings of both magnetic recording and beam addressed memories while still sharing transducers to reduce cost, have ranged from the use of continuous media employing different effects and therefore different transducers such as, surface wave acoustic delay lines, to semicontinuous media such as, magnetic bubble delay lines where the stored information propagates in a continuous media but bits are moved by means of discrete magnetic spots which do not require electrical connection to each bit. Discrete component memory systems circumvent both the mechanical motion as well as the slower speed encountered when the transducers are shared; of course the cost is usually higher and hence a cost/performance tradeoff is necessary.

9.1.2 Semicontinuous Media Storage

To circumvent the difficulties associated with continuous media storage, different schemes have been proposed in the last few years. These schemes overcome the mechanical motion of a moving medium with the intrinsically faster movement of magnetic domains in a stationary media. They use special geometrical arrangements and specially for magnetic bubbles much smaller bits can be stored efficiently. The basic difference between bubbles and other devices is the fact that the magnetization is normal to the substrate in case of bubbles while for the other magnetic film type devices, the magnetization lies within the plane of the film. Thus, the self-demagnetizing field in those devices varies with the linear dimension in the direction of magnetization. These devices, therefore, will be limited in their ultimate packing density on a two dimensional substrate.

Magnetic bubbles—an emerging storage technique—also offer data storage by remanent magnetization and serial access. The access, however, is nonmechanical. The material and circuit processing techniques used for bubbles are similar to those used in semiconductor industry. It has been predicted that bubbles will bridge the access gap between LSI, cores, etc., on one extreme and drum, disk, and tape on the other. This is a very viable technology and one can expect continued effort to improve both performance and cost.

Magnetic bubbles are mobile cylindrical domains that can be generated in thin magnetic layer and moved within the layer and magnetized by external magnetic fields. They remain in stable condition under a delicate balance of two opposing forces—one is the combined force of the applied field and domain wall energies and the other is that of the magnetostatic energy which acts to decrease the surface area of the large magnetized region of the platelet. Accordingly, the optimum range for bubble stability is approximately,

$$d = 2T$$

and
$$T = \frac{4\sigma_W}{4\pi M_s^2}$$

But the domain wall energy density σ_W is empirically given by
$$\sigma_W = 4\sqrt{AK} \text{ ergs/cm}^2$$

so that
$$d = \frac{32\sqrt{AK}}{4\pi M_s^2} \quad \text{(C.G.S. unit)}$$

where
$\quad d$ = bubble diameter
$\quad A$ = exchange constant
$\quad K$ = crystal anisotropy
$\quad T$ = platelet thickness

Hence the bubble diameter is a function of material parameters.

Two areas of major emphasis in the development of magnetic bubble memories are the bit packing density and the operating speed. The technical problem at present concerns obtaining crystals with adequate parameters. Several classes (orthoferrites, garnets, magnetoplumbites) can exhibit bubble behaviour, but only a few materials have attractive parameters for reasonable density and speed. Present prototype mode of bubble memory which has a capacity of 500 k bit (Bell Laboratory) consists of 28 chips, each of which contains 16k bits arranged in a major/minor loop configuration. Garnets are used as the memory medium, with bubbles 6 μm. in diameter propagating at 100 KHz by field access in T-bar tracks of 25 μm. period in the minor loops. The limitation in obtaining increased density in magnetic bubbles lie not only in the lithography and fabrication process, but also in the problems of obtaining small bubbles with desirable magnetic properties. At present, two bubble materials, garnet films and amorphous magnetic films are being considered for use in practical bubble memories. Considerable progress has been made in the development of large area low-defect-count liquid-phase epitaxy garnet films, while the capability of sputtered amorphous films for bubble device fabrication has recently been demonstrated. High density chips may be obtained with at least three different chip configurations: (i) the bubble-lattice-file (BLF) employing closely packed bubbles with a novel wall-structure data coding schemes, (ii) the familiar permalloy-bar-file (PBF) employing T-bar figures fabricating with electron beam lithography and single level masking, and (iii) the contiguous-disk-file (CDF) which utilizes relatively coarse permalloy patterns and hence eases lithography requirements. At present, X-ray lithography is being employed to fabricate 2 μm. bubble in single-level-masking experimental devices whose performance is comparable to those of devices fabricated by direct electron-beam exposure. With the present knowledge of bubbles, it appears that the density of bubble is limited to 1.55×10^5 bits/cm^2 (10^6 bits/

in^2) at a 10^6 bits/sec data rate for inductive sensing via bubble expansion, or 10^7 bits/sec. with Hall or magnetoresistive sensing devices. This bubble size is a characteristic of the material. Higher densities appear plausible with a decrease in material mobility which lowers the data rate substantially.

Regarding the operating speed of a bubble memory two factors are considered: the velocity of propagation of a bubble, and the organization of a memory so as to achieve the shortest possible access and latency time. Present knowledge reveals that during bubble motion, wall structure changes in a complex manner. Hagedron hypothesized that the bubbles which have initially a simple wall structure are converted into a complex structure when they interact with imperfections. The nature of imperfections in question is not clear, so that the basic mechanisms governing bubble motion are poorly understood. The second factor of improved access time may be achieved by proper organization of the memory. Both major/minor loop and on chip decoding schemes permit the organization of a large capacity array into small shift registers which share interconnections and read and write circuitry. The short length, as well as the fast access to such short shift resisters, drastically reduces the access and latency time.

9.1.3. Discrete Component Storages

The discrete component storage systems include cryotron, transistors, switchable resistors, etc., and are distinguished from continuous media systems by their electrical connections. Any devices capable of exhibiting variable resistance with a threshold in voltage or current can be used in the construction of memory unit. In switchable resistors, generally three technologies have received particular attention in the construction of memory unit, the first group is based on telluride compounds while the second class consists of niobium oxide devices, and the third group consists of similar effects in heterojunctions between ZnSe and Ge, and heterojunctions between GaP and Si. These resistances are basically two terminal devices and they require a diode in series in memory operation. This diode is used to prevent the "sneak paths", so that during reading no false signal appears in the sense wire. These devices are very much sensitive to small changes in the material composition. The reliability of chalcogenide glass memory belonging to the first group, lies within the physical mechanism of the device operation. For these devices, speed is one major problem with reliability as a potential problem.

The present growth of computer system has stimulated the need for larger and more complex circuits. The desire for reducing cost has led the integrated circuit industry to the development of large scale integration. It describes the simultaneous realization of large area circuit chips and component packing density compatible with a maximum number of system connections done at chip level. But in this LSI approach also interconnection constitutes one of the most serious problem. Though stacking factor and chip size has improved considerably (from 5 % to more than 60% in 1975. number of circuits per chip 100 to 1200 and more), but still at present both of them are compromised with yield, power dissipation, and propagation delay. These limitations, however, reflect present technological capabilities.

The semiconductor components will play an important role in large digital storage system of the future. Compared to moving surface magnetic storage systems, such as drums, disks, and tapes semiconductor techniques offer greater physical compactness, reduced access times, reduced power consumption, and greater reliability at a given level of storage capacity. The cost per bit of a semiconductor memory of any capacity is strongly affected by the silicon slice area used for an integrated circuit realization. Cell area depends on the device technology, circuit configuration, number of lines to each cell, and minimum photolithographic mask clearances allotted for reasonable yield in fabrication. The fabrication process, limits the uniformity of size of the devices. Wallmark and Marcus (1962) determined the minimum size of a device as a function of doping level of the semiconductor. At present various technologies exist, such as, planer semiconductor, bipolar MOSFET, metal nitride oxide silicon (MNOS), CCD, etc. The physics of MOS device implies that the larger devices may be inherently slower. Bipolar speed is highly dependent upon the memory size in relation to the rest of the computer. Transient time delays are negligible in MOS and resistance-capacitance time constants constitute the primary speed limitations. The MNOS devices which offer potential for high density are basically a variable threshold MOSFET device exhibiting memory in a single device. They provide a simpler fabrication technique but are slower than a MOS random access memory. Their speed can be increased at the cost of more complex fabrication technique. At present both charge transfer (CCD) and MNOS devices appear to be slow in main memory application and hence are more suitable for large storage where writing time is not so critical. Moreover, the major technical problems with MNOS device are the reproducibility and integrity of the thin oxide layer. Their operations depend critically on the oxide thickness, greater than 35 Å gives no tunnelling (an insulator) action, while less than 15 Å gives a short circuit and/or inadequate surface states. All these integrated circuit memories, however, offer the major advantage of speed and density over the other technologies. But their cost is pretty large. In addition, the charge transfer device suffers from speed and transfer efficiency while MNOS suffers from uncertain fabrication processes and will require considerable effort to demonstrate feasible devices.

The standby power requirements for these memories are a drawback, more or less serious depending on system application. The other factor that limits the performances of computers is the heat produced by the power necessarily dissipated in switching operations. Consequently the temperature of the computing system rises and eventually a temperature is reached at which the physical process used for switching action no longer holds. The fundamental measure of the power dissipated per logic stage of an electro-magnetic computer is given by $P = (KT/e)^2/Z,$ where e is the electronic charge, and Z is the impedance of free space. The temperature rise due to this power flow through a thermal resistance R is $\Delta T = RP.$ This power should be taken out from the logic elements. In fact, the problem of disposal of the heat sets a lower limit or the size of the element, and if the size of the element is too small, then temperature rise will exceed some acceptable limit. It has been found that at high doping levels (low resistivity), it is the heat generated that sets the lowers bound on device size, while at low doping levels (high resistivity) the minimum size memory element is determined by cosmic radiation.

Lastly the packaging and interconnection techniques have a major bearing on the reliability, cost, and physical size of potential large capacity semiconductor memories. The reliability and aging characteristics of semiconductor memories are yet to be clearly demonstrated. At present packaging and interconnections are probably the dominant causes of failure for semiconductor memory component rates. The different packaging techniques, such as, dual-in-line package (DIP), solder-reflow flip-chip packaging, and beam lead flip-chip packaging, with particular attention to reliability and cost considerations are crucial to feasibility of large capacity memories. There are marked differences in potential component packing density for the above three approaches. Of course, the maximum useful size of a semiconductor memory is limited by the attainable reliability. Component screening consists of special tests designed to reveal component susceptibility to particular failure modes. For example, plastic encapsulated DIP components and flip-chip solder-reflow packaged components are susceptible to breakage of internal leads during thermal cycling. Ceramic encapsulated DIP components are susceptible to breakage of internal leads due to shock and vibration.

9.2 MEMORY RELIABILITY AND STABILITY

A set of objectives for the reliability and maintainability of large memory systems can be inferred from the stability characteristics of small memory elements. The physical implications of reliability requirement were recognized by Von Neumann in 1949 when he compared the thermodynamic minimum energy dissipated in a binary decision with the dissipation in a neuron. The enormous gap between the two was, he conjectured, due to the need for reliability. The stability of individual element is affected by thermal fluctuations, shot noise, crosstalk, etc. The necessity of having a high probability of error free operation over a period in which many switching operations take place, puts severe requirements on the performance of individual elements.

In order to derive the relationship of the stability of individual element and the computer reliabilities, consider N identical and independent elements, $P_N(t)$ be the probability that at least one error has been made in the entire computer in a time t. Then $Q_N(t) = 1 - P_N(t)$ is the probability that no error has been made. If $p(t)$ and $q(t)$ are the corresponding probabilities for a single element, then we have

$$Q_N(t) = [q(t)]^N = [1-p(t)]^N \simeq \exp(-Np(t))$$

This is true if N is large. If $1/\tau$ be the probability per unit time that a single element will switch spontaneously, then

$$p(t) = 1 - e^{-t/\tau} \simeq t/\tau$$

so that $Q_N(t) \simeq e^{-Nt/\tau}$

or $\tau = Nt[-\ln Q_N(t)]$

now, if $N = 10^7$, $t = 1$ year, and we require that $P_N(t) = 10^{-2}$ then

$$\tau = Nt/P_N = 3 \times 10^{16} \text{ seconds}$$

i.e., a very long life of single element is required.

The above equation for spontaneous switching time is deduced assuming that there is no redundancy. However, logical redundancy and additional coding, decoding circuits can reduce this time. Swanson (1960) has shown that the spontaneous switching time (with mean life time of a single element record) increases exponentially with the size of the system. This is true for thermally activated and for tunnelling processes if one assumes that the effective inertia and the energy barrier of the collective co-ordinate being switched are both proportional to the volume. This physical redundancy, though has an advantage over logical redundancy in the ease with which the configuration is read, but a disadvantage in that external perturbations tending to switch one component of the physical element may have a tendency to switch many or all components at the same time.

The other source of noise is crosstalk. A common mode of storage, however, utilizes the steady states of dissipative devices, such as, bistable transistor or diode circuits. Landauer (1961) has noted that in order that a bistable element does not revert to its initial state after it has been switched, it must be able to dissipate the energy that had enabled it to surmount the barrier. If this energy is absorbed by a neighbouring element, that element will undergo an unwanted switching. The likelihood of such an event depends on whether the energy is dissipated as a single quantum of excitation in the intervening medium or as many quanta. In fact, a reliable computer cannot be made of single particle elements without redundancy. One can argue that the single particle that is switched from one potential well to another need not emit only a single quantum of excitation. However, for the probability of this event to be strictly zero, one would require an exact symmetry so that the matrix element for the process vanishes. This sort of perfection is impossible to attain in real situation.

9.3 ULTRA DENSE BIOCHEMICAL MEMORIES

There is enough evidence to suggest that information processing storage or retrieval by the brain cannot be explained totally by the analogy of nerve nets having element that are activated solely by a 'wiring diagram' of synaptic connection. Two very important group of experiments prove beyond doubt, that at least, as far as the storage of information is concerned, bioelectrical activity cannot be the sole repository. Animals hibernated and frozen to low temperature so as to abolish all detectable bioelectrical activity, when revived did not manifest any loss of stored 'memory'. This brings us to the consideration of 'role of chemical codes' in information processing.

There have been proposed several hypotheses on the mechanism of the memory in the brain, such as, network theory, in which it is postulated that the synaptic connections between the neurons change in accordance with the progress of learning and memory; and in chemical theory, in which it is postulated that memory is stored in a form of chemical substance such as nucleic acid or protein in the same way as the herditory information. We do not know, however, which is the correct hypothesis. Among the brain models based upon the network theory, there are Caianiello's (1961) neuron equation and other models. If we restrict our attention only to the several particular functions of the brain, however, some of these models show very much similar characteristics as the brain. The famous experiment of Lashelay (1964), although the results are a little questionable, suggests that the memory is stored distributedly over the whole brain. The situation is quite different from the core memory of the computer. In Westlake's (1970) model it is postulated that the memory in the brain is stored in a similar way as holography and Nakano's 'associations' have such a distributed memory structure. In constructing these models, mainly the static features of the brain functions have been considered and it seems to be difficult to process the time variant patterns directly with these models.

Nature stores genetic information in DNA molecules made up of long sequences of nucleotides of four different species. The information is in fact stored redundantly since the nucleotides occur in correlated pairs. This redundancy provides a conceptually simple means of replication as well as a means for preserving the integrity of the stored information so that the repairing mechanisms within the cell can restore damaged sections of the molecule. Since arbitrary sequences of the nucleotides are chemically possible, the information content of a single DNA molecule is very large. For example, a typical bacterial DNA molecule contains about 1500 nucleotides pairs. The information content of this molecule is then $\log_2 (4^{1500}) \simeq 3000$ bits. From this view point the total amount of information stored in a bacterium (containing $\sim 2 \times 10^4$ DNA molecules) is of the order of 6×10^7 bits. If we consider the entire cell (ignoring the fact that the DNA is present only in nucleus of the cell), the density of information stored in a bacterium (of volume $\sim 2 \times 10^{-12}$ cm³) is $\sim 3 \times 10^{19}$ bits/cm³. We note in passing that the information is stored stably at temperature of at least 18.6°F.

This mode of information storage, while very compact, does not lend itself to easy recording nor, most assuredly, to easy reading. The times for recording genetic information in nature are measured on the scale of evolutionary processes. The information stored in DNA is read out (or transcribed) by the cell machinery for protein synthesis since this information gives, in coded form the amino acid sequences in the proteins produced by the cell, so to speak, the printout of the genetic memory. A crude estimate of the time for reading out this information is obtained from consideration of the replication time of a bacterium, which is about 20 minutes. During this time all of the genetic information is transcribed, which means a rate of 5×10^{-4} bits/sec. (Note that the fastest laboratory synthesis of protein to date proceeds at the rate of about 11 minutes per amino acid, Since each specification of an amino acid involves about 4 bits, laboratory synthesis of protein proceeds at rate of 6×10^{-3} bits/sec.)

A currently debated question is whether DNA is used by nature as a storage medium where rapid access and ability to update records are a requirement. There are experiments that implicate the nucleic acid RNA in the memory trace and there is also evidence that implicated small protein molecules. In either case the common presumption is that the memory trace consists of neural paths with a high degree of coherent excitability possibly attained through chemical modification of the neural connections (synapses) along the path.

The packing density of information in the human brain, while small compared with the density of genetic information, is nonetheless impressively large. The brain contains 10^{10} neurons each of which forms connections with about 10^3 other neurons. If each synapse stored one bit of information (which is probably an undeterministic since synapse is very likely an analog storage cell capable of storing far more than two states) then the capacity of human brain would be about 10^{13} bits in a volume of $\sim 10^3$ cm³. Thus the storage density is $\sim 10^{10}$ bits/cm³. Von Neumann in the book Computer and the Brain, estimated the lifetime input of information to the brain to be 2.8×10^{20} bits. He assumed that none of this information was truely erased but this is unlikely. It now appears most reasonable that at least two memory mechanisms are operative, a long term memory of the sort sketched above and a short term memory. It seems quite probable that most of Von Neumann's 2.8×10^{20} bits arrive at the short term memory but never get to the long term memory. What is of interest, however, is Von Neumann's estimate of the rate of input of information through the memory system, namely, 14×10^{10} bits/sec. All of these informations are in some sense processed although only a small fractions are stored.

Though the density of components in the human brain is attractively large, these components are quite slow, since the cycle time of a neuron is of the order of several msec. Von Neumann also pointed out that the overall speed of human mental processes is attained with the use of great deal of parallelism.

References

Broadbent, D.E. (1958): 'Perception and communication (Pergamon Press, New York); G.Sperling, Human factors, V.5, pp. 19, 1963.

Burns, B.D., Ferch, W. and Mandl, G. (1965): 'A neurophysiological computer', *Electronic Engineering*, V.37, No. 443, pp. 20-24.

Burns, B.D. and Smith, G.K. (1960): 'A biological interval analyser', *Nature*, V.187, pp. 512.

Caianiello, E.R. (1961): 'Outline of a theory of thought processes and thinking machines,' *J. Theor. Biol.*, V. 1, pp. 204-235.

Feynman, R.P. (1960): 'There's plenty of room at the bottom', *Engg. Sci.* (California Institute Tech.), February, pp. 22.

Freiser, M.J. and Marcus, P.M. (1919): 'A survey of some physical limitations on computer elements', *IEEE Trans. on Magnetics*, V.MAG-5, No.2, pp. 86.

Fukushima, K. (1973): 'A model of associative memory in the brain,' *Kybernetik*, V. 10, February, pp. 129.

Gerstein, G.L. and Kiang, N.Y.S. (1960): 'An approach to the quantitative analysis of electrophysiological data from single neurons', *Biophysics, J.*, V.1, pp. 15.

Hawkins, J.K. (1961): 'Self organizing systems—a review and commentary', *Proc. IRE* V.49, No. 1, pp. 31.

Hunter, I.M.L. (1964): *Memory*. Penguin.

Kelly, P.M. (1960): 'Problems in bio computer design', presented at the Symp. on Bionics, Dayton, Ohio, September.

Keyes, R.W. (1965): 'On power dissipation in cryogenic computers', *IBM J. Res. Note* NC-436.

Keyes, R.W. (1962): 'On power dissipation in semiconductor computing elements', *Proc. IRE.* (Correspondence), V.50, pp. 2485.

Landauer, R. (1961): 'Irreversibility and heat generation in the computing process', *IBM J. Res. and Dev.*, V.5, pp. 183-191.

Lashelay, K.S. (1964): 'Brain mechanisms and intelligence—A quantitative studies of injuries to the brains,' New York, Hafner, 1964.

McCulloch, W.S. and Pitts, W. (1948): 'The statistical organization of nervous activity', *J. Am. Assoc.*, V.4, pp. 91-99.

McCulloch, W.S. and Pitts, W. (1943): 'A logical calculus of the ideas immanent in nervous activity', *Bull. Math. Biophysics*, V.5, pp. 115-133.

Rosenblatt, F. (1958): 'The perception—a theory of statistical separability in cognitive systems', *Cornell Aeronautical Lab.*, Buffalo, Report No. VG-1196-G-1, January.

Spinelli, D.N. (1970): 'Computer model for a content addressable memory in the central nervous system, In: Biology of memory (K. Pribram and D. Broadbent, eds.), New York, Academic Press, pp. 293-306.

Swanson, J.A. (1960): 'Physical versus logical coupling in memory systems', *IBM J. Res. and Dev.*, V.4, pp. 305-310.

Von Neumann. J. (1966): *Theory of Self Reproducing Automata*, University of Illinois Press, Urbana, p. 67.

Von Neurann, J. (1958): *The Computer and the Brain*, Yale University Press, New Haven, Conn.

Wallmak, J. T. and Marcus, S.M. (1962): 'Minimum size and maximum packing density of nonredundant semiconductor devices', *Proc. IRE*, V.50, pp. 286-298.

Westlake, P.R. (1970): 'The possibilities of neural holographic processes within the brain,' *Kybernetik*, V. 7, pp. 129.

Wills, D.G. (1959): 'Plastic neurons as memory elements', *IRE WESCON Conv. Rec.*, pt.4, pp. 55-65.

INDEX